The Treasure Within

An Archetypal Unfolding To Your Infinite Potential

Shannon Pernetti and Diane Steinbrecher LCSW

Inspired by the work of Michael Conforti PhD and Erich Neumann PhD

Edited by Ruth Matinko-Wald

Archetypal Associates
Portland, Oregon

Copyright © 2019 by Shannon Pernetti and Diane Steinbrecher
Second Printing, 2020

All rights reserved. No part of this book may be reproduced or transmitted in any form or by any means without written permission from the publisher.

All quotes from Erich Neumann's *The Origins and History of Consciousness* are reprinted herein by permission of Princeton University Press (Copyright Clearance Center Conf. No. 11623516).

Published by
Archetypal Associates
3942 SE Hawthorne Boulevard
Portland, Oregon 97214
ArchetypalAssociates.com
archetypalassociates@gmail.com

ISBN 978-0-692-99432-0 (paperback)
ISBN 978-0-578-43067-6 (e-book)
Library of Congress Control Number 2018961652

Editing / Ruth Matinko-Wald
Cover and graphic design concept / Machele Brass
Interior layout / Alana Orzol
Diagrams and charts / Rachel Wald
Index / Mary Harper

Printed in the United States of America

*We dedicate this book to our mentor, Michael Conforti PhD,
and to Erich Neumann PhD,
who inspired and informed this book
—they have our gratitude forever—
and to all those on the path to their Treasure Within.*

With Gratitude

To Brook, Casey and Xin Xin; Drew and Pattie; Nina, Joseph Sr., and Jaylun, Jovon, and Joseph Jr.; and Janiyah and Joe Jr.—along with our dear friends and students who provided so much support during the years of writing this book.

Thank you also to those who housed us as we wrote—BJ Byron, Gerry and Nancy Brown, and Jeffrey Sher as well as Melissa at the Surfside Resort in Rockaway Beach, Oregon; to our heroic readers—Chad Stewart, Gerry Brown, Nancy Stevens, Kent Layden, and Susan Paidrin; to our friend Molly Strong for taking our photos for this book; to Machele Brass, Alana Orzol, Rachel Wald, and Mary Harper for lending their time and talent to the production of this book; and to our dedicated editor, Ruthie Matinko-Wald.

Last but not least, we extend heartfelt gratitude to Michael Conforti for writing the book's foreword, reviewing sections one and two, and, in general, being supportive of our work.

Contents

Foreword		13
Preface		17
PART ONE: *Foundational Theories*		**23**
1	Introduction to Archetypal Pattern Analysis	25
2	The Mystery of the Archetypal Domain	31
3	The Archetype of the Container and Archetypal Alignments	39
4	Patterns in the Natural World and the Psyche	45
5	The Profound Influence of Fields	59
PART TWO: *Erich Neumann's Archetypal Developmental Theory: Individuation and the Ego-Self Journey*		**75**
6	Neumann's Archetypal Exploration of Individuation: The Next Step in the Evolution of Consciousness	77
7	Neumann's Creation Myths	91
8	Neumann's Hero Myths	111
9	Neumann's Transformation Myths	121
10	Archetypal Developmental Stages of Life	131
PART THREE: *Application of Erich Neumann's Archetypal Developmental Theory: Rescuing the Captive to Gain the Treasure*		**135**
11	Rescuing the Captive: Its Importance to Living Our Full Potential	137
12	Application of Rescuing the Captive in Neumann's Creation Myths	143
13	Application of Rescuing the Captive in Neumann's Hero Myths	175
14	Application of Rescuing the Captive in Neumann's Transformation Myths	199
15	The Archetypal Approach to Gaining the Treasure	205

PART FOUR: *The Unconscious Expression of the Psyche*   **211**

16	Working with Pre-Cognitive Experience: Implicit Memory	213
17	The Archetypal Nature of Attachment	225
18	Early Development's Relationship with Our Journey to the Treasure	233
19	Unconscious Communication: Translating the Expression of the Psyche	243
20	Images Appearing in Dreams, Visions, and Daydreams in Each Archetypal Stage	265
21	The Wisdom of the Body	281
22	Life Fields and Death Fields	291

PART FIVE: *Three Parallel Maps of Development*   **299**

23	Three Models of Developmental Knowledge	301
24	Evaluating Developmental Stages	323
25	The Difficult Transitions Between Stages	333
26	Attaining the Later Stages Held in Potential	339
27	Challenges of the Later Stages	347
28	Unfolding Our Infinite Potential with a Generative Inner Refuge	353

Epilogue   363

Appendices

A	Supportive Practices for the Later Stages of Development	367
B	For Practitioners	377

Glossary   413
Notes   423
Bibliography   439
Index   449
About the Authors   465

Diagrams and Charts

PART ONE

Domains of Knowledge in Archetypal Pattern Analysis diagram	27
Facets of the Mother Archetype diagram	37
Field Theory diagram	62
Michael Conforti's Four-Tiered Field Theory diagram	72

PART TWO

Ego-Self Journey (beginning) diagram	83
Mythological Stages in the Evolution of Consciousness diagram	87
Erich Neumann's Archetypal Developmental Theory diagram	92
Early Life Stages chart	97
Myths and Archetypal Stages chart	129
Archetypal Developmental Stages of Life chart	132

PART THREE

Three Stages of the Great Mother chart	164

PART FOUR

Rescuing in the Implicit Memory (without perspectives) chart	223
Insecure Attachment Styles chart	230
Reactive vs. Generative Refuge chart	237

PART FIVE

Three Models of Developmental Knowledge diagrams	304
Ego-Self Journey (with consciousness) diagram	307
Developmental Progression of Perspectives chart	310
Researched Developmental Model chart	318
Comparison of Archetypal and Researched Development diagram	321
Rescuing in the Implicit Memory (with perspectives) chart	330
Gaining the Treasure diagram	345

EPILOGUE

Ego-Self Journey with Archetypes diagram	364

APPENDIX B
Holding Environment for Growth and Development chart   393
Therapist Position in Building a Generative Refuge chart   411

Making Use of This Book

Part One
Introduces Archetypal Pattern Analysis; its founder, Dr. Michael Conforti; and its foundational theories relating to archetypes, alignments, patterns, and fields. These are concepts that will help the reader understand the following sections of the book.

Part Two
Introduces Dr. Erich Neumann, his view of individuation, a summary of his Archetypal Developmental Theory of the unconscious, and a visual mapping of the ego-Self journey.

It also includes a template of the archetypal stages of life, inspired by Michael Conforti, showing the contemporary development congruent with each age of maturation.

Part Three
Outlines the application of each stage of Archetypal Developmental Theory. This is the main thrust of our work: to facilitate moving into later stages of adult development to reach our greatest potential, the treasure within, the Self.

Part Four
Is an in-depth study of the unconscious expression of the psyche and how we use it in the journey to the treasure within. In particular, you will find our applications of working with changing the alignment of deep unconscious patterning that veils the treasure. We explore different aspects of unconscious expression including dreams, images, narrative stories, and synchronicities, along with how the wisdom of the body expresses our belief systems and can present through disease processes. Part Four also contains a study of the different images and symbols found in each archetypal stage of development.

Part Five
Introduces the current research in developmental studies that maps the later stages of adult development, which, we found, corresponds with the later stages of Neumann's Archetypal Developmental Theory. You will find the specific capacities and perspectives of each level of both researched development and the Archetypal Development Theory of the unconscious, as we attempt to answer the question: "What does the ego look like in its relational journey toward the treasure of the Self?"

Appendix A
Introduces mindfulness and mindful awareness practices that support releasing limited beliefs of the ego, listening to and releasing our inner dialogue, and movement into the later stages of development and the treasure within, the Self.

Appendix B
Is for clinicians and clients. Its contents describes, from both client and therapist perspective, what our training was actually like and how we changed in the process. We have done our best to lay out this map and hope it will be useful for both therapists and interested travelers.

Foreword

by Michael Conforti PhD

The year was 1954 when Erich Neumann published his seminal work, *Origins and History of Consciousness*. Considered by many to be one of the most brilliant and innovative of Jung's students, Neumann succeeded in demonstrating that the myths emerging during the different historical epochs captured the development of the individual and the ego, as both emerged from within the Great Round of the unconscious. He helped us to see, for instance, that the development from hunting to agrarian societies and the accompanying myths spoke to a profound transition occurring within the psyche. Specifically, by shifting from migratory patterns to planting crops and farming, the individual/ego showcased the ability to survive and thrive in the world.

While Neumann's work is recognized as far reaching and truly innovative, it has only been within the past five years that his contributions have received the prominence they deserve. We have to credit Erel Shalit, the gifted Israeli Jungian Analyst, for helping to organize the first international conference on Neumann's work in 2015. With renewed interest in Neumann's work, we have seen the posthumous publication of *Jacob and Esau: On the Collective Symbolism of the Brother Motif* (2016); *The Relationship Between C.G. Jung and Erich Neumann Based on Their Correspondence* (2016), written by Neumann's son, Micha Neumann; and *Turbulent Times, Creative Minds* (2017). Each speaks to Neumann's profound understanding of archetypal symbolism and the role of archetypes in shaping individual and collective behavior and history.

While the centrality of Neumann's work is now acknowledged, the application of his Archetypal Developmental Theory within the clinical domain has yet to be fully mined. Fortunately, with the publication of *The Treasure Within: An Archetypal Unfolding to Your Infinite Potential*, Shannon Pernetti and Diane Steinbrecher offer a fresh and clinically astute perspective on the importance of Neumann's developmental theory in therapeutic work. From The Great and Devouring Mother and Father, The Hero,

Slaying of the World Parents, and on to The Treasure Hard to Attain, the authors present a series of clinical vignettes illustrating how these archetypal stages are often manifested in the treatment relationship. Here we find that the actual conditions of treatment offered by the therapist and either accepted or rejected by the client, and the interventions made or unconsciously avoided by the therapist, provide a living experience of these archetypal dynamics. All these dynamics serve to create conditions whereby the constellated archetype is manifested and re-enacted in the therapeutic dyad, offering both the client and therapist a unique opportunity for understanding these central life issues. It was the brilliance of Neumann to carefully articulate how these specific mandates are evidenced in dreams, symbols, and the various ways we respond to life's challenges, and how an understanding of these creates conditions for the individual to enter and transit these various archetypal thresholds.

In addition to their attention and articulation of Neumann's work, the authors have thoughtfully captured the spirit of my work in Archetypal Fields and Archetypal Patterning. For more than thirty-five years, I have looked at this Confluence of Matter and Spirit through the lens of Jungian Psychology and the discoveries emerging from The New Sciences of Dynamical Systems, Chaos Theory, and the Science of Emergence. Where Jung found in alchemy a meaningful description of those inherent archetypal processes, the discoveries emerging from these New Sciences also speak to the inherent ordering processes within the psyche shaping individual and collective behavior. Pernetti and Steinbrecher artfully capture the nature of this work, and it is an honor to see so much of my life's work and discoveries so prominently represented in this new book.

The seeds for this work in Archetypal Fields, which winds its way through this book, germinated during the course of seminars I taught in Portland, Oregon, over twenty years. Originally, I was invited to speak at The Oregon Friends of Jung by Jolinda Osborne, and then again by Greg Smith, both presidents of this wonderful group. The Oregon Friends of Jung, one of the most active and largest Jungian organizations in the world, continues to present the richness of Jungian thought in the world. As a result of these invitations, a number of local practitioners asked if I would teach an ongoing seminar on my work in Archetypal Fields and Archetypal Patterning in Portland. Perhaps it was the spirit and energy of a younger man that allowed me to overlook the fact that this teaching would require a bi-monthly commute from the East Coast to the Pacific Northwest, and, as also with many experiences and opportunities occurring in our younger years, I had no way of knowing the importance these experiences and relationships would have for my career and personal life. It was the kindness, coupled with a sense of there being something important about this work, that fueled the generosity of many individuals—including Larry and Elizabeth Kirkhart,

Martha Blake, Rufus Yent, Lola Bessey, and Nancy Stevens—whose encouragement, generosity of spirit, and love allowed these ideas and work to flourish and continue for more than twenty years in Portland, this wonderful City of Roses.

Both Shannon and Diane were members of this original group. For more than twelve years, they fully dedicated themselves to this material, which involved an in-depth study of archetypes, Archetypal Patterns and Fields, the work of Robert Langs, and, especially, a multi-year study of Neumann's *Origins and History of Consciousness*. This was quite an undertaking. While the work challenged their personal and professional limits, they both stayed with and flourished with this material. In time, they emerged as the first graduate Archetypal Pattern Analysts in the Pacific Northwest. They then incorporated this learning into their respective practices, which led to the creation of Archetypal Associates, a Center offering trainings and seminars in the Pacific Northwest on this work.

In time, Shannon and Diane realized they needed to take this work to the next level. For years they had looked at the clinical application of Neumann's work and had decided to publish this material. After dedicating an additional eight years of research and time to reflect upon the work, this book is now completed. With it, they have not only extended the reach of Neumann's work, but they have also done a fine job in presenting the body of my work to a new audience. For all these reasons, I am deeply impressed by their tremendous commitment to this work, and I am proud and grateful for what they have added to our growing understanding of archetypal dynamics.

For clinicians and interested laypersons seeking to understand the relevance and workings of archetypes in clinical practice and personal life, this book is an important contribution, as it provides a readable and understandable approach to archetypal dynamics. So too, this work helps us to better understand the intricacies of Neumann's and Jung's work on archetypal dynamics and to find ways to bring the richness of the life of spirit and soul into our lives. For all these reasons, this is an important work.

Michael Conforti
Stonington, Connecticut
September 2018

Preface

Our journey writing this book started in 1995 when we were introduced to Michael Conforti PhD and his work with Archetypal Pattern Recognition and Jungian studies. We are still astonished that, fourteen years later, we would discover Erich Neumann's step-by-step archetypal developmental map of what is lying in potential for all humanity, apply the work of the two pioneers to our clinical practice, and begin writing this book about the fundamentals of Archetypal Pattern Analysis.

At that time in 1995, both of us were seasoned therapists with at least twenty-five years of training, and we had successful private practices. In addition, both of us had been schooled in psychodynamic psychotherapy, been expertly trained in subjective and somatic therapies, and undergone years of psychotherapy ourselves. Plus, we both pursued spiritual paths, had participated in a three-year spiritual teacher training program, shared an avid interest in nondual philosophy and thought, and engaged in a rigorous study of Advaita Vedanta and Buddhist psychology. We did not come to Archtypal Pattern Analysis with a Jungian focus, although we were drawn to the theories of C.G. Jung.

Archetypal Pattern Recognition, as it was called in 1995, spoke a language that unified Western psychology with Eastern philosophical thought, in Western scientific terms. Dr. Conforti introduced us to the mystery of the archetypal realm—to archetypes, alignments, patterns, the power of fields, the new sciences, as well as patterns in nature and Jungian theory. We became excited by the depth of the ideas abounding in this archetypal work and how they resonated with our own studies, discoveries, experiences, and deep knowing. We steeped ourselves in this study during group meetings with Michael through the Portland Seminars, offered on weekends every other month at that time. We both also participated in weekly clinical supervision by phone with Michael and met weekly for a decade with a peer study group. The work was challenging, as we were exposed to the power of the objective psyche and began to experience the limitations of practicing from a subjective viewpoint. We found ourselves in awe of the psyche's relentless capacity to stand for what is in a person's highest good!

During those transformative Portland Seminars, we explored the theory of Archetypal Pattern Analysis and its application in multidisciplinary fields through case examples and dreams. During supervision, we learned applications in our clinical cases by identifying patterns and their archetypal alignments, hearing unconscious communication and themes, and holding a secure archetypal container for healing. We were exposed to the archetypal nature of development, what is appropriate at each age, and how to help people shift into new and generative alignments. We learned about unconscious guilt, how this can be destructive in one's life, the process needed to resolve unconscious guilt, and how to move into a more generative way of living. And we graduated from the Assisi Institute as Archetypal Pattern Analysts in 2006, at which time Michael encouraged us to begin teaching the "Fundamentals of Archetypal Pattern Analysis."

Through our intimate work with Michael, we were exposed to the work of his own brilliant mentors and the wisdom of their work. From Yoram Kaufmann's work, we learned the Orientational Approach and the power of the image, the informational field each image introduces, and how to stay true to the image in its objective nature, the dominant of an image's expression. We do this by translating, rather than by interpreting the image through the lens of the dreamer or our own associations.

Through Robert Langs' work, we learned how to hold a solid archetypal framework for healing the core patterns of the psyche, about the amazing teachings of unconscious communication, how to hold our own anxiety rather than evacuate it to feel better, and how to help clients learn to contain and process their own anxiety.

From Ervin Laszlo, Fred Abraham, Ralph Abraham, David Peat, David Bohm, Rupert Sheldrake, Beverly Rubik, and Mae-Wan Ho, we began seeing patterns through the lens of Dynamical Systems Theory, Chaos Theory, Complexity Theory, Morphogenesis and Morphic Fields, Self-organizing Systems, the eternal wisdom of patterns in nature, and the importance of fields as they predate form—that matter is shaped and formed by the field it is in, rather than form creating a field in which it is held, which is a common belief.

Through Michael's mentoring, we also delved deeply into the wisdom traditions of the world, their archetypal nature and indigenous knowledge. We devoured numerous assigned books that opened the knowledge of each domain. To pass forward this knowledge, we have shared those books in our bibliography.

With Dr. Conforti's insight into clinical cases, we came to understand the archetypal power of the Devouring Mother and the Crushing Father through the magnificent work of Dr. Erich Neumann, his Archetypal Developmental Theory of the unconscious, and what lies in potential developmentally for us all. Michael peaked our interest in Neumann's work, and we began to study Neumann in earnest. We spent a year in a peer group dedicated to Neumann's book, *The Origins and History of Consciousness*, and three years in further study, attempting to metabolize his findings and learning how to apply the knowledge in our trainings and clinical work.

We found that Erich Neumann had articulated the developmental stages of consciousness, giving us a true, orienting map of human psychological development by translating the myths as they relate to the unconscious dynamics of the psyche. This helped to ground us. In simplifying the main thrust of each stage, we discovered we could use Neumann's in-depth mapping throughout the course of therapy. We saw in his work an arc of unfolding development from conception to the greatest potential of humankind. This helped us to make more in-depth assessments of where clients are developmentally, what their next step would be, and what needs to be consolidated from the past level of development in order to make an easier passage to the next. His work helped us to see that each stage builds on the successful integration of the prior stage, and that what isn't integrated leaves unintegrated "captives" in the younger levels of development. We had been, as therapists, working instinctively with these elements for years, but Neumann gave us both the language and a precise map to follow, shining a light on the dynamics that build unconscious beliefs of who we are, beliefs that must be later confronted and cleared in order to individuate and thrive in our lives.

Neumann's mythic language helped us to see the archetypes of Mother and Father and their generative and nongenerative roles. He outlined the power of the early mothering time and its stages, and how our value, worth, and authority are laid down in the psyche before our brain is developed, leaving "captives" in the implicit memory. He explained the importance of the Father archetype in helping us to move into our place in the outer world through skills, education, career, and relationships. We also found his view of individuation compelling, as it reflected the philosophical underpinnings of our Eastern studies that aligned with "rescuing the captive" to "gain the Treasure" of our true nature, the Self.

We also must acknowledge the impact of the work of Ken Wilber. Wilber translated and applied Neumann's work in both *Up from Eden* and in *The Atman Project*. We found his application very helpful in understanding the gifts that Neumann was bringing to psychotherapy. Through studying Ken Wilber, we acquired an integral lens through which to view and assess development and the numerous "heroic quests" most of us go through to strengthen the ego and then integrate its shadow aspects. This entails our responsibility as clinicians: to assess the developmental stage in which our clients are embedded and to help set a foundation to enable progression to the next developmental level, realizing that the steps between stages contain an "ego death," are challenging to navigate, and need our support, guidance, and mentoring.

We also discovered that there were models of stages of development that extended into later adult stages being researched by Susanne Cook-Greuter and Terri O'Fallon. Through their research, we learned more specifically how the ego changes as it develops, mirroring the map that Edward Edinger showed us of the relationship and journey between the ego and the Self. Through connecting their contemporary developmental research and theories with Neumann's Archetypal Developmental Theory, we began our study of these later stages of adult development in earnest—and excitedly began to see and map the connections between the theories.

In a weekend intensive with us, Terri O'Fallon focused on the later adult stages of development that have been articulated through personal experiences by the Eastern traditions of Aurobindo and Advaita Vedanta. This helped us to connect our two-decades-long study of Advaita Vedanta and nondual theory with these researched levels of adult development and the final stages of Neumann's Archetypal Developmental Theory, deepening insight into the dance between the ego and the Self.

With the rich foundation Michael gave us in Archetypal Pattern Analysis, we have been able to pursue and attempt to assimilate Erich Neumann's equally rich teachings, leadership, and archetypal mapping. In fact, we find what we are learning from Erich Neumann is continually unfolding.

In our personal spiritual journey, many teachers assisted us in increasing our capacity to witness and create the needed internal structures and experiences to comprehend and follow Neumann's path of archetypal development and integrate Archetypal Pattern Analysis into our lives. In the early 1990s, we studied with Leslie Temple Thurston in a three-year teacher training course. We learned how to work with patterned knots in the unconscious and nervous system as well as with the patterns of polarization in society and in the individual. She helped us elucidate the underlying dynamic of our culture's victim-tyrant polarity so prevalent in our time, and how to release and transcend layers of this unconscious patterning in ourselves and in others.

This foundation gave us an experiential concept of the ego-Self relationship that Edinger's writing and pictorial images later catalyzed into a teaching chart of the ego-Self journey found in this book. His contributions mapped a course that the ego takes that eclipses the Self, until the later stages of adult development bring the ego into a purer, less limited form. This gave us enough of a structure to recognize the great gift that Erich Neumann's work offered: rescuing the parts of ourselves still held "captive," seeing that our projections and perceptions are purely our own created lens, and moving into what Neumann calls "gaining the Treasure" of our soul, while having access to more numinous experiences of the Self.

Our years of Tibetan Chi Kung, meditation, and mindfulness practices physically released knots of patterns in the body, nervous system, and the psyche and assisted us in grounding in the deep wisdom of the body. This process released and integrated somatic memories, which then aided us in clearing more and more of the ego's eclipse of the Self.

Our study over two decades of Advaita Vedanta with Babaji Bob Kindler gave us an oral and visual transmission of the ancient Vedic scriptures in a contemporary fashion. He offered us a structured environment in which to be exposed to personal experiences of the archetypal realm, helped us see beyond the mind and inner dialogue, and empowered us to stabilize our minds, quiet them, and give them room to experience the mystery.

Archetypal Pattern Analysis then gave us contemporary scientific names for our personal experience and a process of dissolving what Jung called "shadow," or Edinger called "eclipsing the Self by the ego." We found that the nondual terms of Advaita Vedanta were echoed in Jungian terms. Simultaneously learning Advaita Vedanta and Archetypal Pattern Analysis gave us access to the core of our being and a capacity to recognize the importance of Neumann's teachings.

Our training with Peter Fenner began with a year-long Natural Awakening Program and led to our becoming nondual therapists in 2010. We have been training with Dr. Fenner since then, finding that nondual psychotherapy and Buddhist psychology inform the developmental stage of Gaining the Treasure, deepen our internal releasing, and provide a means in which to help clients align with their true nature, the Self. He has been instrumental in his continual support and mentoring of us as clinicians and as authors in the long process of writing this book.

Truly, we stand in awe of the titans from whom we have been blessed to learn and hope our attempt to shine a light on this material will be useful to those who are excited to learn this inspiring work and to undergo the transformative process it offers.

Diane and Shannon
Portland, Oregon
September 2018

Note: Any cases presented in this book are fictional and not taken from client examples. In order to protect our past and current clients' confidentiality, we, instead, created examples to demonstrate the application of the theories we present herein.

Part One

Foundational Theories

"Life is [the] story of the self-realization of the unconscious. Everything in the unconscious seeks outward manifestation, and the personality, too, desires to evolve out of its unconscious conditions to experience itself as a whole."[1]

- C.G. Jung -

1

Introduction to Archetypal Pattern Analysis

*"The universe is full of magical things
patiently waiting for our wits to grow sharper."*[2]

- Eden Phillpotts -

This book expresses what we have learned in our dedicated study of Archetypal Pattern Analysis and its application in our lives and in our work as psychotherapists, consultants, and teachers of the "Fundamentals of Archetypal Pattern Analysis." Through studying with the founder, Dr. Michael Conforti, we also were introduced to the work of Dr. Erich Neumann, which is at the core of our work and of the application of Archetypal Pattern Analysis. In this opening chapter, we want to introduce you to what Archetypal Pattern Analysis is and how it was developed as well as give you a general overview of its tenants as a meta theory.

Part One of this book contains the fundamental underlying concepts and theories of Archetypal Pattern Analysis as we understand them; we introduce the archetypal domain and talk about archetypal alignments, patterns as they manifest in nature and in the psyche, and the influence energy fields have in shaping the matter they contain. This foundation will help you better understand the Archetypal Developmental Theory in Part Two and how the theory is applied in Part Three.

Archetypal patterns are shaped by underlying forces that influence the behavior of all living systems. Archetypal Pattern Analysis works directly with these archetypal forces by identifying these patterns and their archetypal alignments, intervening, and changing them into their most generative form, whether it be in the human psyche, the natural world, or in systems such as various organizations.

Archetypal Pattern Analysis is an integral theory, an in-depth knowledge and broad lens through which to view the archetypal realm and its profound mystery. It investigates what is attempting to be expressed and known through the patterns that are manifesting, what archetypal fields and alignments these patterns favor, and how to archetypally impact the system—creating and mentoring new pathways for its greatest potential.

In developing this theory, Michael Conforti PhD, Jungian analyst, held numerous seminars and conferences annually over the course of over thirty years. His seminars and conferences featured experts from many different fields who studied patterns such as weather, X-rays, homeopathy, biology, architecture, forensics, dance and choreography, psychology, cinema, physics, fiction, marketing, and branding. By having each expert speak about what he or she discovered about patterns, a meta theory was created regarding how patterns form and repeat, and how interventions can facilitate changing a pattern on a fundamental level. (See the following diagram that shows the synthesis of the many domains of knowledge that form Archetypal Pattern Analysis.) As a result, Dr. Conforti founded Assisi Institute: The International Center for the Study of Archetypal Patterns, a teaching institute and certification program in Archetypal Pattern Analysis.

The Application of Archetypal Pattern Analysis

Because of the universality of archetypal wisdom and because form is expressed through patterns, Archetypal Pattern Analysis is applied across multidisciplinary fields including psychotherapy, cinema, bodywork, consultation in business, diplomacy, the legal system, and health care, just to name a few. Here are some examples of the ways we have seen it applied.

Psychotherapy: As noted, Archetypal Pattern Analysis is an integral approach that investigates what the psyche is attempting to express through the patterns that are manifesting, what archetypal alignments these patterns favor, and how to archetypally intervene in these patterns to create and mentor new pathways to our greatest potential.

Archetypal Pattern Analysis doesn't look at patterns in terms of disorders, pathology, or diagnostic codes but in terms of what the pattern is attempting to express or bring into generativity as a coherent whole and in its full potential. It is the psyche's attempt to point to exactly what is needed for this to unfold. Archetypal Pattern Analysis immediately involves us in looking at the mystery of our own unconscious behavior and suggests new ways of aligning to the life we most want to live. In so doing, this

Domains of Knowledge in Archetypal Pattern Analysis

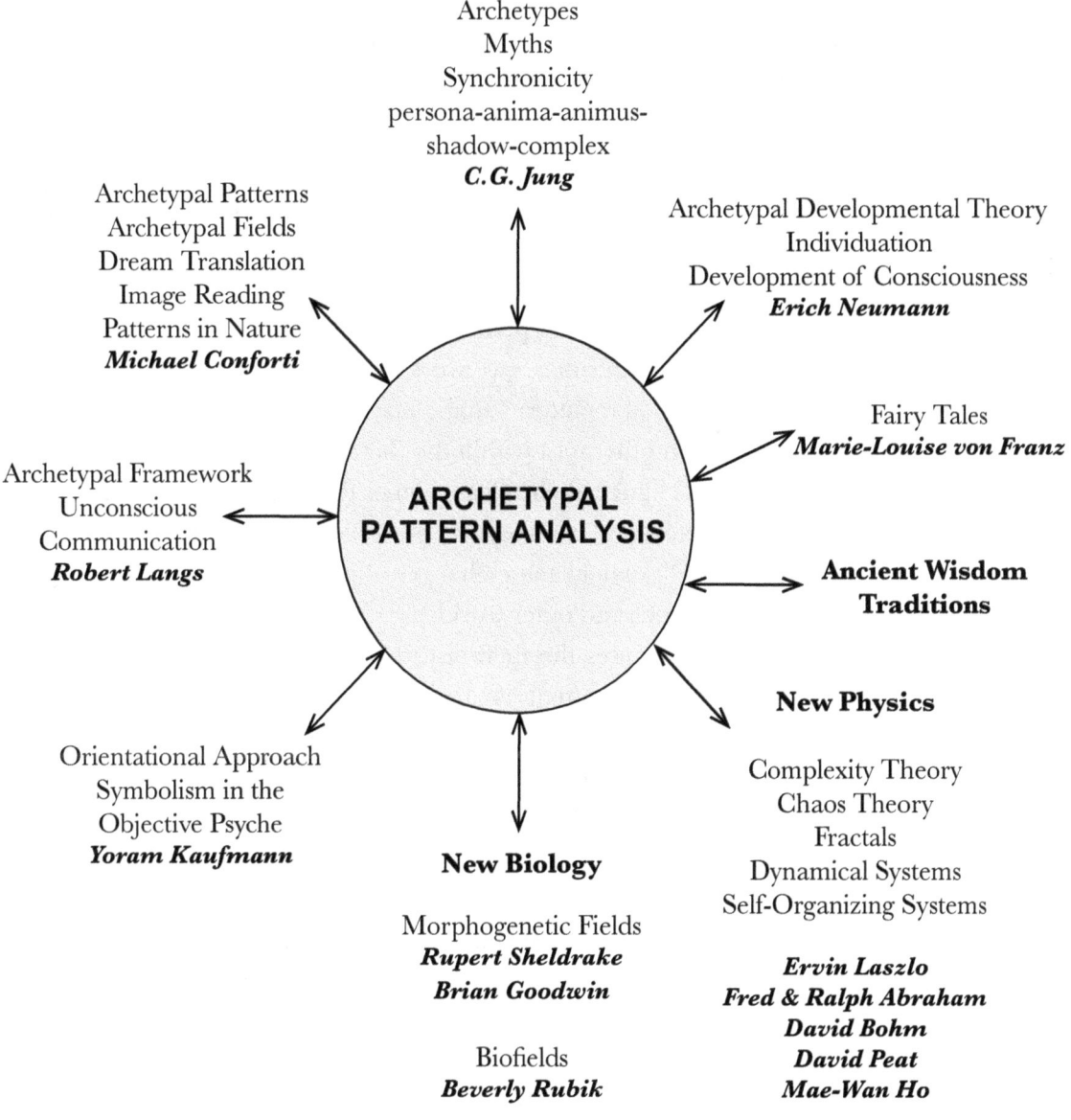

approach moves people into a deep relationship with the fundamental level of our being, our true nature as the Self.

Archetypal Pattern Analysis articulates the specifics of the essential patterns of human nature. Whereas most therapies provide understanding, insight, and clarity regarding one's patterning, working with the underlying archetypal and unconscious material creates an actual clearing of existing repetitive nongenerative patterning by changing archetypal alignments and triggering new and unknown experiences in life.

Many therapies work to develop the ego's ability and to strengthen its capacities to work in the outer world. That is part of this approach, too, but we hold a wider vision. This is a different form of therapy that actually changes patterns and moves people to a deep level of relationship with the Self. During analysis, we see the client as the Self that is unlimited, and we continually examine the client's alignments that facilitate the greatest generativity. We also consistently work to bridge communication between the Self and the conscious mind, to develop a working relationship between the conscious mind and the wisdom of the deep unconscious.

Because patterns are holographic and present across each layer of our being—physical, emotional, mental, and spiritual—we work with the pattern on each level as it emerges. We attend to how the patterns shape our experiences and the themes that manifest between client and therapist within the therapeutic relationship. As the patterns and their alignments change, their release comes through an integrative process that expands the parameters and confines of a person's life and, hopefully, opens a relationship with the Self. Ultimately, these changes affect what a person holds as important in both his or her inner and outer world.

This archetypal approach requires the therapist to continually listen for and address our own patterning and shadow material arising during therapy and to tolerate a great depth of intimacy. From this therapeutic field, clients are able to import this new experience into their own psyches and to align with their true purpose. It becomes a transformational process for both the therapist and client. (To learn more about the clinical application, refer to Appendix B: For Practitioners.)

Cinema: Many films now have an archetypal cinematic consultant who helps the story achieve archetypal congruence. For example, Michael Conforti acted in such a role for *Pride and Glory*. Movies with such a consultant tend to live on in our memory and have success at the box office, as they embody universal truth. Contrary to this, we all have seen movies with outstanding leading actors that hold great promise but seem to go flat and have little attention or popularity; these have missed the mark in acheiving archetypal congruence.

Bodywork: The patterns we embody are congruent in all systems of our life. For example, Annie Duggan and Brigitte Hansmann, in their DFA approach to applying Archetypal Pattern Analysis, look at how we hold ourselves and walk, our facial expressions or lack of affect, our body structure and its strengths and weaknesses are all congruent with the behavioral patterns they express in all areas of our life. Changing such patterns in the body, thus, affects our ability to change repetitive patterns in our relationship to ourselves and to others.

Business: Applying Archetypal Pattern Analysis in business enables employers, by reading patterns both in employees and in the business itself, to work with the most difficult employees in an effective and easy manner. Archetypal Pattern Analysis also helps employers to read patterns in job applicants' resumes, cover letters, and interviews, thus facilitating more successful hiring of new employees and improving the contracts they are hired to fulfill. In addition, many internal conflicts and issues with productivity can be rectified or prevented by aligning with a congruent archetypal mission for the business.

Advertising: Finding the underlying archetype helps companies effectively market what they have to offer to humanity. Branding stems from archetypal pattern reading and explains why branding has become so popular in advertising and the corporate world: It touches consumers at an essential level. Carol Pearson PhD is a pioneer contributor of archetypal pattern reading in the world of advertising and branding.

The Arts: Fine artists, choreographers, fiction writers, and cinematographers have used Archetypal Pattern Analysis to more deeply communicate their vision with a foundational emphasis on the archetypal properties of the informational field of an image. For example, Loralee Scott Conforti and Michael Barber are two choreographers currently integrating Archetypal Pattern Analysis into their work.

Health Care: The authors, as Archetypal Pattern Analysts, look at physical illnesses as archetypal patterns that are attempting to express what is needed to restore health and well-being in the psyche and to release nongenerative patterns and archetypal alignments.

Archetypal Mentoring: This archetypal process facilitates a partnership that supports clients moving to their next developmental stage and engaging in the change process. Without a supportive guide, it is difficult to see our next step and how to get there. It is used in coaching, organizational development, psychotherapy, and counseling.

Because of its use in multiple domains and because it has gained recognition for its scholarly application, Archetypal Pattern Analysis has become an international certification program and field of study, available at Assisi Institute: The International Center for the Study of Archetypal Patterns. The examples we use in this book are how we learned to apply Archetypal Pattern Analysis in psychotherapy, coaching, consulting, archetypal mentoring, and somatic health.

2

The Mystery of the Archetypal Domain

"One does not learn from anybody or from experience about the platonic forms; one remembers them from one's own deep inner resources."

- Socrates -

We are often asked, "What are archetypes, anyway?" The famous Jungian analyst Marie-Louise von Franz defined them as "nature's universal constants." Simply put, they are phenomena that have been found to be congruent worldwide, across all cultures. Current popular culture portrays archetypes primarily through roles people play—such as the hero, trickster, magician, or sage. However, if we look at the origins of their meaning, our view becomes more wide-ranging to encompass the original patterns underlying form, images, and behavior.

The word *archetype* comes from the Greek words *arche* and *typos*. *Arche* means "the first in a series or the origin," and *typos* means "form." *Arche-typos*, therefore, translates into "the origin of form" or "the original pattern of forms." Simply put, archetypes lie underneath form and are dynamic forces that shape matter. Each archetype has an objective mandate to fulfill, which is the essence of the archetype itself.

Although C.G. Jung is usually credited with developing the concept of "archetypes," his work is based on classic sources such as Cicero, Pliny, and Aristotle. In fact, Plato called them "elementary forms" and saw them as the "idea structures" forming the template for material reality. Socrates dubbed them "platonic forms." In the late 1800s, Adolf Bastian labeled them "elementary ideas" or "reconstructed folk ideas," and Joseph Campbell tells us that in Australia they were known as the "eternal ones of the dream."

As noted earlier, archetypes are the original patterns underlying all form, images, and behavior. They guide growth and development through a field in which form can manifest an innate structure. The dynamics of an archetype are captured and coalesce into a pattern of the information itself.

Archetypes are not static; rather, they are dynamic processes. A human experience of this coalescing, for example, might be having an underlying plan to combine materials in such a way that a new form is created. As biologist Rupert Sheldrake says, "Random piles of building materials cannot assemble themselves into buildings."[3]

It is also important to note that archetypes are not "things." They are nonlocal,[4] exist beyond time and space, and can carry many dimensions: physical/material, emotional/feeling, mental/conceptual, and/or spiritual/transcendent. In fact, you cannot see archetypes themselves, although you can see their manifestation, like a wave arising from the ocean. As explanation, Jung saw archetypes as the mediators or as a bridge of the *undus mundus*,[5] organizing not only ideas in the psyche but also the fundamental principles of matter and energy in the physical world.

Consider "bridge" as an archetype:
- *Physical*: Bridge connecting two pieces of land
- *Emotional*: Bridge as a relationship that connects people
- *Mental*: Bridge as a connection between two separate ideas
- *Spiritual*: Bridge between man and creation/universe/nature
- *Archetypal*: Bridge as a connection between the conscious and unconscious

This very chapter you are reading is itself a bridge to understanding!

Consider "container" as an archetype:
- *Physical*: Container as a cup or glass
- *Emotional*: Container as a vow such as in marriage or a memorial such as the Vietnam Veterans Memorial Wall
- *Mental*: Container as the starting and ending time of a group meeting
- *Spiritual*: Container as a hymn, symbol, or chant such as "OM"
- *Archetypal*: Container as a receptacle of archetypal information

This specific page you are reading right now is a container of information. In that way, it falls under the archetypal category of Containers.

You have had an *emotional* experience of an archetype when you felt moved by love, were taken over by a creative project, or felt part of a crowd's emotion—like love at Burning Man or grief at a funeral. You have had a *mental* experience of an archetype when you felt yourself in a Catch 22, when you had a metaphoric understanding that portrays a human dilemma. You have had a *spiritual* experience of an archetype when you felt awe looking at the night sky in the wilderness. And you have had an *archetypal* experience of an archetype when you recognized your similarities with people of a different culture.

Interestingly, symbols have dynamic power through the gathering of the energy of representing an archetype, an energy that cannot be simply or easily expressed through intellectual understanding. Consider many of the mandalas and yantras from Eastern religions. Some symbols, in fact, express a dynamic acting outside the realm of cause and effect, such as the Star of David, which expresses an archetypal portrayal of the fusion of opposites.

The Archetypal Basis of Myths, Fairy and Folk Tales, Tribal Rites, Urban Legends, and Contemporary Movies

We all have sat enthralled in the movie theater watching dramas unfold on the screen. Even watching the same movie thirty years later is still a thrill. Why? The archetypal knowledge contained in the film is eternal. For example, plots taken from the battle of good and evil—where the victim, perpetrator, and rescuer play out their very specific roles—are in our dreams, workplace, and children's video games as well as on the world political stage and cinema screens. And we encounter dramas facing the monster, whether it be a terrorist, Nazi, vampire, or shapeless creature. Nature also appears as a monster in many of our stories—as fire taking on malevolent qualities or as a storm chasing humans.

Being the original patterns of forms, archetypes also are the stored records of the continually repeated experiences of humanity. Their messages are universal yet told in the language of a specific time, place, and cultural custom. Jung considered these tales to be accounts of the activity of the archetypes and, therefore, the workings of the psyche. He would say that all the dramas of good and evil and monsters noted earlier contain hidden knowledge for how to deal with the Beast within each of us.

To archetypally express aspects of our own psyche, we align with mythical figures—such as a fairy godmother, mermaid, giant, fairies, elves, aliens, or even SpongeBob. These mythical figures are examples of universal experiences and their expression in all of our lives. This is true, too, of our comic book superheroes: Wolverine, Iron Man, Superman, Spiderman, Wonder Woman, and the like.

In addition to aligning with specific mythical figures to act out our archetypal stories, fairy tales and folk tales play a major role as well. Throughout history, humanity has preserved knowledge over thousands of years through these oral traditions. Today, our current way of taking in and preserving collective knowledge may take the form of movies, plays, videos, and video games. Whatever the form, archetypal dramas act as living records of the patterns, roles, and outcomes of specific human behaviors, circumstances, and situations. Archetypal stories are our living heritage of what is innate. They act as moral beacons, helping us to navigate what we need to know for the survival of the human race during changing or chaotic times of love, war, peace, and strife.

> Have you ever wondered why certain chants and games from childhood seem to skip a generation and then reappear again? The old rhymes we recited in childhood, now buried in the depth of our memory, hold archetypal knowledge from previous historical times and instruction of how to navigate those particular kinds of times.

Other types of archetypal stories include urban legends, myths, tales, and contemporary legends. These are forms of modern folklore consisting of stories that may or may not have been believed by their tellers to be true. They often carry archetypal information about what is needed for collective evolution. For instance, the "hundredth monkey effect" is a studied phenomenon in which a new behavior or idea is claimed to spread rapidly by unexplained means from one group to all related groups, once a critical number of members of one group exhibit the new behavior or acknowledge the new idea. Research ultimately disproved the hundreth monkey effect—but only years after it had become a common way of talking about nonlocal effects in learning. While the phenomenon may not have been an outer truth, it appears to represent a psychic truth. It seems that in order for psychic facts to come into consciousness, some sort of urban legend will surface, pointing to a way of understanding.

In today's Internet-webbed world, urban legends are rampant; we even have websites to check their accuracy. The deep psyche and the collective unconscious are constantly producing expressions of meaning to bridge that which is unconscious into consciousness.

The Mandate of an Archetype

Because archetypes are nonlocal, existing outside time and space, their most generative or life-fulfilling form is what Michael Conforti refers to as the "mandate" of an archetype. Every archetype has an objective mandate to fulfill, and that mandate holds the essential elements required to meet the most generative expression of the archetype.

There are inherent characteristics needed to meet the mandate. For example, the archetypal figures of the trickster, wise sage, teacher, and fool all have specific mandates, as do the different gods and goddesses, angels, and devas, all who portray different manifestations of powers and attributes. Specifically, the trickster will always open a situation in which a trick or switch is contained, and the wise sage must stay a witness and counsel.

Here are some additional examples of archetypal mandates:

Archetype of Marriage: A universal constant or dominant of marriage is a lifelong commitment, legalized by a state, to be together as a couple. This is different from a couple living together in a committed relationship, which is not fulfilling the mandate of the archetype of marriage.

Archetype of Pregnancy: The mandate of the archetype of human pregnancy is the carrying of new life, an unborn child, through a nine-month cycle, to a healthy birth. Upon conception, this archetype is activated and brought into this dimension of time and space or locality through an archetypal field of pregnancy. This is an a priori field of influence that takes the developing fetus along a predictable course through a set of stages that we can see and follow day-by-day, week-by-week, and month-by-month.

Archetype of Parenting: There is a universal constant for what is needed to parent a child. This is true whether in the human or animal kingdom. The primary task is to provide a safe, secure environment for healthy growth and development. It is within that environment the parent cares for and provides for the daily needs of one who is young, needy, virtually helpless, and highly dependent upon its caregivers. This archetypal mandate is so strong that we see many instances of cross-species mothering. Even species classified as predator-prey relationships can fall under the power of the mothering archetype.

When the mandate is fulfilled, we feel the fullness or essence of the archetype. When the inherent characteristics are not fulfilled or they are accomplished in a non-generative manner, the experience is felt as being archetypally incoherent. We notice this particularly in movies when the screenwriters have the characters do something "out of character" or, put in archetypal terms, out of the mandate of the archetypal role. Movies that are archetypally coherent are usually very successful at the box office; people feel impacted by the strength of the archetypal drama. Movies that are not archetypally coherent leave an audience feeling unfulfilled, even if brilliant actors are performing.

Facets of an Archetype

Archetypes are activated and then brought into this dimension of time and space through energy fields. (See Chapter Five on field theories for further explanation.) When an archetype is activated and brought into time and space, it holds all the potential and future possibilities of manifestation of that particular archetype. It has inherent in it an entire informational field of the many facets possible—and those facets can be generative or nongenerative.[6] We define *generative* as being in alignment with thriving and *nongenerative* as more of an expression of merely surviving.

Let's examine the archetype of motility through the facets of shoes, in which each choice of shoe expresses a different facet of motility while also communicating symbolically the different features of one's archetypal standpoint in life. An alignment with motility is voiced when a particular choice of foot protection is archetypally coherent with the demands of the environment, the appropriateness for the conditions, and the movement required. Choosing footwear inappropriate for particular conditions—for instance, wearing flip-flops in the snow or high heels on the beach—can point to a person not being aligned to their "footing" in life.

Now let's use the archetype of divination as another example. We know divination has the mandate to seek knowledge of the future or the unknown by supernatural means—and there are many different ways in which it manifests: channeling, palmistry, tarot reading, runes, fortune telling, I Ching, oracles, Ouija board, tea leaf or bone readings, shamanic practices, and more. Like the faces of a clock, all these practices are different facets of the archetype of divination, different ways in which divination occurs.

Finally, consider the facets of the archetype of the mother. The central issue of the archetypal mandate of the mother is tending to one who has been birthed and helping that child build a generative inner world by seeing the child's essence and providing conditions to support full potential at each developmental stage. When an archetype is activated, however, it comes into form with both generative and nongenerative aspects. This is true for the mother archetype as well. Examples of generative mothering include loving; nurturing; being protective, wise, and tender; providing a solid container for growth and development; providing good nutrition, guidance, and

Facets of the Mother Archetype

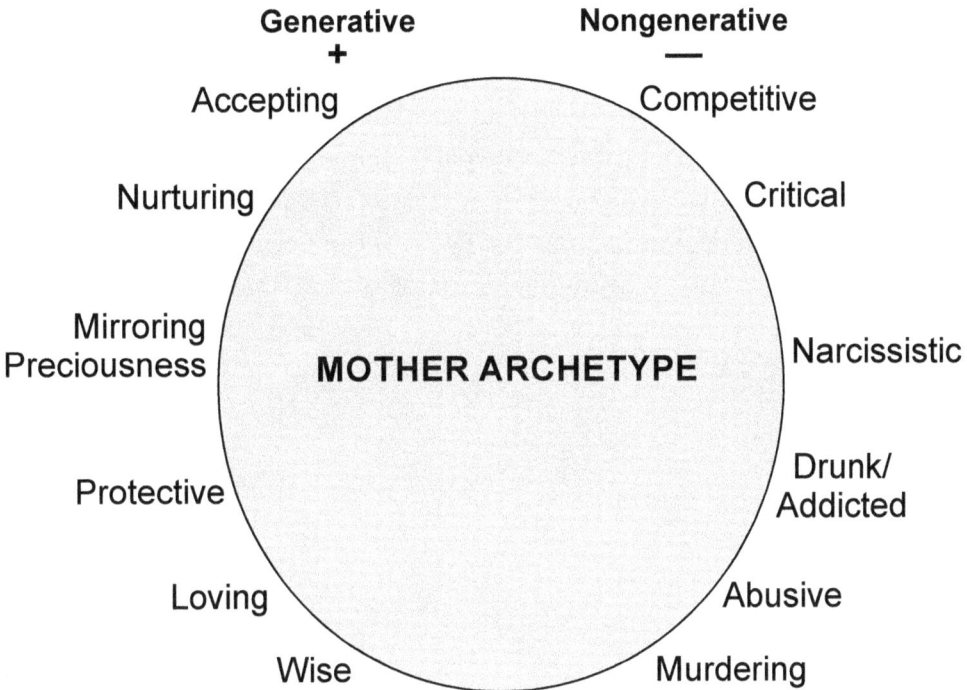

Mandate of the Mother Archetype:
To build the child's inner world by seeing the child's essence and providing conditions to support full potential at each developmental stage.

encouragement; and mirroring preciousness. Nongenerative aspects comprise being competitive, selfish, narcissistic, jealous, fearful, abusive, murdering, and so on.

Depending on your upbringing and what your experience of mothering was like, you will have a conditioned experience that begins a patterned expectation, an alignment toward the generative or nongenerative archetypal mother. A generative alignment would be nurturing yourself as an adult in all aspects of life. A nongenerative alignment might show up as starting a business and then failing to bring it into full potential for success. Other examples of nongenerative alignment would be completing your doctoral classwork and research but not writing your dissertation to finish the degree, or writing a book and then opting out of going through the editing and production process.

In summary, archetypes, with their mandates and facets, are like different perspectives that catch a glimpse of the archetypal dimension. They open the door to a greater mystery beyond explanation and show the powers that underlie all of what we generally take for granted. With a practiced eye, one can begin to perceive glimmers of the numinous, activating a primordial knowing and awareness of the profound influences on all existence.

3

The Archetype of the Container and Archetypal Alignments

"There are transpersonal, archetypal factors that orient and guide much of life. We do well to realize the autonomy of these archetypal dynamics and see that individual consciousness has little to do with the actual activation of the alignment. Here we can consider the unfolding of the archetype as the manifestation of a fated factor intrinsic to the individual's life, since the archetypal alignment tends to create an enduring influence, similar to the influence of one's birth order or cultural and spiritual inheritance. Like them, the field is a carrier of the destiny factor and provides an orientational blueprint for life."[7]

- Michael Conforti -

It is an archetypal phenomenon that all living systems grow and develop within a container, a holding environment that provides protection, safety, and security while maintaining its integrity. The word *container* comes from the Latin words *con* and *tenere*. *Con* means "together," and *tenere* means "to hold." The word *container*, thus, means "to hold together." In keeping with the meaning of the word, the mandate of the archetype of the container is to:

- Have or hold (someone or something) within
- Have the capacity for holding
- Be able to restrain within fixed limits

The container archetype has many facets. Recall that facets are all the potential and future possibilities of manifestation of a particular archetype. For example, on the *physical* level, containers hold liquid and food, showing up as archetypal facets known as cups, soup pots, Tupperware for leftovers, tins for keeping crackers fresh, and so on. Consider also how mailing boxes hold presents, luggage contains clothes, and purses carry personal items. In addition, think breadbaskets, trashcans with lids, refrigerators to keep food cold, and cars and airplanes for transporting people. Even caskets and nuclear waste holding tanks are facets of the archetype of the container! On an *emotional* level, we have "containers" for promises; we call them vows or agreements. In addition, memorial statues and structures can hold the feelings and meaning of whole informational fields for an entire nation; consider the Vietnam Veterans Memorial Wall as an example. Photographs, movies, and novels also can provide the same emotion-containing function. On a *mental* level, think about the starting and ending times that define the "container" of a meeting. Mortgages, business contracts, and computer warranties also "hold" mental currency. On the *spiritual* level, prayers from all the different religions are "containers" for mankind's deepest feelings, as are spiritual rites and rituals performed for hundreds and thousands of years.

Containers for Growth and Development

One of life's sacred mysteries is that everything needs to be held securely for generative development to unfold. In other words, with regard to the processes of growth and development of every sort, the container acts as an alchemical cauldron, protecting as well as organizing the matter contained within. Given the complexity of the processes, the container for growth and development demands the full extent of the mandate of the container archetype.

Let's first consider "protection" as it relates to the mandate of a container archetype. For example, hard outer shells protect the inside of nuts and seeds, whereas outer skin protects fruits. Likewise, shells protect eggs, just as the cranium protects the growing brain of a baby. Even the way we hold a baby's head, egg, nut, or fruit is a "container," by which we protect that which is fragile and precious.

Now consider "organizing the matter within" as it relates to the container archetypal mandate. When a butterfly or moth emerges from a cocoon, we know that everything that created the butterfly came from the elements of the caterpillar; the cocoon acted as a sacred vessel for a metamorphosis. Similarly, the womb acts as a sacred vessel for the metamorphosis of human life. It is where the sperm (a container for the male lineage) and the egg (a container for the female lineage) unite to create a fetus, and where that fetus grows and develops until birth.

Unstable Containers

As we learned in the last chapter, facets of an archetype can be generative or non-generative. What happens, for example, when a container is not able to maintain its full mandate, when its capacity to hold or its ability to restrain is compromised? The cracked glass, cup, or bowl will no longer be able to hold liquid; the apple with wormholes will not taste very good; the damaged luggage will have clothes hanging out; the soda in the open can will taste flat after an hour; and the overflowing toilet will need immediate attention! On a more profound level, when the Fukushima Nuclear Plant leaks, a dam does not hold all the water, or an airplane goes down in the ocean, we shake in our boots. These are containers we need to trust!

Let's also consider what happens if the archetype of the container for human growth and development is not able to maintain its full mandate. For example, we know that, for normal or generative development to occur, specific times and set conditions are required; doctors can predict with good accuracy the development of a fetus and when birth will occur. If the gestational timing is interrupted, a baby will not be fully developed at birth and will need to be held in the container of an incubator to complete its development.

As noted, it is an archetypal phenomenon that all living things be held safely and securely for specific times and under set conditions until they have matured enough to no longer need the container. How well that is carried out predicts the trajectory of that entity's life. When containers for growth and development are not able to hold their stability, whatever is growing inside begins a path toward abnormality. In other words, when a container is secure and its required conditions are fulfilled, archetypal forces create the intended growth. When a container is not secure, however, the mandate of the archetype cannot hold and abnormalities occur.[8]

Imagine a caterpillar's cocoon being torn as an animal brushes past, compromising the cocoon. Now, the likelihood of this butterfly coming into its full potential is greatly compromised. Similarly, if in pregnancy a mother consumes alcohol or drugs, the container of her womb does not supply adequate nourishment for her baby's healthy growth and development. Consequences can include birth defects, impeded brain development, and fetal alcohol spectrum disorders manifesting as a small head size, poor coordination, low intelligence, low birth weight, and often addiction to the substance the baby was exposed to in the womb.

Archetypal Alignments

These early, primal containers of growth and development are imprinted on all living things and create "archetypal alignments." As Conforti states, the alignments are "analogous to having access to just one room in a multi-leveled house."[9] These alignments act as force fields, or "attractor sites,"[10] for each facet of an archetype. With both negative and positive magnetic poles, the attractor sites attract or beckon consciousness and, ultimately, manifestation of generative or nongenerative facets of an archetype, triggering similar kinds of situations to repeat. Specifically, once we develop an alignment to a particular archetype, a pattern is established and kept in place or repeated through the influence of fields and what Rupert Sheldrake calls "morphic resonance"; the alignment resonates with what is "like" and repels what is "not like."[11]

In human terms, this process begins our relationship to generative or nongenerative experiences of the archetypes in our lives. That is, out of our early experiences of our containers—our *in utereo*, environmental, and parenting experiences—we begin to form our archetypal alignments and, ultimately, our life patterning.

Let's consider, for example, what happens if a mother dies and her baby is not able to stay in her womb for the complete gestational period. The container of the womb is replaced with a sophisticated medical container, an incubator. But incubators do not have a human nervous system, mind, and heart with which the baby can connect and develop a generative alignment to attachment, empathy, love, and a sense of significance and belonging. Instead, the incubated baby will experience a loss of containment (a loss of being held safely and securely), and an attractor site to a particular archetypal alignment will begin in the baby's psyche for the loss of containment—the loss of the mother. This translates into the beginning of a nongenerative alignment to the archetype of container and to the archetype of mother.

At this stage, the incubated baby has two possible trajectories: adapt or die. Rather than die, he or she adapts to the new environment, whereby the metal container of the incubator becomes the substitute for the real womb, with the memory of the real or primal container becoming a ghost-like feeling in the infant. In essence, his or her psyche compensates by accepting the substitute container and aligning with it; he or she loses a fully generative alignment with the primal container and, instead, develops an attractor site for and resonance with nongenerative containers or substitute containers and substitute mothers. These initial conditions create a trajectory of patterning in this child's life, a trajectory in which "real" containers are just beyond reach and the feeling of abandonment persists into adulthood.

Granted, alignment with the substitute container can attract adequate containment and mothering, but not rich, full-of-life containers. In the long term, such a nongenerative alignment to the archetype of the "real" container and mother can lead to a child's dreams never being realized, his or her blindly accepting substitutes for real wants and desires, and his or her inability to be content. Specifically, the orphan who is aligned with the abandonment he or she experienced early in life will consistently be surprised that he or she ends up in challenging situations and with people who are abandoning and neglectful. He or she also will be unable to envision what would be supportive, and much of his or her behavioral patterning will be developed by this alignment. There even may be two possible mates for this person: the partner with whom he or she lives who is not very caring or intimately available; and another who is out of reach but would have been nurturing.

Practical Application of Archetypal Alignments

Ideally, we all want to have a generative alignment to each facet of the archetypes in our lives—whether or not the alignment was initially patterned in a generative or nongenerative manner. The good news is that, although we cannot change the archetypes of our lives nor our past experiences, we can change our *alignment* to those archetypes and open our perspective and experience to a wider view.

In an archetypal approach to therapy, an aspect of our initial assessment will include exploring a client's experiences with the primal containers and beginning conditions of life, identifying his or her archetypal alignment. Our providing a solid container and secure conditions in therapy allows for a new experience—one in which to reconnect with the feelings of the "real" container and the generative mother. With the two magnetic poles of generative and nongenerative in the archetypes of the container and the archetype of the mother reunited, the patterns of accepting substitutes can disappear for the client. (In Appendix B of this book, you will find a detailed explanation of the application of archetypal alignments in a therapeutic setting.)

4

Patterns in the Natural World and the Psyche

"Patterns exist in every facet of life, and, through the intricate, fascinating, and beautiful designs they assume, we can see the high degree of self-organization, complexity, and stability working to create them. Every organism simply lives with a mandate to express its natural and unique characteristics. Jung's view was that the Self is constantly striving for expression."[12]

- Michael Conforti -

Our clinical as well as teaching experiences over time have enabled us to explore archetypal patterns through a broad lens and to gain a profound appreciation for their meaning and expression. Through our years of study with Dr. Michael Conforti, we became excited to see how systems function and how the principles underlying patterns forming in nature can be applied to the way patterns form in the human psyche. This helped build our fundamental understanding of how to intervene as well as how to change nongenerative patterns in thinking and behavior. Recall that "nongenerative patterns" are patterns that do not lead to growth but shut down potentiality.

As we approach this archetypal work, we have been challenged by Dr. Conforti and the Assisi Institute to always consult the natural world as a reference when reading patterns in the human psyche and in human behavior. This means looking through the lens of research into dynamical systems, the new sciences and biology, the patterns found in nature, and their consistent similarities to the way human nature is patterned. This leads us to believe it is imperative to use terminology and processes found in these systems to explain the patterns and dynamics of human behavior and the psyche. It is through this union of matter and spirit that we can now find validity in what is witnessed and experienced.

Understanding Repetition and Patterns

In the history of looking at patterns, early Greek philosophers strove to explain order in nature. Plato, looking at natural patterns, argued for the existence of what he called "universal" or "ideal forms." He contended that physical objects are only imperfect copies; a flower may be roughly circular, but it is never a perfect mathematical circle. Pythagoras compared patterns in nature to the harmonies of music arising from numbers, which he took to be the basic elements of existence.

From the early Greeks on, we have learned that the emergence of form in any system seems based on replicative, "iterative" processes. *Iteration* is the act of repeating a process with the aim of approaching a desired end result. Each repetition of the process is also called an iteration, and the results of one iteration are used as the starting point for the next iteration. For example, the shape of a fern can be turned into a mathematically generated pattern that can be reproducible at any magnification or reduction.

From a biological perspective, repetition uses "creodes" and "canalization" to ensure the underlying archetypal form will be maintained. *Creode* derives from the Greek words *chre* (it is necessary) and *hodos* (route or path), combining to create a word meaning, "a necessary route or path." *Canalization* refers to the habitual grooves of repetition.

C.H. Waddington, an embryologist in the 1930s who coined the words *creode* and *canalization*, studied unfolding information in DNA strands and genetics. In his research of embryonic regulation in DNA strands, he found that creodes, or developmental pathways, tend to repeat their development and, even with disturbances, stay canalized in grooves of repetition. This is why an acorn from an oak tree does not become a pine tree. Creodic pathways insure the completion of specific form. Waddington called these "attractors."[13] An *attractor* is the configuration or pattern into which a dynamic eventually settles into a canalized pathway, like the routines that emerge in our life after we move to a new house in a new neighborhood.

Returning to the example of the acorn, an acorn's journey to becoming an oak tree is a biological developmental pathway or habit, canalized into a groove. All acorns have the possibility to become an oak tree, but not a pine tree; of all the potentials possible, only the oak tree possibilities are available. Dr. Conforti calls this a "collapse into a singularity," because, out of all the choices of Nature, she creates a pattern that produces a specific form. To do that, the pattern is reduced to a single unfolding.

Different Types of Patterns

In his seminal text, *Field, Form, and Fate*, Conforti defines *patterns* as "a coalescing of multiple trajectories into a singularity. They exist as a clustering of preexistent information and energetic potential that then emerge into recognizable forms."[14] He goes on to say, "[Patterns] exist as external mappings of internal processes, be it morphogenetic promptings in the biological domain or symbolic, archetypal expressions found in the human psyche."[15] In short, nature's tendency toward the replication, production, and conservation of patterns serves to inform and ensure the existence of life on *all* levels.

Whether in nature or relating to the human psyche, three types of patterns exist: Those that 1) repeat in an orderly fashion, 2) repeat in a sporadic way, and 3) repeat only in certain domains. Patterns that repeat in an orderly fashion are part of a "linear system." Linear systems are logical, incremental, and predictable. Many patterns unfold in a predictable way, like the pattern of a fetus developing in the womb.

Chaos Theory, however, predicts that events and patterns in nature never exactly repeat, because extremely small differences in their "initial conditions" (those conditions present at the beginning of something new) can lead to widely different outcomes.[16] Many natural patterns, the second type of pattern noted above, are shaped by this apparent randomness—creating a non-linear system. Examples include coastlines and tree shapes, which repeat their shape regardless of what magnification from which you view them. Even though the future of these systems is governed by their initial conditions, they are not necessarily predictable. Natural systems, like the human psyche, cannot be anticipated, because random processes can intercede and change their trajectory. You can see by their initial conditions that there is a trajectory, but, like the weather, prediction is not always accurate, as other factors can interrupt the predicted pattern.

Obviously, patterns that repeat look orderly. But patterns that repeat sporadically when looked at in a larger scale reveal a "fractal" pattern[17]—that is, you see elements of a dynamic that cannot be defined or categorized. Fractal-like patterns occur widely in nature, in phenomena as diverse as clouds, river networks, geologic fault lines, mountains, coastlines, animal coloration, blood vessel branching, and ocean waves. Each part of a fractal is a reduced part of the whole, and each part creates a seed to reproduce the whole.

Fractals record what happens in the transition zones between order and chaos. They describe the roughness of the world, its energy and dynamics, and the way things fold and unfold, feeding back into each other and themselves in an iterative process. And they show the dynamics of what underlies form.

The mathematical formula that describes ferns was one of the first to show that what looks like chaos, when viewed from a huge distance, actually reveals a pattern. Even though chaos looks unpredictable, it does follow deterministic rules, based on non-linear mathematics, called "fractal geometry."[18] Using fractal geometry formulas, we can comprehend the irregular yet patterned aspects of nature in a way that conventional geometry never could. In fact, these same formulas are currently used in Hollywood to create the high degree of "realness" in movie special effects and animation.

The third type of pattern is that which repeats only in certain domains and typically goes unrecognized because of its chaotic nature. Sometimes referred to as a "strange attractor,"[19] this pattern type is always doing something new yet confines itself to only certain facets of the archetype. Such patterns also don't appear to have a canalized pathway of expression, making them very difficult to identify. Michael Conforti calls these "patterns not recognized." For example, current deadly viruses such as the AIDS virus, the Ebola virus, or COVID-19 have been challenging to cure because we are not able to see a clear pattern and the appropriate intervention.

The holographic nature of fractals shows up in human behavioral patterns. If someone acts in a certain way in one part of his or her life, the fractal pattern is most predictably there in other parts of his or her life as well. For instance, if someone lies at work, you can expect to find lies or secrets in other parts of his or her life; perhaps a lie or secret may even be underlying that person's behavior in general. Or, if a person is unkind to certain types of people, he or she has the capacity to be unkind to you.

Archetypal alignments are stabilized by the attractor sites with which they align. These "attractor sites then determine the trajectory and confines of the system."[20] This insures the continuity of patterns. What looks chaotic, when seen as a whole, often expresses unconscious dynamics that are being influenced by some outside stimulus. For example, non-metabolized trauma is often expressed as a concretized pattern of behavior that is very confusing, but, when the whole picture of trauma is considered, the expression makes complete sense.

This concept is used in many TV plots in which an insane serial killer's motives are revealed by profilers using pattern recognition techniques; the pattern analysis almost always reveals that the killer is reenacting the kind of abuse he or she experienced in early life. Or imagine the little first-grade boy who is continually disruptive. His behavior may make no sense—until you see the family he comes from interacting in a confusing and disruptive way.

Think of this important concept like this: What appears disordered or chaotic is actually a system automatically evolving toward its attractor, leaving behind all non-attractor states or possible trajectories. Called a "self-organizing system,"[21] this process of organization spontaneously arises out of all the components of a disordered system. It is the lake with all its ecosystems keeping a balance of pH in the water to stabilize the local flora and fauna. Other examples of self-organizing systems that seem chaotic are: the flocking of birds (which never seem to bump into each other), the swarming of bees, migrating animals in large herds moving together, traffic flows, ocean currents, and weather patterns. The human body is also a good example of the self-maintaining nature of systems—from the cells on up to the entire organism, all working together to function as a whole and yet containing mutual dependency or coordination between all the sub-systems. Each sub-system has adapted to the environment formed by all other sub-systems, like individual neurons of the brain coordinating to create a unified sense of a coherent mind.

Applying the Principles of Systems in Nature to Human Systems

By exploring the underpinnings of how our natural world is created, we can learn how patterns form in our minds, emotions, and behavior. In other words, just as each plant and tree unfolds from a series of patterns that have an innate ordering process toward an end result—the acorn toward becoming an oak tree, the seed becoming a carrot—the psyche, too, is a "self-organizing entity that unfolds according to its innate destiny factor."[22]

Basically, the outer world of nature and form mirrors the inner world of archetypal patterns. As Conforti notes, "Patterns can be viewed as material representations of archetypal informational fields expressed in space and time."[23] In art and architecture, for example, decorations or visual motifs may be combined and repeated to form patterns designed to have a chosen effect on the viewer. In a similar way, we create emotional, mental, and behavioral patterns though repetition and canalization.

Regarding the human application of Archetypal Pattern Analysis, Conforti tells us: "Repetition creates a number of crucial dynamics in an individual's life. The first involves the stabilization of a specific behavioral archetypal pattern lived out despite the distress it causes the individual. Second, the repetitive pattern, usually established in early childhood, is lived out in adulthood with a precision that ensures a fidelity and obedience to the original event. Third, because the repetition demands the continual recreation of a specific, relational pattern, it limits the individual's freedom of thought and behavior. Lastly, many new experiences in an individual's life constellate around the hub of the replicative-archetypal order tending to fit the original pattern."[24]

We are what we are! Without an intervention in the pattern, other possibilities are just not available. Similar to Sigmund Freud, who said that we repeat patterns in order to avoid feeling internal distress or anxiety, and as a defense against remembering,[25] we see that we repeat patterns over and over again as a way to maintain the stability of our unconscious patterning.

On a positive note, psyche's relentless attempts to repeat and be heard can serve to bring us into our full potential. Depending upon our early childhood experiences of self, however, our innate archetypal patterns may not be fully supportive of our wholeness and full potential. For example, infants who, at each developmental level, are mirrored the preciousness of their being and offered opportunities promoting their expression and full potential tend to thrive throughout life and to have the ability to weather hardships and losses. In contrast, infants who are mirrored their mother's limitations and stresses or are treated abusively form early nongenerative patterning that repeatedly points to not being "good enough," worthy, or important. Their life trajectory is then compromised by these early impressions and patterns that shape their thinking, behaviors, and future relationship to self and others; these early patterns become concretized as the children go through their developmental stages of life.

In archetypal terms, patterns of thinking, patterns of behaving, and relationships with similar archetypal alignments and attractor sites maintain canalization. With repetition being the key to canalization, a system can open to new, generative options by taking small steps to interrupt the repetition of a pattern. For instance, interrupting a pattern of illness by going to bed one-half hour earlier, or letting go of drinking Diet Coke one day at a time, begins to create a generative alignment to health and opens the door to new possibilities.

Putting This Archetypal Approach to Therapy into Practice

As therapists, when we work with clients, we are assessing the generative or nongenerative trajectory of their patterning and their openness to change. To determine whether someone is open to new information or closed off from it, we need to understand some basic principles of systems and what is needed for change.

Initial Conditions

Perhaps the most obvious requirement for a generative trajectory is having optimal initial conditions (again, those conditions present at the beginning of something new). Conforti studied initial conditions under numerous circumstances, from initial clinical interviews to forms and patterns in the natural world. He found in his studies that, repeatedly, initial conditions provided a predictable trajectory for how something unfolds into a stable, consistent pattern. Further, he discovered that this trajectory can be affected only if there is a strong enough "perturbation" or intervention to change its course.[26]

Let's explore this in more depth. Form lies in potential, waiting for the right corresponding conditions to occur; the seed will not sprout without the right combination of temperature, water, light, and proper soil conditions. When those appropriate initial conditions are provided, they activate archetypal alignments that set a trajectory for future patterning on a course of generativity. If the conditions are not satisfactory or adequate, the trajectory will lead to unhealthy outcomes.

Through resonance, similar patterns are attracted (like attracts like), they become attuned to one another, and the initial conditions begin to replicate. This attunement and continual replication process, called "entrainment," stabilizes the pattern and its trajectory and facilitates a set self-organizing pattern, similar to clocks in a clock shop ticking in unison.

We look through a non-linear lens at a system's patterns. This means that small effects can have large consequences. Small interventions in core patterns also can create large changes. Bringing awareness to the initial conditions and the replicative patterns in place for an individual or a system can begin to open the system to change.

For example, in gardening, we need to focus on the initial conditions in order to have success in the maturation process. To enjoy the fruits of a scrumptious tomato in the summer and fall, the tomato seedling would best be planted in rich, loamy, fertilized soil after the threat of night frost, in an area of full sun and ample daily water. These conditions can set a trajectory for delicious tomatoes when ripened, a generative course toward maturation.

If, however, a novice gardener plants a healthy tomato start in clay soil in a mostly shady location, the seedling will have a poor prognosis for health, a nongenerative trajectory. But this could be rectified. If an experienced gardener were to offer advice that the seedling needs different conditions, and the gardener followed the advice and transplanted the seedling into the generative conditions needed for healthy growth (a strong enough perturbation/intervention), then the plant's maturation trajectory can change course.

Similar to plants needing rich soil and proper conditions to begin life, we want the best for us as humans in our early stages of life. We also want the best conditions possible when we begin psychotherapy!

Open and Closed Systems

In addition to assessing initial conditions in determining the potential for a generative trajectory, we also can look at whether a particular system is "open" or "closed." Open systems are generative, allowing for new energy and information, novelty, and complexity and changes that promote growth and healthy development. Like a family with many ties in the community, an open system provides new possibilities of interaction and activities that create dynamism and aliveness. Similarly, people who as infants were seen for their preciousness and thrived at each level of development create generative alignments. They are likely to be open to new information and meaningful changes at each new developmental stage, ultimately living to their full potential.

Closed systems, on the other hand, limit possibilities for change. They demand that everything organize around what is familiar and known, and they find it difficult to weather a threat to habitual patterns of canalization or to any unfamiliar or unknown territory. For example, consider the ecosystem of a small pool. If it does not have a source of renewing itself with more rain, the pool would be at risk of drying up, which would create a cascading collapse of all the life and ecosystems in that little pool. Similarly, people who faced early trauma, or who as infants began to perceive themselves as being inadequate and unimportant in relationship with their caregivers, commonly face their lives and development by shutting down potentiality with attempts to control outcomes; new changes and new information often feel threatening and terrifying to these "closed" individuals. Their inability to take in complexity or new information that challenges their need to control creates a closed system in motion.

Studying nature and natural systems and then translating the information for use in human systems is at the heart of this archetypal approach. For instance, look at how the earth relieves stress. When an earthquake occurs, cracks form to relieve the stress. If the earth is very hard, or has concrete laid on top of it, the cracking will be much worse (a closed system) than if the dirt is "flexible," perhaps made of clay or sandstone (an open system). Another good example is buildings. Those constructed so they can absorb the sway or shock of an earthquake have a flexibility that supports the likelihood of their surviving tremors intact. Overly rigid structures cannot absorb shock and may crumble under the pressure. This is true in the material world as well as with the psyche!

Consider how stress manifests in different families. Families that have the capacity to receive outside assistance and be open to a wide array of options when they are under stress can be considered open systems. On the other hand, a closed-system family will not be flexible enough to accept new ideas and options; it will feel threatened and "crack" under stress, calling on a need to protect its habitual patterns. By determining whether a family is an open or closed system, we can predict a likely prognosis and future outcome; the quantity and quality of options the family sees will set a trajectory of how it will weather stress.

Specifically, unconscious patterning from pre-cognitive, pre-verbal childhood development—when nongenerative and hurtful parenting patterns are experienced—can create inflexible or closed systems that can pass unconscious behavioral patterns through multiple generations of families. For example, children who lived with parents who had secret illicit affairs often find themselves tempted as adults to have affairs themselves, even when they love their spouse. This can happen when the conditions are ripe, as when a family is under stress. If a family is an open system, it has many possibilities and potential for help, whereas a closed-system family will often experience emergencies and limit itself to not seeing any options, or only poor options, when faced with stress.

As archetypal analysts, our job is to help the closed-system family by intervening with small, incremental perturbations that create small changes and facilitate a more open system, which means helping them create more generative attractor sites and archetypal alignments. Otherwise, the old closed, unconscious system will mature and be available for repetition.

Morphic Resonance

The above-mentioned family with a pattern of secret affairs is an example of what's called "morphic resonance." *Morphic resonance* is the term expressing the means by which information or a pattern is transferred from one system to a subsequent system of the same kind. This can happen across space and time and from past to present. The greater the degree of similarity of the systems, the greater the influence of morphic resonance.[27] Again, like attracts like.

We all have had the experience of meeting someone who reminds us of a close, dear friend. Often, we will find ourselves treating the new person with a kind of trust and intimacy usually reserved for that long-known special person. The morphic resonance is so strong that we begin attributing the trust we have for our dear friend to our new acquaintance.

We all also have had the opposite experience of meeting someone and feeling a consciously unexplainable aversion. In this case, the resonance is a negative one and makes us want to move away from this person. A similar resonance is common when we enter a group of people. There are some we feel drawn to and with whom we easily start up a conversation, and others to whom we feel an aversion and walk away from. Many relationships begin based on these initial feelings and on what Sheldrake is calling morphic resonance. This resonance, while it feels comfortable, is actually because of a similarity in patterning that compels one toward another. Some call this a "good fit" or having a "good vibe." And the replication of patterns continues.

Patterns developed during the initial conditions of childhood are canalized through repetition and are unconscious. Such patterns hold a morphic resonance that dictates what occurs under similar situations. For instance, a man who came from an abusive family, when looking for a significant other, finds and marries someone who eventually turns out to be an abusive partner. How did this occur? Beginning in childhood, when the man as a young boy was repeatedly abused, a stabilized pattern formed, creating in him an archetypal alignment to similar relationships and situations. Through morphic resonance, he gravitated, like a magnetic forcefield, toward the likes of uncaring friends, critical teachers, and punitive bosses. Through this kind of repetition, the nongenerative pattern was reinforced and all generative relationships seemed unavailable and nonexistent. The man unconsciously expected to be treated unkindly and abusively. Even if he consciously believed he was entering a relationship with someone who was caring and loving, the relationship ultimately turned out to be abusive.

As noted earlier, patterns of thinking, patterns of behaving, and relationships with similar archetypal alignments and attractor sites maintain canalization. Putting this in human terms, early patterns are repeated and concretized by unconsciously attracting people who will play out the drama as the psyche hopes that the unconscious pattern will be identified, brought into awareness, and shifted to generativity. This is morphic resonance in action. By acting out a pattern, we keep it externalized and away from the internal upset that accompanies unconscious patterns. It is also a way to keep from remembering traumatic events or traumatic relationships. In this way, we simply pass them on to another person, replicating the earlier dynamics.

For example, an employee or business associate may consistently say she is going to do a task that needs to be done and then, we will find, with surprise, the job never gets done. The employee, too, will be surprised and puzzled by her own lack of action or forgetfulness, and everyone will feel disconcerted. When this happens for a second and third time, this repeated pattern can teach us, through resonance, about a central facet of this person's early experience: Promises made to her, by those upon whom she depended as a young child, were just not kept. Through resonance, we now experience what is out of awareness for that individual; that is, when someone does not keep a promise, it is truly upsetting and disorienting.

Because repetition is the key to canalization, by taking small steps to interrupt the repetition of a pattern, we can help a system open to new, generative options. Interestingly, the embryologist C.H. Waddington found in biology that it takes a larger perturbation[28] than the replicative process the system is in to change the course of a canalized, habitual pattern. Specifically, the stable, replicative pattern needs to be brought to a choice point, a "bifurcation,"[29] where there is an opening for greater complexity and new growth becomes possible. The system must switch into a kind of chaos in order to open to a new pathway that is more generative. In the above example of the employee who does not complete the tasks she has chosen, a new response that takes into accord the unconscious replicative system must challenge her confusion in a way that begins to name and acknowledge the nongenerative pattern; the perturbation must be larger than the original patterned system and call forward new insight and behavior. This will create the beginnings of a new archetypal alignment.

In Archetypal Pattern Analysis, we design archetypal interventions for this purpose, to bring one to a choice point, where a new way of being (or a new attractor) can be chosen. As in the case of choosing to go to bed earlier because it would be healthier, although staying up is desired, the system has to self-organize into a new pattern. This change can only happen if we choose to leave our comfort zone (canalized pathway).

When interruptions halt the replication process, a bifurcation, like a fork in the road that divides into two branches, is created. Bifurcations make us conscious of our replicative processes and familiar patterns. If we choose to move toward change, a new archetypal attractor site opens, and we can shift our archetypal alignment to new behaviors that are generative. The bifurcation allows us to decide whether to choose the new attractor or to continue replicating the familiar pattern. We must consciously choose between staying comfortable in what we know or taking a leap of faith into the unknown, which is required for change to take place.

Symmetry

Finally, Archetypal Pattern Analysis and its interventions are often based on reading symmetry, or the lack of symmetry and lack of congruence. The origins of the word *symmetry* point us to the Greek *symmetric*, "an agreement in dimensions, proportion, and arrangement." According to particle physics, all laws of nature originate in symmetries. In biology, it is the balanced distribution of duplicate body parts or shapes—for instance, two legs, two arms, etc. In chemistry, it is the symmetry of molecules.

Visually, symmetry conveys the likely health or fitness of other living beings. Consider that our hormonal pathways are unconsciously stimulated by symmetry in another person as a likely biological mate. In fact, our need for symmetry is deeply connected to the laws of nature and the symmetry of the natural world. It is so wired in us that the human mind associates asymmetry with threat and danger, probably because it is unconsciously recognized as going against the underlying forms of nature.

Think about walking into someone's home and immediately having an experience of feeling comfortable or uneasy. These "gut" reactions often come from an intuitive grasp of proportions and a sense of correspondence between the objects in the room. This can be understood as an underlying experience of the ancient practice of *feng shui* with a generative outcome. Patterns structure and organize a system; create a balance of dimensions, proportions, and arrangement that creates symmetry in, for instance, our therapy office; and, as a result, send a felt experience that safety is possible here. We have many words for a system without a well-patterned plan; it is asymmetrical and, therefore, seen and experienced as "inferior" and "undesirable."

Studies of descriptions of patterns on diverse cultural objects from all over the world, from Turkish textiles to Zulu beadwork, show that cultural information is embedded in the symmetrical structure of the pattern itself. With a practiced eye, these symmetrical structures actually describe aspects of each culture's fundamental principles for living in the world.[30] And, so it is with individuals, families, and businesses. A coherence or an asymmetry in expression shows us the fundamental principles that are presently operating out of awareness.

Many archetypal interventions are based on the reading of symmetry or the lack of congruence and point out non-symmetrical facts. A pattern interruption might be: "You say you want to earn a business degree, but you are also telling me you aren't turning in your required papers." This statement acts as a perturbation that can interrupt the current unconscious pattern, calling forward the lack of coherence in one's stated desire and actual behavior. From these types of interruptions, psychotherapy clients are brought to a conscious bifurcation in which a choice must be made: to keep the patterns repeating in a nongenerative fashion (a closed system of trajectories collapsing into a singularity) or to enter into the unknown that feels chaotic in order to move toward change.

When some change has been made, many clients will say, "I want to take a break. Things are so much better in my life." As archetypal analysts, we know this is frequently another stage in treatment; the person has come to an unconscious bifurcation or choice point. Fear of the unknown can often be underneath the wish to take a break, indicating an attempt to return to the prior pattern and cancel out potential change. We can interrupt this and its likely trajectory by naming the stage and by identifying the choices: staying with what is familiar or moving into the unknown with therapists, guides, and mentors to help open generative opportunities. This journey is how new archetypal alignments are made, new patterns are developed, and lasting change takes place.

Understanding archetypes and their manifestation leads us to an exploration of Field

5

The Profound Influence of Fields

"A field is the energetic component of an archetype which exerts its influence over space and time. This influence is not bound by space and time constraints. Rather, we find that, in contrast to fields in the outer world which are space-time dependent, such as gravitational and electromagnetic fields, archetypal fields are nonlocal, as evidenced, for instance, in telepathy, synchronicities, and the nonlocal transmission of information, etc. Essential to the concept of archetypal fields is the finding that they are dynamic, not static, and involve interrelationships."[31]

- Michael Conforti -

Theory. Remember, archetypes are nonlocal (not in time and space), so they need certain specific matter configurations to activate an energy field that then brings them into time and space. In developing Archetypal Pattern Analysis, Michael Conforti has created an overarching theory of fields. His work synthesizes many different scientific fields, marrying them with both the Jungian principles of an archetype and with the knowledge of how nature comes into form and grows.

As in any meta theory, many terms are borrowed from diverse scientific disciplines to create a complex and dynamic understanding of the manifestation of an archetype through a field. For example, the terms *morphogenetic fields*, *informational fields*, *thought fields*, *behavior fields*, and *biofields* are all borrowed from various scientific disciplines and their corresponding research, yet all are nested under the category of an *archetypal field*. A basic grasp of these different terms can establish a viewing platform, whereby you can catch a glimpse of the mystery of an archetype's materialization into "gross form" as well as into "subtle form" as thought, behavior, and emotional experience.

Exploring Fields

We all have had experiences of being moved by the influence of energy fields. We might walk into a room of people, the room feels warm and friendly, and we are attracted to one person or group and easily start a conversation. Or we return to our family of origin for a visit, reverting to old relationship patterns and dynamics similar to when we were growing up. Likewise, in some people's presence, we feel good and resonate with them. With others, we react negatively with non-resonance. These instinctual attractions, aversions, and patterns occur because of the information and memory held in each particular person's energy field.

We also may feel moved by the power and mystery of energy fields when we admire flocks of birds swooping in unison or herds of deer or elk running together at breakneck speed. Animal navigation, migration, and homing depend on energy fields connecting the animals to their destinations—like invisible elastic bands linking them to their homes and attracting them through energetic resonance.

Or consider the marvel of plants: They instinctively know what form to take each year as they poke out of the ground, bud, and bloom into beauty. Each plant species has its unique blueprint and archetypal information directing whether it needs sunlight or shade, its length of time to mature, whether it is a perennial or annual, edible, medicinal, or poisonous, flowering or ornamental. Similarly, cultures of people naturally have certain traits, body shapes and sizes, facial features, skin color, and ways of behaving and relating, each with their own specificities. But how? All these scenarios and characteristics—in fact, all forms, thoughts, behaviors, and systems—occur because of precise information contained in the archetypal field innate to the particular entity.

Conforti defines *fields* as non-material regions of influence that shape all that is in them. They are "the energetic component of an archetype, which exerts its influence over space and time. This influence is not bound by space or time constraints."[32] They seem to be invisible, in that we cannot see them with the naked eye, yet they determine all aspects of our world. When we look out to space, for example, it appears to be empty, but space is actually filled with field upon field of archetypal information in the form of energy. Rupert Sheldrake says, "Fields cannot be explained in terms of matter; rather, matter is explained in terms of energy with fields."[33]

Given that information is at the root of archetypes, archetypal fields are often called *informational fields*, a term that came into Archetypal Pattern Analysis through the work of Ervin Laszlo.[34] We can witness the power of informational fields in the simple exercise we did as children with a magnet underneath a sheet of paper topped with iron filings. Recall that the filings quickly organize themselves in a pattern of arcs that begin at the northern pole of the magnet and swing up and around to the magnet's southern pole. This pattern of filings is visual evidence that the magnet creates a field, albeit invisible. The field permeates the space around the magnet, exerting a force or influence beyond the magnet's physical boundaries.

Energy fields are integral to and underlie the organization of all systems—from atoms to galaxies. Although they predate form, they contain the information enabling physical matter to exist and archetypes and forms to manifest. That is, fields continually shape and influence that which they contain. They organize all forms, structures, and patterned interactions of systems under their influence—including those of animals, plants, cells, proteins, crystals, brains, and minds. In truth, fields shape all matter, thoughts, behaviors, cultures, and societies. They hold the "destiny factor" (or "entelechy") of an organism;[35] everything unfolds from this explicative order through energy fields. For example, similar to magnets, our modern technology is dependent upon invisible electromagnetic fields. Our cell phones, Internet, wireless networks, cloud storage of data, MRIs, airport security, and the like are only possible through access to the information and energy from available electromagnetic fields.

Researchers have identified distinct energy fields, as illustrated in the following "**Field Theory**" diagram.[36] These fields range from nonlocal fields (beyond time and space), formless and spaceless, to the different states before coming into form as physical matter. Specifically, the diagram showcases: the formless, unconditioned space of the Absolute in Field 0; the "causal" Field 1 that holds form in potential; the "subtle" realm of Field 2; Field 3 with its dimensions of time and space; and, finally, the gross material world of Field 4.

Delving deeper, **Field 0** is the nondual, unconditioned space permeating all other fields and from which all in the other fields arises. It is the open, empty, non-separate space of unconditioned awareness and is referenced in numerous ways. Depending upon the wisdom tradition, it is known as the Absolute, God, Spirit, Buddha Mind, Brahman, Pure Presence, and what C.G. Jung called "the Self."

Field 1 comprises the "causal" realm—nonlocal, or beyond time and space boundaries. It is a vast, nearly infinite and expansive consciousness where form is held in a potential a priori state referred to as eternal memory or the Akashic field, a Sanskrit word meaning "ether" or "all-pervasive space."[37] Field 1 is thought to contain the archetypal grid and templates, held in formless, creative potential. Seeming to be a blank or nothingness, formless state, unaware of our embodiment or existence, this is the field we enter in deep sleep each night when we return to a state of unity with the Self. As the diagram illustrates, Field 0 permeates Field 1 and all subsequent fields.

The "subtle" realm of **Field 2** cannot be seen, tasted, touched, or smelled but

Field Theory

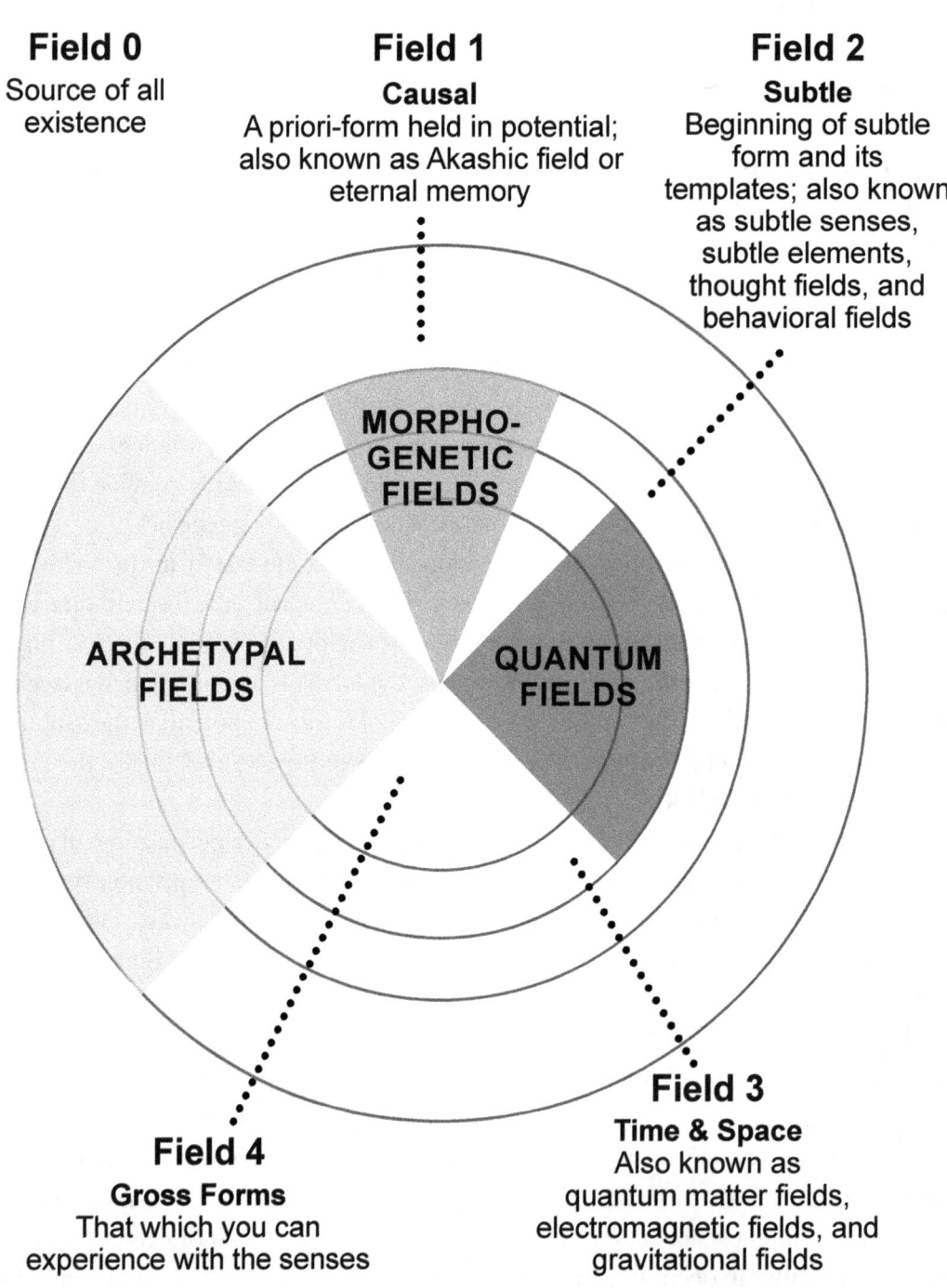

Field 0
Source of all existence

Field 1
Causal
A priori-form held in potential; also known as Akashic field or eternal memory

Field 2
Subtle
Beginning of subtle form and its templates; also known as subtle senses, subtle elements, thought fields, and behavioral fields

Field 3
Time & Space
Also known as quantum matter fields, electromagnetic fields, and gravitational fields

Field 4
Gross Forms
That which you can experience with the senses

Based on the wisdom tradition of Advaita Vedanta and Integral Theory can be felt through energy in and around our bodies. Herein lies the beginning of subtle form, subtle senses, and subtle elements that remain in templates from which form will arise but is not yet manifested. These templates are mere ideas of form, like the in-the-dream state we enter during sleep that contains images, feelings, emotions, light, and energy. As in the dream state, we have inner visions, sounds, smells, and tastes that are not yet in physical form.

Field 3 is the beginning of time, space, gravity, and duality of opposites, or objects being in separate states. We feel ourselves as a subject (I, me) seeing an object outside ourselves that may be good or bad, right or wrong, inside us or outside us, and the like. This duality exists because time measures from event to event and space measures from object to object, causing the appearance of separate states, separate things, and separate beings. Field 3 is the beginning of form through quanta of energy in quantum matter fields, electromagnetic fields, and gravitational fields. Form begins with microscopic quarks, atoms, and molecules and becomes denser and larger, eventually becoming gross forms.[38]

Field 4 is the physical realm of gross form, our embodied form, and what we experience with our senses. It contains all that can be seen with the naked eye in the physical, material world.

When viewing the "Field Theory" diagram, notice how the four fields nest within one another like Russian matryoshka dolls, ordered by levels of density and degrees of form or formlessness, ultimately resting in and being permeated with the Absolute or Self. Let's explain this important relationship through an archetypal lens: Arising from the unconditioned, formless space (Field 0) are archetypes in the causal realm beyond time and space that transcend all cultural differences (Field 1). These archetypes are constellated when activated and are manifested in this locality by energy fields called archetypal fields (Field 2). In these are nested morphogenetic fields that contain quantum, gravitational, and electromagnetic fields (Field 3). These fields give way to gross form and our physical reality (Field 4). The bottom line is that each field influences and is nested within the other.

....

Archetypal Fields

As Conforti notes, archetypes are nonlocal in that they exist beyond time, space, and gravity, as well as across cultures. Archetypes themselves are believed to be absent of energy until they are constellated and activated by energy fields in time and space, thus being called "archetypal fields."[39] As stated before, these archetypal fields are constellated and activated by specific configurations in the material world. This process is a part of the awe, the vast mystery and beauty of the world; science is limited in its ability to explain the unexplainable. We can possibly describe it by saying that all in the causal, subtle, and gross form arises from and is permeated by the Absolute, unconditioned source of all that exists. These archetypal fields are thought to originate on the cusp of the line between the Absolute and the causal realms (between Field 0 and Field 1).[40]

Although archetypes do not contain energy themselves, each has a specific informational field and mandate that contains the "eternal memory" of the archetype. Based on this eternal memory, the blueprint for the archetype lies in potential. When the archetype is activated, that blueprint is laid down and its form is brought into time, space, and gravity through energy fields and a process called "morphogenesis."[41]

When an archetype is activated and manifested through fields, these fields are referred to as "archetypal fields." As you can see on the diagram, archetypal fields begin in Field 1 and penetrate all through Field 2, Field 3, and Field 4. Archetypal fields contain all the information needed to bring that archetype into form. The archetypal field shapes and stabilizes this form, because fields configure the matter within them. For example, innate in the archetypal field of a tomato seed is everything needed to grow a tomato. It cannot become an eggplant or a green bean but only a tomato. Consider the following additional examples of material configurations that activate specific archetypal fields:

Pregnancy: With conception, the archetype is activated and manifested through an energy field filled with all the information and blueprint for the pregnancy of the species: nine months for humans, three months for dogs, two months for cats, twelve months for elephants, and so on. Due to the archetypal template for the species, within each of these cycles is a predictable process of growth and development at each particular stage until maturation is complete.

Containers: Containers as archetypal fields and archetypal structures are responsible for holding what is being contained in them. For example, the womb during pregnancy is the container responsible for keeping the fetus safe during growth and development to birth. Like a fetus, all living systems are held and contained throughout their growth and developmental process. If the container is compromised, so is the growth and development—and the survival—of that which it contains. Containers for other things such as liquids are similar in their mandate, in that, if there were a fracture in the container, it could no longer maintain its function of holding.

Orphans: When someone is given up for adoption or parents die, the orphan archetypal field is activated. Due to the information held in this archetypal field, those orphaned, even if placed at birth into a loving family, tend to carry similar feelings and patterns of behavior. Common feelings can include a sense of not being wanted and fears of abandonment and rejection. These feelings are integrated and often acted out in the orphans' lives. Even as adults, when both of our parents die, we feel the sense of orphan-hood, an untethered aloneness, as the archetypal field of the orphan is activated.

Cultures: Each culture practices certain traditions, rites, dress, and ways of being specific to that culture. As with Native American traditions and indigenous cultures globally, each tribe has different ways of practicing and expressing very similar rites and traditions. These traditions and practices are archetypal in nature, each having its own informational field.

Morphogenesis and Self-Organizing Systems

As noted, it is the process of "morphogenesis," which begins in Field 1 and is nested within an archetypal field, that moves the potential and blueprint of an archetype into form. The word *morphogenesis* has Greek origins: *Morpho* means "form," and *genesis* means "the bringing into." Thus, *morphogenesis* can be translated as "the coming into form" as a "morphogenetic field." Morphogenetic fields are a way of looking at archetypal fields.

In his revolutionary works—*A New Science of Life*, *The Presence of the Past*, and, most recently, *Morphic Resonance*—Rupert Sheldrake discusses how things come into form. According to Sheldrake, morphogenetic fields (also known as "morpho fields"), like other fields, contain all the information, memory, and intelligence needed to organize all form, structure, and patterns of relating. The morphogenetic field shapes and orders that which is being formed in it and contains a memory that then converts the information into form. This is true and consistent in animals, plants, cells, proteins, crystals, brains, and the mind—in the entire natural world. For example, the morphogenetic field of a dragonfly has all the information to transition a swimming larval creature called a nympth through a metamorphosis into an adult flying insect with two pairs of wings without going through a pupal stage. The field of the dragonfly cannot produce a butterfly or another flying insect other than a dragonfly.

Similar to archetypal fields, morphogenetic fields provide a structure but, in and of themselves, do not contain the energy to build the structure. That energy is found through interacting with energetic processes. Like building a new home, there needs to be an architectural blueprint or plan, building materials, as well as the energy and activity of builders. Basically, morphogenetic fields are part of an archetypal field as it begins to bring a structure to an archetype. Conforti often uses Sheldrake's scientific language in describing the power of archetypal fields and its many examples in our daily life.

Sheldrake refers to this as the innate intelligence of an entity, the "entelechy." The entelechy holds the blueprint, the goal, and the directing force in the development and functioning of an organism or system within a field. Sheldrake says that the entelechy actually organizes and controls the process of morphogenesis, or the unfolding of destiny itself. If the normal pathway to the unfolding destiny is disturbed, the system will try to redirect to reach the destiny in a different way. Specifically, the entelechy is one of the intelligent forces that motivates and guides us toward the wholeness inherent with the Self.

> **"Entelechy"** comes from the Greek word, *entelecheia*, which means: "that which realizes or makes actual what is otherwise merely potential." The concept is intimately connected with Aristotle's distinction between matter and form, or the potential and the actual.
> — From Britannica.com/topic/entelechy

Delving more deeply, according to Sheldrake, morphogenetic fields play a causal role in the development and maintenance of *all* living systems. That is, the information contained in a morphogenetic field organizes all living systems it relates to; it also maintains their development and structural form. And this is consistent at all levels of complexity.

Further, Sheldrake says that morphogenetic fields have "self-organizing capacities" and calls their process of organizing "formative causation."[42] Generally, morphogenetic fields behave as if nature's habits govern them. For example, morphogenetic fields of different plant species hold all the information needed to regenerate the plant from a plant cutting. In the suitable medium needed for each species, the plant cutting will begin to grow as a new plant, independent of the parent. Similarly, the amputated limbs of starfish will later regenerate, and earth worms, if cut in half, will regrow their tails. The morphogenetic field and the entelechy hold all the information for the different possibilities and potentials of the species.

Interestingly, as evidenced in the "Field Theory" diagram, morphogenetic fields are nested within one another, as well as within archetypal fields, and contribute to the memory and organization of larger systems. One of Sheldrake's striking contributions is that morphogenetic fields contain an inherent memory that becomes the source of information for all future self-organizing systems. Therefore, morphogenetic fields of similar organisms—whether plants, animals, or humans—can access the memory of other morphogenetic fields in order to continue the reproduction of their own species. Without this inherent memory, it would not be possible to continue a species, because there would be no memory to organize its structure.

Because of this nesting of morphogenetic fields and the access of information and memory, morphogenetic fields of similar species can share similar habitual patterns related to growth, development, and general functioning. These habitual patterns are stored in the memory of the morphogenetic fields and have influence over future organisms through the process of formative causation. In this theory, new systems show an increasing tendency to come into form the more often they are repeated. This replicative process tends to concretize its form and increase its probability to continue replication, similar to the hundredth monkey phenomena mentioned earlier.

Morphic Resonance

The term *resonance* is used in many domains: electricity, music, math, chemistry, physics, phonetics, as a feeling of emotion, or describing a richness of expression. Our understanding of morphic resonance, from studying Rupert Sheldrake's work, is that similar forms, or "fields of information," reverberate and exchange information within a subtle field, which we have labeled "Field 2" on the "**Field Theory**" diagram.

Morphic resonance is a prime example of the power archetypal informational fields hold in shaping what is in them and their attunement process (like attracting like). For example, Sheldrake notes that, through morphic resonance, members of certain species can tune in or resonate with similar species and to the larger collective morphic field of the entire species. Through resonance, species may begin to share behavioral patterns, and a repetitive process begins to establish behavioral pathways. Through repetition, these patterns can begin to organize and become increasingly habitual. The more that patterns are repeated, the more concretized they become, as noted in the last chapter.

Morphic resonance provides the inherent memory in morphogenetic fields through the vibration of similarity, based on past vibratory patterns. We are attracted to what is similar and resonate with it, attunement of the systems occurs, and repetitive patterns and habits are formed. In this way, information and behavioral patterns can be transferred from an a priori system to a new one.

As an example, Sheldrake believes it is through resonance with the innate memory held in the morphogenetic field that birds access their instructions related to nesting, flocking, migrating, mating, and the like. He has found no evidence that this information is stored in DNA. In this age of climate change, bird flocks are quickly changing their migrating and nesting patterns as a whole species. This raises many questions. Is this change based upon experience of the previous migration? How does a whole specific species of bird simultaneoulsy get this new information of where to nest? As Sheldrake states: "Through morphic resonance, newly learned patterns of behavior can spread rapidly throughout a species."[43] In order to continue to propagate the species, there must have been an urgent need for a swift response to new nesting grounds, and a change in timing of migration itself. When the flock had one or two catastrophic years, the field retained its wholeness and moved to recover its coherence by instituting new nesting sites and a new time for migration. Similarly, the human experience of a "phantom limb" after an amputation is an experience of the system's resonance with its own initial form.

Sheldrake further states: "In human psychology, the activities of the mind can be interpreted in terms of morphic fields interacting with the physicochemical patterns of activity in the brain. But these fields are not confined to the brain. They extend outward beyond the body into the environment. These extended mental fields underlie perception and behavior. They also enable phenomena that is without current science's understanding."[44]

Similar to Sheldrake's theory of morphic resonance and how everything is affected by everything else is Beverly Rubik's hypothesis on "biofields." Rubik's research attempts to explain the underlying dynamics and effectiveness of our current energy medicines such as acupuncture, Reike, and homeopathy, to name a few.

Rubik defines a *biofield* as the electromagnetic field in organisms that contains biological information and helps regulate the "homeodynamics" central to our lives. They are holistic organizing fields that involve subtle field interactions and biological information conveyed by electromagnetic signals throughout our bodies, as well as emanating from them.[45]

In Rubik's words, biofields are "the intelligent energy of living systems. They are a living communication network derived from bioelectrical phenomena inherent in our living tissues—the subtle body of an individual."[46] She goes on to say that energy medicines act "informationally" on our subtle energy fields and that we only need small interventions interacting with our natural system's dynamics to restore balance and harmony.[47] For example, to stimulate and impact biofields to carry information throughout the body, an acupuncturist inserts needles into acupuncture points. Similarly, Reike practitioners emit electromagnetic fields of frequency from their biofields that then impact the biofields of their patients. In homeopathy, the remedies are intended to interact directly with the biofields of the patient to effect change. All these therapies impact the biofields and supply information to the body to help maintain health and well-being.

Quantum Fields

Quantum fields are most noted because of the field of quantum physics and its research studies. As can be viewed on our "Field Theory" diagram, quantum fields begin with quanta of energy in time and space and describe the process of morphogenesis and where form originates. They include the continuum from the tiniest microscopic forms, like quarks and atoms, to forms that appear very solid to our eye, like furniture, food, and physical structures.

Quantum fields arise from and are contained within archetypal and morphogenetic fields. They are important in the diagram of fields only in that they represent where gross form begins to manifest.

Examples of Morphic Resonance and Morphic Fields

Termite colonies, bees, herds, packs, and other animal groups are held together and structured by morphic fields. The information from these morphic fields shapes and forms their own kind of collective memory. Morphic fields link members to a social group. A field enfolds all the members of the group within itself. Sheldrake says that these fields can stretch like an elastic band, enabling communication at a distance.

As we watch birds fly in flocks, wheeling and turning as if they are of one mind, each bird is navigating through a resonance to the field of the whole. Similarly, fish swim in schools, darting and whirling, maneuvering swiftly without running into each other, seemingly moving as one large organism, even creating defensive bunching against predators—all through resonance. In addition, we have all watched ants move in a single-file line, not touching each other, but pacing at an equal distance from one another over great distances, to get to some goal that's larger than themselves.

As for humans, we know that family members can have invisible emotional connections that persist over time, despite geographic distance from each other. Many people even intuit when a family member is in trouble or having a health crisis. Another example is when a mother's milk begins dropping from her breast when her infant, at home with caregivers, becomes hungry and begins to cry. Many of us also have experienced returning home for a family visit as an independent adult only to find that the family field is so strong that we begin to act in similar ways as we did as a child within those family dynamics. And, how do we explain immediately falling into easy conversation with an old friend to whom we haven't spoken in years?

In his book *Dogs That Know When Their Owners Are Coming Home*, Rupert Sheldrake shared his research about dogs and their humans. He found that dogs seem to know when their owners are coming home—even when the owners come at non-routine times in unfamiliar vehicles, even when no one at home knows when they are on their way, even when they left for the airport on a different continent to come home. The dogs went to the door or window and waited when the owner was on the way home, as if there were an invisible band of energy between them.[48]

Where romantic love is concerned, morphic resonance also plays a starring role. Recall that morphic resonance is an unconscious dynamic based on our patterning; like attracts like. When we feel romantically attracted to another person, we feel a strong resonance. We think we have much in common, despite barely knowing the person. This is an example of feeling a "shared resonance." But that resonance might be based on our nongenerative patterns; the psyche may be attempting to understand the dynamic and move toward generativity.

The HeartMath Institute has done fascinating research regarding the body's heart energy field and the powerful magnetic field that extends up to twelve feet from the body in the shape of a torus (surface of revolution generated by revolving a circle in three-dimensional space about an axis coplanar with the circle). Also, in measuring magnetic fields between people feeling love and affection for one other, the heart waves could instantly be measured as an increase in brain wave activity in the other.[49]

Similar research states: "It appears the heart has its own powerful and unique intelligence, which tells us that it's not simply the organ that pumps our blood and keeps us alive. Take the large number of heart transplant recipients who've reported incredible changes after transplant surgery: There have been reports of odd cravings, handwriting changes, new musical preferences, and even strange new memories that don't seem to be their own. These are simply transplanted along with the heart through a field of information, similar to a biofield, and the recipient experiences them as if they were his own, just like the heart's owner previously did."[50]

Such profound experiences, consistently reported by heart transplant recipients, demonstrate the power of fields to shape the matter in them. And it is not just the transplanted heart, but the entire informational energy field of the heart as well! Additional research from the HeartMath Institute reveals that the heart field of a pregnant mother creates a rudimentary heart field in the fetus before the heart is in form. From this heart field, the heart of the fetus is formed and the bonding process begins. It is also found that, in addition to the nine months needed in the womb, the baby needs another nine months in the mother's arms for the prefrontal cortex to grow, activate, and stabilize all bodily functions, particularly the heart, which requires constant reciprocal interaction with the DNA of the mother's body, heart, and emotional system as well as attunement with her electromagnetic fields. This is critical for a child's brain development and system stabilization.[51]

The power of fields and how we affect one another is also illustrated in Michael Conforti's "**Four-Tiered Field Theory**"[52] diagram. Although the diagram can be used in any setting, we often use it in psychotherapy to demonstrate how the therapist and client relationship is affected by one other's informational field. We begin the explanation of the diagram by discussing the middle of the diagram. There, the client and therapist each enter the room with a unique informational energy field. These two energy fields then form another combined energy field of shared information and relationship. All three of these fields are full of information about the therapist, the client, and their relationship. These informational fields are then contained within the archetypal field of psychotherapy and its mandate. Finally, these four fields are nested within the field of the Absolute from which all arises and with which all is permeated.

Why is this relevant and important? Without this knowledge, we tend to overlook the power of fields and how we attune to one another through similar patterns and experiences, what Sheldrake calls "morphic resonance." With attunement, unresolved patterns are more likely to be replicated. Avoiding this unconscious "blind spot" is what clients and therapists are typically looking for in finding "a good fit."

A common example is a therapist with a familial abuse history treating a client with an abuse history and blurring boundaries or not maintaining a solid "container" and conditions for treatment, even without conscious intent. Boundaries and the failure of families to maintain solid conditions for generative growth and development are the life history of both the therapist and the client, and they can be replicated during therapy. Think about the circle surrounding both the therapist and the client of the "Four-Tiered Field Theory" diagram and all the information available in these two fields that is then held in one informational energy field.

When the therapist is able to keep solid conditions and boundaries, this information is then imported from the therapist's psyche (subtle field) to the client's thought field as someone who is strong enough and has the client's best interests at heart. (This will be explained in more detail in Appendix B.)

Thought fields go way beyond the boundaries of our bodies; we have all sensed when someone was looking at us from a distance. Bruce Lipton, one of the frontrunners in epigenetics research and the author of the book, *The Biology of Belief*, acclaims the power of our perceptions. He notes that how we *perceive* things forms our thought structures. Most of these thought structures and aligning perceptions are formed in early childhood based on the impressions and the ways we were treated by our

Michael Conforti's Four-Tiered Field Theory

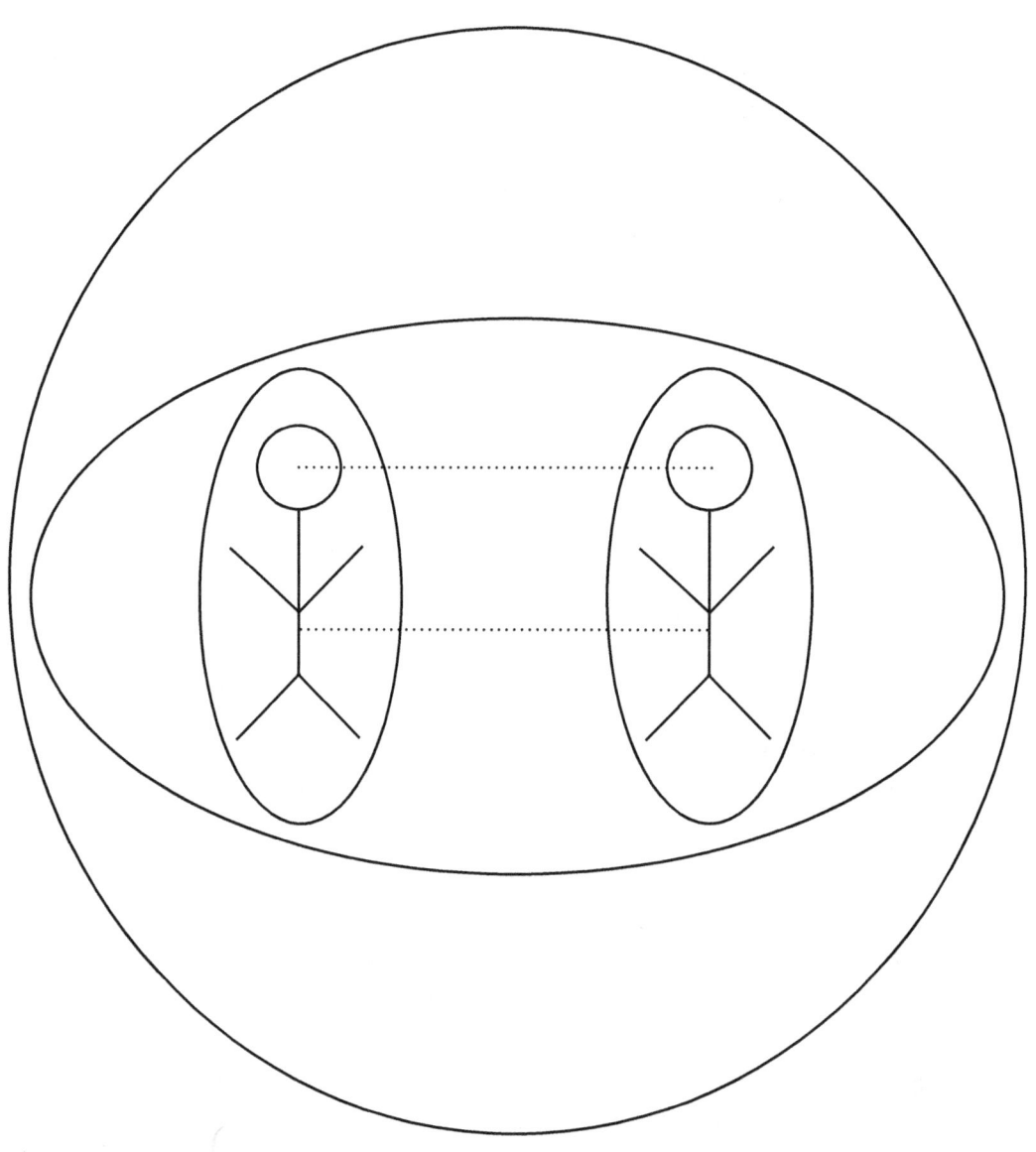

parents. These thought structures then affect which chemicals are released from the brain. And the chemicals and stress hormones permeate our cellular structure and the body's genes. In effect, according to Dr. Lipton, our perception can alter our very genetic makeup.[53]

Another fascinating study was conducted by Masaru Emoto. Dr. Emoto attached labels with words such as love, compassion, gratitude, evil, killing, and the like to the outside of containers holding water. When he microscopically viewed the water crystals within the containers, he found that each word he introduced changed the formation of the water crystals, depending upon the morphogenetic field introduced.[54] This demonstrates the power of the field that each word carries with it and the effects the thought field can have on us physically—given that our physical structure's primary component is water!

Here's the concept in a nutshell: Thoughts we think, experiences to which we are exposed, movies we watch, and the ways others relate to us can all impact who we are on a cellular level. That's why, when we walk into a room, we feel an attraction or an aversion to certain people or activities; relationships and friendships are based upon our resonance with each other! Women living together for a length of time tend to attune to the same hormonal rhythm and menstruation. And that's why a new clock in a clock shop will begin a similar ticking pattern of the other clocks (examples of morphic resonance and behavioral fields within archetypal fields).

The presence of an archetype and the energy components of archetypal, electromagnetic, and morphogenetic fields are profoundly felt by their effects on us in terms of feelings, behaviors, thoughts, and ways of relating to others and the world. By being more conscious of their existence and impact on us and our world, we can make more intentional choices in how we conduct our lives, in the perceptions we hold, in the thoughts we believe, and what is of most importance to each of us individually.

Part Two

Erich Neumann's Archetypal Developmental Theory:
Individuation and the Ego-Self Journey

"Once we have understood that the ego can never exist and develop without the Self that underlies it, . . . we see that it is the Self around which the ego revolves, as the earth revolves around the sun. Then we realize that the ego-Self axis is the foundation of the personality [and see] the dynamics of human life as a unity in which conscious and unconscious process, 'inner' psychic contents and 'outward' world contents, form an indissoluble whole."[1]

- Erich Neumann -

6

Neumann's Archetypal Exploration of Individuation: The Next Step in the Evolution of Consciousness

"Where the ego is not developed, the conventional collective ethic (or the Law) will be adequate. For the personality in whom wholeness has unfolded its flower, the authority of the (inner) 'voice' will replace the collective law of conscience."[2]

- Erich Neumann -

Along with Archetypal Pattern Analysis, it is the groundbreaking work of Dr. Erich Neumann that has fueled our study and clinical practice over the last few decades. In this section of the book, we would like to introduce you to Erich Neumann and to share why his work has been so captivating to us.

Erich Neumann PhD (1905 -1960) met C.G. Jung after finishing his medical training in 1934. By all accounts, Neumann was transformed by Jung's belief in the objective psyche, and a life-long relationship ensued. When Neumann subsequently moved to Israel, the two maintained contact through letters and visits, although from 1939 to 1945, World War II kept Neumann isolated and out of communication. During that time, "Neumann, having no other choice, took what he learned from Jung and applied it, imagined into it, and expanded it,"[3] synthesizing it with his deep Jewish studies. When he could finally communicate with Jung after the war, in 1945, he shared "massive amounts of content, including *The Origins and History of Consciousness*," which Jung deemed "brilliant."[4] In this landmark book, Neumann laid the "grand plan for a comprehensive archetypal theory of human development."[5] He outlined a unique history of the evolution of consciousness, representing the phenomenological journey of the ego and the Self, showing the birth, growth, and transformation of the ego reflected in three great cycles of myth: the creation myth, the hero myth, and the transformation myth.

By this time, Neumann and Jung were colleagues and friends, with Jung endearingly calling Neumann a "companion on the road."[6] In retrospect, Dr. Gerhard Adler notes, "Erich Neumann was the one truly creative spirit among the second generation of Jung's pupils, the only one who seemed destined to build on Jung's work and to continue it. This was . . . due to the fact that his work did not spring from his intellect but from a deep and living contact with the unconscious sources of creativity."[7] We particularly resonate with the concept of Neumann's "living contact with the unconscious sources of creativity," because it aptly describes our own experience with Neumann's depth of intellect and his extraordinary work.

Looking forward, the rest of Part Two features:
- Overview of Neumann's vision of individuation
- Explanation of the myths that underlie the archetypal developmental stages
- Summary of each of these myths
- Visual diagram of the Ego-Self Journey
- Visual diagram of the archetypal developmental stages
- Model of contemporary ages and tasks congruent with each of the stages

We hope we do justice by interpreting Neumann's work in a contemporary and clinical language that will be of service to others.

....

Overview of Neumann's Vision of Individuation

Erich Neumann paints a rich picture of individuation in his book *Depth Psychology and a New Ethic*, calling *individuation* "a necessary next step in the evolution of consciousness."[8] This next step, he says, is the deep acceptance of the unconscious and of our own negative tendencies. The step allows humankind to not just be rooted in the conscious mind, but to be rooted in our total psychic structure—the Treasure of the Self, which is so difficult to attain.

In the past, society's general moral code, collective values, rules, and law held us in a "stable container" that allowed the ego to stabilize and strengthen, keeping us from being overwhelmed by our unconscious and of acting out unconscious tendencies.[9] Yet, to individuate[10] is to discover and assimilate our own aggressive and negative tendencies, taking us beyond using our introjection of an external moral standard of conventional values and rules (which were taught to us from outside ourselves) to gaining our own inner moral code, not based on the conscious mind alone, but coming internally from our total psychic structure[11] and experience of the Self. It is the vital difference between a plant grown in water and a plant grown in the earth.

Erich Neumann's vision of the future of individuation reveals a society of matured individuals who have metabolized our "shadow," found our center as the Self, and achieved an ethical sovereignty, which comes internally. With this ethical sovereignty coming from the total psyche, we no longer need to project unconscious tendencies onto others. Instead, we can act as the stewards and purifiers of the collective. As we withdraw psychological projections, we begin to experience the creative fullness of our own primal psychic ground, the Self.[12] Of course, this is a gradual process and is experienced as a shifting away from the dominance of the ego and the conscious mind toward the Self and the phenomenon of the wholeness of the psyche. We are a long way from this extraordinary vision. We can only hope, as individuals, that we can make a contribution toward this reality.

Erich Neumann's Eight Great Myths

Showing us the way, Neumann found, through his intensive study of world mythology, that **eight great myths** symbolically express the developmental stages of the individual ego and the collective unconscious in human culture.[13] These eight myths reflect the birth, growth, and transformation of the ego on its journey toward consciousness. They express a comprehensive view of the development of consciousness and the stages of individuation.

> **Erich Neumann's Eight Great Myths**
>
> Uroborus
> Great Mother
> Separation of the World Parents
> Birth of the Hero
> Slaying of the Parents
> Rescuing the Captive
> Gaining the Treasure
> Transformation: Unification of Opposites

Each myth expresses an alignment with the stages of individual development; these stages are archetypal and exist in potential for all humanity. This rich vantage point provides a lens through which to examine the developmental stages from birth through the highest level of consciousness available to us as humans.

For clinicians, these stages and the dynamics within each of them offer a powerful archetypal diagnostic tool through which we can map where a person is in these stages of development, what the next stage is, what is helpful to reach that next stage, and the likely obstacles. We also can work simultaneously with the ego aspects and the psyche's overall intention to move toward wholeness with the Self.

One of mythology's primary functions is to initiate the individual into the magnificent ordering of the psyche. Mythology also shows how the symbolic can inspire awe and activate the innate inner wisdom that guides us toward deeper meaning and Self-realization. In *The Origins and History of Consciousness*, Neumann outlines the relationship between the ego and the unconscious as well as the personal and the transpersonal. Each myth shows specific stages of this archetypal process as well as the crisis bifurcation, or choice point, that needs to be faced at each stage—whether to move forward into the unknown in order to advance in consciousness and development, or to remain in the comfort of what is familiar. Each developmental crisis takes new choices and deep wrestling with fears and inner demons to change behavioral patterns aligned with the next stage of generative development. The stages build on one another; when the foundational stages of the Great Mother are compromised in any way, our inner world and the ego's impressions compromise the development at each successive stage. Of course, with a large enough perturbation—such as a loving relative, teacher, or therapist—this course can correct itself into greater generativity.

Seeing the therapeutic application of Neumann's brilliant synthesis of these eight myths, their symbolic meaning, and his articulation of the development of the unconscious, we began building on his work by translating the stages of the myths into clinically recognizable features and applying them to the individual's archetypal journey to attaining unity with the Self, the Treasure of our being. Each stage has tendencies and behaviors that are different expressions of archetypal processes, from the beginning of life through the highest stages of consciousness. This book is our attempt to share our translation of Erich Neumann's Archetypal Developmental Theory, our articulation of the ego's tasks as it traverses the archetypal map of life, how we use the translation and articulation in our clinical practice, and how it might be applied to life. The understanding of this framework offers a way to chart the navigation on this archetypal journey, for ourselves and those with whom we work—to see what transpires at each stage through the course of development, which stage someone is at currently, and the next step to be mastered of both conscious and unconscious development.

In the rest of this section of the book, we will explain the eight myths Neumann laid out in *The Origins and History of Consciousness* and walk you through the aligning stages in his Archetypal Developmental Theory related to individual human development. We also will present a visual view of this journey, inspired by Edward Edinger's work on the Ego-Self Axis,[14] which gives us an archetypal blueprint and overview from the perspective of the relationship between the ego and the Self and their dance of individuation. The subsequent section will focus on the application of this archetypal knowledge and its use in working with others. It also can be used as a framework for individuals and other practitioners.

....

Introduction to Neumann's Archetypal Developmental Theory: The Ego–Self Journey Toward Individuation

"Individuation" is the process in which a unique individual identity develops out of an undifferentiated unconscious. Once mature, we become fascinated with a conscious rediscovery of that from which we individuated—the vastness of the Self, which is the center and foundation of our very being.

The Self is not located in the psyche nor in the physical world; it is beyond these realms. The Self also is simultaneously permeating and inseparable from all existence. In order to speak about them, we often refer to our unique individual identity as the "ego" and the vastness of our true nature as the "Self," as if they are two separate entities. But nothing can truly be separate from the Self, as it is the underlying source from which all arises.

In Archetypal Developmental Theory, the ego is seen as the masculine part of ourselves (our relationship to the outer world) and the unconscious is the feminine part of ourselves (our relationship with our inner world). It is through the ego-Self journey that lies in potential that we have the opportunity to develop more consciousness and begin having experiences of our true nature, the Self. Innately, this process contains the possibility of our masculine and feminine aspects coming into balance and unity.

In terms of our development, at first, the emerging ego can only differentiate itself from its environment. For example, think, "I am different from my blanket." Then it differentiates itself from caregivers, as in perceiving, "My mother can go away from me. I am different from her." Eventually, the ego becomes an identity called "me" and establishes a social personality that can interact with others and with the culture within which it is embedded. In general, the ego is the center of our field of consciousness. Once it matures and can look back on itself and witness its own functioning, it can then intuit itself as an object of an unknown vast subject, which we call the Self, the center and totality of the psyche.

Through ego development theory and research, we know that the ego, our instrument for individuating from the unconscious, has the innate potential to reach a state of unity with the Self. To accomplish this, development demands that we separate from both the personal and the collective qualities with which the ego has formerly identified (e.g., parental injunctions, cultural dictates, etc.). This takes conscious effort and attention. We must release and bring to awareness the archetypal nature of the psyche itself. Like the process of digestion, the refinement and separation of the archetypal psyche from the ego's identifications evolves by keeping what is truly nourishing for the unity of the psyche while integrating disowned aspects developed during earlier conditioning. The journey's end is for the ego to position itself as a servant of the Self, thus completing the archetypal journey of individuation into conscious unity, metabolizing a knowing awareness of body, mind, and spirit.

Carl Jung divided this process of development into the first half of life and the second half of life, because they represent two quite different phases of the life cycle. As we mature, the Self reveals itself in small increments, most particularly in the second part of life. He explains this developmental progression as being similar to the sun's daily cycles: rising in the morning, reaching its zenith around noon, continuing its descent throughout the afternoon until its completion, and setting in the evening.[15]

As described, there are specific stages in which the ego matures and passes through in its dance with the Self—a journey toward individuation.[16] From the work of Dr. Edward Edinger (1922-1998), we were inspired to create a diagram of this dance. In our **"Ego-Self Journey"** diagram, the Self is illustrated by large grey circles, whereas the ego is illustrated by smaller black circles. Note that the Self starts out nearly empty at first, showing that the ego is undifferentiated. At birth, the ego begins and then gradually grows larger, carrying more consciousness as the individual ages, yet always at the mercy of being pulled back into its smaller, undifferentiated mode. To deal with this conflict of "push-pull," the ego continually tries to rid itself of whatever in its nature it considers unhelpful to the growth process by relegating it out of awareness, hiding it in the unconscious. The ego eventually moves outside the circle of the Self to stand independently, secure in the outer world, feeling its difference and uniqueness from all others.

Once the ego reaches this zenith and stands alone, without the fear of being drawn back into the unconscious, it is then strong enough to feel its innate longing for wholeness and for knowing the Self. Pulled by this knowledge and fortified by its strength, the ego begins the journey back to ego-Self unity, gaining deeper consciousness in the process. This entails reintegration of all that it had to leave behind as it tried to move out of the gravitational pull of the Self. As it reintegrates, the ego moves back into relationship with the Self, but it is now able to feel both its own uniqueness as well as an embeddedness in the mystery of life. Then the ego becomes conscious of a reality beyond the mind, begins to form a numinous relationship with the Self, and finally dissolves from its separate state into a vast unification with the Self.

In human development, this dance between the ego and Self, when understood, can open up a vast view of reality. It maps a course that leads us beyond our condi-

Neumann's Archetypal Exploration of Individuation   83

Ego-Self Journey

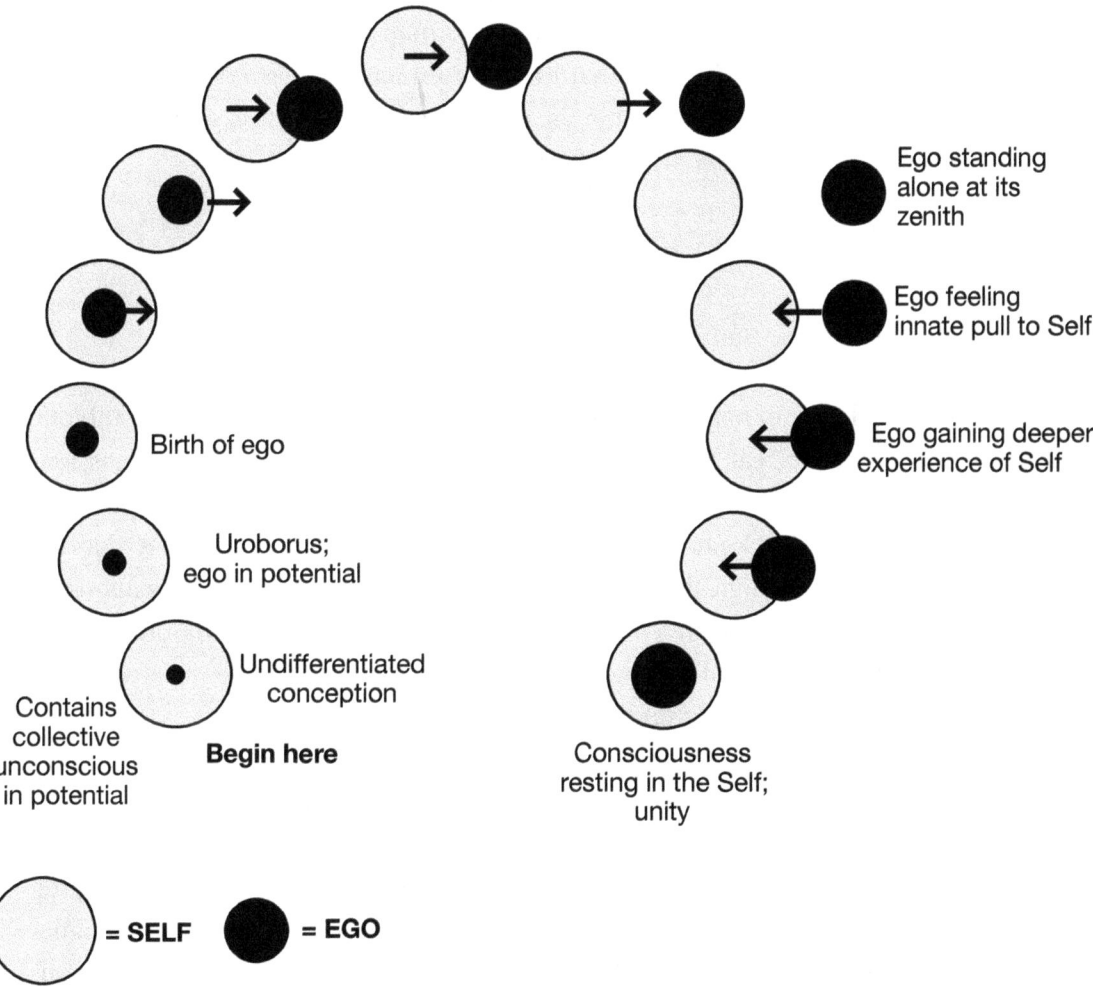

Inspired by the work of Edward Edinger

tioned ego and its thought structures of early childhood that are unconscious and which the ego believes to be our truth. When we begin experiencing the Self, we start to see the conditioning and our early impressions for what they are, and their power dissolves. Compassion and love can fill some of the spaces where critical thoughts and suffering once had root. Embracing our conditioned ego and vast numinous Self as undivided opens a threshold for living the full potential of our life and for sharing the unique gifts each of us brings to humanity. Similar to Neumann's vision, we hope to live as much as we can in relationship and alignment with what the Self asks of us.

We find the ego-Self diagram to be a shorthand map of the process outlined in the Archetypal Developmental Theory that Erich Neumann synthesized from his extensive studies of the world's myths. Put in the language of ego and Self, we hope it helps to show you the landscape we are about to enter in detail.

....

Overview of Neumann's Archetypal Developmental Theory

Archetypal development begins with the undifferentiated state of unity and symbiotic relationship with the Great Mother of early infancy. The early stages are unconscious and somatic, given that they are pre-cognitive, pre-verbal, and based on impressions taken in during the development of our inner world. It is during that time that the Self is experienced through the body. As we move from this symbiotic relationship with the mother into some differentiation from her, the early conditioning of the pre-ego begins the process of veiling our true nature, setting the stage for the beliefs, perceptions, and thought structures of the early ego.

From the parental impressions during early development, the "anima" and "animus" (archetypal imprints in the form of parental introjects) also take root and, later, form our outer projections in the world of relationships. The anima represents the psychic feminine archetype, and the animus, the masculine archetype. Emma Jung described these as "the outer personality behaving as if they are inner personalities and exhibiting the characteristics which are lacking in the outer, manifest, conscious personality. [They] are conditioned by the experience each person has had in the course of his or her life with representatives of the other sex, and also the collective image of *woman* carried in the psyche of the individual man, and the collective image of *man* carried by a woman."[17]

It takes the activation of the Father archetype for us to turn to the outside world relationships and be pulled from the Great Mother forces. This shift from inner life and a focus on bodily needs (the Great Mother) to the mind, concepts, and outer world accomplishments of the Father archetype begins the stage called the Separation of the World Parents. This shift also lays the groundwork for the development of the "superego" and early "persona" (the self-image we have as our identity and want others to see). As development proceeds, the outer world, peer group influences, and the conditioned ego gain importance. To individuate from parental and societal influences and embrace our own sense of self, we must take the hero's journey.

In developing the ego, the unconscious is veiled and in the background but is manifested and expressed by outer projections and reactions that feel very true and real. The journey to becoming a hero (the ego and masculine aspect of self that is not gender specific) is to have the strength and courage to face early childhood experiences and parental impressions we have believed about ourselves, the inner world of the maiden (feminine aspects of our young self/the unconscious inner world), and perceptions left behind in early childhood. At this point, the "ego ideal" that began in our early impressions dictates the qualities of the hero we will become. The ego ideal is a symbolic figure, formed in our unconscious, that empowers us with the authority to find our way in the outer world through heroic quests of mastery (outer accomplishments such as completing an education, playing sports, creating a home, and having children) and to face old confusions and beliefs that were relegated to "shadow" realms (the unconscious).

Influenced by the Father archetype of the outer world, the ego is also the part of self that projects onto others the hurt, reactive states from early childhood unconscious impressions; forms our perceptions (that which we believe to be true); and impacts our relationships and outer activities (based on the early anima and animus impressions of parental experiences). These dynamics become the foundation of most of adult life—and our unhappiness. When we come to the realization that all endeavors in the outer world do not lead to lasting fulfillment, happiness, or a sense of inner peace, we reach a bifurcation or choice point. Do we continue living life from the same vantage point, or do we turn back to our inner life of the feminine Great Mother forces and face the aspects of self left behind that may be painful and frightening to face? The hero chooses the latter.

Equating that latter part of the hero's journey with the Great Myths, the Rescuing the Captive stage depicts the return of the hero to the hurt or confused places inside us that were created when we were not seen or acknowledged for our true nature. Those aspects went into hiding, split off into sub-personalities, and were walled off to protect our innocence and heart. During the Rescuing the Captive stage, however, anima and animus are revealed from the unconscious, allowing us to have a deeper relationship with ourselves and others.

To become a hero in our own power and authority is to have the capacity to face the unconscious forces of the Great Mother that feel as though they will take over and annihilate us. Once we face our fears and rescue our unconscious feminine, we can then integrate it and make a marriage of both the ego and the unconscious, the masculine hero and the feminine maiden, the Mother and Father archetypes. This integration of the Mother and Father archetypes will reveal the Treasure—our full potential and fullness of life. Also, with this unity, we become empowered to bring our unique gifts into the world.

Neumann's Great Myths: A Summary

The Archetypal Developmental Theory is a blueprint or grid for the developmental stages of human existence based on the eight myths Erich Neumann used to explain the origins, history, and development of consciousness. He organized these myths into three major categories:

Creation Myths include myths related to the Uroborus, the Great Mother, and the Separation of the World Parents. These myths orient us to the beginning of our lives when we are in an undifferentiated state of unity and a symbiotic relationship with the Great Mother, called the uroborus. During these early creation stages, the archetypal dynamics are present in the inter-relationship with the Great Mother and her infant, who is developing its inner world of feelings, emotions, perceptions, and sense of how to take in the world related to self and the body.

As noted in the last section, it takes the activation of the Father archetype to help free the child from the forces of the Great Mother and her devouring tendencies. This shift enables a move into the outer world of the mind, concepts, and early ego development in the Separation of the World Parents stage. The journey continues as the ego develops through its conditioning and outer world accomplishments, with the material world eventually becoming paramount.

Hero Myths include myths related to the Birth of the Hero and the Slaying of the Parents, meaning the Mother and Father archetypes. To truly become a hero may take numerous "dragon fights," both inner and outer. These dragon fights are necessary, in fact, to gain autonomy from the significant influence of the parental archetypal forces and to embrace our own unique sense of self. A

Erich Neumann's Mythological Stages in the Evolution of Consciousness

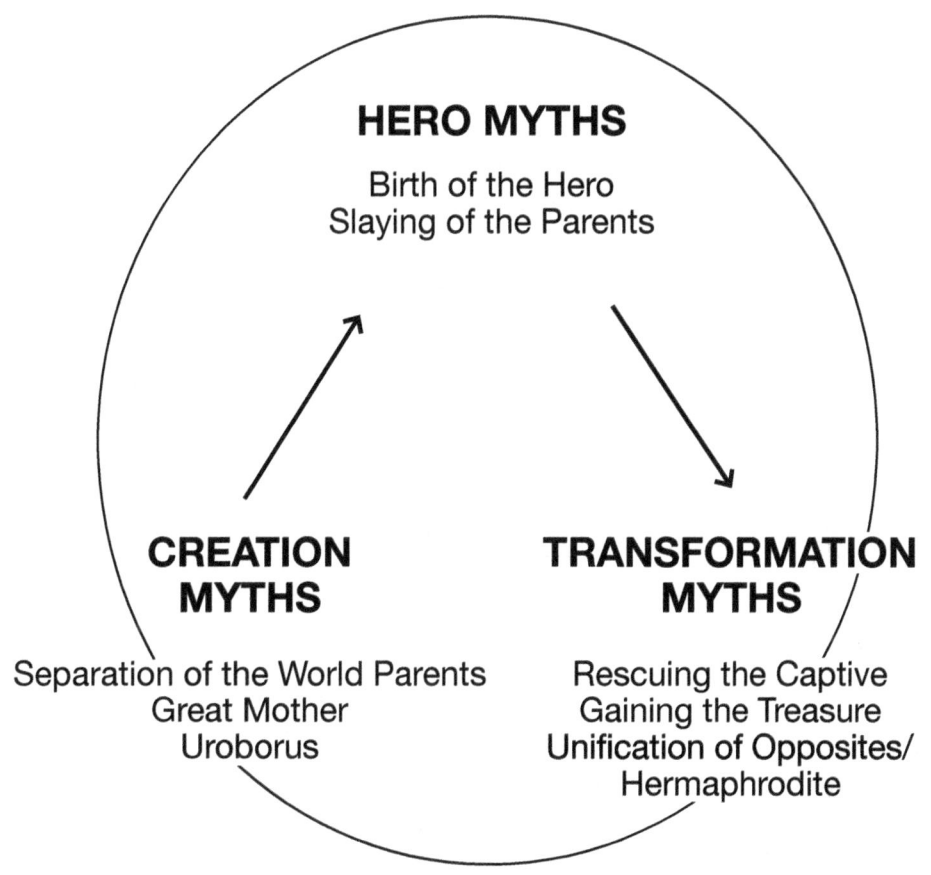

common example is ending attempts to get approval from parents and peers by building our own internal approval.

The hero (not gender specific) is called to do two things: firstly, to learn the mandates of the culture, and, secondly, to bring a new order into the culture. Archetypal movies such as *Lord of the Rings*, *Harry Potter*, *Indiana Jones,* and *Wonder Woman* depict that effort and the dragon fights that ensue. Such movies are popular because they show us a process for a meaningful relationship with life that fulfills the mandates of the hero. Common themes are: 1) answering the call and saying, "yes," to the endeavor; 2) leaving the ordinary life we know behind; and 3) facing our inner fears and demons by facing death and annihilation in order to capture the treasure and share it with humanity. It is the hero's task to return to the Mother world to rescue, capture, and return the "feminine maiden," becoming increasingly more conscious and opening to the transformational stages.

Transformation Myths include myths related to Rescuing the Captive, Gaining the Treasure, and the Unification of Opposites. To live our Treasure and unveil the awareness of the Self that has remained our source and ground of being means seeing through, releasing, and integrating aspects of self and their aligning patterns by rescuing parts held captive during the Great Mother, pre-cognitive, pre-verbal early years of childhood. This is the hero "rescuing the captive." As we do this, more aspects of the Treasure of the Self are revealed, and the ego morphs into being clearer and less reactive, allowing increased unity with all humanity. In our increased unity, the polarities of ego (the masculine aspects represented by the ego and the feminine unconscious aspects) also unify and balance. The mythic symbol Neumann uses to represent this transformation is the hermaphrodite, an androgynous figure with a diamond glowing from the heart who is wearing a crown of the Self and standing on a dragon.

> In honor of Neumann's work, we will be using his symbol of the **"hermaphrodite"** throughout our text. We are aware that the hermaphrodite depicts undifferentiated genitalia, rather than a unity or balance of masculine and feminine aspects which is present in the more contemporary symbol of the androgyne.

These eight myths begin with our birth, when we are in unification with the central archetype of the Self but in an undifferentiated, unconscious state. The process continues with the emergence of the ego that, as it develops and is conditioned through parental and societal influences, becomes central to our lives. During this process, we focus externally, turning away from the Self, the source and ground of being. Our relationship with the Self remains unconscious and seems to be veiled from our knowledge. In this apparent separation, we feel disconnected from others, experiencing the duality of an inside self and the outside world, and we lose the capacity to view and inhabit the vast unity of all existence.

The ego in its process of developing and individuating is transformed with the gaining of consciousness, and eventually it is able to turn back toward the Self and see the unity that has always been present. As the developmental process continues, we carry on the transformation process of Rescuing the Captive and Gaining the Treasure in subtler forms. The more of us rescued from the captive, the more the Self/Treasure is revealed and the more the ego morphs into a clearer form, free from the earlier conditioning. When we realize and live from the Treasure of the Self, the masculine and feminine energies become balanced and unified, and the opposites the ego holds from early infancy—such as life-death, self-other, inside-outside, good-evil, light-dark, and victim-tyrant—begin to dissolve.

At each stage on our way to discovering our unity with the Self, the Treasure, we are faced with a dilemma and a bifurcation, a choice point: Do we move toward the desire for a deep, meaningful life and a realization of our unity with the Self? Or do we choose to stay with what is known and familiar out of fear that we may face death or annihilation? It is the hero who faces the fears and demons to interact with the archetypal forces through the stages to the Self.

The desire for unity with the Self is the archetypal force of Eros. Love and deep desire for wholeness pulls us through each stage toward realization of the Treasure. Although the unconscious forces of fear of death and annihilation create obstacles toward moving forward, constellating a strong wish to stay comfortable in the familiar, if we flow with the forces lovingly pushing us toward wholeness, we begin to move toward our unique destiny.

7

Neumann's Creation Myths: Uroborus, Great Mother, and Separation of the World Parents

"The mother-child relationship is archetypal in that it elicits a psychic field where the Divine child archetype is constellated in the mother as the Mother archetype is simultaneously constellated in the child and is ready to be evoked at any time. This archetypal image sets in motion a complex interplay of psychic functions in the child that lays the foundation for the development between the ego and unconscious as well as the Eros-bond attachment between the mother and child."[18]

- Erich Neumann -

Archetypal Developmental Theory includes both Erich Neumann's interpretation of the myths and the human developmental tasks of gaining consciousness. Starting with the Creation Myths, Neumann shows that consciousness begins in an undifferentiated, purely unconscious unification, the uroborus. This stage is also known as the eternal womb of the Great Mother. From this space, the ego is born and held in a "germ-like state" of potential until further development has taken place. For generative development to occur, trust, safety, and security are paramount.

During pre-ego times, when the ego is in potential, we are developing an inner emotional world tempered by the feminine forces of the Great Mother archetype. As this early conditioning takes place, great courage and strength is required to free from her grips if she is not helpful and supportive in the process. In fact, much of our original self can be left behind in the unconscious while transversing this early developmental journey. The state in which the young developing ego leaves the Great Mother sets the foundation for moving from the feminine, body-centered, inner world to conquering the outer world of the masculine forces of the mind and the concepts of the Father archetype. Neumann says that the ego begins to take form as the Separation of the World Parents unfolds and the Father archetype becomes primary in influencing the mind, concepts, and outer accomplishments. Once the ego integrates enough aspects of both the feminine and masculine worlds and has developed more consciousness, the Separation of the World Parents opens to the hero being born.

Erich Neumann's Archetypal Developmental Theory

HERO MYTHS

Separation of the World Parents   Dragon Fights

(Father Archetype activated)   Birth of the Hero

Slaying of the Parents

TRANSFORMATION MYTHS

Great Mother Archetype

Stage 3

Stage 2   Rescuing the Captive

Stage 1   Gaining the Treasure

Uroborus   Unification of Opposites / Hermaphrodite

CREATION MYTHS

Uroborus: The Primal Relationship of Mother and Child in the First Phases of Life

The primal relationship of early development is about being held in the arms of the mother and is symbolized by the mythological uroborus, often depicted as a serpent eating its tail, a mandala, or Vishnu sucking his toe. These symbols are borrowed from alchemy and represent the symbiotic relationship of the mother and the infant. In that relationship, the baby is unable to differentiate "self" from "other."

Neumann, in *The Origins and History of Consciousness*, describes the uroborus as the "grand round" that is more than just a womb of the mother. He says the uroborus stage is the World Parents joined in uroboric union, not to be divided. Within this union are held all the potential and archetypal images of the Mother as well as all opposites of existence yet to be birthed later in development: father and mother, birth and death, heaven and earth, good and evil, light and dark, and the feminine and masculine principles. This grand round union is symbolic of the universe, of eternal life, and of the perfection and ground from which all springs—and it holds the union of the opposites in their purest form as the new beginning.[19]

This uroboric union dominates the initial phases of our young, developing consciousness. At this stage, from birth through approximately six to eight months old, the ego exists as budding potential, in an undifferentiated, symbiotic state with the mother, while also in unity with the Self. While being held in the arms or at the breast of the mother, the infant is being conditioned by taking in impressions somatically, and its inner emotional world is being built by those impressions and attempts toward secure attachment.

In *The Child*, Neumann explains this prime importance of the mother in a child's early development. He writes, "The mother-child relationship is archetypal in that it elicits a psychic field where the Divine child archetype is constellated in the mother as the Mother archetype is simultaneously constellated in the child and is ready to be evoked at any time. This archetypal image sets in motion a complex interplay of psychic functions in the child that lays the foundation for the development between the ego and unconscious as well as the Eros-bond attachment between the mother and child."[20] He notes that, during this early symbiotic relationship, the mother and child appear like an enclosed, omnipotent system with a shared boundary.

Neumann goes on to say, this intra-uterine and extra-uterine primal experience is all under the influence and care of the Great Mother and her archetypal forces and mandate—which is to care for her dependent being's needs with loving attendance.

She is to put her needs secondary and provide safe and secure holding, while mirroring, through gazing, the baby's radiance, preciousness, value, and essential nature of being. Because the child and Great Mother are in a unified psychic field and the child experiences the mother as the Self, the child is open and vulnerable to all her forces, generative as well as hurtful and destructive.[21]

In our over forty years of clinical practice, we have observed that, because of their own limitations, too many mothers become more aligned and possessed by the nongenerative aspects of the Great Mother and, instead, focus more on themselves and their own needs. It is unfortunate that these narcissistic limitations are then mirrored to their child and taken in somatically in the unified symbiosis while there is no delineation between self and other. Specifically, while taking in food and milk from her breast, the infant takes in the negative projection held by the mother, which ultimately compromises the child's needs: basic holding, security, and trust. This narcissistic wounding is stored somatically and injures the later sense of identity, which can be felt as, "I'm bad, not important, and not good enough." It is from this seeding that later belief structures and aligning patterns take root as a background presence and feel core to one's being.

In mythology, the archetypal drama of the Mother devouring the pure and beautiful aspects of her child is often symbolically represented as a devouring mother or as a dragon devouring a child. Another way to look at the dual nature of the uroboric Mother archetype is that, while infants can feel a state of blissfulness held in the symbolic arms of the Great Mother, in this oral time of dependence, they also can have a primordial fear of being swallowed, engulfed, or annihilated by the uroboric other, referred to, by Neumann, as "uroboric castration."

Many developmental theorists, such as Melanie Klein and Donald Winnicott, talk about the extreme importance of a "protective container" and the necessary conditions of the mothering environment. This primal relationship sets the foundation for all subsequent dependencies as well as the relationship with self and others. Ultimately, how well a baby is cared for determines the solidity and stability of its early foundation and the integration of its sense of self.

Because being in the arms of the Mother can feel like paradise or hell, the powerful uroboric state can be our unconscious go-to in certain situations throughout life. For example, when we face a difficult task, feel vulnerable and intimate, or fear being overrun by another, to avoid the tension and discomfort, we might regress. This might manifest and lead to our unconsciously distracting ourselves with pleasurable activities such as eating, drinking alcohol, doing drugs, smoking, masturbating, watching TV or movies, surfing the Internet, and hoarding, to name a few.

Again, the uroboric period of early development is of prime significance. The uroboric, unconscious state is the time when our needs for nourishment, comfort, attachment, and being seen as the purity of the Self are foremost in our conditioning. It is the root of implicit memory and the time that sets the foundation for the Great Mother's first (oral) stage and beyond. It is these somatic memories that are triggered and expressed as reactive states in later development.

When the objective psyche that is monitoring the child's self senses there is no future at the uroboric stage, the "uroboric slumber" is withdrawn. This takes the infant into the next developmental stage, corresponding with the Great Mother archetype in Neumann's archetypal theory. The infant starts to shift from the symbiotic relationship to experiencing its body and its separateness from the mother and its surroundings. This manifests as the baby beginning to smile and coo at its mother and to suck its fingers and toes.

Great Mother Archetype

When awakening from the uroboric slumber, the Great Mother is the first to be experienced, so she becomes associated with one's relationship with existence itself. She literally becomes the focus of an infant's entire world. She is the central figure who dominates not only early development in life but also acts as an underlying archetypal force throughout life, a force that can easily draw us back into her uroboric belly and the unconscious state of being.

It is important to note that, within her womb, the Great Mother embraces all pairs of opposites innate in our existence—life and death, self and other, inside and outside, good and evil, light and dark. Thus, the Great Mother is capable of being nurturing and the source of all our nourishment in her loving greatness. But, like the goddess Kali, she also is capable of destroying as the devouring negative Mother who can threaten the ongoing development of the ego/child. This dynamic activates the innate polarity of victim-tyrant and an alignment with one side while feeling the other side being "done to us."

Thus, during the Great Mother stage, the child unconsciously wonders, "How will I get my needs met? Lovingly, benevolently, and nurturingly? Or in terrifying and devouring ways?" To gain nourishment and loving support and to avoid destructive actions, an infant will try in numerous ways to please the Great Mother and to ease the anxiety caused by separating from the Great Mother as well as the anxiety of potential annihilation at the hands of a devouring negative Mother. This is the reason it is so tempting to return to the uroborus—why, in darkness, the Great Mother can pull us back into the depths of the unconscious slumber.

As Robert Langs has taught us, any time we open ourself to being vulnerable, we also are open to annihilation and death. These early states of vulnerability are significant, in that we are totally dependent on the mothering one to meet all physical and emotional needs, to hold us securely and safely, to see our preciousness and essence and mirror that to us. When all this is done with love and tenderness, we learn to trust in the world. We become confident that it is safe to be open and vulnerable. And we are less defensive about the outer world and more comfortable taking risks, striving toward growth, and honing the personal essence of our being. Many people, however, are faced with the negative aspects of the Great Mother, who mirrors to her child her own negative inner feelings and limitations. These are then integrated by the infant as attempts to devour the child's life and the budding young ego.

Three Stages of the Great Mother

To continue on the developmental journey means integrating the inner feminine world of emotions and feelings, our value and worth, our sense of young authority and power, our body-focused desires and functions, and how we begin to take in the world and metabolize the forces of the Great Mother. If the mother world is safe, nurturing, and loving, the mother will mirror the infant's essential nature as a precious being and there will be an integration in the inner world of the child of self-love, nurturing, tenderness, self-care, self-worth and value, and an ability to take in the abundance of goodness available in the world. Because the Great Mother archetype is about our inner world of feelings, emotions, and instincts, and is body focused, there are three major stages of the Great Mother: oral, anal, and genital (often referenced in Psychoanalytic Development). These three Great Mother stages complete the foundational piece of developing our inner world that ultimately conditions the pre-ego self and establishes the platform from which we enter the outer world.

Oral Stage

The uroborus stage segues into the first stage of the Great Mother: the oral stage. This particular stage actually can best be viewed on a continuum from the extra-uterine phase of undifferentiated unity with the Self, to the symbiotic intra-relationship of early infancy with the Mother, to early stages of differentiation between the child and the Mother. In the oral stage, the infant's first attempt at unity with the Self and its innate wholeness is through what it takes in orally. In other words, the infant takes in the world by "swallowing it," and union is directed toward the mothering one. The Great Mother is "seen" by swallowing her and incorporating her into oneself through the breast, thumb, and, later, food. Taking in the material world of *Mater* or Mother opens the door to feeling either loved and seen as a precious being—or to feeling afraid of being swallowed, eaten, and devoured by the negative Mother's strong archetypal forces. How does this manifest developmentally? The dominant archetypal feature of the oral stage is one of satiation and fascination with taking in through the mouth. What is also being taken in is our sense of value and worth.

As Melanie Klein states, the infant longs for attachment to the mother. This longing is a universal phenomenon that is archetypal. Separation feels like and can equal death. Because mother and child were once experienced in a symbiotic unity, differ-

Early Life Stages

Archetypal Stage	Internal Structure	How It's Built
Uroborus	Undifferentiated	Trust, safety, and security
Early Ego Generative Development	Early differentiation	Seeing preciousness, potential, true nature; gazing
Great Mother Stage 1 Oral	Self-worth & value	Giving baby's needs priority; providing the expectation of safety and security
Great Mother Stage 2 Anal	Empowerment & authority	Supporting autonomy and young authority; Allowing disagreement; Ensuring safety and security
Great Mother Stage 3 Genital	Embodying early sexuality	Supporting budding sexuality and full creative expression

entiation now seems very threatening, like death. If this fear of death and of being devoured are not accepted and embraced, the infant ego will continue to be caught in the throes of the Great Mother forces.

It takes a nurturing, loving, generative mother to help her infant navigate the new differentiation from her. If supported and encouraged by a generative mother, the child will begin to integrate a strong sense of a young self, to feel valued and important (as mirrored by the mother). In addition, the child will gain mastery to move into the next stage of the Great Mother, with a sound foundation.

All too often, however, the mother is nongenerative and unable to see the true nature of her infant, due to her own limitations. The child of a nongenerative mother ultimately integrates a poor sense of self, value, and worth and aligns with similar behaviors and beliefs. Left feeling a deep sense of separation anxiety, this child may attempt to soothe the pain of separation from the unconditional love of the Self and the integration of the devouring forces of the Great Mother with oral fixations such as those related to food and thumb sucking. In adulthood, this pain of separation, unresolved, may manifest as an internalized inner critic and not feeling "good enough" or important. This negative sense of self then shows up in behaviors such as eating disorders, smoking, alcohol and drug use or addictions, shopping, and the like.

To further our discussion of the oral stage of development, let's consider the work of renowned developmental psychologist and psychoanalyst Erik Erikson (1902-1994). In *Childhood and Society*, Erickson delineates eight stages during the course of the life cycle. The first is "Basic Trust vs. Basic Mistrust," the stage that correlates to the oral stage about which we are speaking.[22]

As noted earlier, this early stage is characterized by the primal body-self relationship with the mothering one. Erikson says that, in order to build internal basic trust, during this stage the child must have a deep sense of continuity and consistency, which can only be provided by another, presumably the mothering one. Further, for optimal development, the child during this stage needs similar experiences that can provide a rudimentary sense of early ego identity from which to build upon. The child also needs a sense of trust in the continuity of its own bodily actions and sensations.

Specifically, according to Erikson, basic trust is built through a quality maternal relationship—being able to count on consistent, sensitive care—and a firm sense of personal trustworthiness. When these requirements are not fulfilled, the child builds levels of basic mistrust and feels a sense of being deprived. Also, parts of the child's self feel abandoned. Further, when basic trust is compromised, the child goes forth in its development into the next stage without a firm foundation and is ultimately not able to trust in the world as a safe and supportive environment. In particularly traumatic situations of having a nongenerative mother during this stage, a child's nervous system also can become overstimulated, and hypervigilant behavior patterns may replace basic trust. That child's nervous system, then, is patterned with negative alignments to the Great Mother archetype.

This theme is also echoed in the work of author and spiritual teacher A.H. Almaas (b. 1944) who speaks of the need for holding in order to build basic trust. He says that without holding there is a loss of basic trust, first in the environment, then within ourselves. Finally, Almaas says, without holding, we lose basic trust in being helped by the universe and its divine presence. He writes that through basic trust we learn that life is safe enough and manageable, so we can relax and trust that the universe is supporting us and that we have whatever resources we need to deal with what life presents.[23]

The bottom line is, when mistrust is built during a child's oral stage, parts of the child's early developing self are left behind. If the child is ever to feel safe in the world, those abandoned parts of the child's early developing self need to be rescued at some later stage of the inner journey. Neumann refers to this as "rescuing the captive." Others such as relatives, teachers, neighbors, and mentors might help the child form trust. If not, the child lives from a mistrusting place and proceeds through the life journey compromised, feeling alone in the world.

Anal Stage

The anal stage follows the oral stage and has different developmental tasks and characteristics. As its title implies, during the anal stage, the focus shifts from oral needs to the body. "I am the body" becomes the identity that sets the stage for much of the archetypal development of life when the material world of desires and attachments takes precedence. The archetypal dominant of this stage is retention and expulsion as well as gaining our sense of authority and empowerment.

One of the primary developmental tasks of this stage is to gain autonomy and not need the mother's continual attention. The young child begins to do this by playing alone or with others for short periods. The child, however, expects the mother to be readily available to return as needed or wanted.

Gaining autonomy can ultimately build a sense of empowerment and authority, another developmental task of the anal stage. Specifically, the anal stage is about the desire to possess, conquer, master, and control the world, in fairly primitive forms, while wanting some autonomy from the mothering one. This may manifest as control of feces and wanting control over potty training, trying to exercise authority by trying to control the feminine forces, flexing the muscles, pushing away help from the outside world, and being resistant and defiant, saying, "No! I can do it myself!" These behaviors are in defense of the fears of being open to the archetypal forces of the Great Mother's control, domination, and possession.

The readiness and the capacity to gain the new skills of autonomy and a sense of empowerment and authority are dependent upon how successful the child integrated self-value and being "good enough" in the prior oral stage, which sets the foundation for all future stages. We need to know we are important and "worth it" before we can fully move into feeling empowered rather than taking power over others.

While children make strides toward differentiation during this stage, their inner world is still being developed. That development is dependent upon the parental impressions of who they are to their parents. A generative, loving mother knows the tasks of this stage and allows her child to exercise authority and make some decisions, as long as safety is not compromised. She realizes that her child wants autonomy but simultaneously expects her to be available—and she flows with these needs. The demands can be difficult, however, especially for a mother with self-limitations and childhood wounds of her own. These mothers might struggle with their young children, want to control their behaviors, or shame them for mistakes or for not doing well enough. Recall our discussion in the "Oral Stage" section of Erik Erikson's delineation of eight stages of the life cycle in his seminal book, *Childhood and Society*. Erikson's stage at this juncture is called "Autonomy vs. Shame and Doubt" and aptly so, as this is ultimately the dilemma presented to mother and child at this stage.

Also included with autonomy and authority are the actions of holding on or letting go. Consider these actions both in terms of physical control as well as of building our inner world of feelings, emotions, fears, and compensations. As young children, we are very sensitive to our new sense of autonomy and power, so we can be easily hurt, feel a sense of shame for our actions, and doubt our capabilities. This shame and doubt lays the foundation for feeling exposed and self-conscious, which becomes "baggage" as we grow and develop into adulthood.

Erikson goes on to say that this stage becomes decisive for the ratio of love and hate, cooperation and willfulness, and freedom of self-expression or suppression throughout life. That is, from a sense of self-control, without damage to self-esteem, comes a lasting sense of good will and pride. If the young child struggles with or feels humiliated by the mother, a lasting propensity for shame and doubt is likely.

When mothers, in collaboration with their partners, allow independence with dignity, the child will feel good will and confident that this kind of autonomy, fostered during childhood, will not lead to undue shame and doubt later in adulthood. The child can then move into the next developmental stage, confident it is safe to own his or her power and authority. He or she will not need to control and will be ready for new developmental tasks.

However, should the opposite be true and mothers (with their partners) not allow independence with dignity during the anal stage, the child will go forward in development hindered by fears of empowerment. He or she will likely be controlling and fearful of trusting in the safety of letting go. Or he or she might be passive, submissive, and lack autonomy. The fears that hold the need to control in place are related to not feeling safe to be open and vulnerable. In other words, children not allowed independence with dignity during the anal stage often feel a need to "keep a lid" on control so as not to feel inner chaos and traumas.

Genital Stage

The genital stage brings to a close the purely body identity that is unconscious and forms our implicit memory. In this stage, we deal with many inner feelings, drives, and new body sensations while simultaneously struggling with the desire to remain in unity with the Great Mother, to not leave her arms and uroboric slumber to further mature. There is an ongoing conflict between wanting to feel her love, comfort, and security, while also feeling the inner drive for more initiative and autonomy from her.

The archetypal dominant of this stage is arousal, both genital and creative. As the name suggests, the early focus of this stage centers around the genitals and sexual impulses. Much attention is given to genital satisfaction, and often masturbating, as these new sensations are discovered and enjoyed. A new curiosity with the difference in genitals between the sexes may lead to exploration. In general, during the genital stage, the focus turns to taking in the world through genital satisfaction and sexualizing it in young attempts to find unity with the Self. Many may get stuck in this stage, if not properly navigated with helpful parents, and continue their search for unity with the Self through genital satisfaction and sexual addictions into adulthood.

With the new feelings and urges during the genital stage also come new fears and conflict, because intimacy with the Great Mother leaves us vulnerable to physical castration and to emotionally having the rug pulled out from under our new autonomy and zest for initiative. That is, we have a great desire for intimacy, acceptance, and love from the mother but also want to pull away from her. If we prioritize intimacy, we are at risk for engulfment. But too much distance feels like alienation.

Now the child enters what has historically been called "the Oedipal conflict." There are varying interpretations of the Oedipal myth associated with this developmental time. Richard Nicoletti says, in his diploma thesis for the Jung Institute of Boston: "Oedipus is a family myth depicting archetypal re-enactment in every generation of an erotic triangulation pattern"[24] of parents and child.

In the myth, Oedipus, having been given away by his biological parents, is driven by a terrible prophecy: He unconsciously returns to his homeland and unknowingly kills his biological father, answers the riddle of the Devouring Sphinx who has been terrorizing the countryside, and subsequently marries his biological mother. Once conscious of the reality of what has happened, he blinds himself and must face the consequences by going on an inner journey toward gaining consciousness.[25]

We do not see this conflict as being gender specific, as is often interpreted. Rather, we see this conflict as the archetypal transition children make during the genital stage of development. The conflict entails the child being torn between two worlds and triangulated between remaining embedded in the grips of the Great Mother and the inner world of feelings and emotions versus moving into the masculine world of the Father archetype and developing an ego, concepts, and outer world skills. In other words, as the Father archetype is activated in the psyche, the child is split between staying in a "marriage" with the Great Mother or venturing into the unknown outer world of the Father. The former choice would, consequently, kill off the archetypal Father and keep the forces and consciousness of the ego in a dormant state. With the latter choice, the child develops skills to eventually gift to humanity.

How this looks developmentally at this juncture is that the child sees the father enjoying an intimate relationship with the mother. Because the child desperately wants that same closeness, the objective becomes to replace the father in this role. This leads to a triangulation with the parental figures and to the child attempting to pull them apart to gain this intimacy. The child may say, "I want to marry Mommy, too!" (It is important to note that the roles of mother and father are not gender related. Rather they are the roles played in developing the inner world of the feminine and the outer world of the ego and masculine in a child's life. These roles can be successfully met by any gender parent.)

The rivalry ensues until the child realizes all attempts are futile. The shift occurs when the child is able to see the father as not only an intimate partner with the mother but also as a model for how to have autonomy and independence from her. As Michael Washburn observes in *The Ego and the Dynamic Ground*, "The child's choice is between confrontation with and acceptance by the father: to pursue intimacy with the caregiver is to risk confrontation with the father as rival, and to pursue distance from the caregiver is to win acceptance from the father as role model."[26] Now the child has the assistance of the father in his or her attempts to gain autonomy from the Great Mother forces, and with this can come new conflict.

According to Neumann, in order to leave the emotional and body realms of the Great Mother, the young ego self must have a "dragon fight" with her to break the bond and not be castrated or dissolved back into her influence. We need to fight and defeat her archetypal influence and prevent being pulled back into the unconscious so as to move into the higher realms of concepts and the outer world. The "dragon" is her power to seduce the young ego self, leaving it vulnerable to castration, destruction, being devoured, and, thus, returning to the unconscious realms. The young ego self must expose the dragon, conquer fear, and not let itself be destroyed by regressing, dissolving, repressing, or dissociating. Once this is accomplished, the ego no longer identifies with the genitals and must surrender the body focus to move into the higher mental realms of the masculine world of the Father archetype.[27]

Pulling from the magnetic archetypal forces of the Great Mother and her influence takes great power and initiative; the Mother-child relationship is fundamental to our existence! Until this point we have either basked in the comfort and love of her holding, or we have longed for this kind of relationship with her. Either pole brings its challenges in moving out of her powerful influence. With the aid of the father's modeling, we can leave the body and inner world focus of the Great Mother as our main identity, and we can move toward the functions of the ego and outer world.

Loving parents will help their child navigate through this stage, its fears and conflicts, by collaboratively supporting one another as a couple and as a parental unit, informing the child of their love, and not shaming the child for the desires for intimacy or sexual gratification. Loving mothers will see this as a time for their children to differentiate and to turn attention toward the outer world, rather than encourage continued dependence upon them. Generative mothers support this process, while simultaneously loving the child and being available for support as needed. Fathers will see this as a time to become more active in modeling independence and showcasing outer world activities.

In *Childhood and Society*, Erikson calls this stage "Initiative vs. Guilt."[28] The child suddenly seems to "grow together" in person and in body. There is a sense of early "growing into" oneself. Initiative adds to this growing autonomy, and there are tasks for the sake of being active and on the move. This is different from the anal stage, during which self-will often inspires acts of defiance or protests of independence. The bottom line is that initiative is very important to the developing ego, which will soon be taking more shape and precedence in life.

With a child's new locomotor and mental power during this developmental stage, goals are often contemplated and acts initiated with exuberance and enjoyment. If these endeavors are encouraged, children continue the actions feeling very proud of their accomplishments. If they are discouraged or put down, guilt typically ensues and children feel disempowered, not good enough. While the child fantasizes and attempts to exercise power, parental interference of guilt can activate a "castration complex" in which the child fears genital harm, has an overarching fear of bodily harm, and/or senses that accomplishments will draw crushing discouragement. Such parental interference of guilt also may set the stage for later repression of urges and an inner powerhouse of rage, as some of the child's fondest hopes and wildest fantasies are repressed and inhibited, acting to obstruct creativity as an adult. In addition, it may activate guilt from an earlier phase. Neumann notes that a "central symptom of a disturbed primal relationship is the primary feeling of guilt." He goes on to say that, "not to feel loved can feel identical with being abnormal, sick, leprous, and condemned."[29]

It is also important to note that the genital stage can be compromised in a number of other ways. With prior incompletion of the oral and anal inner world needs, a child may enter the genital stage clinging to the mother or feeling alienated, fearful, or submissive in relationship to the mother. Also, when a mother who wants to hang onto her child shames the child for sexual urges and/or masturbating rather than allowing some independence, she can cause her child lasting harm. Obviously, overt or covert sexual abuse during this stage also can be devastating to the developing child. The long-term harm shows up in our current culture as promiscuity, sexual and pornography addictions, sexually objectifying partners, failed relationships, and viewing the world as a sexual arena. In adulthood, we find that those who had generative experiences during the genital stage, whether male or female, live "erect" and potent lives with much initiative to fulfill their goals and dreams, and those who had nongenerative experiences live an impotent, more limp way of being that lacks an inner sense of empowerment and drive.

In summary, when parents are present, actively involved, and express love for their children, those children successfully integrate the genital stage and complete the Great Mother period. These children often show up acting with confidence and esteem, taking initiative free of fears, freely expressing themselves and their creativity, and ready to face the world.

Separation of the World Parents

Erich Neumann's three great mythic categories, which we have outlined—the Creation, Hero, and Transformation myths—correspond to three life passages available to humans: the passage into the body, the passage into the mind and ego, and the return to our true nature as the Self. The Separation of the World Parents stage marks the transition between the Creation and Hero myths. It comprises the movement from an identification with the body to an identification with the mind and the ego. During this transition, the identification with the body is finally consolidated, and then, as the brain develops, there is a growing identification with the conditioned mind. This transition spans many years of growth and development, from toddler to adolescent. Over the course of those many years, a significant number of dynamic activities take place.

To explain in more depth, let's return to the Great Mother stage. During that time, the very young child is in a state of unity with his or her body and the Self. This unity gives the child a sense of mystical participation, a partial identity with "all that is." In this state, all the polarities exist simultaneously; for the child there is no polarization. Good and bad, love and hate, pleasure and pain all exist simultaneously. Even both genders of male and female exist at the same time within the child.

As children move from the Great Mother stage into the Separation of the World Parents stage, four major shifts occur:

1. They introject, or take in as whole, the psyches of their parents; this introjection becomes a stable structure known as the "personal superego."
2. They then leave behind the undivided world where there are no polarities, and they also leave behind their original identification with their body, feelings, instincts, and emotions.
3. Even though the natural disposition of every individual inclines to be physically and psychically bisexual, the child can no longer rest in the hermaphroditic state where both masculine and feminine exist together.[30]
4. The activation of the Father archetype is instrumental to this development, which ultimately drives the transition from the Creation Myths to the Hero Myths—from an identification with the body to an identification with the mind.

> **"Introject"** is a term from Gestalt therapy that describes the process of swallowing whole, without chewing into parts. For example, the whole of the parents' psyches are taken inside the child's psyche without any process of discrimination.

Once children introject, or take in as whole, the psyches of their parents, they no longer need the parents to be external and close by, as they once required. As noted earlier, this introjection becomes their "personal superego," their very own set of internal suggestions, commands, and prohibitions (albeit they are patterned by the personal superegos of their caregivers).

With the development of the personal superego, children leave behind their original identification with their body, feelings, instincts, and emotions, unconsciously pushing this unity, which they have felt through the body, into the background. This fundamental alienation of their true nature has a massive impact on the psyche. This alienation becomes deeply embedded as a psychic structure of consciousness and unconsciousness, inside and outside. This force in development takes an act of aggression, which leaves the ego in later stages feeling a dividedness and what Neumann calls a "genuine and necessary guilt." This act of development coincides with a new focus on developing the mental aspects of the ego, creates the dual system of consciousness and unconsciousness, and is necessary in order to protect the growing mental ego, to engage with the Father archetype, and to begin the heroic journey into the outer world.

Despite its importance as a means to necessary development, the alienation of a child's identification with his or her body, feelings, instincts, and emotions constitutes the first self-imposed loss in the child's life. The unconscious experiences this as a loss of huge proportion, often described as "leaving the Garden of Eden." Wholeness is now unavailable to the conscious mind. Later, in the Rescuing the Captive stage, the child will need to confront this loss to regain conscious awareness of his or her unity.

With this newfound development, a child starts to build his or her unique persona with input from the personal and cultural superegos. The "shadow" also begins to form based on the opposite gender with which the child did not align. For example, in our culture, little boys are not supposed to be soulful or emotional, so those aspects are often relegated to the unconscious and begin to establish the seeds of the anima/animus.[31]

Because this particular stage of the Separation of the World Parents spans toddlerhood through adolescence, it seems important to outline the changes the ego undergoes to reach the next stage of the Birth of the Hero. At the start of this stage, the ego begins to build its authority to facilitate its move away from a paradisiacal state of unity. Instead of just knowing itself through names and words, it is evolving a self-concept that contains images, fantasies, and ideas of being a separate entity. In contemporary development terms, the ego develops from a magical primary process to an ability to use representational thinking and then moves into, what Piaget calls, concrete operational thinking. In mythical terms, the ego develops from being animal like (identified with its instinctive unconscious), to being in an active, "I want" stage, mythically named a "magic-phallic stage," in which the unity of the body becomes its first expression of individuality.

Next, the ego moves to what Neumann calls a "magic-warlike stage," in which the young child is able to hold an aggressive, stable stance against the unconscious that is trying to reabsorb it. This eventually leads to a "solar-warlike stage," in which the ego gains power and control of the destructive tendency of the unconscious. This new power is needed in order to move toward the next stage, the Birth of the Hero,[32] which is still many steps of maturation away.

Later in this stage, children will project their personal superego onto a peer group and also take in their culture's ideas of what and who they *should* be, thus initiating their "cultural superego." The cultural superego is built through injunctions from school and church, society, media, and more. The injunctions include messages such as "I have to be thin," "Girls can't be smart," or "Boys don't cry." Obviously, the culture has been in the background behind the parents, influencing their behavior and attitudes, but now it comes into focus as the child's own internalized cultural superego. This contemporary "collective conscience," along with the Father archetype, eventually will guide the child in working with and mastering the tools of the adult world.

The shift in the personal superego being projected onto a group of peers, as well as the cultural superego being integrated into the psyche, naturally advances children toward independence. But, in the process, they continue to lose an unconscious integration with the foundation of their being. In other words, as the ego and personal and collective superegos take the "inner controls" and the Self is relegated to the background, there is a lasting loss in the psyche, a loss of knowing the true ground of being: "Inner knowing" is traded for "outer belonging." How much of their inner knowing a child will lose—the amount of the "trade" they are making—will depend upon the generativity of a child's early parenting. Without generative parenting, a child might stay locked in the world of the ego, stranded from knowing his or her true nature.

Also during this stage, a heroic "ego ideal" begins to solidify and come to the foreground, eventually supporting children in their quest for knowledge of their true nature. In other words, the undivided world that a child used to inhabit back in the Great Mother stage begins to coalesce during the Separation of the World Parents stage in the mind of the child as the "ego ideal." Arising from the child's unconscious, the ego ideal is experienced as a symbolic hero figure that can gain mastery of forces both within and without. Examples of this magical, powerful figure can be found in our many films of comic book superheroes. Children use this heroic ego ideal, sometimes simply called the "heroic ideal," to strengthen their own ego, to help them move out of range of the Great Mother's archetypal pull, back into the unconscious, or to call on it when they need help. This shift out of the realm of being a satellite in the Great Mother's world allows children to move into the next stage of the Hero, where they will fully wrestle with and, hopefully, release those aspects of their parents and the culture that do not portray their true self. This will ultimately empower children to reunite directly with their own unity and eventually bring their true gifts to the collective.

Activation of the Father Archetype

In archetypal terms, the movement from the feminine inner world to the masculine outer world involves the activation of the Father archetype. Recall that the Great Mother world of the feminine, which represents the unconscious aspects of the psyche, focuses on the inner world of emotions, feelings, love, protection, tenderness, and bodily functions. To shift from that feminine inner world to the masculine outer world of the ego and the mental realms of concepts, will, reason, logic, morals, and values takes a shift from the Great Mother archetype to the Father archetype, which also deals with the skills of the outer world including education and preparing oneself for a career.

Generally, development proceeds from the Great Mother to the Father (sometimes called the patriarchy), assisted by the ego and superego, which are also "masculine." It is important to note here that the archetypal symbolism of male and female, or matriarchal and patriarchal, is not biological nor gender specific. Feminine people can be bearers of masculinity and vice versa. The roles of Mother and Father archetypes, the feminine and masculine aspects of self, are roles necessary to facilitate the growth and development of our inner and outer life. These roles can be demonstrated by one parent or more and, again, are not dependent upon the gender of the parent(s).

As noted earlier, during the early years of a child's inner world development, the mother, or mothering one, is the most relevant and intimately important. The father, or fathering one, however, can be imminently helpful during this early development: He can hold a strong, "protective container" for the mother and child by creating the environment necessary for secure attachment, healthy mirroring, and optimal neuro-network development.

How this time is navigated depends upon the support the mother has for the child's differentiation from her and how generative and available the fathering one is. A generative father sees his role during a child's very early years as the holder of the protective container of the outer world. He fosters the environment by providing the outer needs. This enables the mother and child to relax and focus their energy on bonding and building a healthy inner world.

The father also plays a generative role by allowing and encouraging the child to be age-appropriately empowered and by being a good role model, alongside the mother, during the Oedipal stage. He helps steward the child through this period and through the intimacy wanted with the mother, while allowing the mother and child to play out the various developmental stages necessary during this time.

It is during ego development in the Separation of the World Parents stage that the father's importance becomes more active and necessary. Once the child has gained some degree of separation from the mother's influence, the father and the world of the Father archetype then play a key role in teaching the child the rules, norms, and roles of the outer world and all that is needed to set a firm foundation in strong ego development, sense of self-esteem, and autonomy from the archetypal influence of the mother. Neumann explains the importance of the Father archetype thus: "Collective masculinity is a value-creating and educative force. Every ego and every consciousness is gripped and formed by it. In this way, the masculine side helps the developing ego to live through the archetypal stages individually and to establish contact with the Hero Myth."[33]

By partnering and working closely during the early years, the mother and father together can build a healthy platform from which the child can begin building the ego, conceptualization, healthy activities, and relationships. That healthy early foundation also offers an early integration of how to protect oneself and be grounded in the necessary activities and skills to promote success in one's life and to align to one's contributions and goals related to career and independence.

In therapy, we often see women who were deficient in father mentoring during their early life. These women repeatedly put themselves in dangerous and compromising situations and have not integrated a sense of how to protect themselves. Also, in the media, we often hear about women getting intoxicated with men they just met—and then being raped or abducted. These women, too, typically had nongenerative fathering.

Other examples of people without generative fathering include those we often see in therapy who have few or no skills in how to handle finances. They do not know how to create a budget or prioritize their spending (without large credit card debt and monthly interest fees), and they are unable to pay their loans. Others are unprepared to interview for employment in a way that demonstrates their strengths and cannot answer why an employer would want to hire them. Another common trait of these individuals is that they are often impulsive in decision-making and do not adequately think through the steps necessary to achieve their goals.

8

Neumann's Hero Myths: Birth of the Hero, Dragon Fights, and Slaying of the Parents

Eventually, we unconsciously ask: "How will I overcome the depths of the unconscious (my dragons) and bring my gifts to humankind?"

The archetypal hero always has an archetypal, trans-human parent and one human parent with whom we have our more personal experiences. Mentors such as Obi-Wan Kenobi, Meister Eckhart, and the great master teachers have their roots in the transpersonal. They meet the archetypal mandate of a hero by supporting the supreme health and well-being of the collective or larger whole. Other examples of the archetypal hero include athletes who perform far beyond their competitors, those who give their lives to the service of humanity such as Mother Teresa and the Dalai Lama, and those who reach stardom and then use their elevated position to benefit the greater public.

Birth of the Hero

As noted in the last chapter, during the Separation of the World Parents stage, heroic images arise from the unconscious, forming a child's heroic ego ideal. That heroic ego ideal is the child's unconscious identification with an archetypal form of the father and mother and with the lost unconscious unity with the Self.

Early manifestations of the hero (not gender specific) who grows from the ego ideal take the form of childhood proclamations such as the likes of: "I want to be a policewoman," "I want to be a fireman," "I want to be a veterinarian," "I want to be an Olympic runner," "I want to be Superman," or "I want to be Wonder Woman."

Although all the elements of the hero are in the unconscious, images of the hero, as noted in these examples, often embody wishes for perfection, for the power to support the collective, or for the ability to lead the collective into new realms.

What children align with in the outer world to fulfill these wishes ultimately will be tailormade by their own entelechy or internal guiding principles. As they mature and become old enough to choose their own school friends, peer groups, hobbies, and interests, we see more concrete images awaken in their unconscious that constitute the alignment they will take to eventually fight the "dragons" of the introjections taken in during the Separation of the World Parents stage. Ultimately, particular behaviors manifest from this alignment. For example, many young people question rules and

HERO MYTHS

Separation of the World Parents   **Dragon Fights**

(Father Archetype activated)

Birth of the Hero

Slaying of the Parents

TRANSFORMATION MYTHS

Great Mother Archetype

Stage 3

Stage 2

Rescuing the Captive

Stage 1

Gaining the Treasure

Uroborus

Unification of Opposites / Hermaphrodite

CREATION MYTHS

seek peer groups that hold values that are often counter to those of the parents and/or the culture. In addition, at this developmental stage, they begin to set their own goals and look for the internal and external support to work toward those goals. A good example is the adolescent girl who finds ways to take a bus into the city by herself to take dance lessons—which her parents do not support.

These generative behaviors are possible because the heroic ego ideal functions within the psyche as the will and energy to do the foundational work of learning valuable skills. Other examples of such foundational work include doing repetitive lay-up drills in basketball, sitting through classes in summer school, and practicing endless scales on the piano.

The heroic ego ideal, which eventually shapes the persona and the shadow (to be explained in the next section), also inspires one to take on rites of passages and initiation. In addition, it functions as a "protective container," protecting the psyche from feeling the reality of death, mortality, and fear. In other words, through fashioning the internal image as being heroically invincible—"I will help all beings like Superman does, or go to infinity and beyond as Buzz Lightyear does"—we think, "This is who I am and whom I want the world to see." (At this time in development, the ego feels the unity of the Self and innocently borrows the Self's invincibility as its own, a confusion that will eventually need to be cleared.) With this sense of invincibility, youth are empowered to move out into the world, try new things, fight the internal dragons, and gain mastery over the external forces of nature and marketplace. This includes being able to compete for mates beyond family and small village, which ultimately strengthens humankind.

Major Dragon Fights in Stages of the Creation and Hero Myths

Looming in the unconscious of children is the unlived lives of the parents, the parents' ways of relating to the children, and what they think and feel about the child. If the parenting is not generative, "dragons" abound in a child's unconscious. The "dragon" is that which has been taken in (whole) that is not in alignment with the full generative mandate of the Mother and Father archetypes. Particular dragons can be identified as the devouring mother and the castrating or crushing father. The devouring, negative mother takes over a child's inner world, and the castrating father crushes a child's attempts in the outer world.

Eventually, the child unconsciously asks: "How will I overcome the depths of the unconscious (my dragons) and bring my gifts to humankind?" During the Birth of the Hero stage, a child begins to connect unconsciously with images of the kind of hero with whom to align and, therefore, what the child's tasks in life will be. Then, during their first dragon fights, youths stand as subjects confronting an objective world. They unconsciously realize that, to manifest strongly enough to begin a conscious life in the outer world, they must first face fights against the pull of the unconscious forces of the Great Mother. To attain power over outside forces, they must first master the unconscious inner forces.

The archetypal images of the hero, aligned with a higher calling, shape the choices the child's ego makes as it fights for freedom from the unconscious and wrestles with clearing nongenerative aspects of the introjected parents and culture. This builds character and strengthens the child for the real journey of life: gaining the Treasure.

What happens when a child's heroic image has aligned with resonance to an icon that becomes a nongenerative hero? Consider cultural icons such as the cyclist Lance Armstrong who met the mandate of the Hero archetype by overcoming huge obstacles, performing at a super human capacity, and doing service for humanity, but did not maintain the hero's mandate. What about the spiritual teacher Rajneesh, who let down thousands of followers? Or a dad who seems like Superman to his child but becomes an alcoholic and begins to focus only on his own needs rather than on the developmental needs of his child? This shattering of the alignment to the hero can create an internal crisis that will taint all further development.

The heroic ideal is an internal support for navigating a generative potential at each developmental stage. Without proper help to resolve and repair a breach, a child's development can be completely derailed. "I'm never going to count on anyone again," might become the lens through which the child lives life, well into adulthood. With good mentoring, however, the child might be able to get back on track and think, "I can be a hero even though ___ let me down; not everyone will let me down." The shattering and its repair can be part of building the strength and character needed to be on course for the Transformation stages.

....

Heroic Quests[34]

As the Birth of the Hero stage unfolds during later adolescence, the would-be hero begins to ask yet another question, "What do I really want?" With the activation of this entelechy or guiding principle, the heroic ego ideal is projected into the outer world, triggering aspects of the outer world to beckon with greater importance. One young person decides he wants to become a surgeon, and medical school seems to light up as his goal. Another decides she wants to be wealthy and begins seeing opportunities to begin a business or apply to business school. Another wants to be a mother, and particular young men seem to shine as potential mates. Yet another decides he wants to be creative and "original" and pursues art or music. These attempts by young people to experience a completion of desire are called "heroic quests." During these quests, the ego whispers, "If I have or do this, I will be fulfilled."

Many of the culturally approved pathways of available heroic quests are ways of strengthening the human race. For example, consider the collective benefits of going to an excellent college, becoming a sought-after sports player, becoming an entrepreneur, or joining the military. But heroic quests also are often begun as a way to either prove that the superego introjections from the parents are true or that they are false, or to rebel against parental or cultural expectations. In addition, depending on what might be held captive in the unconscious from the Great Mother stages, particular heroic quests can be attempts to get confirmation of one's own worth and value from the outside world. They also may be attempts to find a way to "take in" the world or "be taken in" by it—attempts to create a place in the world, find a niche, or find a calling for oneself. Yet other heroic quests are attempts at cosmic perfection.

Youthful heroic quests also function to create the "shadow." Those parts of us that do not fit what is needed for the quest or that do not fit the ego ideal are relegated to the shadow. For instance, if our quest is to be an elite mountain climber, most of our human weaknesses will be assigned to the shadow and will not be permitted to be seen as part of our conscious self. In other words, the ego ideal develops a persona that works hand in hand with the shadow, thus presenting to the world only the features and strengths of the hero. Interestingly, some heroic quests are even undertaken simply to pump up the persona and to keep what is in the shadow stable. Consider how participation in an extreme sport with great danger can keep a feeling of weakness at bay and strengthen the view of heroism shown to the world.

As we need all our value, worth, and authority to fulfill our heroic quests, this also can be a time for working through what we have left behind in earlier developmental stages. We might need to shore up confidence as we stumble across weak places in ourselves during dragon fights, or we might need to face a perception of perfectionism we cannot humanly live up to. Work on a PhD thesis might reveal a lack of authority, or a negative office relationship might showcase that we don't have all our worth in place. With the knowledge uncovered during a heroic quest, we can begin to slay the dragons of our early life.

No matter the trigger or rationale for our heroic quests, all of them ultimately are attempts to unify with and gain the Treasure, although the Treasure is comprehended differently during each developmental stage. During the heroic stages, the Treasure seems as if it is in the physical world, that it is something you could attain, own, or have. In truth, however, the Treasure is inside each of us, and the underlying purpose of our heroic quests is to bring something new to humankind and to strengthen the ego for its most important task of finding that inner Treasure. Looked at another way, the mandate of the Hero archetype is to bring "the new" to the world while also gaining our sense of value, worth, and new inner authority.

In general, heroic quests contain the seeds of what the ego ideal wants to express. Perhaps by going to business school as a heroic quest, we hope to open or facilitate a mind-body business so we can offer a healing service to others. Or perhaps our goal is to gain great power over others, or to create a business that will enhance large-scale communication. Our conscious mind may be thinking about money and ease of work, but our ego ideal is busy creating a business that will eventually bring something new to humankind while simultaneously strengthening the ego's ability for introspection and fulfillment.

Anima/Animus

A major heroic quest for most of us relates to our relationships with intimate partners or sexual mates. We tend to attract people who represent unconscious aspects left in our alignments to the Great Mother and Father archetypes in an effort for unity and for a doorway to a deeper fate, psychological development, and transformation.

According to Neumann, the anima and animus projection is the basis of life between the sexes. Jung defined *anima* as being the inner feminine of man, the hidden side of a man's personality. Similarly, *animus* is the inner masculine of woman, the inner, hidden side of a woman's personality. The anima connects man to his interior world, and the animus connects woman to her interior connections to the outside world. The beauty of the anima and animus is that they connect us to our soul and the Self. Neumann said that, as long as the alignments to the anima and animus are unconscious, they are projected out, and these projections magnetically force us into attractions and relationships. By encountering our opposite in another, our ego is strengthened.

Our sexual projections are deep, unconscious processes that result from what is introjected from the Mother and Father archetypes and the masculine and feminine underlying principles in the psyche. In terms of masculine and feminine, they are not gender specific; rather, the role of the ego is identified as masculine, and the role of the unconscious is identified as feminine.

To explain this further, note that we carry an external image of our inner self and see it in the people to whom we are attracted. Depending on what is trying to be revealed from early introjections, the anima/animus can be negative or positive, hurtful or helpful. The negative anima/animus can persuade us to be irresponsible or lazy, whereas a positive anima/animus can encourage us to feel more deeply or become more loving. The negative anima/animus can persuade us to be overly self-critical and judgmental, whereas a positive anima/animus can encourage us to make bold and courageous changes in our outer life.[35] These positive or negative anima/animus representations are related to a person's alignments to the Great Mother and Father archetypes during the introjects of early development, when aspects of the Great Mother and Father were taken in whole.

Later during development, these anima/animus representations lovingly point us back inside, to what needs to be rescued in the second part of life, that which is held captive. In completing this journey, we see that the anima and animus, ultimately, are guides to our fate, guides to our relationship with our true Self.

In summary, heroic quests are opportunities to establish and strengthen the ego as well as to achieve in the outer world; they are often about "winning" the truth or power or the bride. Because the next developmental stage is the Slaying of the Parents, we, as heroes, must be strengthened and have developed enough through our heroic quests to be able to stand up for our own beliefs, views, and meaning of life, not just to live solely based on the conditioning of our parents, school, church, and culture.

Ultimately, the Hero Myth is fulfilled once we are strong enough to go back into the underworld and expose ourselves to annihilating forces of the unconscious to rescue what is held captive in the Great Mother and restore to wholeness that which was separated into the shadow and held in place by the persona. We must be able to withstand the forces both from inside (the unconscious) and the outside (conscious) world without being destroyed, regressing, dissolving, or repressing. We must even be able to withstand attacks on our heroic quests themselves. Only when the ego turns to go back toward the Self, rather than trying to find the Treasure outside itself, will the transformation and journey to gaining the true Treasure begin.

Slaying of the Parents

Recall that, during the Separation of the World Parents stage, young children take in whole the psyches of their mothers and fathers, including their unlived lives, and project these into the world as their own personal superegos. With the development of the heroic ego ideal during the Birth of the Hero stage, however, teens begin to pursue their own interests and goals and to establish their own set of trusted friends who reflect their values. To gain autonomy, discover their own Treasure, and manifest their unique gifts to the world, teens must continue growing by moving to the next developmental stage and creating unique lives of their own. Called the Slaying of the Parents stage, this is the hero's time of chewing, digesting, metabolizing, and/or spitting out what had been swallowed during the Separation of the World Parents stage.

> **"Spitting out"** is a quite literal usage of the term *rejecting*. People have actual feelings of wanting to vomit when they are in dragon fights. Many people have lost their instinct to vomit because they were forced to "swallow whole" so much. These people must regain their ability to vomit instinctively.

Autonomy, authority, and differentiation mark the hero's development during the Slaying of the Parents stage, and the dragon fights during this stage build upon those begun in the Birth of the Hero stage. These fights consist of the conscious examination of the personal superego and the spitting out of the negative aspects of the parents' psyches, their unlived lives (teens may feel they have to live for their parents), and their early conditioning. In general, they consider: "This is what my parents thought was important and what they thought of me when I was young. Do I believe this? What do I think and how do I feel about this?" This can be a painful process for many parents, as one or both parents can be seen as a dragon that must be slain.

When the hero wins the dragon fight related to the *personal* superegos, a pure form of the anima/animus crystalizes in the hero's psyche. This emboldens the hero to face subsequent dragon fights to clear the *cultural* superego. During these dragon fights, the hero thinks: "I am a product of a certain place and time. What do I carry in my psyche that I have not examined from the context in which I was conditioned? Do I want to retain this? What are *my* values, morals, and ethics?" This type of dragon fight carries a mandate to deconstruct the old ways, traditions, and taboos, in order to bring the new to humankind.

Erich Neumann, in *Art and the Creative Unconscious*, uses the example of an artist to describe the dominant dynamic of the Slaying of the Parents stage. He says that the artist is compelled to ". . . leave the land of his birth, his mother, and the house of his father, and seek out the land to which the godhead leads him."[36] This signifies that the artist is creatively moved to bring in the "new" through his or her art by aligning with the Self and building upon, but transcending the father world (which represents the existing presiding values and rules). In other words, the creative artist becomes a hero by deconstructing society's old paradigms and ushering in the new. But this new

> ### Major Dragon Fights in Stages of the Creation and Hero Myths
>
> **Separation of the World Parents**
> * Shifting alliance from the Great Mother archetype to the Father archetype by creating a psychic structure that seemingly veils the true nature of the Self, relegating it to the background, while the ego takes precedence in the foreground
>
> **Separation of the World Parents and Birth of the Hero**
> * Fighting with the feelings, urges, emotions, and forces that want to pull us back into the unconscious forces of the uroborus and the Great Mother
>
> **Birth of the Hero and Slaying of the Parents**
> * Slaying the personal superego, the negative aspects of the internalized parental introjections, by replacing them with our own values, ethics, opinions, and ideas
>
> **Slaying of the Parents**
> * Clearing the cultural superego—the conditioning of family, institutions, and culture—and leaving behind the tribe of our peer group and culture
>
> *Note: These fights are not linear. Each usually takes many dragon fights within each stage to accomplish.*

is often unwelcomed, criticized, and seen as violating the contemporary rules of art. The artist also is often demeaned and faces harsh opposition from the conventional art community. In fact, much of society often rejects both the art and the artist. For instance, the paintings of the Impressionists did not sell well during the artists' lifetimes, although they now sell for millions, having taken many years to be viewed as masterpieces.

As a contemporary creative example, consider musicians who bring in the "new." Although originally rebuffed by the general public, rap music now constitutes 82 percent of all music sold in the United States! Another good example is the internationally touring drummer and percussionist Kasiva Mutua, who grew up in Kenya. Ever since she was a child, Kasiva played rhythms with her hands and on objects around her. Early on, however, she felt she had to hide her love of rhythm, because, according to African tradition and culture, only men were drummers. Along her creative journey, Kasiva was questioned, criticized, attacked, and ostracized by both Kenyan society and her family. Somehow, she faced down her dragons and followed her calling. Today, in addition to be an international star, she also teaches the significance and importance of the drum and percussion to young boys, women, and girls. Her passion to preserve her people's expression of drumming is especially important work as the art has begun to lose its popularity in contemporary culture.[37]

Ultimately, the Slaying of the Parents stage is a dragon fight that culminates in stepping into our own authority and having the ability to say no to the values, beliefs, and dreams our parents and the culture have for us. We step on to our own internal path, which connects us to our soul and destiny. Think about the young man whose parents demand he become a surgeon, while he longs to be a graphic artist. For him to follow his calling, he must "leave the tribe"—his parents' demands or the culture's contemporary values with which he has been aligned—to function from an internal, rather than an external, compass. Through this process, identity solidifies and the ego becomes fully developed, although not yet mature. On our **"Ego-Self Journey"** diagram, this stage is illustrated as the ego being at is furthest point outside the circle of the Self.

When we realize the heroic quests we once thought would satisfy actually fail to deliver lasting satisfaction, we face a crisis, often known as a mid-life crisis. We see that the ego has taken us as far as it can. Now we must embark on an inner journey on the road to Transformation, starting with Rescuing the Captive.

9

Neumann's Transformation Myths: Rescuing the Captive, Gaining the Treasure, and Unification of Opposites: Hermaphrodite

"While in the beginning the ego germ lay in the embrace of the hermaphroditic uroborus, at the end, the Self proves to be the golden core of a sublimated uroborus, combining in itself masculine and feminine, conscious and unconscious elements, a unity in which the ego does not perish but experiences itself, in the Self, as the uniting symbol, the hermaphrodite!"[38]

- Erich Neumann -

The term *transformation* is used in many different domains to describe a process that makes a complete or dramatic change in form, appearance, or character. It also can signify the recreation of an old being into a new being—metamorphosis. On the life journey to this new mythic stage, we have gone through many transformations. As we strengthened our heroic ego, we relied on our sense of worth and value (which may have been under great attack), tolerated leaving the known path of social order, and walked into our own dark forests. As heroes, we confronted the dragon of the Great Mother in the unconscious many times and retrieved what was captive there. We may even have experienced versions of dismemberment as we uncovered over and over aspects of our shadow. Then we experienced the predictable shattering of our persona, only to rise again with an intention toward reuniting with our own projections, releasing our known identity, and releasing any defenses we held toward our complete vulnerability to our own spirit of wholeness. In this final mythic stage of Transformation, we face the dissolution of our ego in its familiar form and patterns. Its morphing to a clearer, less conditioned state allows for a life more solidly anchored in the Self.

HERO MYTHS

Separation of the World Parents   Dragon Fights

(Father Archetype activated)

Birth of the Hero

Slaying of the Parents

TRANSFORMATION MYTHS

Great Mother Archetype

Stage 3

Rescuing the Captive

Stage 2

Stage 1

Gaining the Treasure

Uroborus

Unification of Opposites / Hermaphrodite

CREATION MYTHS

Rescuing the Captive

Up until this point in development, through the Slaying of the Parents stage, the ego/hero has been building itself through a vast array of heroic quests to prove its value and worth, gain authority, and feel empowered—with the ultimate goal of fulfillment. The process has involved attaining achievements and possessions in the outer world. Other aspects of the process have comprised projecting the parental internalized objects as the anima/animus onto the world and relationships, and believing these projections to be real and true rather than a lens of perception unique to oneself.

The completion of the Slaying of the Parents archetypal stage marks the beginning of the Rescuing the Captive stage, named the "introversion" stage by Erich Neumann. But, this inner journey of heroism is not taken by all. Many remain glued in the projections based on early unconscious impressions and implicit memories that cause reactions throughout our lives. Or we may linger on its edges, fearful to take the plunge into the underworld of the unconscious, split-off parts, the shadow aspects of our psyche. And those of us who do not undertake the journey remain unfulfilled.

This stage of Rescuing the Captive asks the ego/hero to turn the projections toward oneself, enter into the depths of the psyche, and acknowledge the parts of the self left undeveloped and split off in earlier parts of childhood development. We must reach into our depths for the courage and strength to embark on this hero's journey and be willing to face the early experiences, pain, fears, and inner demons needed to gain the Treasure!

In mythology, the hero has amassed enough inner strength from "slaying the parents" that it becomes clear that the only next step is to return to the depths of the Great Mother with fierceness, not to be overcome by her forces, to save the "captive maiden," and to bring her to safety. It takes the outer masculine hero force that holds our intellect, understanding, and muscle to return to the Great Mother, to capture the parts of our real self that are left there when we believed our immature impressions and introjects to be our true essence. In other words, the inner feminine world that says, "I am not good enough or important," is the underworld of demons that must be seen through and slain in order to rescue the pure maiden of our authentic nature. During the process of "rescuing the captive," the conditioned self of early childhood starts to unravel, and the light of the Self begins to shine through. As more of the authentic self is revealed, the Treasure is illumined.

To accomplish this feat, the hero is asked to examine his or her own unconscious shadow, the disowned contents that did not fit the heroic image or heroic quests in the world nor fit parental expectations. In movies, this effort is depicted by the hero traveling into the underground to fight the monsters guarding the treasure. In fact, the process we must go through to encounter and re-own our unconscious shadow of the captive maiden is as terrifying as scary movie scenes. When we encounter aspects of our shadow, they feel alien and monstrous. In movies, this is often represented as the hero moving through snake pits, swamps, or other such terrifying spaces; dealing with wild and scary creatures; or tolerating spiders crawling on him or her.

To survive and thrive, our persona must reunite with the disowned aspects. Our idea of who we are must expand, our defenses must be examined and revealed, and our denial and fears must be fully faced and put to death. We must be strong enough to expand our sense of self and embrace a new identity that is more in alignment with who we really are. Doing this feels like going down into the underground to face our vulnerability and neediness that was disowned into the unconscious shadow when support was not available. Ultimately, our internal heroic image becomes one of helping others and of self-reliance, like a superhero!

In archetypal language, during the first part of the Rescuing the Captive stage, we begin to examine our alignments with the Mother and Father archetypes by broadening our perspectives of our earlier experiences and by withdrawing blame for our conditions, our feelings about the world, or how our parents treated us. We start to see that it was the introjects we accepted to be true from our early experiences that caused us to turn away from the Self and our authenticity. This ownership creates an emotional maturing which, ultimately, leads to a sense of feeling "grown up" and integrated.

Once we have accomplished a major part of this first task of owning and integrating the introjects left in the unconscious shadow, we enter a second stage of Rescuing the Captive. Now, our hero is strong enough to develop a new capacity to witness his or her experience and perception, and to fine tune and withdraw projections that are not congruent with who we are. We transfer our own desires and emotions that are hidden from our awareness to another person or situation that has similarities to our past experiences, even though something new could now be occurring in the present. By looking at our attractions and aversions, we can begin to come into contact with what we felt we had to hide from ourselves in the past.

In our previous stage, the main projections were: "There isn't any help available" and "I can't trust help anyway." From that perspective, we developed patterns of thought and constructed stories of how the world "is." Rather than ask for help, we would withdraw from a situation, assuming there would be no support. At this new stage, though, we begin to let in that we really do not know what is possible. We also recognize we have been running on decisions and alignments made very early in life. Once we begin to see through the old constructed stories, we can release our old predictions and experiment with becoming open to new possibilities.

This effort is an ongoing process. The hero must return many times to rescue what is held captive in the unconscious and engage in many dragon fights. Before each pass at a dragon, the hero's ego must reorganize and tolerate the newness of identity. With each layer of releasing the captive, more of the true nature of the hero is available, and more of the hero's persona falls away. The destruction and metabolization of the internalized dragons ("There is no help!") ultimately results in the liberation of the captive, the dismemberment of the dragons leads to an assimilation of the unconscious, eventually giving the Self authority, and the soul begins to reveal itself! Then we are tasked with listening to what the soul is calling for, finding the soul's purpose in the world, and answering the question, "What is the Treasure of our life really about?"

At this point, the masculine and feminine aspects of Self begin to integrate and balance, and our inner emotional world and outer expression of our gifts lights the way to experience the Treasure. Through the Treasure, we gain fulfillment, purpose, and deep meaning.

Gaining the Treasure

To recap, the Hero Myth is fulfilled once we are strong enough to return to the underworld, expose ourselves to annihilating forces, and rescue what is held captive in the Great Mother, restoring to wholeness what was separated off into the shadow and held in place by the persona. With vulnerability and openness as our armor, we must be able to withstand both inside (the unconscious) and outside (what is conscious) forces without being deflated, regressing, dissolving, or repressing. With heroic effort, we may uncover the Treasure. The Treasure is on the infinite continuum of the realization of the Self, its integration into beingness, and the dropping away of the ego as the center of the psyche. Once gaining the Treasure, the psyche is consciously reoriented, with the ego now orbiting the Self as the center of the psyche rather than the other way around.

When the ego commits to rescuing the captive, many archetypal forces are released to help in that quest. In movies, this assistance is portrayed as magical powers, magical tools, fairy godmothers, or wizards. In this next stage of Gaining the Treasure, help also emanates from the organizing power of the Self, which is experienced as incidents of synchronicity. In fact, the organizing power of the centrality of the Self takes over in earnest; intention, clarity, and creativity shine clearly. What were once heroic ego projects now effortlessly unfold. As in fairy tales, the unification of the masculine and feminine live happily ever after in the golden light of love and integration. The captive is the generative feminine principle, and the hero, the masculine principle. The rescue of the captive by the hero creates a balance of the two principles, and the Treasure is attained in its unity, with the Treasure of the soul and the gift of life unfolding from that as the fullness of emotion of our inner world and the expression of our soul into the outer world of our work and relationships..

As we gain the Treasure, our identification with the body and mind begins to shift to our soul's purpose, to living from our heart with love and generosity, and to the messages coming from the unconscious as teachings to support our Self-realization. Ultimately, we make the link with the unconscious truly creative. Creativity in all its forms is always the product of the meeting between the masculine world of ego consciousness and the feminine world of the soul. More balanced and enlightened, we are now able to bring our creativity in its full form to our communities and to continue the ongoing process of owning our projections, rescuing parts held captive.

Unification of Opposites: Hermaphrodite

During the Transformation Myth stages, we find ourselves back at the psychological place we inhabited unconsciously as children, before the Separation of the World Parents, when we became, as it were, twins (i.e., the one who existed whole and the one who went on to have a place in the outer world). More conscious, having survived our dragon fights and having been transformed, we return to oneness, to a state of unity where all the possible opposites simultaneously exist together—where inside and outside dissolve into one and the stability and morphing of the ego allows the archetypal energy of the Self to integrate and then to flow into the world.

As further explanation of this transformation, let's return to the work and words of Erich Neumann. In *The Origins and History of Consciousness*, Neumann wrote: "Only in this paradoxical situation, when the personality experiences dying as a simultaneous act of self-reproduction, will the twofold man be reborn as the total man." He goes on to say, "While in the beginning the ego germ lay in the embrace of the hermaphroditic uroborus, at the end, the Self proves to be the golden core of a sublimated uroborus, combining in itself masculine and feminine, conscious and unconscious elements, a unity in which the ego does not perish but experiences itself, in the Self, as the uniting symbol, the hermaphrodite!" Further, he depicts the transformation as "an alchemical picture, with the hermaphrodite standing upon [a] dragon: By virtue of its own synthetic being, [the hermaphrodite] has overcome the primal situation; above it hangs the crown of the Self and in its heart glows the diamond."[39] Note: As stated earlier, we are honoring Erich Neumann's work, and we are aware that the hermaphrodite depicts undifferentiated genitalia, rather than a unity or balance of masculine and feminine aspects present in the more contemporary symbol of the androgyne.

Transforming into the hermaphrodite entails three stages.[40] In the first stage, we exist in an undivided state in which the conscious and unconscious have not yet been established as two distinct fields. In the second stage, the original double-sexed figure is divided; the splitting of the original unity gives birth to "the opposites." In all myths, this splitting is the price of consciousness, just as the Separation of the World Parents moves us into a split between the conscious and unconscious. During the third stage, the opposites reunite. This union is depicted as asexual, and the resulting mythic image is of the hermaphrodite—one with both genitalia (the union of the masculine and feminine) who stands on the slain dragon wearing the crown of the realization of the Self, while a diamond glows in the heart.

Transformed, we find our heroic Self back at the psychological place we inhabited unconsciously as children, before the Separation of the World Parents and now with consciousness. With the journey complete, we return to our true nature, united in the subtle realm, conscious of that which we exist within and of that which exists within us. The seeming separation we have held between self and other, and inside and outside, now begins dissolving into experiences of unity and illumination of the Self as our essential being.

The Return with the Treasure

Every good Hero myth has the hero return, either alive or dead, to the community. The hero comes bearing gifts such as leadership, stands for integrity, models truth and generativity, works in service to others, or lives in service to the betterment of humanity—all while holding a heroic vision. For this to happen, the psyche must be strong enough to attain the Treasure within, the goal of life.

In broad terms, Erich Neumann would have our heroic gifts be in service of bringing about an integration of all nations, tribes, races, and groups. He envisions a future humanity that would cast out the primordial uroboric dragon and reconcile, through integration, a new synthesis for all beings. This ultimate gift—establishment of a structure of humankind that can no longer be split apart by opposites—would eliminate the ability of the uroboric states to manifest in the world and cause atrocities such as the Holocaust and the Rwandan genocide. What a wonderful dream Neumann held for us all! The potential of this outcome seems illusive now, but, by many of us undergoing this journey to the Treasure, we hold the promise of Neumann's vision.

Dragon Fights During Stages of the Transformation Myths

Rescuing the Captive
* Rescuing any aspects we left in the uroborus and Great Mother stages
* Becoming a true hero within by rescuing our value and worth and finding our true sense of power and inner authority

Rescuing the Captive and Gaining the Treasure
* Beginning to clear the shadow and release identification with our persona
* Ending heroic quests in service of the ego
* Bringing in projections of anima/animus and working these internally

Gaining the Treasure
* Clearing the psychic structure made in Separation of the World Parents that separates us into conscious and unconscious, from natural unity with the Self into the ego and the outer world
* Bringing in all projections and seeing them as outer reflections of our inner processes
* Shifting and changing the egoic patterns revealing the Self
* Living in service of the Self as our true nature

Unification of Opposites
* Dissolving the separation between ego and the Self

Note: These fights are not linear. Each usually takes many dragon fights within each stage to accomplish.

Myths and Archetypal Stages

Overall Mythic Stages	Eight Myths	Archetypal Stages	Processes within the Stages
Creation Myths	Uroborus	Uroborus	
	Great Mother	Great Mother Stage 1 (Oral) Great Mother Stage 2 (Anal) Great Mother Stage 3 (Genital)	Anima/Animus laid down
	Separation of the World Parents	Separation of the World Parents	• Father archetype activated (which moves person into next Hero Myths) • Heroic ego ideal • Persona • Superego (personal and cultural)
Hero Myths	Birth of the Hero	Birth of the Hero	• Wrestling with nongenerative aspects of introjected parental psyches (personal superego) • Heroic ego ideal • 3 main dragon fights • Heroic quests • Anima/Animus • Different kinds of heroes (defines introjection, projection, shadow, and persona)
	Slaying of the Parents	Slaying of the Parents	
Transformation Myths	Rescuing the Captive	Rescuing the Captive	• Withdrawing projections • Dragon fights
	Gaining the Treasure	Gaining the Treasure	
	Transformation	Unification of Opposites	

10

Archetypal Developmental Stages of Life

Love and deep desire for wholeness pulls us through each stage toward realization of the Treasure.

All human development and behaviors have an underlying propensity toward unity and the discovery of our natural state, the Self. This guiding principle enables us to identify and label what each developmental stage attempts to manifest in its generative form.

Based on our years of clinical practice and supervision with Dr. Michael Conforti, we also are able to correlate chronological ages with archetypal developmental stages. (Note: Dr. Conforti uses his own template of applying congruence in archetypal stages with specific ages in chronological development.) This correlation helps us to hold the mental question as to whether a client is congruent with his or her chronological age, and, if not, what kind of behavioral changes and mentoring is needed for that individual to go into congruence with his or her contemporaries? In other words, what are the behaviors that need to be put in place for the client to be in line with his or her peers who are on track for their age?

To learn how to assess these stages and their congruence, we have created a chart that outlines the archetypal developmental stages of life, each stage's attempts at unity of Self, and how the stages correlate with chronological age. We have found that the chronology is archetypal throughout different cultures, but it is obviously contemporary. If or when life-expectancy ages change and as we evolve developmentally as a culture, the chronology of archetypal stages will change as well.

Archetypal Developmental Stages of Life

Stages	Developmental	Attempt at Unity
Conception & Birth	Pleuromatic	Undifferentiated unity with Mother
Infant & Toddler	Uroborus • Great Mother	Symbiotic stage, differentiates into Self vs. other
	Great Mother Stage 1	Oral relating to world • Value and worth established
	Great Mother Stage 2	Anal • Autonomy and control as way of relating to world
	Great Mother Stage 3	Genital • Way of union with the world
Pre-school Age & School Age	Separation of the World Parents Father Archetype begins	Superego begins • Parents introjected whole • Child turns away from wholeness to have place in world • Gender chosen • Opposites begin • Establishng in society outside the home
Puberty	Dragon Fights	Hero catalyzed • Ego ideal begins to fill out • Superego, shadow, and persona develop • Society gaining importance
Adolescence into Teens - 19	Birth of the Hero Slaying of the Parents	Beginning independence • Peer group becomes central • Parental images projected as anima/animus • Forming independent identity • Beginning development of own values and goals
Young Adult (20s)	Still Slaying of the Parents	Striving for external life achievement • Heroic quests become dominant • Relationships with anima/animus figures • Dealing with self-image

Established Adult (30s)	Continued Individuation	Finding oneself in relation to the collective • Heroic projects, career, family, autonomy, individuation
40s	Begin Rescuing the Captive	Forming strong foundations • Trying to unite with spirit through heroic projects • Trying to expand life achievements to maximum potential
50s	Rescuing the Captive	Birth of the mature ego • Death of false persona • Taking back projections of anima/animus • Questioning the meaning of life • Beginning to leave collective's expectations
60s	Rescuing the Captive Gaining the Treasure Unification of Opposites	Looking at old age and death • "Have I done what I came for?" • Leaving ego's projects, feeling the pull of the entelechy • Starting to align with the soul's purpose by shifting to internally driven identity • Bringing gifts of soul's purpose to community
70s	Gaining the Treasure Unification of Opposites	Endeavors based on significance • Internal identity aligning with the soul • Recognizing mortality
80s - 90s	Gaining the Treasure Unification of Opposites	Winter of one's life • Communicating experience and wisdom to the next generation • Coming to terms with dropping the body
90+	Unification of Opposites	Courting a relationship with death • Leaving a legacy for the next generations • Using wisdom to help set up structure for your own legacy

Inspired by Michael Conforti

Part Three

Application of Erich Neumann's Archetypal Developmental Theory:
Rescuing the Captive to Gain the Treasure

"It is only the captive's connection with the 'treasure hard to attain' that reveals her nature, for the captive is herself the treasure."[1]

- Erich Neumann -

11

Rescuing the Captive: Its Importance to Living Our Full Potential

According to Neumann, the mandate of this archetypal dragon fight is to free the feminine aspects that form our inner emotional life and to help us integrate the knowing of our true value and worth. Feeling fully empowered and in our authority, we take a stance of maturity that is also integrated in our sexual being, creative potential, and expression. Then we can find union with the Self and the world as the Treasure of our true nature. This communion ultimately allows us to shine from the heart in love, tenderness, nurturing, protectiveness, caring, compassion, empathy, and gratitude.

As an overview, recall that, at each archetypal developmental stage, we want to foster the consolidation of that specific stage as well as plant the seeds of the skills needed for the transition to the next stage. Simultaneously, we want to reintegrate aspects of earlier stages that have been left behind. This allows us to integrate arrested development and shadow aspects while dissolving defensive boundaries and liberating the persona to become more open and flexible. Ultimately, we are cultivating the awareness and skills for learning to live from an alignment with the Self.

By the time we reach the advanced developmental stage of the Transformation Myths, we already have experienced a demanding process of struggling to find our own opinions and knowing, but our developmental work as humans does not stop there. As noted in the last section, to truly "gain the Treasure," we must journey inside the psyche to clear any patterns interfering with living fully. And this takes ever more heroic action.

In our clinical practice, helping our clients to begin or stay the course on their heroic quest to "gain the Treasure" is our goal. To help them with their efforts in this endeavor, we focus on the Transformation Myths' Rescuing the Captive stage, on walking the path with them as they muster the courage to rescue their captive maiden and live from the Treasure of their true nature. Most therapies stop with helping the ego/hero strengthen his or her quests in the world; they do not necessarily go deep and spend the time needed to complete the rescue of all that is captive, particularly those aspects of self that were split off during the Great Mother stage. In our clinical practice, however, we concentrate on assisting the ego of our clients to gain more consciousness and morph into a clearer, natural state. This takes dissolving the ego's defensive boundaries, so it can begin to be absorbed into the Self.

As we explained in Part Two, the Self is our essential nature. It is always present, but during our early conditioning of childhood the Self becomes veiled from conscious awareness and goes into the background. As therapists, we see the Self in each client and stay focused there, while we read the patterns and themes of their early conditioning and serve as a bridge between the conscious mind of the ego and the deep unconscious of the inner world of the psyche. Our goal and destination, at all times, is to help our clients realize the Self that is underlying and permeating their ego and all aspects of their being. Significant in the depth of our work are the therapeutic conditions we provide. These conditions offer an archetypal container that intervenes in replicative patterns from early conditioning and repairs any compromised containers provided by our clients' families during early childhood.

HERO MYTHS

Separation of World Parents

Dragon Fights

(Father Archetype activated)

Birth of the Hero

Slaying of the Parents

TRANSFORMATION MYTHS

Great Mother Archetype

Stage 3

Stage 2

Rescuing the Captive

Stage 1

Gaining the Treasure

Uroborus

Unification of Opposites / Hermaphrodite

CREATION MYTHS

To give you a road map of our psychotherapy work, here in Part Three we walk you through each developmental stage and the path through the many rescues. This constitutes a detailed description of our application process related to rescuing the captive—and to ultimately fulfilling humankind's potential. Such an application process can be useful for other therapists as well as for anyone of any age who desires wholeness, who wants to experience the full potential of life.

Overview of Rescuing the Captive

To summarize what we discussed in Part Two, our human life is archetypal with archetypal aspects and archetypal stages that coincide with certain parts of our lives and certain chronological ages, when these stages typically become available. Rescuing the Captive is that particular developmental stage when we might turn the corner from being ego driven and identifying with accomplishments and material possessions as the source of our value. We might begin to see that, no matter how hard we try or how many attempts we make, lasting happiness and fulfillment are not found in the outer world.

When we only seek happiness and fulfillment in the external world, all our anima and animus projections lead us to the same place: emptiness. Despite everything we try, we still feel empty! We try eating all things yummy or starving ourselves to look thin. We try drinking or smoking cigarettes or mind-altering drugs. We try through numerous relationships and sexual experiences. We try through taking care of others. We try through our careers and making enough money to buy the material items that make us happy for a day or so. We try through having a nice house with a white picket fence or by buying shiny new cars and big trucks. Having exhausted the possibilities, we lament and acknowledge that none of these external things brings lasting inner peace or happiness. With nowhere else to look for those elusive desires, we finally realize that finding lasting happiness and contentment comes through a connection on the inside. In other words, "This is an *inside* job!"

The experience of shifting gears from seeking our heart's desire in the outside to the realization that the inner Self holds the potential for all our joy and fulfillment is well depicted in *The Wizard of Oz*. Dorothy, Tin Man, Scarecrow, and Lion travel together on the yellow brick road to find the Wizard. Each seeks the Wizard for a different purpose: Dorothy wants help to find her way home; Tin Man seeks his heart; Scarecrow is looking for his brain; and the Lion desires courage. At the end of the road, though, the foursome eventually discover that the Wizard is actually a fraud. They learn that each holds his or her own power to realize his or her dreams and desires. This wonderful archetypal story parallels the human journey of looking for someone or something in our outer life to bring us home—to the Self. Like Dorothy, Tin Man, Scarecrow, and Lion, we, too, must get to the point of realizing that the wise wizard is in each of us, as the essence of our being. There truly is no place like home!

Most of us make many attempts to find our "home"—our value and worth, our sense of empowerment, our ability to be in lasting, loving, and intimate relationships, and our sense of inner peace and happiness. When we see our patterning over and over bringing us back to an empty place, we finally realize the true treasure in life—the treasure of our being, the preciousness of our essence—is not found through outside means. And then we shift gears into taking an inner journey back to wholeness and the treasure of the Self.

In Erich Neumann's depiction of the Rescuing the Captive myth, the hero has searched for meaning and fulfillment from the outer material world through numerous heroic quests. Although disappointed by this search to ease the heart, the hero is empowered enough by past heroic experiences to embark on the inner journey. There, the hero finds the captive maiden of the beautiful feminine self. In their marriage is the union of masculine and feminine aspects of self, with wholeness and essence revealed.

Remember, though, that the hero's journey is not a one-shot deal. The hero must delve into the depths of the unconscious many times to rescue that which is held captive. With each quest, a layer of the captive is released and more of the true self is integrated. As the hero's shadow is revealed and more of the hero's persona dissolves, the ego must reorganize and tolerate the newness of identity before standing up to the next fierce dragon, again and again.

We see this theme of the hero having many dragon fights to free the feminine captive often in movies. For example, in *Indiana Jones* movies, Indiana Jones goes through many fights and near-death experiences to free the treasure and bring it home. In *Pan's Labyrinth*, Pan must run from relentless demonic characters and free herself from the powerful glue of giant spider webs to find the magic key and escape from the underworld. Another good example is *Clash of the Titans* and the story of Perseus. In this epic film, in order to rescue the captive Andromeda, the beautiful maiden (the anima figure of his psyche), Perseus must slay the archetypal Father and Mother (portrayed by the sea monster, the Kraken; and Medusa, who, if Perseus looks at her during the slaying, will turn him to stone).

Liberation of the captive means the destruction and metabolization of the internalized dragon. As Neumann puts it, in a sense, the liberation of the captive and the dismemberment of the dragon mean the assimilation of the unconscious, of the anima and animus introjects and projections. This ongoing process of assimilation ultimately allows for the crystallization and integration of the pure archetypal forms and for the Unification of Opposites, the union of masculine and feminine forces.

Like the hero in Neumann's archetypal myth, we, too, must rally the hero inside ourself to face the inner fears and demons, hurts, pain, shame, and doubt of our underworld. We must find the courage and heart to face the dragons of the devouring Mother and crushing Father, to rescue the parts of Self left in their grips. We can then integrate enough parts to feel a sense of wholeness, live the fullness of our life, live our purpose, gain the Treasure of the Self, and share our gifts with the collective world.

Typically, the inner journey, the developmental stage of Rescuing the Captive, occurs in the second part of our lives. It may be attained earlier if we experienced generative parenting during childhood, if our caregivers supported and encouraged our essential nature and were strong, inner guiding forces. But if there were a history of trauma or a lack of attachment with the mother, the rescue could take a very long time.

Whenever one embarks upon the inner journey, the task is not easy work! Fearful to take the plunge into the underworld of the unconscious, split-off parts, the shadow aspects of our psyche, too many of us linger on the edges of this important developmental stage. We remain in the familiar, yet unfulfilled, place in our lives where we project our inner experiences from perspectives based upon our early development and conditioning by the Great Mother and the Father world, the anima and animus projections. We continue the search for the Treasure through outer means—just like Dorothy, Tin Man, Scarecrow, and Lion sought the Wizard in the Emerald City to make them whole.

But many of us feel the hunger for "home," for living from our essential nature. We are tired of the same patterns playing out in our lives and want to find the deeper meaning for "Why am I here? What is the purpose of my life? Who am I?" At a bifurcation or fork in the road, we are ready for the journey into the depth of our being. We just need a guide or mentor to walk with us through the new territory.

Saying "yes" to the Rescuing the Captive process begins a commitment to look at our inner world, thought structures, feelings, and emotional states. It requires us to pull in our unconscious anima/animus projections, to own our perceptions and our stories, and to see through the untruths and constructions we created about ourself and others. Saying "yes" crosses the first threshold of "answering the call for transformation," and the hero emerges with a sense of fierceness and strength to face the dragons, to fight off the demons without being overcome by the Great Mother forces, and to rescue the beautiful maiden of our being.

Specifically, the mandate of this archetypal dragon fight is to free the feminine aspects that form our inner emotional life and dialogue to help us integrate the knowing of our true value and worth. Feeling empowered and in our authority, we can also integrate our sexual being and creative potential. Then we begin to find union with the Self and the world as the Treasure of our true nature. This communion ultimately allows us to shine from the heart in love, tenderness, nurturing, protectiveness, caring, compassion, empathy, and gratitude.

> ## Neumann's Rescuing the Captive Myth
>
> Because we base so much of our psychotherapy work on the Rescuing the Captive myth, it is important to know the elements of the myth, as described by Erich Neumann himself. In *The Origins and History of Consciousness*, Neumann views rescuing the captive as rescuing our soul, the Treasure of our essential being, and the coming into our fullness of the Self and our essence. According to Neumann, the hero is our archetypal masculine force of ego, "the embodiment of heaven and the Father archetype."[2] Further, the archetypal feminine of our inner psyche that is unconscious is "the fruitful side of the Mother archetype embodied in the rejuvenated and humanized figure of the rescued virgin."[3] Neumann says that the feminine image must extricate herself from the grips of the devouring Mother, a process known in analytic psychology as "the crystallization of the anima/animus from the Mother archetype."[4]
>
> Moving forward developmentally, the mandate of the hero is to rescue that which has been held captive. That journey consists of many dragon fights with inner and outer demons until the hero and captive marry, forming a union and balancing the masculine and feminine, the inner and outer parts of self. Neumann notes, "What the hero [masculine and ego] kills is only the terrible side of the feminine [unconscious captive], as this he does in order to set free the fruitful and joyous side with which she joins herself to him."[5] He goes on to say that this union is "the essential outcome of dragon fights the world over,"[6] ... that "[t]he task of the hero is to free, through her, the living relation to 'you,' to the world at large."[7]
>
> Delving even more deeply, Neumann writes, "Thus, the hero's rescue corresponds to the discovery of the psychic world. This world is already a vast extent as the world of Eros, embracing everything that he has ever done for woman, everything he has experienced and created for her sake."[8] Finally, Neumann proposes that "Personality is built up largely by acts of introjections; contents that were before experienced outside are taken inside and seen as contents of the psychic world of objects within."[9] In other words, rescuing what is held captive allows the anima to be revealed from the unconscious feminine so that we can have a deeper relationship with ourself and others.

12

Application of Rescuing the Captive in Neumann's Creation Myths

"Value is our first state of Being, second is Love, and third is Nourishment. These are... universal givens for what is our essential nature."[10]

- A. H. Almaas -

Application of Rescuing the Captive in the Great Mother Stages

Whatever the young psyche experienced in the womb, with birth, and then took in during the early formative stages of dependency and bonding that was too painful and traumatic to be metabolized is split off and left behind during the Great Mother stages of early childhood. These life experiences, held in implicit memories in the cellular structure of our body, become shadow sub-personalities,[11] unconscious aspects of self, as the inner parts of self are developing. They then become the triggered, reactive states that take form in our inner thought structures of how we perceive ourselves and our world. We then project these perceptions of how we feel about ourselves and what we believe others think of us into the outer world and onto our relationships in adulthood. Recall that Jung referred to these projections as "anima" and "animus."

What we have learned in our decades of clinical practice coincides with what Neumann lays out: Our conditioning during life's early, unconscious, undifferentiated stages are organized not only around trust and security but also around our feelings of value and worth, our power and authority, and our sexuality and union with life. When we are mothered by someone who has psychological limitations, aspects of self are "devoured" and need to be taken back, healed, and integrated. In doing this, we free the feminine and heal the inner world of our psyche.

Archetypal Aspects of the Great Mother Stages

The aspects of the Great Mother are archetypal and held in potential as a part of our universal imprinting as humans. As noted in Part Two, we see three major stages associated with this early childhood and attachment that mark significant times in this developmental process. Recall that the dominant feature of the oral stage is satiation while in a symbiotic merging that includes the intra-uterine, birth, and extra-uterine experiences, and it is the time when we begin to lay the foundation of our value and worth based on that very thing that has been introjected from the mothering experience at that time. During this stage, as we take in food and nourishment from the breast or bottle, our projections and introjections are in union with our mother's thoughts and feelings. Our experience from this undifferentiated union with her is introjected into the implicit memory of our body and into the patterns lying in potential for our thought structures, emotions, and feelings. We take this forward into the developing ego structure.

If our merging with the mothering one is generative, we integrate that we are of value and worth and are prepared for the next stage. If it is nongenerative, we are compromised as we enter the stage of early autonomy that occurs during the second stage of the Great Mother, the anal stage of retention and expulsion. If our budding, immature sense of flexing our muscles with our power and authority is undermined, or if we are shamed, the anal stage is compromised: We try to control or not be controlled, we try not to feel the oppressed pain, or we act superior to cover feelings of inferiority.

The third stage of the Great Mother archetype is focused on arousal, genital satisfaction, sexuality, our budding creative potential, and how we unite with the outer world. How well we navigate the Oedipal dilemma and triangulation with the parents and their messages about our sexual body during this stage, along with prior stages' alignments to the mothering aspects, sets the stage for the developing ego structures going forward.[12]

These three stages of the Great Mother are archetypal and universal for all human beings. We all have alignments to these aspects of the Mother, whether generative or nongenerative, and these alignments determine our inner stories, thought structures, feelings, and emotions. They define how we take in the world and view our value and worth, our power and authority, sexual expression, creative potential, and life flow. They shape our view of the world and our relationships to others.

Almaas' Platonic Forms

Based on our alignments, we develop either generatively or nongeneratively around our power and authority, sexual expression, creative potential, and ways of being. These are the fundamental qualities we all have in common that need to be rescued during the Great Mother stages. A.H. Almaas says that, "Value is our first state of Being, second is Love, and third is Nourishment. These are Platonic forms,"[13] universal givens for what is our essential nature. These are all a part of the human imprinting of the oral stage of the Great Mother.

How we experience these platonic forms—value, love, and nourishment—establishes alignments to them. For example, consider "value." If as infants we received loving attendance and were mirrored the preciousness of our essential nature, we become generatively aligned to believing we are valued as a human being. However, if we introjected a feeling of not being worthy or good enough for our mother's approval and appreciation while taking in the milk from her breast, then we may have a nongenerative alignment and doubt our value and assume that the outer world also doubts our value; this sense of worthlessness becomes a general theme or undertone of our inner dialogue and of the feeling states that play out throughout our lives.

Almaas' second quality or universal form that is "a given" for humans is love. Love fully develops when object constancy and secure attachment are obtained. It is a state of our essential being and exists from the inception of life. Although this is the state of existence for babies much of the time, with our conditioning over time, we can lose touch with feeling our essence as "being love."

We form alignments to generative or nongenerative aspects of love, again, based on our experiences in the womb, at birth, and, once delivered, with the mothering one. Does she express love in pure form and mirror our preciousness, or does she express her wounding and limitations through narcissistic means? That is, when one experiences from the mothering one a sense of, "Who I am is valuable and lovable, even though I'm not perfect," there is an integration of "being as love." Often, however, the mother carries a narcissistic wounding from her own childhood. Manifesting that wounding, she might put her needs above those of her baby. This nongenerative dynamic sets up the child to wish for love and seek outer approval from others.

The third state of being or platonic form to which Almaas refers is nourishment. Nourishment was once experienced as the conditions of the womb; it also is equivalent to the mother's breast on a physical level and to

> the particulars of this oral stage which comprise nursing, oral gratification, and how issues around weaning are experienced.[14] Just as mother's milk is needed to nourish the infant physically, essential nourishment is also needed for the realization and development of our essence.
>
> We all have deep longings for a nurturing presence, the nourishment that comes from the mother. This longing made conscious and concrete is needed for complete autonomy. Generative alignment to nourishment is demonstrated by taking good care to nurture ourselves in all parts of our life, by creating a "generative womb" for our adult existence. A nongenerative alignment to nourishment sets the stage for oral fixations related to food, addictions, sugar, smoking, and general care of oneself. To permanently realize a generative alignment to nourishment, one must deal with the deepest structures of the internalized Mother's image, such as a sense of being a hungry mouth relating to the world as a breast. The loss relating to this aspect feels like "big hunger" or an empty stomach. Almaas notes that this empty stomach can be manifested in the form of needing to be fed by the world, by our successes, by being acknowledged, and by how much money we have, as well as by food addictions, smoking, alcohol and drug addiction, the need for love, and so on. This hunger, in fact, underlies all hungers of addictions.[15]

Merging with the Mothering One

One way of understanding this important developmental stage and the subsequent behaviors that often occur is by considering the need for merging with the mothering one during the symbiotic early months, when attachment and bonding is so critical. Merging is central to development; it conditions the ego for its journey in life, and it conditions our ability to individuate and to find the Treasure of our being. Merging is particularly present in times of gratification as well as in ways we attempt to recreate the Great Mother image, even as adults.

Our gratification needs are on a continuum, depending upon our internalized experience during our symbiotic relationship—depending upon the feelings we had while taking in the milk of our mother's breast, being held, and being attended to. We all have a need for a good and gratifying internal mother image. If that need is not adequately met during the merging time with Mother, we look for it to be gratified "in much of life, food, comfort, protection, safety, pleasure, warmth, contact, discharge of tension, etc."[16] According to Almaas, this unmet need can later manifest in adults "as love relationships, overeating, smoking, drug addiction, greed, idealization of community, and belongingness. The need for being is directed to external objects and activities."[17]

Our means of dealing with "negative merging," a defense against separating from the mother image that is internalized in the individuation process, is a wish to remain connected and to do so based on our alignments to aspects of the archetype of the Great Mother. We may then attach to a love object according to what was internalized at that time. These become our desires for outer objects and attachments to people and things in order to feel a sense of gratification. But this sort of gratification is short lived, and we need to find yet another object to bring satisfaction. This negative cycle goes on and on, is held in our unconscious, and is the source of most human suffering, emotional and relational.

To allow the merging and absorption of the ego into our essential essence, the Self, we must surrender our defenses and the identifications associated with any negative merging experiences and impressions taken in. When we feel loved and valued by the mothering one during symbiosis and merging time in development, a trajectory is established for our providing ourselves full nourishment, love, and care in all aspects of living. If not, we project into the world a need for acknowledgement of our value and worth, a need for love—and we give away aspects of our power and creative flow in the process. The efforts of seeking value, worth, and love externally—and the associated behaviors to self-soothe and compensate—are actually attempts to merge with a Great Mother image, albeit in an external way. To truly facilitate healthy attachment and full integration, these attempts must be faced, honored, and met in a loving, therapeutic manner.

General Examples of Rescuing the Captive During the Great Mother Stages

To summarize in clinical terms, Rescuing the Captive is the fight undertaken to free those aspects of the self that are fragmented, split off, and/or held in the devouring negative Mother stages of early life. Many of the nongenerative aspects are the unconscious, pre-verbal, and pre-cognitive thought structures and archetypal images that are held in the implicit memory of the body and that become our inner dialogue. They are what has prevented our clients from living fully and expressing their full potential, and they are the areas we assess and assist our clients in rescuing. This work ultimately prepares our clients for opening to the Treasure of their being.

We have many examples of adult symptoms that express the need for rescuing the captive. We have chosen to share here the ones that reflect a cultural expression of the psyche's call to embark on the hero's journey—to have the courage to rescue the captive maiden and to gain the Treasure.

Let's start with obesity. Obesity often correlates with a captive in the first stage of the Great Mother. During this oral stage, when all is identified with what is taken in through the mouth, the baby felt unmet and unseen for its preciousness by the Mother or caregiver. Having felt unmet orally as a baby, the adult attempts to soothe through oral means. The work here is in the implicit memory of the unconscious. To mend the early attachment disruption requires a strong bond in the therapeutic work.

Hoarding is another example. This behavior shows a captive in the second stage of the Great Mother, when the toddler is learning about a sense of authority and control in life. If attempts to be in control early in childhood were thwarted, hoarding is one outer expression pointing to what was missed. The repair work is also in the implicit memory and takes a clinician who has done her or his own work. That is, to empower our clients, we as therapists must have gained our own authority and sense of being empowered, so as not to need to be in control through rescuing our own captives in the second stage of the Great Mother.

Finally, pornography and sexual objectifying show a captive in the third stage of the Great Mother, the genital stage, when the child is discovering a sense of pleasure in the genitals and/or the desire for the opposite sex parent. This genital stage often can be challenging for parents, particularly if they have histories of boundary blurring or violations and don't feel comfortable with their own sexuality. It takes a strong couple relationship to help the child find a healthy sexual expression. The clinical work here also involves delving into the implicit memory as well as into fragments of memories and feelings of shame.

Interestingly, the specific pattern in which a physical disease manifests can point to which stage we need to address as clinicians and what needs to be rescued. For instance, an environmental disorder often is an outer expression of inner fears that the world is not a safe place. We have learned to translate this as parts of self held captive in the first or second stages of the Great Mother and have developed strategies to help people release this pattern from their bodies.

	Attempt at Unity	**Fear**	**Adult Symptoms**	**Integration**
Great Mother Stage 1 Oral	Through the mouth Incorporating into one's self what is given	Fear of being devoured, swallowed, eaten	Destructive inner critic For example: Eating disorder Smoking Alcohol abuse Drug use	Taking in generative nourishment Being a "good mother" to yourself Stopping destructive behavior

What Is Held Captive and Needs Rescuing in the Oral Stage

What is primary during the oral stage is satiation, taking in the mothering relationship and what is focused on the mouth, the stomach, and basic survival needs. This begins in the embryonic stage when the fetus is attached to the mother's placenta for nutrients of life via the umbilical cord.

Bruce Lipton PhD, cell biologist at Stanford University School of Medicine, tells us that current epigenetic research indicates that the mother transfers not only food nutrients to the fetus in utero but information as well.[18] This information includes what the mother perceives from her outside world that is then forming her inner thoughts and beliefs about herself and the world in which she lives. These perceptions, and the subsequent thought structures created, cause a release of hormones and chemicals from her brain, through the placenta, into the fetus. These hormones and chemicals influence brain activity that then affects the cellular structure of the fetus' body, ultimately influencing genetic activity.

All this information, and any stress of the mother during pregnancy, is transferred to the fetus in the womb. If the mother is stressed or fearful, the fetus feels it and reacts. If she is feeling love, the fetus feels this and is able to be at rest and feel safe. In short, signals from the environment program the genetics of the fetus, and the fetus is programmed by the mother's perception of her world. In the long term, our embryonic environment determines our own "inner" environment—our sense of security, trust, and ability to establish and maintain close relationships. This environment is the basis for a generative or nongenerative alignment to the Mother archetype.

Based on current epigenetic research, we also know that the "download" of information through the placenta includes information and patterns of at least four generations of the family lineage. These unconscious messages, relayed into our genetic makeup, program us and program our patterns regarding our responses to love and fear. Similarly, external experience also influences our genetic makeup. Someone tells a child who he or she is, and it is all recorded in Theta brain waves, as in hypnosis. This recording is primarily unconscious; controls the chemical reactions in the brain and our resulting perceptions, thoughts, reactions, and behavior; and programs us into our habitual patterns.[19]

A.H. Almaas also explores the impact of our early environment. He notes that, after birth and for the first year of life, the primary focus is on "Mommy, my tummy, and the breast that fills it." It is understandable that we begin to see life as functioning this way: We feel empty and the milk coming from our mother relieves the feelings of hunger. Our deepest identification with the body is the condition of our stomach. Thus, the stomach and whether it is empty or full, being fed or not being fed, begins to underlie all we act out in our life. This is then connected to any time we feel a sense of emptiness; it is the stomach that needs to be filled.[20]

Almaas goes on to say: "The central object relation is founded on the identification with the body and its relationship to the body of the mother, whether as a stomach relating to the breast or as the embryo relating to the placenta. This is how it is in the beginning with the breast. You had an empty stomach, you were at the breast, and the nutrients came from the breast into you."[21] It then makes sense that we see this is how the world functions. This begins with our first year of life and what is our basic early experience as we take in the world. This experience is one of a food source/breast, a mommy, a "me," and a stomach. According to Almaas, "The breast is either there or not there, good or bad, full or empty—and the stomach is either being fed or not being fed. These sensations of hunger that are relieved by breast-feeding are what eventually feel like our stomach and are at the core of the object relations we enact in our life. Our earliest relationship with our mother is as an embryo attached through the umbilical cord and later as an infant suckling at the breast. Our deepest identification is that we're a stomach."[22]

While this is yet a differentiated state of unity, the wanting of the breast begins our separate state of being a subject with a longing for an object (the breast) and for a full stomach. When we feel emptiness, that feeling is followed by our feeling the fear that we will not be able to fill the stomach. We, thus, begin unconsciously to set up a system of attuning to the unified state as the emptiness related to not feeling our belly being full. This goes along with the conditioning of the separate state and losing awareness of our true nature and unity.

Overview of What Is Held Captive and Needs Rescuing in the Oral Stage

1. **Turning away from unity**
   What underlies all that needs to be rescued in the Great Mother is our recognition of our essential nature as a magnificent being, the fullness of life of the Treasure of our soul, and living in relationship with the Self and its interconnectedness with all. This is veiled and turned away from, as we are conditioned to focus on the body as our definition of self—and on the physical world where this is experienced.

2. **Basic trust and safety due to fear of being devoured, swallowed, and annihilated**
   In the symbiotic state, we are totally vulnerable and feel little to no separation from the one on whom we are dependent for our safety, nourishment, consistency, love, and basic needs. Our unity with Self is projected onto the mothering one, as we turn from our essential nature and essence toward a budding ego and identification with being the body.

   The quality of care and the maternal relationship is the basis by which basic trust is developed. For this to happen, the infant must have a sense of continuity, consistency, sensitivity, and similar experiences that can be relied on to form a rudimentary sense of early ego identity from which to build upon. When solid conditions of holding and caregiving are not met, mistrust forms and the world feels unsafe. Fears of being devoured or annihilated by the mother develop. Fears of death and fears of living also take root at this time.

3. **Feelings of Self-Worth and Value**
   The baby is in a symbiotic state of little to no differentiation from Self and mother during the early Great Mother stages. If the mothering one is unable to mirror our beauty and value as we are suckling at the breast, we instead take the milk in with the introject of her limited feelings about herself. These limited feelings are taken in as being our essential nature, and the truth of our being as pure preciousness is left behind. In this way, the mother's narcissistic wounding and its limiting thought structures are passed intergenerationally.

Daniel J. Siegel MD, professor of clinical psychiatry at the UCLA School of Medicine and executive director of the Mindsight Institute, has coined a phrase to explain and emphasize the significance of this early mother and baby time of breast-feeding and gazing: "Neurons that fire together, wire together." He refers to the process as our having "neuroplasticity."[23] During the symbiotic time and early brain development, because of their synapse linkage, the mirror neurons activate the perception of the mother and her internal stimulation and the attunement of neuron firing. This is yet another way we introject the information from the mother as being the truth of who we are.

4. Healthy attachment and feeling loved

The infant longs for attachment and for feeling loved by the mothering one. Separation and differentiation from her feels threatening and deathlike. When the mother is unable to embrace her infant's need to be seen and dependent upon her, and to provide the conditions necessary for security to be built, the child feels a deep sense of separation anxiety. Because this may be too painful to experience, the child develops a defensive structure to compensate. For example, consider hearing or exclaiming, "I don't need anyone. I can do it myself!" Other ways of compensating are to not allow closeness with others and to not permit ourselves to feel anything.

In archetypal terms, an empty stomach is related to the devouring forces of the Great Mother and to our leaving the purity of our essence behind. To try to soothe the pain of separation from unconditional love of Self, to attempt to mitigate our feelings of lack, and in our struggle to integrate the devouring forces of the Great Mother, we then crave a full stomach and engage in oral fixations such as thumb sucking, over eating, chain smoking, and the like. Even throughout adulthood we have a recurring wish to return to the arms of the mother and her breast, to the uroboric slumber, in hopes of feeling full and finding safety, security, peace, and happiness—that which can only be truly found in a relationship with the Self.

How This Manifests in Adult Behaviors

Adult behaviors are the psyche's attempts at pointing to the hurts and unmet needs held captive in the Great Mother. They also point to the aspects of self that need rescuing, healing, and integration. All adults—even those who had a loving, nurturing, mothering experience—have some aspects of self left behind in the Great Mother stages. If someone feels "empty" and exhibits oral fixations, for example, we as therapists would look to the oral stage for clues as to what needs to be rescued. Because the primary experience in the oral stage is the mother, the breast, and the stomach, we self-soothe and avoid feelings of emptiness by putting something in the mouth.

In adults, this commonly shows up as smoking cigarettes, drinking alcohol, abusing drugs, or having an eating disorder. Eating disorders are both over eating in attempts to take in more of mother or starving oneself in attempts to avoid taking in what feels like a toxic, terrifying mother.

Most addictive behaviors are rooted in the oral stage and are in service of avoiding a sense of emptiness. These behaviors tend to trigger the early oral memories with the mothering one, her lack of attentiveness and loving presence, and the initial turning away from our true essence and magnificence of being. Materialism and the resultant shopping is another prime example of addictive behavior rooted in the oral stage; some "go shopping" in search of happiness and feeling "full-filled," which happens only momentarily with something new.

Displays of not feeling good enough or of not feeling valued or worthy can take many other forms as well. For example, there are those who think they always need to be more advanced developmentally than they are and cannot accept who or where they are currently. Other examples are those who criticize themselves and those who present themselves as being superior to others—each representing a side of feeling inferior and worthless or superior and inflated.

As stated previously, safety, trust, and security are at the foundation of our being during the oral stage. Those who experienced unsafe conditions or sensed it was unsafe to be oneself or vulnerable may hide who they are out of fear of humiliation. Or they may project living in and being allergic to an unsafe world, that which was introjected in relationship to narcissistic mothering. This shows up as environmental illnesses or sensitivities to environmental factors that cause sickness and the need to avoid being in the world. For those who endured traumatic and abusive early experiences, a "death field" is often created that arrests healthy growth and development and "kills off" opportunities to live in the fullness of life and our life's purpose. (Refer to the chapter on "Life and Death Fields.")

What needs to be rescued in the oral stage is our deep knowing of inner safety and security and our complete belief in our own value and worth as human beings. We need to feel that we can handle anything that comes in life. We need to know that value and worth are our birthright and that they have no basis on what we do or accomplish. Rather, our value and worth are at the core of who we are, our personal essence and presence of being. This knowing opens us to the Treasure of living from our true calling and purpose. It clears the veils to the preciousness of being human—and to seeing that this preciousness has always been present as the ground of all that is.

If there is pain associated with the initial mirroring from the mothering one and we turn away from our true nature as a knowing presence, we forget our true nature and our conditioning creates a seeming amnesic barrier to this reality. When we begin to clear the veils and realize our truth, we must face the emptiness and the spaciousness of our pure presence that is unconditioned awareness. We then see that what we have been covering with oral fixations and soothing with the mouth is the fear of being empty and "nothing."

In his book *The Origins of History and Consciousness,* Neumann notes that C.G. Jung also referred to this when he discussed the discovery of our "nothingness," which once again brings us back to the emptiness of the stomach and facing the Great Mother.[24] Jung is referring to the unconditioned essence of our true nature and the essence of all that is arising from this mystery, which is not a "thing." Rather, this awareness of our essence is experienced as "nothing" and as emptiness that, paradoxically, is filled with everything. We have experienced this emptiness many times. Consider when we don't know what to do and kill time by, for example, standing in front of an open refrigerator. In general, feelings arise of discomfort and self-soothing, and then oral fixations come to the forefront.

Through our life experiences, and in the rescuing process, Almaas says that we feel and realize we are empty and attempt to fill this feeling of emptiness with outer world manifestations such as a partner, sex, cigarettes, alcohol, drugs, God, what feels like our essence, and the absolute spiritual discovery. We begin to realize we are this emptiness, and we are trying to fill this with various outer world manifestations. But we never feel full.[25] He concludes: "The ultimate truth is that there is no breast."[26]

When we have rescued the aspects of self left in the oral period of the Great Mother and are living its integration, self-destructive behaviors are replaced with being a "good mother to ourselves." We provide good nourishment in all aspects of life: food, exercise, work, relationships, family, meditation, and daily mindfulness practice. From this integration, we begin to face the emptiness and embrace its beauty, silence, and stillness as the core of our essence and all experiencing.

Beneath the entire Rescuing the Captive stage of archetypal development is the oral stage and the introjected information and generational downloads that need clearing to move into Gaining the Treasure. What happens in the womb and this early stage of life forms the foundation on which all future stages are built. We can intervene at any future stage, but, ultimately, we will be guided to return to the initial conditions of our life.

Integration of the Oral Stage through Rescuing the Captive
When the rescue of the aspects from the Great Mother is integrating, clients begin to nourish and nurture themselves generally in all ways in life. The nongenerative alignment to the mother has been released, and the client has moved to a generative

alignment. Generally, this generative alignment shows up as clients being able to experience what is of value in their experience. They learn what will nourish and lead to growth for themselves and others. They also can see what needs to *not* be taken in and what is *not* good for them or others in any situation.

With this integration, the archetype of value shines fully. The alignments to valuing, not valuing, or undervaluing self have all been acknowledged or seen through and, therefore, brought into balance. The search for external appreciation and recognition ceases, and being itself becomes the self-existing value that contains the generative facets of value.

Through integration, clients also experience love archetypally, as a state of being. Love is no longer structured by the conditioning of the ego or by the persona attempting to find fulfillment through accomplishments and objects. Instead, they experience a freedom from the past. Love no longer needs to be directed to only one person or close ones but can be experienced toward anything or any being in any situation.

What Is Held Captive and Needs Rescuing in the Anal Stage

When our development is compromised during the oral stage, we enter the next stage, the anal stage, at a disadvantage. Defenses and fears built during the oral stage can handicap us as we move into "I am the body" as a focus.

	Attempt at Unity	**Fear**	**Adult Symptoms**	**Integration**
Great Mother Stage 2 **Anal**	Through mastery and possession of world autonomy and control	Fear of being controlled and dominated Possessions rule you	Controlling others Your needs come first For example: Hoarding Cutting Caretaking Lying & stealing	Being able to: Stand in your own authority and power in all actions Release control Embrace what is

Overview of What Is Held Captive and Needs Rescuing in the Anal Stage

What is held captive and needs rescuing in the anal stage falls into two categories: mastery and possession of the world; and autonomy, control, and empowerment.

Mastery and Possession of the World
During the anal stage, infants move from purely oral gratification and dependency on the mother to mastering skills. Walking, early language, eating on one's own, and potty training are a few examples of the skills learned at this time. To begin this differentiation from the mother, there may be some flexing of muscles and pushing away from her by saying, "No! I can do it myself." This comes as a defense to fears of being vulnerable to the archetypal Great Mother's domination, possession, and control. Also, if a mother cannot support and guide her child's growth and differentiation from her, the child's early skill building and mastery may he hindered; this leaves the psyche wanting to dominate and possess, or these needs remain split off and unconscious and must be rescued later in development.

Mastery over potty training and control of feces is an important step in the budding exercising of power and authority, particularly at the time the child is identifying as "I am the body." When we are shamed, undermined, or pushed by parents toward being potty trained prematurely, these feelings are introjected as our true identity and later become a subtle part of the structure of the superego. Also, a narcissistic wound of feeling deeply unseen can develop, as children feel the mother's needs are more important than their own needs and pace. With the pain of this wounding and rejection, aspects of self are split off and left behind in the Great Mother, undermining and compromising mastery and empowerment as we move forward in development. In short, we find that our need to be in charge and in possession of feces and potty training sets the stage for whether or not "possession" rules our life later on.

Control, Autonomy, and Empowerment
With generative, loving mothering, we begin to feel empowered rather than feeling the need to control or to fight being controlled, dominated, or manipulated. As adults who experienced generative mothering, we are able to stand in our own authority in our actions without needing to be in control. On the other hand, if the mother is unable to help the child navigate his or her new power successfully, the child tends to be

controlling and selfishly demanding. This behavior occurs in response to the mother's similar needs, with the child pushing back for authority. Alternatively, a child may begin hiding feelings and vulnerabilities because life feels unsafe.

With muscle maturation at this stage comes a new sense of growing autonomy and independence. Included in this autonomy are actions around holding on or letting go, retention and expulsion. When autonomy is hindered and not supported by the mothering one, shame and doubt are felt, because the child is still very sensitive to this new sense of autonomy and power. This shame and doubt lays the foundation for feeling exposed, vulnerable, and self-conscious.[27]

Whether the child feels safe and encouraged during the anal stage to have mastery and control—or not—is crucial to the foundation we form to adapt to the world. With mother's support for our power and control, we integrate a sense of our own authority and go into the next stages with more ease to express our power and our self. If our authority is unsupported and undermined, many other patterns form: We might, for example, force power over others, need to control, or feel compelled to take care of others. On the other hand, Erikson notes that, when parents allow autonomy during this time, children feel a sense of good will and confidence and will be less susceptible to shame and doubt later on and into adulthood.[28]

How This Manifests in Adult Behaviors

Much of how the anal stage and what needs to be rescued shows itself in adulthood involves how an adult deals with fears of being controlled and dominated. This is true particularly if the mother was devouring of the child's life, sense of own control, and autonomy. As mentioned over and over already, mothers like this are quite injured in their own needs! This prevents them from allowing, let alone encouraging, their child's behavior of testing his or her strength, control, and possessiveness.

Adults often compensate either by being very controlling or by giving up their control to others; they either flex their muscles to feel powerful or give up and go limp, as though impotent. Those being controlling of others and situations convince themselves, "If I don't do it, it won't be done right!" Those who "go limp" think, "It's too hard!" Both positions need to be abandoned. The pain and the hurt that underlie both positions must be faced in order to move into a true sense of being in our own power and authority.

Mothers with narcissistic injuries of their own pass the injuries on to their children, as their mothers did to them. When our mother's needs are more important than our own, we typically respond either by being narcissistic ourselves (our needs come first), or by hiding and expressing little or no needs. Often these polarities are both expressed, going back and forth depending upon life circumstances. For example, we might react to a mother's narcissistic wounding by feeling a need to take care of others, at our expense, thus building little to no identity or sense of importance beyond that of a caregiver. On the other hand, we might feel a need to be taken care of in a childlike manner, acting as though we are not capable of managing on our own. Beneath the narcissistic wounding is a rage related to turning away from our true essence and empowerment as well as a rage related to how much was lost and sacrificed. Inherent in the rescuing process is a shift from anger and hurt toward the outer devouring Mother to realizing that the devouring Mother is within us and needs attention and "decommissioning."

> **"Narcissistic injury or wounding"** also can occur when a mother believes her children exist only to fulfill her wishes or needs. She may be unable to view the world from the perspective of the baby or child who has unique needs.

Another area that needs rescuing from the anal stage relates to possession. When children feel dominated, manipulated, and controlled during the anal stage of development, they were not allowed to feel in control of themselves or their possessions. As a result, they find it challenging to be able to "hang on" or "let go" on their own. As adults, this wounding manifests as a need to possess, and that need shows up in various behaviors such as hoarding, lying and stealing, and materialism and the "power" shopping needed to buy the stuff. Obviously, these behaviors are reactions to taking back control and our own dominance, but doing so not in a truly empowered way.

When control is rescued from the Great Mother, we can embody our empowerment and let others in our life be in theirs in a loving manner. In addition, we do not need a sense of glory nor acknowledgement for accomplishments, but we feel the sense of inner joy that comes from our hard work. An integrated form of the anal stage is when we are able to embody a true sense of our inner authority and power in all actions such as by:

- Providing a nurturing life for ourselves in all areas
- Knowing we are safe in the world, that we can handle anything that happens in our life
- Refusing and standing in protection of any further abuse, disrespect, cruelty, or manipulation in our lives (from self or other)
- Releasing any need to control but also taking charge when necessary
- Embracing and accepting what is rather than dwelling on how we want things to be
- Inviting in all that is needed to be healed, released, and integrated in order to live from our essential nature

What Is Held Captive and Needs Rescuing in the Genital Stage

The genital stage is focused on attempting unity with the Self through arousal: genital satisfaction, impulses, and bodily union. Again, if major building blocks in development were compromised in the earlier stages of the Great Mother, we come to this stage already disadvantaged. Fears underlying this stage are that union with the archetypal forces of the Great Mother, through the mothering one, will lead to the ground being pulled out from under our budding zest for empowerment. We fear being crushed in our endeavors versus encouraged and supported. Quite literally, as Neumann states, we actually fear being castrated by her.

	Attempt at Unity	Fear	Adult Symptoms	Integration
Great Mother Stage 3 **Genital**	Through bodily union and genital satisfaction	Fear of castration Feel as though ground is pulled out from under you Feel crushed in all your endeavors	World seen as sexual arena For example: Pornography Promiscuity Sexual objectifying	Generative communion with self and others Free of addictive behaviors Integration through all three stages

Overview of What is Held Captive and Needs Rescuing in the Genital Stage

What is held captive and needs rescuing in the genital stage can be broken into three categories: 1) Healthy expression of sexual sensations, 2) Navigation of the Oedipal complex when the Father archetype is activated, and 3) Gaining initiative and increased autonomy.

1. Healthy Expression of Sexual Sensations

When children begin feeling their sexual self through the good feelings of touching their genitals, they often begin masturbating. This frequently frightens parents, who then attempt to stop the process. Children then introject shame and fear about sensations that feel good. They equate their "unacceptable" behavior with their essence not being acceptable. Consequently, they identify their sexual selves as disgusting. These feelings then are split off and become unconscious, shadow aspects of self that are later acted out or repressed. These thwarting actions of parents can literally crush the budding ego of a child, resulting in much of the creative life forces being withheld from consciousness. Children then actually feel shameful being themselves and expressing how they feel.

2. Navigation of the Oedipal Complex/Father Archetype Activated

The Oedipal complex is a myth of consciousness based on the story of Oedipus. (Recall the Oedipus myth explained in Chapter Seven.) The myth conveys our being torn between two worlds: that of the body-focused world of the Great Mother and that of the rising mental world of the Father archetype. When this bifurcation point occurs developmentally, children can move from a focus on the emotional-sexual inner world to unity with the mind and conceptual outer world.

Neumann identifies this stage as being when we leave behind the young childhood time of being held in the Great Mother, which is not an easy feat. Mother has been our inner world, our attachment, and our sense of self as a body identity while it is being formed and while the ego germ is being birthed. When a mother encourages her child's autonomy, the child can navigate leaving the Great Mother stage with more ease. But when a mother holds on with her grip of control, shame, or guilt, the child must undergo a dragon fight to break the bond and not be castrated or dissolve back into her influence. The father can be a great help in advocating for the child's autonomy and initiative. He also can encourage and support the mother to allow the child to further grow and develop beyond her influence and mentor the child in the outer world of skills and concepts. To develop in a generative manner, we must fight and defeat the Great Mother influence. By not being pulled back into the unconscious, we move into the higher realms of concepts and reasoning and into the outer world of the Father archetype.

If parents partner collaboratively and let go of any jealousy, they can provide together what their child needs to complete this stage successfully. When children can feel accepted by their parents for their young expression of sexual desires and needs—but not acted upon in any way—the children can move forward developmentally.

Successful navigation of this time occurs when the parents do not become triangulated with the child and they do not permit the child to be in the middle of their conflicts. This might happen when a child is aligned more with the same sex parent or with mothers who have a difficult time letting their child grow up, develop an ego, and differentiate from her. If parents triangulate with the child during the genital stage, the time is very confusing and individuation is obstructed; children then feel an alliance with one of the parents and a need to take care of him or her rather than focusing on their own growth and development. In fact, being left out of the parental union in a generative, loving way is paramount to successfully making the shift from the body and emotionally focused world to the conceptual outer world of the Father archetype. Children who are freed from the parental union naturally begin to construct a higher order of union, one that is not part of the body identity but a shift to developing the mind and mental realms.

3. Gaining Initiative and Increased Autonomy

This is a delicate time when children begin to take increasingly more initiative, exercise their independence, and seem to grow into their self as more than a body. They begin to undertake, plan, and carry out tasks on their own—but not from a place of willfulness or defiance. Their budding initiative at this stage establishes the foundation for the developing ego, empowering the child to learn and take action as he or she journeys into the outer world and into his or her unfolding future.

If children are not nurtured and encouraged at this stage, they may feel a sense of guilt when contemplating goals and when they initiate action. Also, when a child's expression of exuberance and enjoyment toward new locomotor and mental powers is discouraged by the parents, particularly the mothering one, the child's initiative may be halted.[29] In this case, parts of the natural expression of initiative may be left behind, replaced with feeling guilty and wrong for differentiating and for seeking greater autonomy from the mother's control and influence. Even generative mothers may be reluctant to encourage initiative, knowing this also means her child is gaining autonomy and their special, close, bonding years are passing.

When children's fantasies and attempts to exercise power are halted, parental interference of guilt can activate a castration complex in which children fear genital harm as well as fear and repress their own life force. Nongenerative parenting in this regard can set the stage for later repression of urges. If such occurs, an inner rage is split off;

some of the fondest hopes and wildest fantasies may be repressed and inhibited and then acted out in nongenerative form during childhood and adolescence as well as later in adulthood. In addition, with nongenerative parenting, the Oedipal stage and the coinciding initiative and increased autonomy can be hindered by an oppressed moral sense. This can restrict all that is possible—or it can set the direction toward that which is tangible and permit the dreams of early childhood to be attached to the goals of an active adult life.[30] That is, in later childhood or adulthood, individuals either own their power and authority and are very "potent and erect" in their lives, or they are "limp" and lack an inner sense of empowerment and willingness to conquer what feels difficult.

How This Manifests in Adult Behaviors
As stated earlier, adult behaviors are the psyche's attempt to point to the hurts and unmet needs in the Great Mother that need to be met by us as adults, to those aspects of self that need rescuing, healing, and integration. For example, children who were shamed or traumatized in relation to their sexuality, touching genitals, masturbating, or feeling crushed in their endeavors by the mother (or father who becomes more active at this time) tend to show these hurts and fears by acting out sexually. This stage can be further complicated if there has been sexual abuse. Any such traumatic experience can confuse and arrest healthy development going forward and can result in an array of adult behaviors— such as seeing the world as only a sexual arena and engaging in pornography viewing and masturbating (even at the expense of their relationships), promiscuity, prostitution, or child sexual abuse. The partners of adults hurt during the genital stage are often treated as sexual objects rather than treated with love. Much of what the psyche is attempting to express through the behavior is the deep grief that results from not feeling loved, important enough, or worthy to be protected and not used as an object for adult needs.

Adult behaviors and their extremes will directly relate to how many disruptions happened in each of the Great Mother stages and how severe these were to the individual. For example, abuse, neglect, and traumatic events early in a child's life cause significantly more disruption than in situations related to generative, loving mothers who, at times, were unavailable but whose intentions were sincere and caring. No matter the extent of the loss or pain, to rescue any and all aspects of self means grieving the losses and the lost time in our lives. We also must face these hurts and fears and be the generative mother to ourselves. Looking for the "rescue" in our relationships or in the outer world is a bottomless pit, impossible to ever fill. This realization is typically painful, but it is necessary in order to make room for true and deep healing to take place. All addictive and self-destructive behaviors need to be given up for love and deep respect for the Self, to discover our true nature.

What also gets integrated from the genital stage is how to love another human being deeply, including ourself—and how to meet another in a sexual union that is a pure expression of that love. Viewing pornography and masturbating is a solitary activity focused only on our own needs, much like the narcissistic mother. The union of making love is feeling fulfilled through giving to another whom we love deeply. Such generative behavior begins to dissolve the boundaries of self and other and empowers us to rest in the ultimate and absolute of pure unconditioned love.

Integration of the Genital Stage Through Rescuing the Captive

Until all major aspects of self are rescued, we tend to feel a sense of loss and sadness that the mother did not recognize our true essence. Rescuing the Captive from the Great Mother is integrating when we see our value and worth as our birthright, when we see that all humans have the same amount of value and worth underlying their conditioned selves with no relevance to what we do in the world and when we know to the core of our being that our sheer essence gives us value and worth. We then can integrate our full authority and feel empowered to bring our gifts into the world. From this vantage point, we shift toward feeling love for our partners rather than using them for sexual self-gratification. And we hold our sexual energy and impulses and express these as a sacred union with the one we love.

Acting from the center of our being strengthens our inner world. This process thins the veils seeming to separate us from the Self and the boundaries of "inside me" and the outside world. We align more and more with our essence and the interconnectedness of all life. We feel love in our hearts, and exquisite beauty is mirrored in what we see and perceive in our lives. We align with our deep knowing of awareness as the eternal "I"—our experience of the presence of our true nature. And we shift from finding meaning in life from what we are "doing" to finding purpose in "being." Ultimately, the natural unfolding of the expression of this shift is through service in the world. We are then actualizing our essential being and divine nature. From this stance, we enter the stage of Gaining the Treasure.

	Attempt at Unity	Fear	Adult Symptoms	Integration
Great Mother Stage 1 Oral	Through the mouth Incorporating into one's self what is given	Fear of being devoured, swallowed, eaten	Destructive inner critic For example: Eating disorder Smoking Alcohol abuse Drug use	Taking in generative nourishment Being a "good mother" to yourself Stopping destructive behavior
Great Mother Stage 2 Anal	Through mastery and possession of world autonomy and control	Fear of being controlled and dominated Possessions rule you	Controlling others Your needs come first For example: Hoarding Cutting Caretaking Lying & stealing	Being able to: Stand in your own authority and power in all actions Release control Embrace what is
Great Mother Stage 3 Genital	Through bodily union and genital satisfaction	Fear of castration Feel as though ground is pulled out from under you Feel crushed in all your endeavors	World seen as sexual arena For example: Pornography Promiscuity Sexual objectifying	Generative communion with self and others Free of addictive behaviors Integration through all three stages

Application of Rescuing the Captive in the Separation of the World Parents Stage

Eight major activities of the psyche occur during the Separation of the World Parents stage:

1. Completing the introjection of the parents' whole psyches from patterned experiences occurring from conception through the Great Mother stages
2. Pushing our felt sense of unity to the background of our awareness, while also beginning to create the ego
3. Leaving behind our felt unity with the body of feelings, instincts, and emotions for a mental world of symbols and concepts by creating a psychic barrier to our own true nature
4. Unconsciously pouring the undivided world of feelings and instincts into a projected ego ideal that contains the seeds of heroic action in later life
5. Aligning with a gender and beginning to develop a persona
6. Coalescing of the personal superego as an introjected auditory conceptual set of impressions, suggestions, commands, injunctions, and prohibitions absorbed from all early patterned experiences

> Recall that **"introjection"** refers to taking in or swallowing something whole without chewing, leaving it undigested in the psyche. As adults, we often experience these introjections as "shoulds" or "ought tos." Introjections stay with us as unexamined material and form our internal guiding structure. Some are generative, whereas others are nongenerative. "Don't cross the street without looking" is a generative introject, whereas "You will fail" is a nongenerative introject.

7. Creating the shadow for disowned aspects that do not fit the ego ideal and persona, often including the opposite gender that was not aligned with
8. Coalescing of the cultural superego as an introjected cultural authority that leads as our "collective conscience," guiding our development while working with the persona and the shadow necessary for the continuation of culture

These eight activities are placed here in a linear structure in order to be able to recognize and work with them, but many of them occur concurrently and/or simultaneously. With so much developmental work to do, children have many potential reasons to be unable to navigate this passage well. Conversely, having so much developmental work to do also can offer children many opportunities to navigate this passage too well, meaning that these activities can become so solidified in the psyche that they can become thick, unyielding, and often leave us as adults stranded from our true nature. In any case, there is a need to "rescue the captive" in this stage.

Let's examine what needs to be rescued during the Separation of the World Parents from the perspective of the stage's eight major activities.

Activity #1: Completing the introjection of the parents' psyches. This includes introjecting, or taking in whole, without digesting, both positive and negative aspects of the parents' psyches, including their unconscious, along with their unlived lives and potential. It also involves the introjection of the parents' relationship with each other as well as the introjection of their relationship with the child. In introjecting our parents' psyches, we carry them within us and, therefore, no longer need their physical nearness, which enables us to begin to develop the internal structures that will eventually enable us to turn to the outer world and meet the Father archetype.

This introjection of the parents' psyches has been going on through resonance with:

- Experiences in the womb, the birthing process, and early birthing experiences
- The symbiotic merging in the first (oral) stage of the Great Mother
- The experience of potty training and gaining an attitude toward what is inside us
- The patterning experiences of gaining physical separation and some independence and authority in the second (anal) stage of the Great Mother
- The body identification in the third (genital) stage of the Great Mother

The Rescue: The captive created in the introjection of our parents is undigested material encapsulated in our psyche. In general, this material provides a felt experience of our value and worth, guiding how we will be in relation to ourself and others, what we can expect from the world, and how we expect to be treated. To gain our Treasure, we need to bring conscious awareness to this undigested material, own what is ours, and discard what is not.

Another way to look at this concept is to note that, when we feel we are bad or deficient, what we might really be experiencing are the negative aspects of our parents that we took in as children. Once we recognize the source of our negative feelings, we then have a platform from which to examine other internalized views of self that were developed with our young, immature mind.

So, how do we get to that undigested material in order to rescue it? Remember that the introjections of our early relationships and parental experiences are held in our implicit memory and inner dialogue. Because they are not available to the conscious mind, as such, in order to access our early introjections, we need to explore where we have challenges manifesting what we want and dream of being, or where and when nongenerative patterns keep playing out in our adult life. Perhaps our mother was overwhelmed with child rearing during our infancy and often acted toward us as though we were a burden. This might show up as our unconsciously acting as if we are a burden in our relationships; or we might perceive that our partner sees us as a burden and constantly feel on "pins and needles," wondering if we are disappointing our partner or if we need to do something to make up for our inadequacies, no matter what kind of reassurance our partner gives us.

Another manifestation of this introjection might be finding ourself always in a power struggle with our partner. This can originate because our parents' relationship with one another is internalized and acts as an archetypal model of what to expect in romantic relationships. Another tragic example is introjecting the sense that what is inside of us is bad and makes people unhappy, disappointed, and not want to be with us. For instance, this might cause us to feel we have to be very careful about the way we smell; we might feel we always have to wear deodorant and often catch a scent of ourself that makes us feel bad and shameful. This can come from early introjections of the reactions of our caregivers to changing our diapers or cleaning up our spit. Another example is feeling like a failure and that we will never be able to succeed at our attempts. This can come from our father's unconscious feeling of being unable to care for his family in the way he wanted. We may introject this and begin to help him carry forward this sense of a negative destiny. Yet another example is the unhappy college student who feels compelled to study something in which he or she is not really interested. The crux of the student's problem is an old parental introjection that is not in alignment with the student's own entelechy (destiny), true nature, or purpose. That introjection could be an old dream of the student's parent—that he or she would have chosen that career if his or her life situation had been different. That introjection also might be a secret parental fear that people are only safe pursuing that specific career.

In general, when we feel we must do or feel what other people tell us to do or feel in order to be loved, we will need to rescue what was left behind of ourselves when we introjected this parental material. Without examining and digesting our early introjections, we cannot proceed to remembering our true unity and end up being glued to the Birth of the Hero and the Slaying of the Parents stages. The human process of maturing involves examining the attitudes, ways of thinking, and standards to which we hold ourselves; determining which are truly ours and fit our entelechy (destiny);

and then what is needed in "rescuing the captive" in order to gain the Treasure.

It is also important to note that, the more introjections that have taken root and the more traumatic they are, the less room there is for true discovery of the Self. For instance, the devouring or crushing parents can be so toxic for some that we create splits in the psyche to contain the material, making a place for a "good me" and "bad me." Also, introjections that stay in the unconscious implicit memory, holding us back, often manifest as physical aliments or dis-ease. To rescue the captive from these dilemmas, we need to learn and be mentored in what is actually healthy, what kind of healthy boundaries to have with others, and what our true worth and value really is.

Introjecting is actually a confusion of making ourself responsible for what is actually part of the environment. This process happens developmentally, when we are so young, that we experience our self as the environment. Introjecting moves the boundary between our self and the rest of the world far inside our self. Think about the example of an introjection of the father's sense of failure: When we are babies, that sense of doom and failure is part of our environment, so we experience it as part of ourself, even though it actually is our father's internal dilemma. Or we experience the identity of being a burden, when actually it is our mother who is experiencing being burdened. She, however, directed that sense toward us, and we took it in as if it were us.

Activity #2: Pushing our felt sense of unity into the background of awareness during the beginning stages of ego development and through superego injunctions about what is needed to please those around us.

The Rescue: This is the first self-imposed experience of loss in our life, and our psyche reacts to this choice of sending unity to the background of consciousness with a sense of betrayal (as psychic wholeness is lost). Myths abound that express this loss of unity and the feeling of betrayal. In the Garden of Eden myth, for example, Adam and Eve are accused by God (who feels betrayed) of eating the forbidden apple (of doing something wrong), and they feel shame. Like a Kafka story, the accused feel as though they have done something wrong and agree they are guilty, but they do not really know what the charges are. Only the loss remains. Many images in dreams also manifest working through this "fall from the garden/betrayal" activity of Separation of the World Parents. The dream images show up as a two-headed person or animal, a twin existing somewhere else, or even a younger sister, brother, or child under the age of six representing a second you.

In general, people working to rescue the captive from this activity of the Separation of the World Parents stage often experience a deep sense of having done something wrong or shameful, or that there is something missing in them. The key to the rescue is to articulate the loss as one that every human has, that it was a choice to join the outer world and have a place there. Also, once the impasse is named, a mourning and forgiveness process needs to occur intrapsychically in order to make a bridge back to the natural self, the one still in unity. This often needs facilitation.

Activity #3: Leaving behind our felt unity with the body of feelings, instincts, and emotions for a mental world of symbols and concepts. This triggers the separation of consciousness into two entities: 1) the ego, the conscious mind; and 2) the unconditioned self, which is no longer available to consciousness. A psychic barrier is internally created which seems to keep these separate.

The Rescue: As our brain develops and our verbal mind begins to function, we can become cut off from access to our feelings and instincts, which contain the guiding knowledge of wholeness. On the contrary, if we refuse to shift from feelings to concepts, we may stay connected to our feelings and instincts but be unable to clarify our thinking or use our mind well. This "disconnect" acts as an opaque membrane between the conscious mind and our true nature of unity.

The work here is in resuming brain integration between the conscious and unconscious, recreating felt connections between the mind and body, the heart and spirit. It is major healing we all must face to gain the Treasure! In fact, without this specific rescue of the captive, the mind reigns supreme and the higher stages of development are not as available.

Activity #4: Unconsciously pouring the world of feelings and instincts into a projected ego ideal that contains transpersonal mastery of both the inner and outer worlds.

The Rescue: The ego ideal is internally experienced as an idealized image of our self, a powerful figure that can gain mastery of both what's inside as well as outside. Examples of this powerful figure in the media are comic book and superhero characters such as Superman, Wonder Woman, Buzz Lightyear, Batman, and Spiderman. The unconscious archetypal alignment with a particular figure creates an idealized image of us, and our personality develops as we try to live according to this unconscious ideal. That is, our ego ideal impacts the thoughts we have, the actions we take, the kind of people with whom we associate, and the life we live.

Not surprisingly, the ego ideal has a lot to do with what our parents idealized. Therefore, that voice that directs us, the superego, both personal and cultural, is aligned with the ego ideal. Depending on how much we have to disown our own feelings, there would be a lesser or greater projection on the ideal, the alignment would be stronger or weaker, the personality would be more or less influenced, and the superego would contain a stronger or weaker need to dominate our personality.

Nonetheless, the ego ideal is a mental construct that the psyche chooses. To complete the rescue of the captive or gain the Treasure, we must see that we have developed *an idea* of our self, rather than developing our "being." Looking at the underlying transpersonal entity of the ego ideal, therefore, would be helpful and bring consciousness to an out-of-awareness process.

To do this, most therapies try to make the ego ideal more realistic. Our approach differs. We ask our clients to release having only the positive alignment to the ego ideal and to see it as the *idea* it is. We then encourage them to collapse the polarity of ideal and deficit, leaving them neither ideal nor deficient, but resting in their humanness. In other words, to rescue what is held captive in this activity of the Separation of the World Parents, we must let go of our idealized image as the truth of our being and relegate the mind to taking a subservient position to the Self. This will result in reuniting the mind with the heart, and the body with instincts. Consider, for instance, that Superman has a weakness that takes away his idealized power: He becomes a regular human again when near Kryptonite and must learn how to live with his humanness. That is, Kryptonite, his weakness, is the homeopathic remedy for his healing!

Looking at this idealized character will reveal what the psyche is trying to compensate for and forms the basis for our heroic quests in adult life. For instance, those who find James Bond, 007, a hero will see that he is able to win over "all the women," but he doesn't seem to have an ongoing intimate relationship with any of his romantic partners. The only long-term relationship he has is with his older woman boss.

Activity #5: Choosing a gender and beginning to develop a persona based on that choice. Up until this stage, we rest in a state in which both genders are available simultaneously. The alignment to a gender is based on several things:

- Parents' conscious and unconscious desires that have been introjected
- Actual genital configuration and the conditioning it brings
- Idealized transpersonal figure with which the psyche chooses to identify
- Contemporary cultural status of the genders the child has taken in from family roles, television, media, toys, and so on
- Entelechy existing in the psyche of the young person
- The deep need to be accepted and belong in our family and tribe (i.e., "I want to be what will be accepted." "I want to please my parents and family.")

The Rescue: The gender is aligned with by the developing ego. Once a gender choice is made, the young one begins to develop a persona, that which faces the world. This budding persona is very tenderhearted and afraid of humiliation. This fear recedes when met with loving support. When loving support is unavailable, a layered false persona develops.

In the case of gender choice, if there is support in the family, we will choose the gender with which we most identify. If there is not support, we might build an identity around a false gender to please our parents and/or the culture. Consider someone saying: "I was supposed to be a boy; that's what my parents wanted. So I will build my outer identity around being a boy, but my natural self is feminine." Or, we hear someone stating: "My family already had three girls, so I became the boy my father always wanted by being a tomboy and being interested in all the things my father liked." We also see many contemporary cases of different gender choices, with transgender, transsexual, and bisexual identities emerging in later life.

Rescuing the captive in the different gender choice has, up until this time in history, meant confronting the culture, the family system, and the sexual identity of the person. When we see a lot of shame related to identity and particularly to gender identity, we can often assume that the persona was attacked in this stage and that there is work needed to rescue the captive.

Activity #6: The coalescing of the personal superego. This is a mental internalization of the parents and creates an archetypal alignment with the kind of relationship possible with our own self and also what will be possible with personal relationships in the world. The personal superego is not fundamentally negative, but it is often in an ongoing struggle against our true nature.

The Rescue: The disruption or annihilation of our autonomous rhythms by the authority of the personal or cultural superego violates us, causing a loss of safety and an injury to ego development. The Self, which normally bestows security, is replaced by a superego that creates uncertainty and guilt, because we cannot live up to the superego's demands of perfection.

At this stage, the superego is in the unconscious as a structure that views the world with its own set of rules and ways of relating as well as its own biases and prejudices; in fact, the superego often is an actual internal voice. Rescuing the captive, at this level, is to help the conscious mind see the structure, content, and voice of the superego. Once the superego is recognized as the structure, content, and voice that it is, we can help our clients to find their own natural rules that stem from their own being rather than from an idealized self. We also can help our clients to see any mistranslations their superego has (from being developed so young, with only one perspective), and to transcend its unconscious operation as the voice that suppresses any natural functions and demands a particular face be shown to the world. When we see deep humiliation arise relating to what seems to be antiquated and narrow perspectives cast as strange rules from the superego, we know we are touching into a captive (in the beginning of the persona) who is asking to be rescued.

Activity #7: Creating the shadow. This is the repository for whatever natural aspects we must override and hide in order to be accepted as a part of our family and the culture. The shadow, therefore, often contains the "gold" of the natural self, along with the rejected aspects. It also often contains the opposite gender.

The Rescue: As young children, we take on the role of the parents toward our self by retroflecting, or turning back on our self, those concepts and affects not permissible to the parents or culture at large. We begin to control our self with these same parental and cultural attitudes. This is experienced as our "inner critic" constantly reminding us, "I'm not okay if I am this" or "I can't belong here if I am this."

Everything about our being that does not fit those internalized rules must go somewhere. This is the beginning of the shadow, the entity of our psyche holding aspects of us that we think others won't accept and that we don't want. These aspects might be a feeling that is not allowed in the family, like anger, or a sexual preference that is abhorred, or a talent that is not appreciated or respected. Once our shadow holds our disowned aspects, tendencies, and feelings, then we can't or don't want to see those parts either. They do not fit our idealized image of our self.

To successfully rescue what is held captive in the shadow, having a stable experience of our own essence as well as a stable witness is paramount. It takes much releasing of our set picture of our self to allow our persona to reintegrate aspects disallowed at an early age. Depending on the severity of the superego and parental acceptance of our natural state of being, reintegrating the shadow can be the work of a lifetime and involves not only the initial conditions of a person's conception, birth, and early development, but also the family history. This early conditioning and our integration of these early impressions provides the veiling of our essential nature. As aspects of our self are rescued and integrated, this veiling begins to dissolve and the Self becomes revealed and liberated.

Consider, for instance, "Aunt Hilda," who went crazy and was banished from the family, never to be mentioned again. This old, unconscious family shadow might show up as something to clear and integrate just when we are about to gain the Treasure. Time and space do not exist in the same way in the psyche. Events that predate our birth or early injunctions that did not involve us can still be part of what we have to rescue.

Activity #8: The coalescing of the cultural superego occurs once we are more involved in the outer world through school and cultural activities. This is a part of the superego introjected from what the culture portrays as "the right way to be." It leads in the collectively guided development of the individual to the formation of the persona and the shadow, which are necessary to the continuation of culture.

The Rescue: Because the authority of the superego is transpersonal, both the personal superego and the cultural superego act in the mind as the superior voice of "what is good" and as a "prosecuting attorney" that conducts the internal struggle of good against evil. When that voice is extremely rigid, the developing ego in the child can become crippled with a fear of being infected by evil and of being unable to eliminate the evil in its own nature. In reaction to that fear, the developing ego cuts itself off from the Self and acts as a regulator and rejecter of the lower aspects of the body and certain needs, talents, and desires. Infection, sickness, devil, and death are the images that arise from this impasse in the psyche. This impasse also can cause obsessive rituals such as a constant cleansing of the hands or cleaning of the house, lining up material possessions in highly structured ways, or rituals of always putting on certain clothes in a specific, magical order.

When the developing ego of the child no longer recognizes its own wholeness, our psychic wholeness is replaced by the dualistic principle of opposites, which then governs. Polarization into two psychic systems results in an insulation of the inner world and the building up of command by the ego, rather than the Self. Inner knowing must, in large part, be given up or hidden from the conscious mind. Any felt unity in this condition is only the relative unity of the conscious mind and not that of the whole being. This means moving from being centered in our wholeness to being centered in our ego that is in alignment with both the personal and cultural superegos, rather than with the Self.

The opposition between the Self and the superego is the compelling dynamic in this developmental stage. In our psychotherapy practice, we might hear a plea, "I'm doing everything I *ought* to do, and I don't feel satisfied." This is a clear indication that the superego has caught a person in its grip and that the individual needs to be able to overthrow old messages. Sometimes the trauma of our ancestors holds an unconscious rope around our legs, keeping us stuck and unable to progress toward becoming a hero.

When adults experience events that contain the early demands and injunctions that caused their early ego to cut itself off from its vital center and true nature, despair usually sets in. This triggers them to feel as though they are evil, and a voice of doom can grow from this despair. This voice can begin harping at them, until they feel they must end their life as the only solution to the despair. Our work involves helping such clients revisit this early despair and trace the connections from everyday contemporary events to their early experiences to recover their original feelings and alignment to the Self before the ego developed. In other words, the rescue includes tracing our fears to the early introjected injunctions from the personal or cultural superegos, becoming conscious of them and what we want to keep, and ultimately relieving the anxiety that accompanies our fears.

Naming the ego-Self impasse also gives us a new place to stand in order to look at other introjects. For example, when adults who seek our help feel as though they have no access to their creativity and clearly have lost touch with the knowing of the natural self, we work to restore a connection between the conscious mind and the rejected aspects of the self. This is like curing an autoimmune disease. Wholeness has been exchanged for a workable and successful personality based on a fictional character, and that needs to change. Unity and a relationship with the Self needs to be regained.

By the time we move to the Gaining the Treasure stage, we are actively involved in releasing all of our early conditioning. These first rescues allow us to find our fullness and engage in the necessary dragon fights to clear the old messages that keep us from our purpose of bringing the new way into the world.

13

Application of Rescuing the Captive in Neumann's Hero Myths

"The hero has to . . . awaken the sleeping images of the future which can and must come forth from the night, in order to give the world a new and better face. This necessarily makes him a breaker of the old law."[31]

- Erich Neumann -

Application of Rescuing the Captive Through Dragon Fights During the Hero Myths

What are the dragons? What are the fights? Three main dragon fights need to occur during the stages of the Hero Myths in order for us to progress to the stages of the Transformation Myths and gain the Treasure of our being:

Dragon Fight #1: Beginning of Hero Myth Stage
   Dragon = The uroborus and Great Mother attempting to reabsorb our instincts, body, and emotional realm back into her domain.
   Fight = To leave the pull of the uroborus and Great Mother's domain behind and move into a life in the outer world in order to mature and fully develop as a human.

Dragon Fight #2: Middle of Hero Myth Stage
   Dragon = The internalized devouring or crushing aspects of the personal parents, who, once internalized, become archetypal in nature.
   Fight = To clear the personal superego of internalized messages of constriction, failure, impotence, and repression. This battle is really to strengthen and clear the heroic ego, to enable it to take on its final task of gaining the Treasure.

Dragon Fight #3: End of Hero Myth Stage
Dragon = The old ways of the last generation (the conditioning from family, church, school, and culture).
Fight = To free the cultural superego of internalized messages that constrict and castrate through alignments with cultural convention, taboos, rules, laws, and sterile traditions. The hero's fight is to bring in the new energy of the hero's entelechy (destiny). As Erich Neumann says: "For the hero who represents the new consciousness, the hostile dragon is the old order, the obsolete psychic stage, which threatens to swallow him up again."[32]

Rescuing the captive during any dragon fight usually means winning or at least resuming a particular dragon fight. Because the fights have to do with our early conditioning and the defense mechanisms laid down in our early years when we only had a child's perspective, much of the rescuing has to do with creating an adult witnessing platform. In other words, we need to be able to look back on our early conditioning through adult eyes, with an adult perspective. When we do this, we can see that our original young perspective was just trying to stay safe. Once that reality is acknowledged, named, and honored for its years of duty, a reunion with current-day consciousness can occur.

Dragon Fight with the Great Mother
Neumann emphasizes that the first major dragon fight is a fight against the pull of the unconscious back into an inner life with the mother. It is often dramatized as being absorbed by something larger or of having to fight a way out of something (which is symbolic of the lure of the uroborus, the promise of some kind of merging with the Great Mother).

This first dragon fight manifests in adults as not being able to create a generative life in the outer world. This shows up as people playing video games all day and living in their parents' basements. Others struggling in this dragon fight spend their time getting stoned and partying, or worse, doing drugs that create a stupor. Perhaps they are caught in a crazy love affair that leaves them feeling vacant and unable to function. This dragon fight also can manifest as someone who just cannot figure out what the next step is, what to do to create the life he or she really wants. Being stuck, these individuals may say: "I want most in the world to write my stories (or do my art or . . .), but I just can't seem to do it. I end up playing Solitaire on the computer (or _____) instead!"

Like the whale in the Biblical story of Jonah and the Whale, the above situations are states that absorb the ego but do not nourish it. They are ultimately nongenerative alignments to the Great Mother. Rescuing the captive in these situations takes bringing awareness to the pattern of either wishing to regress or actually regressing back to the comforts and arms of the Great Mother (uroborus) in the face of either not knowing what the next step is or not understanding our own reluctance to fight or find a way out of our current situation. It takes mentoring to create a new alignment to a generative life in the outer world.

Dragon Fight with the Personal Superego
The second major dragon fight focuses on slaying the negative aspects of the personal parents, their unlived lives, and the misalignments to the hero's entelechy (destiny). Through examination and being proactive, this fight involves chewing and digesting all that has been, until now, out of awareness and held in the personal superego.

Although they are unique in certain ways, the first and second dragon fights often overlap, as the superego is commonly part of holding a person in the sluggish, inertia-like states described as exemplary of the first dragon fight. (Recall that the superego is a structure that includes and enforces the heroic ego ideal; the prohibitions, rules, values, and preferences of the parents; and our version of what our parents thought of us.) Through the introjection of the above, we learn—out of fear of disapproval, rejection, or punishment (and also out of love for our parents)—to push down a particular action or feeling. Over time, this negation becomes internalized within our own personal superego. Eventually, whenever a situation elicits the particular action or emotional state, there is a disapproval that punishes us with guilt, shame, and other painful affects. Our fear then becomes a fear of our own punishing, accusing archetypal voice. We learn to defend our self from the internal voice the same way we defended our self against our parents: by pushing down the particular action or feeling and by cutting off our awareness from our own impulses, feelings, and actions.

This whole process is unconscious and happens automatically, with the superego thought structures and values becoming the "enforcing agent." For example, depending upon our introjections, we might inhibit the expansion of our awareness and our inner development. Further, a superego that is structured as a system to keep us "good," approved of, and protected from outer judgment or punishment usually does not lead us to becoming our own unique person, let alone to gaining our Treasure. For we must go into the taboo areas we are guarding to find the Treasure!

To rescue this part of the captive requires looking at the superego with a developing awareness of how different behavioral patterns and beliefs are ruling our current life. We also must risk going beyond what is good and pleasing to others in order to decrease its power and influence. Our goal is to find effective ways to defend against the superego's criticisms and attacks without having to use repression and the other unconscious defensive strategies of the ego.

This archetypal approach helps our clients learn to be aware of their "inner voice" attacks, the content and the judgment. Then we assist our clients in identifying the origins of those destructive thoughts and feelings. For example, let's take the case of a young man who becomes ashamed any time he feels tenderly toward someone. His superego attacks him with shame and belittling, with the judgment that "You are weak and 'girlie' if you feel tender." When he remembers his father's attitude toward weakness and recognizes his father's words in this attack, he can understand where his own punishing voice came from; he introjected his father's attitude at a very young age. Once he recognizes, names, and honors this reality, he can mindfully refuse the voice, tell it to stop, and embody the very natural feeling of tenderness.

When we learn to defend against our superego, we will gradually expose its structure. Remember, the very young superego was merely trying to belong and to protect its innocence from an outer attack. Once we establish a strong "witness," our emerging hero can begin dismantling our punitive aspects. As therapists, we can support our clients by encouraging this dragon fight. Our ultimate goal is to help them develop their own generative inner system they can rely on for innate wisdom, a system that will give them a true sense of their identity and strength.

In the later stages of Rescuing the Captive, we have developed enough awareness and a strong enough witnessing capacity to risk remembering very early assumptions introjected in the oral stages of the Great Mother that were taken in and believed as fact about our identity. These were actually downloads of the mother's feelings of her own life as well as her fears and concerns about the baby that the baby took in as though they were the baby's own. "I am sadness itself," "I'm a bother," "I'm not good enough," and "I'll never get the love I want" are some of the deepest-held knowings that are strong strands woven into the superego. Knowings such as these take the bravest hero to rescue, because they are so strongly linked to survival and the merging with the mother. In such delicate cases, our job is to point to the true nature of our clients as a guide to who they really are. Looking at babies, you can easily see that their true nature is one of love, joy, sensitivity, innocence, and spontaneity. When anchored in the reality of their own spaciousness, our clients can release and unweave old, constricting messages from their inner life. They then can begin to see their truth as being love—the same as when they were babies and have been all along.

Dragon Fight with the Cultural Superego

The third main dragon fight in the Hero Myths stage is against the cultural superego and the old ways held by the parents and the culture. Because this dragon fight can only strongly manifest once the Birth of the Hero stage is achieved and because the content of this third dragon fight makes up the Slaying of the Parents stage, we will look at it more closely in the next section that focuses on those stages.

Major Dragon Fights

Great Mother Stage
* Fighting the Oedipal fight

Separation of World Parents Stage
* Shifting alliance from the Great Mother archetype to the Father archetype by creating a psychic structure that seemingly veils the true nature of the Self, relegating it to the background, while the ego takes precedence in the foreground

Separation of World Parents and Birth of the Hero Stages
* Fighting with the feelings, urges, emotions, and forces that want to pull us back into the unconscious forces of the uroborus and the Great Mother

Birth of the Hero Stage
* Slaying the personal superego, the negative aspects of the internalized parental introjections, by replacing them with our own values, ethics, opinions, and ideas

Slaying of the Parents Stage
* Clearing the cultural superego—the conditioning of family, institutions, and culture—and leaving behind the tribe of our peer group and culture

Rescuing the Captive Stage
* Rescuing any aspects we left in the uroborus and Great Mother stages
* Becoming a true hero within by rescuing our value and worth and finding our true sense of power and inner authority

Rescuing the Captive and Gaining the Treasure Stages
* Beginning to clear the shadow and release identification with our persona
* Ending heroic quests in service of the ego
* Bringing in projections of anima/animus and working these internally

Gaining the Treasure Stage
* Changing the psychic structure made in Separation of the World Parents that separates us into conscious and unconscious, from natural unity with the Self into the ego and the outer world
* Bringing in all projections and seeing them as an outer reflection of our inner processes
* Shifting and changing the egoic patterns revealing the Self
* Living in service of the Self as our true nature

Unification of Opposites
* Dissolving the separation between ego and the Self
* Accepting and loving our humanness and human condition

Note: These fights are not linear. Each usually takes many dragon fights within each stage to complete.

Application of Rescuing the Captive in the Birth of the Hero Stage

As noted in the last section, our first dragon fight involves the fight to leave the Great Mother's domain. This effort takes the birthing of our hero. If our inner hero is not strong enough and we stay in the old domain, we either continue to "inhabit the womb" by living in a sheltered environment provided by the parents or another caregiver, or by becoming a servant to the Great Mother archetype. In the myths, this is portrayed as the Son Lover, who actually has his power castrated and lives in service to the Great Mother's wishes. Some examples of how this shows up in adult form follow:

- The backup singer who really longs to be the solo act
- The young lover living in the shadow of the older woman
- Those people born into wealth who never apply themselves to a quest but merely dabble in possibilities and in pleasure
- The addict who spends his or her time trying to find the money for the next trip into the oblivion of the Great Mother

What Is Rescued in the First Dragon Fight?
What does it take to ensure a person is able to birth his or her inner hero and win the first dragon fight? In short, the heroic energy of our ego needs to be cathected (invested with emotion and feeling) and supported so that positive energy can be applied toward the heroic quests. Often that support and energizing comes through a peer group of respected others who themselves are pursuing what they really want and who are making the necessary sacrifices to accomplish their goals. Examples include the student working night and day to go to medical school, the musician taking small gigs to be able to continue playing his beloved instrument, and the dancer turning down an academic scholarship to dance with an up-and-coming dance company in a junior role. Good role models matter! They show that, to make a dream reality and create a life of one's own, one must put concerted effort into real world tasks.

Through all the dragon fights, the hero in us always has the anima/animus projections to rescue. In the movies, the anima figure (often a damsel in distress) is always standing by, hoping the hero will fight and rescue her from the beasts. In real life, these projections are on those we are attracted to, care about, hate, and compete with. How we relate to them holds the secret as to how we treat our deep inner self and how much there is to rescue through the dragon fights.

What Is Rescued in the Second Dragon Fight?

All heroic quests involve mastering inner criticism and becoming internally congruent with the psychological tasks inherent in whatever the heroic quest contains. The work of the second dragon fight, however, also involves seeing that the inner work can ultimately impact outer world problems. For instance, to be an actor and sell yourself at audition after audition (outer dilemma), you must get good at tolerating rejection (inner work). In other words, to clear the negative aspects of the introjected parents, one must fight on inner as well as outer ground. The particular work that will need to be done to pursue the mandate of a particular heroic quest, what will need to be rescued, will be dependent upon what one brings from the early stages of the Great Mother. Let's return to actors for example: If they want to succeed, they have to do the outer work of going to auditions as well as do the inner work of tolerating rejection. One actor's specific inner work with rejection might be crushing early introjects of "I am not of value" and "I don't really deserve what I want." Another's actor inner work with rejection might include dealing with the discovery that acting was the dream of a parent and not really what he or she wants to do after all. In essence, the second dragon fight is a time of experimenting and finding one's true heroic quest.

Inevitably, during this stage of development, there is always a dragon fight with the void; you must be able to tolerate periods of not really knowing who you are or what is next or where you are really going. This takes being able to sit with what seems like emptiness until the next step appears, or until you once again can see what action to take. Many shy away from this part of a dragon fight. It is a hard task for a solidifying ego! Our young people need to be schooled in mindfulness practices so they have a place and time to rest, rejuvenate, and witness thoughts rather than believe them. This fortifies them to be able to tolerate the storms of rejection and chaos they will undoubtedly encounter on their journey.

Heroic quests also require aspects of personality that have been relegated to the shadow and do not have a place in the persona. Like the young man who could not feel weak without accusing himself of being "girlie," his persona must expand to accommodate what has been hidden in the shadow (both good and bad), and his shadow must open in such a way as to allow an examination of what has been put out of awareness and kept in place by his superego. Recall that the shadow contains what did not fit with the heroic image, with our heroic quests in the world, or with what Mommy or Daddy expected us to be. In the movies, this examination of the shadow is expressed by the hero going into the underground cave to fight the monsters guarding the treasure.

In order to tolerate this opening of the shadow—which feels like something other than us, something alien, something monstrous—we must be strong enough to be able to expand our sense of who we are. This is represented in movies as tolerating spiders crawling all over us or as making our way through snake pits, swamps, or other onerous-feeling spaces. Once we expand our sense of self, then we are able to broaden our perspective of our earlier experiences—to establish the invaluable mature witnessing platform discussed earlier. From this new viewpoint, we will see ourselves for what we are and be able to withdraw blame on the world or our parents for our conditions or feelings. Once we can reveal and examine our defenses, we will then be able to put our denial to death.

This work is not easy and takes time. The hero must be strong enough to return over and over to the shadow world to explore what he or she holds captive. This is shown in movies and myths as the many obstacles located in the path of the hero to even get to the dragon's lands and the many-headed monsters. Plus, before making each pass at a dragon, the hero's ego must reorganize and tolerate the newness of identity. Ultimately, however, with the tackling of each obstacle/dragon and the release of each layer of what is held captive, more of the hero's shadow is revealed, more of the hero's persona falls away, and more of the true self of the hero emerges and shines.

What Is Rescued in the Third Dragon Fight?

The third and final major dragon fight is fighting the old order of society and bringing in the new. This is actually the hero's consummate mandate: to bring into the world something new—the new dance, the new music, the new politics, the new literature, and so on. Some might do this by creating a business and some through actual parenting of a child.

The work of this dragon fight involves combining the earthly world with the wisdom of the ages to bring in the new. It requires maturity and enough strength to go back and rescue what was held captive in the early developmental stages. In essence, a higher mode distinguishes the mature hero, one who has found the high road and walks it in real life. Myths and movies highlight this "higher" power by making the hero the son or daughter of not only a mortal but also a god.

Unfortunately, liberation from the old guard and bringing in new wisdom can take us into situations where we are tempted to give in to instincts to value money above all else, to seek or exert aggressive power, to act out sexually, to go with the status quo, and the like. Having an inner refuge and mature "witness" allows us to examine our own conscience, rescue that which is held captive, and hold fast to our moral balance in the face of temptations.

We all have seen young politicians finally reach their goal of a powerful office, only to watch them treat their underlings poorly or have numerous affairs. Others settle into a place of complacency and rest as a representative of the current norms, arrested in an inertia of tradition, possessed by the ruling Fathers. We also hear stories of highly paid corporate officers who give up their positions after many years because they feel they have been "wasting time," meaning all the work they did over those many years did not follow their true callings; they had given in to the lure of money and power as being the source of fulfillment, and they, too late, learned otherwise. In the myths, this dragon fight is depicted as the task of upholding spiritual wisdom in the face of the Great Mother's mysterious call to lose our self in the pleasures of the world and to give up our true quest. By this final phase, the hero can be guided by inner direction rather than by the outer standards of society.

Rescuing the Captive Applied to Heroic Quests

Rescuing the Ego Ideal

Because we have turned away from our wholeness in the Separation of the World Parents stage and have projected this into a seed idea (embodied in our unconscious as a heroic figure called the ego ideal), we are left unable to feel and know our true Self. We feel empty inside and think to ourselves: "I have love but am not love. I have intelligence but am not intelligence." Then we spend our life trying to fill this hole with an ideal.[33]

When we add not really being seen for our preciousness in infancy and toddlerhood, we can only conclude: "Who I am is not good enough. I reject me, because they reject me." Taking in nongenerative parental introjections, we don't believe we can be loved just for the mere fact of being who we are. We begin to think that, to gain the acknowledgement and admiration we want, we must have certain qualities. Whatever these qualities are, we build into the ego ideal. Then we begin to believe that this ideal is the best part of ourselves and that, if others see this ideal in us, then we will finally feel loved and a sense of belonging. This often becomes a striving to be perfect, or to have the perfect house, the perfect toys, the right car, and the like. As A.H. Almaas says, "The Ego Ideal is a compensation for a certain loss. . . . Ultimately, your gift to the world is being who you are."[34]

Because we believe that only an ideal self will be accepted, we create world quests for this heroic ideal to undertake, in an attempt to gain the Treasure. But, the dilemma of heroic quests is that they are actually a substitute and can never really fulfill us. What we need is to reunite with the undivided wholeness that we truly are.

Until we come close to this knowing, we will chase wholeness in symbolic substitutes known as wealth, fame, power, knowledge, mastery, and the like.

Highlighted are some of the various projected qualities that become the heroic stances people take. We consider these positive qualities—we believe that to become "better" means actualizing our ego ideal—but an idealization is always a distortion of one's reality. Rather, each of these qualities is really a defense against a negative sense of self.

Heroic Quality	How Enacted
Competent	I'm interested in action, using power, and doing things right.
Love as caring	I'm concerned with helping and taking care of things and people.
Protective	I'm committed to protecting and defending.
Knowing	I'm always engaged in trying to know and learn things.
Love as being loving	I'm always trying to be loving toward everyone.
Strong	I'm engaged with ways of trying to be perfect in strength. I don't want to feel weak or take weak action. I'm trying to prove my strength. I'll bring about harmony through revolution.
Knowledgeable	I'm trying to find and bring a new knowledge that no one has had and that could change the world.
Original	I'm incessantly trying to be original, authentic and spontaneous.

Through acknowledging these qualities as idealizations and rescuing that captive, we can return to the underlying strength, knowledge, and lovingness organically inherent in each of us. In other words, to get to our true essence, we must let go of idealizations, because idealizations actually overlay our real qualities, making spontaneity unavailable. As soon as we can tolerate stopping the idealized behavior and allow the emptiness underneath to "be," without trying to substitute another ideal, our wholeness begins to be revealed.

Because the ego ideal is developed partly to suspend the fear of mortality, we often aren't afraid of death. Because the mandate of the hero is to bring in the new to mankind, our ideal hero is often doing just that. And because we are all working our anima/animus projections, our chosen heroes know how to succeed in dealing with their own relationships. Thus, we have heroes of the body, like our Olympians and athletes; heroes of the emotions, like our first responders; heroes of the mind, like our Nobel Prize winners; and heroes of the spirit, usually our revered elders.

Here are several archetypal images of the hero, each with its own higher calling:

- The **Hero as a Warrior** who keeps us safe
    Higher form: The warrior who fights the status quo
- The **Hero as a Lover**, the one who wins the opposite sex
    Highest form: Those who can go into union with the feminine and also keep their own identity
- The **Hero as the Emperor (or Tyrant)** who wins the fruits of life
    Highest form: The one who opens our eyes to the truth
- The **Hero as the Innovator** who brings in the first of something for mankind
- The **Hero as a World Redeemer** who can refute tyranny by his or her personal presence
- The **Hero as a Saint** who renounces the rewards of the world to create the highest for all
- The **Hero as Unafraid of Death**

In our archetypal approach to psychotherapy, we try to help our clients reach an awareness of their ego ideal "above their natural self." Once they can see their ego ideal for the structure it is, they can more easily allow it to dissolve. Sometimes people don't have a good ego ideal structure built at all. In that case, rather than helping clients build this structure, we attempt to help them connect with and rely on the real fullness underlying their whole existence. This work is challenging for clients and not usually accomplished until the Rescuing the Captive stage.

Rescuing What Is Held Captive by the Superego

Our ego ideal often dictates how we will progress in development. Its degree of acting-out strength depends on the success we experienced when we were two and first discovered we were independent from our parents. Because of this role of the ego ideal, part of what is held captive in the superego and needs rescuing is the strength and passion of the "No!" and "Mine!" from the two-year-old. This "No!" and "Mine!" are our superego acting as the enforcer of our ego ideal, because the superego functions as our conscience, implementing the conscious and unconscious rules and norms of the family, school, and society. It is like a net of internalized dialogues we use to scold or praise our self into enacting our ego ideal and restraining our natural self that does not fit these dictates.

> Heroic quests are often taken as a way to either prove superego introjections are true, to prove they are false, to rebel against them, or to deny there are any introjections at all. Here are some examples of heroic quests to rescue the captive of the superego and to subsequently progress in development:
>
> * Gaining autonomy from our parents by disproving their negative thinking about us and life in general. *e.g., "I'll show them I can do this. What do they know?"*
> * Gaining autonomy by getting our parents' approval and proving their negative thinking about the world. *e.g., "I won't study for this test. He thinks I'm stupid anyway. That will help my father feel superior."*
> * Gaining autonomy by getting our parents' approval and proving their positive thinking about us and the world. *e.g., "I'll go to the Olympics with this skill!"*
> * Gaining autonomy by rebelling against our parents' version of life and/or our culture's approved values. *e.g., "So you think you like minorities, huh? I'll start dating one and see if that gets your attention. My parents are such hypocrites."*
> * Gaining autonomy by taking the stance of acting as if we don't care about anything. *e.g., "This is all so lame. Why are they getting so riled up about all this? It's all crap! I'll find my own way."*

When we are helping clients with issues related to development and emancipation, we work with layers of different ages, yet all stages of differentiating can try out the above scenarios. Whether it is the two-year-old trying to feel his or her own sense of authority and strength, the adolescent attempting to choose his or her own friends, the teenager preparing to go away to college and make a place in the world, the twenty-something setting up his or her own first home—real autonomy involves clearing the superego and anything held captive from the earlier stages. Only when we gain autonomy from the personal and cultural superegos will we be able to build our own world, with our own opinions and values, and bring in the new to humankind.

The vehicle for clearing the superego and other captive material is the heroic quest. Based upon their own projections, clients will choose certain quests and not others. In our therapy practice, we encourage their unique choices and help to illuminate obstacles. Remember these obstacles might look like they are in the outer world, but they are actually internalized commands of our superego projected as worldly dilemmas.

An instrumental part of our therapy work is assisting clients in examining their relationships with family, friends, and partners. The process guides people to becoming aware of their anima/animus projections, which greatly impact all relationships. We ask, "What kind of relationships do you have? Long-lasting ones? Short ones? Do you have generative, healthy relationships or volatile, hurtful relationships? How much anxiety is involved in your friendships? In your romantic relationships?" Planting the seeds of knowing that our relationships are a projected part of us held in our unconscious forever changes our perspective and opens us to the possibility of a deeper relationship with our self—and more meaningful and loving relationships with others.

Once the Birth of the Hero and the Slaying of the Parents stages are in full swing, we begin to ask clients to look at their heroic quests in a different light and to point to their quests as an attempt toward wholeness. We may ask, "What actions are needed to realize your true essence, and what would it look like to live from this vantage point?" We then direct them to look inside for this craving and ask them to see their anima/animus projections as a mirror of their inner life directing them to their true nature.

Sometimes heroic quests are simply taken to shore up a sense of identity, to tighten the patterns that keep the shadow out of awareness and keep the persona reigning supreme. We know that the best foundation for anyone is to have a flexible persona that can stand integrating material from the shadow without shame. Often what is in the shadow is kept there by a sense of shame or humiliation, and that sense of shame and humiliation is usually reinforced by our superego. The work of our heroic quests always leads to the integration of what was once humiliating, embarrassing, and shameful. When our witnessing capacity is solid, our persona can tolerate these feelings and the gems of the shadow can be available to the whole personality.

As an example, let's consider a young girl who had a mother who felt very competitive with her, so any kind of advance in skill by the girl had to be kept in low profile. That is not helpful for that girl who is now twenty-something and working at a job where she needs to broadcast her skills. Her persona will have to tolerate being seen as more skillful than some of her colleagues, without regressing or shutting down in fear of losing the friendship of her workmates.

Quests and Stages

Heroic quests look very different in each archetypal developmental stage. In the early stages of the Great Mother, they are about proving worth and value, building authority, and experimenting with sexuality and our creative expression. Even the Oedipal conflict is a heroic quest to free oneself from the Great Mother and come into the Father outer world.

In the Separation of the World Parents stage, quests are about moving from the inner world to the outer world, about trying out the magical heroic figure—like Spiderman or Superwoman—who is the master of both inside and outside worlds and who can bring the outer and inner worlds together. Examples of heroic quests in the Separation of the World Parents stage include:

- Having a tea party with all our animals and one of our parents, with rules about which spoon and plate to use.
- Teaching a doll we take everywhere with us about behaving.
- Any imaginary play that includes what happens in the outer world such as playing store or pretending to drive the car.

In the dragon fights, heroic quests are about creating our own world, even if it is an online world. With the Birth of the Hero and the Slaying of the Parents, heroic quests are about working through the superego; creating our own philosophy about life, perhaps based on a beloved book; and having an identity in our special world, like the athlete at school or the musician with his or her garage band. Even Rescuing the Captive can become a heroic quest itself.

The search for the Treasure goes on at every age. Sometimes that Treasure is of the material realm, and sometimes it is of the emotional, mental, or spiritual realm. As Ken Wilber says: "Each stage or level of growth seeks absolute Unity but in ways, or under constraints, that necessarily prevent it and allow only compromises: substitute unity and substitute gratifications. The more primitive the level, the more primitive the substitute unity. Each successive stage achieves a higher order unity."[35]

Heroic quests from the earliest stages of the Great Mother that have taken over life functioning are the most symptomatic and problematic in society. Let's take a look at some of the substitute gratifications from disruptions in these early stages:

Uroboric heroic quests are undertakings that result in regressions into undifferentiated states as an attempt to experience wholeness. They manifest as:
- Excessive sleeping, laziness, inertia
- Excessive masturbation

- Pornography addictions
- Excessive drinking of alcohol, often until blacking out
- Heroin, opioid, and methamphetamine addictions
- Screen addictions such as watching movie after movie or playing video games on and on

Great Mother Oral Stage heroic quests are undertakings to experience our true essence through activities involving the mouth such as:
- Continual overeating
- Excessive attempts to stay thin, including throwing up
- Smoking cigarettes
- Excessive smoking of marijuana to stay numb
- Excessive drinking
- Certain sexual acts performed frequently
- A great deal of anxiety in relationships
- Co-dependent relationships
- Excessive caretaking of others as a way of life

Great Mother Anal Stage heroic quests are undertakings to experience our true nature through controlling and possessing people and things, manifesting as:
- Attempting to be able to exclaim, "I have the biggest, best, most toys!"
- Being obsessed with exercise and body building (distortions of body building) and attempting to be able to exclaim, "I have the best-looking body!"
- Shopping as the only pleasure in life
- Hoarding
- Sadism and masochism as the life pursuit
- Feeling that life is only about pursuing ways to feel superior to others such as wanting and working to be the best climber, the best dresser, the boss, etc.
- Feeling powerless to live out our dreams
- Domestic violence
- Acting superior to others
- Choosing roles or jobs that give us complete power over others or have people depending on us for their life (e.g., running illegal immigrants, being a pimp, being a loan shark, etc.)
- The need to constantly enforce our will on someone else (particularly on someone who is innocent)
- Stealing, particularly going into other people's houses
- Gun obsession

Great Mother Genital Stage heroic quests are undertakings to experience our natural essence through activities involving the body, particularly the genitals. This can manifest as:
- The overwhelming need to have dangerous sex (i.e., exposing ourself to diseases, sex in public places, risking having dangerous partners, etc.)
- Sexual addictions, pornography addictions, and promiscuity
- Believing that conquests of the opposite sex are paramount in life, even to the point of putting career and/or relationships in danger
- Voyeurism
- Obsessing about having perfect cars (with throbbing speakers)
- Stealing
- Drug addiction with drugs that are injected
- Gun obsession
- All relationships having a great deal of anxiety if intimacy is expected

These manifestations of heroic quests are messages from the deep psyche stating there was a kind of disruption of care experienced in that stage that needs to be rescued. The therapy work in these cases requires a very secure, consistent container, and the work revolves around the real message underlying the gratifications. The real messages might be:

- I need to feel safe, merging love.
- I need to feel nourished, nurtured, and cared for.
- I need to feel safety and trust.
- I need to feel valued and important.
- I need to feel my own autonomy and strength and be celebrated in it.
- I need to feel my own authority and power and be safe to express it.
- I need to feel my sexuality, have it acknowledged, and feel safe in it.
- I need to feel a deep love for myself and others.
- I need to be able to express that love in sexual union with another.

Applying Anima and Animus in Rescuing the Captive

The anima and animus are intimately involved with the stages of consciousness and act as a guiding force toward our conscious emergence of the Self and the transformational journey of humankind. Murray Stein, in his book *Jung's Map of the Soul*, outlines Carl Jung's five stages of consciousness[36] in this journey to the Self, which follow nicely with the archetypal development outlined by Neumann. The first four stages of the development have to do with our ego development and take place in the first half of life. The fifth stage marks the second part of life and goes beyond unconscious projections into conscious relationship and union with the psyche and the natural world. This cannot be attained without a commitment to conscious work and being in relationship with our anima/animus projections.

Jung's first stage of consciousness in the journey to the Self is characterized by the *participation mystique*, a condition in which our consciousness and the world around us (contents of awareness) are the same thing. In this stage, there is an absence of awareness between the subject of awareness (me) and the object of our awareness (not me, but other). This is evident in early life with our mother and particularly until language and brain development mature; as infants we cannot distinguish between the boundaries of self and our mothers or caregivers.

This stage is highly influenced by our conditioning and early undifferentiated relationship with our mother. What is introjected is on a continuum between her limiting beliefs about herself, her mothering, and her ability to mirror the preciousness of her child's true Self. These introjects set the stage for further development and for the seeding of anima or animus in the unconscious. They ultimately impact our feelings of value and empowerment, our loving relationships, and our sexual expression of love.

Some people, at least to some extent, remain stuck in this first stage throughout their lives. For example, those whose identity is their career or the cars they drive find it difficult to delineate any sense of identity separate from those. This is an adult version of this stage.

Jung's second stage of consciousness in the journey to the Self is when projections become more localized. There begins to be some distinctions between "me" and another, and the focus expands to a few objects of consciousness. Slowly, the difference between "me" and another, and inside and outside of "me," begins to emerge.

As this differentiation process continues, the participation mystique changes; some objects of our projection become more important than others, and we become more and more invested in them. For example, important objects, other than mother, are things like favorite fun toys that catch our attention. Also, our father gains importance, as do pets, friends, or family who visit and entertain us.

Jung called these earliest projections of mother and father "our archetypal projections," like gods. These projections begin our introjects and beliefs about who we are, and this conditioning of introjects from the archetypal Mother and Father plants the seeds for later projections as anima and animus figures in our lives. For example, completion of the Oedipal dilemma happens when the external parents become internalized masculine and feminine representations.

The salient feature in this second stage is that a duality emerges that is experienced as 1) a sense of a separate self as me/I; and 2) an object outside of ourselves in which we project our unconscious introjected aspects from our parents. As we mature in this second stage as young children into adolescence, and as our ego develops, we begin projecting our internalized anima and animus on peers, siblings, teachers, and institutions such as school, church, and community. For example, those to whom we are attracted and with whom we fall in love are direct expressions of our anima/animus projections from unconscious aspects of Self, from the archetypal figures of the Great Mother and Father. These projections go on into our child-bearing years, as we then project our own parental introjects. Parents often hear similar phrases from their childhood come out of their own mouths while reprimanding their children—phrases they hoped they would never hear again! For example, have you ever thought, "I sound just like my mother" or "I swore I would never say that to my kids"? Many people do not evolve beyond this second stage but continue to believe that their perceptions, thoughts, feelings, and projections onto others are real and justified. They do not see their outer projections as a mirror of their inner life but, rather, continue to blame the outer world for their suffering.

Jung's stage three of consciousness in the journey to the Self is delineated by the anima and animus projections being focused on a more abstract, mythological, or spiritual figure. These projections remain quite real and concrete. For example, some believe in an outside God who is either loving or punishing, depending upon the belief system involved. In the Christian worldview, people believe in an outside Jesus as their savior. Duality and opposites remain central features of this stage.

Jung's fourth stage of consciousness in the journey to the Self is when there is a radical shift into the second part of life and projections seem to become extinct. This shift leads us to what Jung called the "empty center," a sense of soul, meaning, and purpose, a sense of immortality and experiencing the divine within. Jung saw this stage as potentially dangerous, in that the ego is still very involved and is projecting. One's ego often becomes inflated and invested in the shadow's wish for power and superior attitude.

When we are able to achieve a point of self-reflective ego and not become inflated, we are ripe for the fifth stage. So far, only a minority of humans attain the fifth stage. It is archetypal and open to all who are willing to see their projections of anima/animus as a reflection of their inner experience, and to use those projections as a guide to realizing their essence as the Self. Again, many never reach this stage. It is a huge achievement, particularly when we remove our projections enough to take personal responsibility for our destiny and not get trapped in our ego's shadow.

> **"Reactive states"** are those reactions activated from hurts from implicit memories of early childhood. They originate in the unconscious, somatic states. When triggered by outside experiences, they take over our lives and seem to possess us. C.G. Jung referred to these states as "complexes."[37]

If we do reach **Jung's fifth stage,** we shift into a conscious relationship with the anima and animus archetypal images and their projections as the center of individuation. Our ego and unconscious become joined in this lovely, and sometimes very challenging, introspective process of owning our projections as our inner perception based on anima/animus unconscious introjects. Also, we no longer see others as the source of our pain and suffering or as the source of joy and love. An example of this is a shift away from thinking, "My partner is so demanding of my time. She or he is always asking to spend a part of the weekend on our relationship. Why can't she or he understand I have so many of my own things to do?" When we are in a conscious relationship with our anima/animus projections, we, instead, would look at what this reaction (within me) is about, rather than attributing the cause of our feelings to our partner and/or blaming him or her for our reaction. We may inquire, "Could I be reacting out of fear of being close and being taken over, like what happened with my mother?" By uncovering the truth of our feelings and reactive states, and by being honest with ourself, the introjects impacting our lives begin to dissolve. We can then face the fears and hurts and move into a more loving way of being.

As we continue through this evolution and more introjects (and the patterns built from those introjects) dissolve, we integrate a strong sense of self, value, and worth. We feel empowered and loving, can demonstrate our love in sexual expression with our partner, and our creativity flourishes. In addition, a union between the psyche and the world takes place, and an opening to realizing the Self manifests. Of course, this process is ever evolving and never ending.

We can, thus, see the importance of having a conscious relationship with our projection of anima/animus, as doing so dissolves the veils to our true nature and essence of the Self. Also, once the anima/animus allows the ego to clear and morph, we can enter into and experience the depth of the psyche. If we make a commitment to work with the anima/animus unconscious projections, and stay with this work even when it gets intense and difficult, we can make steady progress in growth and maturity. The result can be an ever richer and more complete synthesis and conscious integration of life's meaning and purpose.

Centroversion

Neumann highlights the important role of "centroversion" in our development and how it expresses itself in the psyche. *Centroversion* is the tension and conflict felt between the conscious mind and the unconscious aspects of our being. Neumann sees this tension as our innate drive and striving for wholeness in the second part of life. He notes it will serve to balance out the one-sidedness of the first half.

In the first part of life, puberty is when the "contrasexual imagos" of the anima/animus are activated from their seeding and when the unconscious projections in relationships and attractions begin to take center stage. The anima/animus projections then constellate in the form of a partner and become the main theme throughout the first part of life, while, simultaneously, the building of our ego takes a central position. These go hand in hand.

It is not until centroversion takes hold in the second part of life that there is a significant change to real depth in our life. This depth requires actively and consciously engaging in the tension between the conscious and unconscious, inquiring into, owning, and seeing through our anima/animus projections. Being in this working relationship between the conscious and unconscious, we can begin to use our projections, and that which manifests in our life, to clear patterns and early introjects and to gain experiences of our true essence.

This process is our innate search for wholeness. When enough of our ego is cleared of its reactive projections, we experience stability, positivity, integrity, strength, and a sense of having moral character. In addition, the conscious mind refuses to be pulled back into the throes of unconscious realms again. This superior power is what Jung called the "transcendent function," that which is the result of holding and tolerating the tension of opposites.

When the conscious mind and unconscious anima/animus projections are no longer in opposition or split off from one another, the continued work in this ego clearing and morphing eventually brings us into experiences of our unified state. As noted earlier, Neumann refers to this state as the hermaphrodite—the union of opposites, masculine-feminine, anima-animus in its conscious form.

It is in our emotional relationships that this increased consciousness is most potent and where we can make the most progress in clearing the early introjects. We can accomplish this by becoming conscious of our anima/animus projections on others, owning them, working with the conditioning underlying them, and transcending the polarities of masculine and feminine. We transcend this polarity when we have developed our inner feminine aspects (feelings, emotions, tenderness, nurturing, authority, and love) and outer masculine aspects (career, education, protection, skills, power, goals, and dreams), embodying them equally and in balance. This would be the natural unfolding when the early introjects, patterning, and anima/animus projections are seen through for what they are and are dissolving.

As noted earlier, to differentiate between the projection and that which is the object of projection (between fantasy and reality), moving to this level of consciousness, is uncommon but very possible. It takes commitment, fierceness, and diligence. The more we are willing to dissolve the persona, defense structures, and the anima/animus, the more doors will open to the deeper layers of the unconscious. To accomplish this challenging work, we must deal with the conflict between ego and the persona and anima/animus. This conflict asks for our deeper commitment and seriousness. Our ego can no longer exist in its past form or get activated if there is no subject to project on or if the projection is seen through for what it is and dissolves.

Neumann states that Rescuing the Captive is complete when the pure images of the masculine and feminine archetypes are revealed and we are no longer caught in the conditioning of the earlier stages and the resulting attitudes we had toward ourself. We begin to see the reality of and purpose for our lives. After dissolving the limiting introjects of the Great Mother and Father, we experience a "crystallization of archetypal purity." This makes way for the masculine and feminine images to reveal their purest form. With the ongoing dissolution of limiting anima/animus projections, we naturally move into a purer relationship with the archetypal union of opposites and cross the threshold to the Self.

Application of Rescuing the Captive to the Slaying of the Parents Stage

The finale of the Hero myth is the Slaying of the Parents, which involves facing the many aspects of the parents that have been taken in and swallowed whole during the Separation of World Parents stage. These parental introjects have been mostly unconscious in the psyche and form the seeds of the underlying masculine and feminine archetypal principles. As explained earlier, these seeds are what Jung referred to as the "anima" (feminine principle) and "animus" (masculine principle).

Having birthed the hero, we become stronger in who we are as individuals. We begin to reject some aspects of the parental introjected beliefs, values, morals, opinions, and hopes for their unlived lives. As we move into the Slaying of the Parents stage, we must engage in a challenging dragon fight to rid ourself of the negative aspects of the mother and father that do not align with our ego ideal and our personal destiny or entelechy.

During the Slaying of the Parents stage of development, the anima and animus seeds take form as the unconscious parts of the feminine principle (called the "anima" for men) and of the masculine principle (called the "animus" for women). These unconscious aspects are then projected into the world as we begin to engage in deeper friendships, intimate relationships, and relationships with cultural establishments such as fraternities, universities, careers, and the like. Much of what is left unresolved in the Great Mother and the Father stages constellate in the anima and animus and are projected onto others, most particularly, onto our close friends and family members.

The anima/animus is not something in itself that can be rescued. Rather, it can only be seen through by studying the patterns of our projections that are revealed in the choices we make in our friends, loved ones, and communities. The anima/animus projections point us back into the depths of our inner world, toward what needs to be rescued to gain the Treasure. This is all in service of (in later development) unifying the polarities/opposites, balancing the feminine and masculine parts of Self, and transcending into the truth of our essential nature.

What Needs Rescuing in the Slaying of the Parents Stage?

The work of this stage is to advance the deconstruction of our personal superego introjects of our parents. Often that means taking stands against both parents, stands around issues that are not in alignment with our ego ideal and destiny. The work of this stage also involves rescuing that held in the Great Mother in terms of worth, value, and our inner authority, as well as in terms of our ability to love and to express ourself creatively and sexually. This often requires facing the unconscious shadow aspects of self to examine that from which we have disconnected. What we find in the shadow must be integrated into creating a new persona, and what we find may include anger, sadness, or whatever was not welcomed in the past.

The work of this stage is also the deconstruction of the cultural superego, those messages taken in from school, church, and popular culture that define the values of that era and culture. For example, we might disagree and fight with our parents about a particular philosophy of religion or a political candidate. Through this fight, both the personal and the cultural superego introjects are being brought into consciousness, chewed on by discussion and argument, and digested into a new form that reflects our own opinion and values.

Such work leaves us feeling as though we are an agent of our own life. Because we know our own mind and values, we can accept the differences with our parents and are able to take authority over our parents, when that could not be done in the past. In archetypal language, we are beginning to examine our one-sided alignments to the different facets of our major archetypes, expanding our knowing of ourselves to reveal both our generative and nongenerative sides.

Recall that rescuing the captive of the Birth of the Hero stage is a fight undertaken to free our generative aspects that are fragmented, split off, and held in the devouring Mother and crushing Father of the early stages of life. Many of these aspects are unconscious, pre-verbal thought structures and archetypal images held in the implicit memory cellular structure of the body that developed into our inner dialogue. What is now left to rescue in the Great Mother, at the Slaying of the Parents stage, is engaged with through relationships in the outer world, both with romantic partners and with institutions. That is, the hero in the Slaying of the Parents stage often seeks the lost parts of self through relationships. For instance, a weak woman will choose to be with a strong, stoic man—and then not feel satisfied with the relationship. Her anima and animus projections triggered her reactive state, left from hurts early in life. Helping this woman to see that what she struggles with in her romantic relationships is rooted in introjects from her relationship with her father is part of understanding the mysterious process of projecting. By clearing the introjections of the devouring Mother and/or crushing Father, she can gain both the internalized feminine image and an internalized masculine image that, as Neumann says, have "archetypal purity." Once the anima/animus is seen and acknowledged in Gaining the Treasure, it becomes our innate wisdom—an internal guide and helpmate to the ego—influencing our way of communicating in the external world as well as impacting the examination and transformation of our internal patterns.

When people need to rescue a captive in this specific stage, they have to gain their true voice—based on their own opinions, values, and beliefs—and be able to express those in a contemporary way. The archetypal approach to Self-actualization will have them learning to listen to the command of their own inner guide. Clients will be helped to hone in on the heroic quest that will be the archetypal container for their destiny or entelechy to manifest in a way that fits with what their generation needs. For example, "Don't trust anyone over thirty" was the battle cry of the dragon fight of the Baby Boom generation.

Heroes of today need to find the "new" inside themselves, not to complacently live according to what is already established. In this conflict, the inner guiding voice within the hero calls forth the new way. Neumann says it best: "The hero has to . . . awaken the sleeping images of the future which can and must come forth from the night, in order to give the world a new and better face. This necessarily makes him a breaker of the old law. He is the enemy of the old ruling system of the cold cultural values and the existing court of conscience, and so he necessarily comes into conflict with the fathers and their spokesman, the personal father."[38]

Having slain our parents by projecting them into the world as the anima/animus, then having gone out to meet those projections and established ourself in the world through different heroic quests, recognizing we have our own opinions and thoughts, and taking on the mantle of overcoming the old phase of existing systems, our hero reaches the second stage of the archetypal life journey that Neumann named "introversion," an inner journey of heroism, the gaining of the Treasure!

14

Application of Rescuing the Captive in Neumann's Transformation Myths

"We are not responsible for our projections, only for not becoming conscious of them, taking them back, or familiarizing them."[39]

- Murray Stein -

Application of Rescuing the Captive Stage One

The focus of our therapy work is to create alignments to the Self and to bring the developing ego to a place that can support living from and being in service to the Self. As we have discussed in the last sections, this work takes rescuing aspects of ourselves held captive during various developmental stages. To rescue the captive also takes a strong and safe therapeutic container.

As therapists, we hold the therapeutic container and conditions for an alignment with the Self that embodies the mandate of the Mother and Father archetypes, in order to facilitate the repair, rescue, and integration of aspects split off and left behind in the unconscious during a client's early life. We begin the process by asking our clients to approach this work from a place of empathy and self-compassion, whenever possible. This is critical to their ability to meet and embrace whatever is keeping them from experiencing their worth and value, their own power and authority in the world, and their creative potential—the culprits likely being the nongenerative facets of the Mother and Father archetypes internalized during the early stages of development.

Although our clients' work often begins in the Slaying of the Parents stage, during the Rescuing the Captive stage they must go into the unconscious to find what needs rescuing. Again, it is imperative that what they find be received with love and without judgment. Clients typically are critical of their younger inner parts and resistant to needing to rescue them. They also assume we feel the same. On the contrary, we invite all the feelings and thoughts to come into the therapy session, and we meet those feelings and thoughts with compassion and love, while focusing on seeing the Self in the person at all times.

In addition to approaching their work with love and non-judgment, clients in the rescuing stage also need to develop a strong narrative of the context in which they grew up. They need to understand what they experienced and felt in their early family life and begin to recognize the imprinting from school, religion, and culture. They must start seeing that they are something much larger than their introjections and imprints, and that their essential nature, the Self, is more vast than the ego structures and its inner narrative from which they have been living.

Meeting our clients' narratives with reverence is important, because their stories reveal what needs rescuing. They carry the patterns and alignments, through morphic resonance to particular archetypal attractor sites, that keep our clients' nongenerative aspects alive in their behavior. Listening to each story and meeting each with love and acceptance is the mandate of the Great Mother archetype! The process allows for the repairing and building of a richer, truer, and stronger inner world and facilitates opening to the Treasure of each person's essence, the Self.

Stories also help us see how canalized and habitual certain archetypal alignments are and how they are experienced in the patterns of current life. They show what polarities are emerging and point to particular archetypal developmental stages. This is important because our rescue-and-repair work involves not only exploring the client's current archetypal life stage but also integrating previous stages and looking at his or her chronological age and life stage and its congruence to its archetypal life stage. (See our "**Archetypal Developmental Stages of Life**" chart in Chapter Ten.)

Unconscious communication also informs us if we are receiving the material we need to rescue, or if there are places in the implicit memory that need help in telling the client's story. Our job as therapists is to remain objective and true to the images, translating them and helping our clients to build a bridge for this information from their unconscious to their conscious mind. Much of this work involves helping our clients to develop a witnessing platform. We encourage them to view their thoughts and feelings from a third- and fourth-person perspective, to become aware of their thoughts or feelings as an observer. This "witness" helps clients see what they went through as a child and what they decided was true about themselves and the world from that early time. From this perspective, they begin to understand that their constructed thoughts and behavior patterns developed from early parental and cultural introjections and were never the truth of their being.

Also present during stage one of Rescuing the Captive is how clients are caught in what we refer to as the "victim-tyrant" polarity. In this dynamic, clients typically move back and forth between feeling victimized by someone or something in the outside world (e.g., institution, religion, race, etc.) and then making that person or thing a tyrant that needs to be killed off or hurt in revenge. In revenging, the client becomes the tyrant who is victimizing whomever or whatever appeared to be his or her tyrant in the first place. This polarity underlies the human condition as a part of our imprinting and needs dissolving to ground solidly in the Treasure stage of development.

We begin working with these alignments as a fundamental part of Rescuing the Captive, as the victim-tyrant polarity holds many of our thought and behavioral patterns locked into place. This polarity is a vicious cycle that maintains a level of functioning that needs to be seen through as a *constructed* reality, a lens of perception, and then resolved if a client is to complete the rescue process. In fact, dealing with the victim-tyrant polarity will be a major part of our work throughout the Rescue stage as well as into the Treasure stage, as subtler aspects become revealed.

Simultaneously with meeting all parts of our clients and their stories and exploring what was introjected, we also mentor our clients so they can see the archetypal mandates of the roles they are currently carrying out in their life and work. In addition, we help them to move to their next developmental stage by teaching them skills that are needed for the second stage of the work of Rescuing the Captive. These skills involve building and strengthening:

- Their witnessing capacity and ability to practice mindful awareness,
- A relationship with their inner guidance and innate wisdom,
- A grounded physical presence,
- An intention toward integration, and
- A norm of valuing openness and being vulnerable.

Through this process, the shadow begins to be exposed and the persona expanded. Any closed systems tend to become more permeable and open for new energy and information to enter. And, a new level of novelty and complexity, which will promote growth and change, begins to emerge.

Application of Rescuing the Captive Stage Two

Once the nongenerative introjections of the Mother and Father archetypes are consciously known, identified, and on their way to dissolution, we are no longer fused in our history. We have gained a perspective of observing our life in context and are beginning to see that we are the creator of our own life. We also develop an interest in looking inside at what is attracting certain patterns into our life and how we are maintaining those patterns.

Granted, we still need to engage in ongoing work on deconstructing shadow aspects and releasing the defensiveness of the persona, of what we are willing to allow the world to see. But, at this developmental stage, we begin to see our own projections into the world and reclaim them as our own perceptions. These projections are the externalization of unconscious psychic contents, a pre-conscious, involuntary process happening outside of consciousness and always originating in the archetypes and in unconscious complexes. Some projections are defensive, and others are projected for developmental and integrative purposes. Murray Stein in *Jung's Map of the Soul* noted, "Jung has always held that projections are created by the unconscious and not by the ego. We are not responsible for our projections, only for not becoming conscious of them, taking them back, or familiarizing them."[40]

The shadow can be an example of a defensive projection. We might deny we have a particular trait because that trait doesn't fit with who we feel we are supposed to be or how we view ourselves. In doing this, we create an alignment with that very trait and begin to see it in other people and situations. An example is jealousy. Too often, one half of a couple will become attracted to and begin having sexual feelings for someone other than his or her partner. He or she will deny the feelings (even to him- or herself) and then accuse the partner of being unfaithful, jealously seeing signs of the unfaithfulness everywhere, even if they are not there in reality. Likewise, many movies show the workings of people having a guilty conscience over something they are covering up, and then they begin to see signs of their guilt everywhere.

The persona can be another example of a defensive projection. For example, a bully who needs to feel superior and look powerful (as a way of compensating for his real insecurity) may take his vulnerability and project it onto others—and then try to beat their vulnerability out of them. This kind of aggressive projection of displaced negative emotion happens in interpersonal relationships as well as on the level of politics and war.

There are also unconscious projections for developmental purposes. For example, we might project an image of the Self on people who have a trait we sense will complete or activate our own entelechy or destiny factor. A good example is that most of America projected hope for a better world onto Barack Obama when he was running for and became our first African American president.

The anima/animus is also a common integrative projection; we project our relationship with our own psyche's unconscious onto other people and attract others into our field through morphic resonance (like attracts like) in order to help bring these deeper unconscious aspects into our conscious awareness. This is how most couples find one another, saying in the beginning how much they have in common and later seeing they seem like opposites. We can use these projections onto our partners as a means to bring aspects of ourselves into conscious awareness in order to rescue and integrate this healing that otherwise may stay hidden. Another example is projecting wisdom onto a teacher but, in the process, ignoring the teacher's human traits or failings. This may actually be an unconscious attempt to develop our own wisdom by working extra hard to be seen as credible by the teacher. Once we begin to feel, "Oh, I created this, and I need to meet myself in the places I was not met, and I need to love and see my own preciousness," we then move into our humanness, releasing the idealization for which we have been striving. We also begin to forgive our imperfection and messiness and start to experience the Self beyond the influence of memory.

In summary, in these later stages of Rescuing the Captive, the focus becomes gaining consciousness of more and more aspects of ourselves that are unconscious introjections from early childhood experiences that we believed to be true about ourselves and which became our inner narratives of the mind from which we have been living our lives. Once we begin to see *through* this creation of ourselves, we also see we were actually the *creators* of the lens of our perceptions, inner thoughts, and projections onto the world. From this vantage point, we can begin a process of meeting these precious unmet aspects of ourselves with love and compassion. And then we can accept and embrace our humanness, realize the idealization for which we have been striving, and forgive and accept our human imperfections. This opens a door to discovering and expressing our true nature and unique gifts that lie beyond our reactive states and the projections influenced by our early childhood introjections. In this process, we begin to feel a new sense of maturity that is more congruent with our chronological age and less tied to younger aspects of Self.

15

The Archetypal Approach to Gaining the Treasure

We help our clients to strengthen the ego to be strong enough and flexible enough to continue its own maturational journey—which includes its own dismantling!

The goal of this archetypal approach to therapy is to help our clients create healthy archetypal alignments and clear nongenerative patterns of thoughts and behaviors so they have more spontaneous experiences of living from their true nature, the Self. In doing so, clients shift their center of gravity from living from their conditioned ego and reactive states from early childhood to living their full potential and bringing their unique gifts into the world—what Neumann calls "the Treasure."

Because the container embodies the mandate of the Mother and Father archetypes, a therapeutic container helps our clients heal aspects from early stages of development. As therapists, thus, we hold the therapeutic container and its conditions to support our clients in shifting from being aligned with the ego (and its inner dialogue and behaviors that relate to early childhood conditioning) to aligning with the Self as their essential essence. Specifically, we help our clients to strengthen the ego to be strong enough and flexible enough to continue its own maturational journey—which includes its own dismantling! Our end goal is to have our clients realize their larger identity, manifesting as an alignment to the Self, their true nature, that includes the experience of:

- I am an expression of the Self.
- I am fully embodied and mature, have a full range of human emotions, and can express those emotions.
- My mind has thought structures and patterns developed in early childhood, but I am larger than my mind and thoughts. My true essence is beyond this inner dialogue.

- My behavior is patterned, but that behavior and those patterns do not define me.
- I have a persona in the world but am not attached to it and can let it go to show others my true Self.
- I have constructed my identity but do not have attachments or aversions to these separate states. I see that letting them dissolve brings me closer to my true expression of Self.
- I am larger than my attachment or aversion to form itself.
- When I inquire within, I cannot find the "me" with which I have been so identified.

With this archetypal approach, we foster the consolidation of each developmental stage while also planting the seeds of skills that will support the transition to the next stage. Simultaneously, we empower our clients to integrate aspects of earlier stages that have been left behind: They integrate arrested development, attachment disruptions, and shadow aspects in the unconscious. They also liberate the persona to become more open and flexible, to become a closer expression of their uniqueness and wholeness. And, they dissolve the defense systems needed to be resilient and to unify opposites and polarities of the ego patterns. Ultimately, our clients develop witnessing abilities, learn the skills, and engage in the behavior modification needed for living from their true nature, the Self.

As noted earlier, one of the main strategies of this archetypal approach is to provide ways for our clients to build a conscious awareness and ability to witness:

- Sensations and experiences
- Emotional states and the thought patterns that created them
- The internal stories thought to be true that created these thought patterns

Through such a witnessing platform, clients are able to observe their own ego and its structures. They learn to recognize how the duality of feeling a separate self and there being a separate "outside other" was developed. And, they open up themselves to the unity and oneness of being.

Working with Neumann's Archetypal Developmental Stages from the Stage of Gaining the Treasure

As therapists, we are always looking for ways to support the integration of material from earlier stages of development while, simultaneously, working with a client's current stage. From this vantage point, we are then able to plant the seeds for the foundational structures the client needs in order to enter the next developmental stage.

Following, we will review each stage of the Great Mother as examples of the role a therapist can play:

Conception, Pre-birth Experience, and Uroborus

All experiences during these stages, including trauma and disrupted attachment, are stored in the implicit memory and in the cellular structure of the body. As such, the experiences of these stages are not available to the conscious mind. Nonetheless, they are manifested through symptoms or behaviors.

To work with this stage takes . . . a secure therapeutic container and a deeply trusting attachment between the therapist and the client. It is very slow work, often taking years. The therapist must listen deeply and consistently; he or she must see and reflect the preciousness of his or her client's being. The work includes translating a client's adult symptoms into their origins and what was internalized in early childhood. This involves understanding the client's early environment. For instance, one client's sense of being unsafe as an adult might have its origin in the Nazi occupation that occurred during the client's first two years of life or even in the womb; this unconscious memory gets relived daily as the feeling that the world is a dangerous place not to be trusted.

Oral Stage of the Great Mother

During the oral stage of the Great Mother archetype, the baby is in a symbiotic union with the mother and takes in all the mother's ways of relating by way of what is being fed to him or her. Thus, the focus of this stage is taking in the world through the mouth; all experiences are interpreted through the perception of food. As in the earlier stages, these experiences are stored in the implicit memory and are not available to the conscious mind, and they manifest throughout life as symptoms or behaviors. For example, trauma and insecure attachment during this stage colors our lens of perception as we mature into and throughout adulthood and triggers certain reactive states.

To work with this stage takes . . . a secure therapeutic container and a trusting relationship between the therapist and the client. Consistency is key with regard to issues of safety, trust, and protection. Clients must be fully seen, heard, and accepted for who they are and how they present themselves; they must be seen as the beautiful beings they are, their natural state as the Self. We accomplish this by focusing on their essential nature and their value and worth, consistently treating our clients with great respect and providing generative mirroring. By mirroring their essence and offering a new experience by how we are experiencing them, we enable clients to develop new neural networks in their brain (through neuroplasticity) and to shift toward integration, healing, and a more balanced nervous system.

In general, during work in this stage, we strive to help clients see that it was their early conditioning that made them feel certain ways, such as unworthy and unvalued. We then help them shift and reframe the nongenerative archetypal alignments to generative aspects of the Great Mother that were previously missing. We must remind them that nothing is, or ever has been, wrong with them, that the information about them introjected from the mother and the environment was never true. The work involves slowly translating their adult symptoms into the origins of those symptoms, which were early occurrences and the conditioning of their early environment. For instance, feeling very alone as an adult often can be traced to a client's early feelings of abandonment during the Great Mother oral stage. Other issues from this stage also show up as eating disorders or drug and alcohol abuse; endorphins not received from Mother are sought during adulthood—but only appease the desire temporarily. No matter how nongenerative the patterns, we welcome all aspects of our clients' lives. They, in turn, begin welcoming repressed parts of their selves, parts held in the unconscious. We ultimately help them to integrate basic trust and safety and to translate unconscious narratives and dreams to bring these into conscious awareness.

Anal Stage of the Great Mother

A few memories from the anal stage of the Great Mother may be conscious. Because the brain is not well developed, however, most experiences from this stage are unconscious, are not available to the conscious mind, and are stored somatically in the implicit memory. As with earlier stages, the early experiences present themselves as symptoms or behaviors throughout life. Our clients don't usually understand their particular behavior or symptoms, even though they feel very real and true to their experience. For example, they may be stymied by their own insecurity regarding their own authority, power, and worth. We help them to understand that they were unable to integrate a healthy sense of self and of their value and importance during the oral stage and so did not step into their authority and power during the anal stage.

To work with this stage takes . . . recognizing the power and authority of our clients. We often will find that clients struggling with issues from this stage are embroiled in victim-tyrant interactions with other people, authorities, and/or the world. Our job is to treat each one with great respect and to stay out of the victim-tyrant mindset, reframing issues as often as possible, not getting caught in a polarity, and providing a larger transcendent perspective.

Sometimes feelings of being bad, of shame, and of doubt are part of toilet training during the anal stage that carried the message, "You have something inside you that is terrible." Often others dominated this process. We work with our clients to help them integrate holding on, letting go, and being in charge of their own decisions—of gaining autonomy without feeling shame and doubt.

In general, clients with issues rooted in the anal stage of the Great Mother need help with rapprochement problems as well as with developing object constancy, autonomy, and emancipation. For instance, some clients will try to "give us their authority." When this occurs, we can say, "You are giving your power to us. Let's help you find it in yourself." They are dealing with integrating their power and importance and, at the same time, with being able to be in close relationship with us. Giving away their authority often has been their pattern for developing close and meaningful relationships, which makes it imminent to help them step into their power with our support and acceptance.

So they can gain a sense of power and practice emancipation, it can be useful for clients to be in charge of when they come to therapy, when they leave, or whether they come at all for a scheduled appointment. By knowing we are there holding the space of a solid therapeutic container and conditions, and that we will lovingly welcome them no matter when they come, can provide a missing experience and subsequent healing and securing of attachment needs. This practice allows them to stand in their own authority and feel connected at the same time; by integrating object constancy, they can begin to develop secure attachment. Also, by slowly translating their adult symptoms into their origins as early occurrences and as the conditioning of their early childhood environment, we help our clients to develop a healthy witnessing platform from which to view the origins of their symptoms and behavior and to integrate aspects of their past that will help them to achieve generative alignments.

Genital Stage of the Great Mother

In the genital stage, children discover the good feelings of their genitals and body. At this time of development, they also take in how their parents or caregivers react to bodily exploration, including masturbation. Do the parents shame the child or provide good boundaries? For example, parents might say, "That's something you can do in your room, but not outside of it."

If a child's bodily exploration was not met in a generative way by the parent or caregiver—or if there has been sexual abuse, physical abuse, or shaming—adult clients may show up with symptoms in the form of sexual acting out, promiscuity, not being able to say "No" to unreasonable demands, suppressed sexuality, and/or an interruption in the flow of creative development.

To work with this stage . . . takes recognizing the power of the fields of incest, sexual abuse, and shaming and how these nongenerative patterns attempt to replicate. The container of the therapist-client relationship and therapeutic setting helps by providing a consistent holding environment, allowing for generative intimacy to be experienced and integrated into a client's relationships.

It is also important to remember that, if parents do not act as a team during this period of development, children learn to triangulate to get their needs met. Because of this, as practitioners, we make sure we do not triangulate with other family members, friends, practitioners, or employers. We also point out triangulation if it occurs, with the goal of supporting clients in developing intimate relationships, both sexual and nonsexual. Ultimately, clients would value their partner's needs as well as their own, and they would be able to say "No" to what doesn't feel right to them as well as ask for what they want.

We cannot leave this section without specifically addressing shaming. Shaming greatly impacts a young one's heart and mind. Therapists can help their clients see from an adult perspective the larger context of early shaming, including the limitations of their parents and caretakers. This new perspective can lead to an exploration of the layers and layers of shame. We can then help our clients recognize and connect with the feelings in their body that may have been repressed or shamed and is, therefore, no longer available to awareness.

As noted earlier in the book, clients with captives in the genital stage are often vulnerable to being seduced into believing the best of others and then having the rug pulled out from under them. This crushing of hopes and dreams can interfere with the natural flow of creativity. For example, some people will believe they have no imagination or they cannot create anything—when that ability is innate in all of us. Once clients have integrated their value and worth, however, they can stand in their own authority in a new way. They will not be fooled by false promises, shaming, or criticism, and they will be able to express what they want and need, while saying "No" to what doesn't work for them. This often opens the flow to imagination and new creative endeavors.

Part Four

The Unconscious Expression of the Psyche

"Day after day we live far beyond the bounds of our own consciousness; without our knowledge, the life of the unconscious is going on within us. The more critical reason dominates, the more impoverished life becomes, but the more of the unconscious and the more of myth we are capable of making conscious, the more of life we integrate. The unconscious helps by communicating things to us, or making figurative allusions. It has other ways, too, of informing us of things which by all logic we could not possibly know."[1]

- C.G. Jung -

16

Working with Pre-Cognitive Experience: Implicit Memory

"Caretakers activate the growth of the brain through emotional availability and reciprocal interactions."[2]

- R.N. Emde -

Shifting our practice from more subjective therapies into working with the deep unconscious and unconscious derivative forms of communication changed our worldview. We went from looking at various behaviors in people as being pathological and problematic to seeing their patterns and behaviors as perfect expressions of the psyche longing for wholeness. We came to understand that patterns and behaviors clue us into what wants to be known, seen, understood, and guided toward full health and a life of thriving, meaning, purpose, and living the unique gifts we all have in potential.

Throughout the years of this work, we have been continually in awe of the relentlessness of the psyche to go to any means of expression to be heard, all in service of the greatest good for each person. We see that, if the psyche is not understood on the mental and emotional level, it will manifest physically as how people inhabit their body and present themselves; it also will sometimes present as a disease. In fact, the psyche will do whatever is needed to express what is needed for wholeness and generativity. Because the psyche is mostly unconscious and the goal of life "development" is to gain more consciousness, being able to understand the psyche's expression opens us to a larger view and deeper love and appreciation for all humanity.

The Inner World of the Child

The amygdala is a part of our primitive brain that is central to processing experience during our early life. As the central hub of social and emotional processing, the amygdala functions as an organ of appraisal for danger, safety, and familiarity in approach-avoidance situations and assists in connecting emotional value to experience, which it then translates into bodily states[3] (somatic states). A child's amygdala and the beginning structure of a child's inner world develop from experiences of existence in the womb, experiences during the three stages of the birth process (the contractions, the passage through the birth canal, and the emergence and first inhale),[4] and in relation to the child's symbiotic relationship with the mother and/or the caring one. This caregiver, who carries the archetype of the Great Mother, can be the mother, father, aunt, grandmother, or some other person; the role is not gender specific. Whoever that person is, recent interpersonal neurobiology research clearly proves: "We now know that the quality of caretaking affects the function, structure, and neurochemical architecture of the brain"[5] and "The human brain is inherently dyadic and is created through interactive interchanges."[6]

The archetype of the Great Mother has a mandate to build the inner, emotional world of the child. This generative mandate is to create an inner world of love, emotions, and feeling states that are anchored in safety, trust, security, nurturing, tenderness, love, and protection. Such generative caring will bring about the eventual fulfillment of a little being's potential. Thus, what a baby most needs is to be at the center of a strong container of love and care. Resting in that secure container, the baby is able to take in the affection and an abundance of attention and care that ultimately wires in that little one a nervous system that is calm, balanced, and able to ease through its natural process of rising stimulation and discharge. This positive bonding between caregiver and baby creates a state of resonance and a sense of joining together called "attunement." What is truly remarkable is that the strength of this resonance continues when the two are separated, because the baby begins to build an *internal experience* of this attunement.[7] Through mirroring the caregiver who is loving and kind, a child slowly learns how to handle rising tensions and stress, how to relax, how to deal with different emotions such as anger, frustration, and love, and how to self-soothe when upset or frightened.

On the other hand, if the container of the family is disrupted by any number of factors and the child cannot rest in the center of the family's care, that child's nervous system learns not to relax. On hyper alert at all times, the baby will react negatively to over-stimulation, under-stimulation, or periodic disruption. Eventually, wired with an "on-alert" nervous system and prepared to consistently meet stress, that child will become reactive to all stimuli and maintain unconsciously a position of hyper vigilance.

Noted psychologist Louis Cozolino, in *The Neuroscience of Human Relationships*, describes the process well: "We all have an internalized [version of our] mother, which is a network of visceral, somatic, and emotional memories of our interactions with our mothers, which are thought to serve as the core of self-esteem, our ability to self-soothe, and the foundation of our adult relationships. . . . This early, pre-verbal dyad [two-person relationship] establishes the biological, behavioral, and psychological structure of our expectations about other people, the world, and the future. . . . Although we don't consciously remember these experiences, they shape the neural infrastructure of our implicit memory [our brain and nervous system], exerting a lifelong influence on us."[8]

The experiences in the womb, at birth, and during at least the first seven months of life outside the womb are instrumental in coding the inner world of a child. Unconsciously, the child begins to file the early experiences and interactions into categories. The files are like computer folders marked:

- What the world is
- What I can expect from big people
- Who I must be, given how I am being treated by others
- How I need to behave to get attention or what I need

The repetition of those experiences forms patterns and, ultimately, a rhythm of connection or of disconnection, depending on the generative quality of the experiences.

In essence, the symbiotic fusion with the mother (or caregiver) contains a download of the emotional patterns of the mother, any close caregiver, and the atmosphere of the household. The child's brain links to the caregiver's (mother's) brain to slowly learn how to (among other things):

- Handle rising internal tensions
- Handle stress
- Relax
- Be soothed when upset or frightened
- Handle different emotions such as anger, frustration, and love

This early linking process of taking in the early relationships and experiences changes the brain of both the child *and* the caregiver. It becomes the child's "inner refuge" or internal base (secure or insecure) that gives him or her the ability (or lack of ability) to cope with the challenges, stresses, and traumas of life.

Renowned British psychologist and psychiatrist John Bowlby purports this inner base is formed on a total of thousands of experiences with caregivers that then become unconscious, involuntary predictions of the behavior of others. These predictions also determine whether we are able to use our outer relationships to maintain emotional and physical stability and well-being,[9] or whether we feel on our own.

In Archetypal Pattern Analysis, we call this inner refuge an "alignment to the Mother archetype." Through patterned repetition, alignments to specific attractor sites occur. Current research calls this "attachment theory"[10] and speaks of the patterns of neural networks that are laid down in the brain in the early period of childhood. These neuronal firings, also called "mental representations,"[11] continue to influence how we see ourselves, others, and the world throughout our lifespan. Think about when children look into their mother's eyes to determine whether the world is safe or dangerous; her expression can tell them to be afraid, even if the situation or environment is benign. If the mother consistently conveys fear and distrust, her children as adults will most likely live lives that revolve around preparing for attacks and violence. Even a person who never directly experienced or even heard about certain traumatic or tragic situations but lived through such circumstances via the unconscious connection with the minds and brains of his or her mother and/or family will be hypervigilant and distrustful as an adult.[12] Brain research and attachment theory demonstrate that, through what Daniel Siegel calls "neuroplasticity," the neural networks between mother and infant actually become attuned. In Siegel's words, "Neurons that fire together, wire together."[13] Because neurons are activated together between mother and infant, they will likely fire together in the future. Siegel's research shows how significantly we all affect one another, and that particularly significant is the relationship between mother and infant during the formative stages of development.[14] (See the next chapter for more on attachment theory.)

Research also shows that trauma experienced by a child's last several generations of ancestors is passed to the child epigenetically in the womb through downloads of information via the umbilical cord before birth.[15] This trauma is wired into a baby's cellular structure, which is then unavailable to the conscious mind as the child develops. Yet many clients, when they consciously discover and explore their ancestors' traumatic experiences, feel a relief of symptoms.

As further evidence of the importance of a child's earliest life in setting the groundwork for a lifetime, consider the work of noted psychoanalyst Daniel N. Stern. In his book *The Interpersonal World of the Infant*, Stern presents evidence concerning the development of a sense of self in pre-linguistic infants. He says their first way of organizing their experience has to do with the body—that infants are always aware of their body, of how its inner feeling states change and flow, of how it moves, and the feelings that go with that movement. He concludes they have a coherent memory of all these.[16]

The truth of the matter is that, even before children learn how objects can function and what will make objects move or stay stable, they are already beginning to organize and encode their experiences into pervasive patterns that will give their ongoing experience form and meaning. They are beginning to build the "filing system" that will be the foundation of how they organize the rest of their experiences throughout life.

As the psyche of the child organizes that underlying feeling sense of the world, a patterned meaning in the form of feeling rhythms or emotions is encoded in the child's brain. This is a large experience of somatic feeling that eventually begins to be sustained by a primitive organization of memory traces, images, and internal memory records of experiences at a pre-verbal, pre-cognitive level. The amygdala in the brain stores these memories as visceral, sensory, motor, and emotional at all levels of the central nervous system,[17] creating overall pattern expectations. That means that the patterned meaning does not crystalize into words or concepts. Rather, they are "atmospheres" locked into the body's cells. Often strong but not realizable nor expressible emotions, these somatic states are "the way things are." They are symbolized versions of interpersonal conditioning with caregivers, but they do not lead to action as an image might. Instead, that patterned meaning might determine whether or not a child can trust others and feel safe. The patterned meaning also might convey a felt sense of "I am valuable" or "I am not valuable." The Italian psychiatrist Silvano Arieti, regarded as one of the world's foremost authorities on schizophrenia, calls this developmental stage an "Endocept." He says the stage only can be communicated to other people when it is translated into expressions that belong to later developed mental levels, which are only in *potential* at this stage of a baby's development.[18]

The science of neurobiology currently calls this "implicit memory." Implicit memory organizes and retains primitive memories of early caregiving, rendering them into permanent psychological significance.[19] It includes perceptual, emotional, behavioral, bodily sensory memory, and "mental models," or the generalizations of repeated experiences, sometimes called "invariant representations." These are generalized experiences grouped into a summation or model of a series of events.[20] Cozolino, in *The Neuroscience of Human Relationships*, says, "These memories form the infrastructure of our lives. We experience them as the 'givens' of life. We seldom realize that they are influencing and guiding our moment-to-moment experiences. They are the emotional background against which all subsequent psychological development takes place."[21] (See the inset, "The Formation of Implicit Memory," at the end of this chapter.)

As explained earlier, the knowing from implicit memory is registered in representations of interpersonal events in a non-symbolic form.[22] As a result, this memory is not retrievable by the conscious mind due to a child's immature brain development and to the brain's inability until later in childhood to register these memories in the "explicit memory" (the conscious memory of narrative representations).[23] Our early knowing only has unconscious ways of expressing itself, which we experience later in life as moods, chronic unexplainable feelings, reactive states projected onto others, and disease. Once we reach the later stages of adult development, implicit memories show themselves again, as pervasive feeling and reactive states. As we mature, these primitive somatic states wired during our earliest experiences lay dormant in our unconscious. They give meaning to the world. They are the unconscious sense that an individual makes of the world.

The Formation of Implicit Memory: Our Early Conditioning for Life

The following delineates what is being encoded in the archetypal developmental stages that occur during the first six or seven years of implicit memory that is not available to the conscious mind. We refer to this information to access that with which a captive in each stage might be dealing.

Conception
* If my conception has a charge of deep love and intimacy, that will be downloaded into my implicit memory. If my conception has an energetic charge to it of rape, incest, an affair, or trauma, that will be downloaded into my implicit memory.
* If my mother is excited and happy when she finds out she is pregnant, that will be anchored in my cellular structure. If she is stressed or frightened at finding out she is pregnant with me, that feeling will be anchored with her stress hormones in my cellular structure.

In Utero
* While floating in utero, I am downloading all my mother's experience into my cells, whether they are generative experiences or nongenerative. I also am taking in at least four generations back of my ancestors' experiences, on my mother's side.[24] I am taking in all my mother's stress hormones and other chemical reactions in her brain related to her present experience of life as they come through the umbilical cord into the placenta with the food/nourishment; I take them in as though these stress hormones and experiences are nourishment, too.
* If my mother tries to miscarry or abort me in utero, I will have the memory in my cells of the intrusion and the feelings that were projected toward me.

* If I am growing in a womb where a sibling died through abortion or miscarriage, that experience will be downloaded into my implicit memory.

Birth

* The three stages of the birth process are: 1) how I experience contractions, 2) what the passage through the birth canal is like, and 3) what I experience when I emerge into light and take my first breath. Like the in utero experiences, the actual birth experiences also stay in my cellular structure and are stored in my implicit memory. For example, if I were born via a late-stage cesarean surgery, that is encoded in my psyche as: "When I try and emerge, I make progress and then get stuck and collapse. Then I am put to sleep (by anesthetic)." This is such a powerful early encoding that I will act out the pattern in my life until it is named, heard, acknowledged, and becomes conscious.

Birth marks the first passage of development, of dying to the inner uterine world.

* If I am premature and have to live in an incubator, the feeling of being separated from my mother and the metal "wrongness" of the container of the incubator will be imprinted in my cellular memory as abandonment. The alignment to the Mother archetype will carry an experience of metal, rather than of flesh and blood.
* If I have operations performed on me, I may experience pain beyond what my nervous system can handle. This pain may be encoded in memory as torture, and the absence from my mother may be encoded as abandonment; any absence from being with my mother is encoded nongeneratively in my memory.

Early Infancy

* I am completely connected to my mother; she and I are one to me. Any life situation that affects her is downloaded by me into feelings. How she treats me is also internalized.
* If I am adopted at birth, I will feel a primal loss and abandonment. I shared a thirty-six to forty-week experience with a person I bonded with in utero, a person with whom I am biologically, genetically, historically, and, even more importantly, psychologically, emotionally, and spiritually connected.[25]
* If my mother is not available after birth because of illness, death, or complications, because I only have the perspective of egocentric information processing, I will encode my mother's absence as a primal abandonment, that she left because I wasn't lovable enough.[26]

Whatever my caregivers in her absence feel about me and about the situation of her illness or loss, I also will take into my implicit memory as a feeling about my worth and value.

Great Mother Archetype
* I am taking in how my mother and caregivers are feeling, how they treat me and feel about me, and I'm beginning to encode those feelings into patterns that are "background affect" stored in my implicit memory.

These patterns are pre-verbal structures of meaning. They are an enduring physical and psychological content that retains the power to affect the child now and in the future. These somatic patterns of feeling remain nonrepresentational at a pre-verbal level. For children as well as adults, they will be experienced as an emotional feeling that does not expand into a clearly felt emotion. They are a primitive somatic state that symbolizes interpersonal conditioning.

* If the content of these atmospheric feelings is positive, it evokes motivation to seek the actual object (e.g., caregiver, food, or help). If the content is conflicted, there will be a push-pull to the motivation of searching out the actual object. If the content is negative, it evokes motivation to withdraw from the actual object. This is how attachment styles and alignments to the Mother archetype are developed.
* Right now, I only know repeated stimuli, which creates a patterned expectation in me.
* I have a body that feels, and the blanket does not have feeling to me. This helps me come to a primitive realization that I am a body.

With this discovery, the self is no longer bound to the pleuromatic (undifferentiated state of unity with the mother that is unconscious) fusion with the world, but primitive identity is now connected to the body.

Great Mother Oral Stage
* I am different from my mother! She can leave me! *We call this "separation anxiety"; the realization can be a terrifying fulcrum of development for a child.*
* I make an image of mother I can hold in mind, a beginning image that has a perception, feelings, and sensations related to her. This helps me when she is absent.

* I make a symbol of mother to feel safe. This is an inner object. It has images and emotions that form an inner object, then I connect them with the binky or my Teddy or my blanket. Binky is Mom!
* I am my body and am separate from people and objects.

The child is now able to experience simple emotions such as tension, fear, rage, and satisfaction as well as anxiety, anger, desire, and security. Anxiety and anger are sustained at this age with images. Images are eventually connected with those atmospheric feelings, and images of the caregivers stabilize.

* I can now have some words stand for bigger ideas (e.g., potty, water, more, etc.).

This is the pre-verbal, oral stage of the Great Mother when the implicit memory is storing information and experiences in relationship to the infant's needs—needs to be touched, soothed, and to be seen in the mother's gaze for the preciousness of being. If any level of deprivation occurs, the infant introjects a compromised message of his or her value, worth, and importance.

Great Mother Anal Stage
* I am an emotional body-self and, if I have enough support, I will learn that my emotions are different from the emotions and feelings of others.
* I need to have the right to say "no" and "this is mine"—and to have that be respected.
* If I am traumatized by my parents (including through sexual, physical, or emotional abuse), I may not have a conscious memory of it, but it will be encoded in my implicit memory. Those memories will be activated when I encounter intimate relationships or when I am faced with trust, security, and boundary issues.
* If I feel trapped in abuse or neglect, I will automatically transfer that feeling into my encoding related to relationships.

This is the second stage of the Great Mother, a time for learning that personal boundaries can be respected. This is an early stage of ego development that is body oriented around the physical self. The child is preoccupied with basic needs, safety, and what others will provide him or her. Thoughts are very concrete and focus on "me," "mine," "I want," and "no." The child's ego is impulsive, protective, and self-centric.

Great Mother Genital Stage

* My genitals feel good to me, but I can easily be shamed if people get upset about my touching myself, and that shame goes into the implicit memory and is activated by intimate relationships.
* I'm integrating being able to feel *and* think. I'm a conceptual self now and can use my mind to repress feelings and needs that I do not think will help me to please others, get attention, or get along. I also can use my mind to integrate what I do feel and need.

As language emerges, the self-identity begins to shift from a solely biological body-self to a verbal-ego self that is no longer bound to the body but bound to a mental-ego self.

* I am trying to please the Great Mother by understanding and going by the rules. I will get rid of any needs or feelings that do not meet these rules. These rules are difficult to keep. I will not be able to hold a whole concept until I am at least six years old, so I do not really know what they are talking about or want from me.
* The questions I am asking are: Am I wanted? Am I safe? Am I important to you? Am I needed? Can I assert my needs and still be connected?

Wanting to be "good," the child can dissociate him- or herself from having a "bad," impulsive side, creating the first mental representation of him- or herself. This will not be available to his or her conscious mind but will be stored in the implicit memory.

* If I feel good about myself and can understand what is wanted of me, I feel valued and worthy. If I cannot understand what is wanted from me and am always getting told "no" and punished, I begin to feel as though I am not worthy and cannot trust my own authority.

Current research shows that explicit memory or a conscious memory begins to be developed by the age of seven when the hippocampus of the brain, responsible for memory, is developed and functioning and memories start to be stored in story form in the mind rather than in the cellular structure. Throughout our lives, however, we continue to store in implicit memory those experiences that are traumatic or stressful—experiences that are too overwhelming for the conscious mind or so stressful that the hippocampus in the brain is bypassed and not activated.[27]

Rescuing in the Implicit Memory

Ability of Stage	Capacity	Archetypal Developmental Stage
Sensorimotor intelligence	Sense of self in physical brain	Uroborus
Sensation, perception	Floating in Mother's womb	Uroborus
Exocept — primitive organization of memory traces and images	Downloads of environment and caregiver's feelings	Uroborus and Great Mother Stage 1
Images	Transitional object of caregiver	Great Mother
Symbols	"I exist as object in the world"	Great Mother
Endocept — preconscious cognition; an interrelationship of feelings and former experiences	Emotional brain comes online; Stage 1 creates magic for events too complex	Great Mother
Words		Great Mother
Rudimentary concepts		Great Mother
Rudimentary schemas		Great Mother
Rules, peer group, in/out group		Great Mother
Symbols		Separation of the World Parents
Goals	Intellectual brain online	Dragon Fights
Contexts		Birth of the Hero

17

The Archetypal Nature of Attachment

We need to shift from an egocentric focus to a focus that is neither negative nor positive—to just embracing what is and the beauty of our human experience. When we own our outer projections as our unique perception based on reactive states and early childhood experiences, we ultimately shift into a later developmental stage that brings us into a state of love toward ourselves and others. And then we are empowered to meet life's situations from this place of love!

Erich Neumann, in *The Child*, reminds us that the human child, in order to attain the degree of maturity that typifies the young of most other mammals at birth, requires a period of a year after birth, which Neumann calls the "extra-uterine embryonic phase."[28] During this time, though the physical body is already born, the Self or core being of the infant is not yet experienced as separate from that of the Mother; it is psychologically contained within her. Also, the baby's ego is still contained in the uroboros through the Mother. In other words, the nature of the relationship between Mother and child is not one of subject and object, but, by a kind of fluidity of being, a relationship of Mother-child-world that transcends both time and space. The Mother provides a "container" for the child's developing ego, just as she had previously provided the container for his or her developing physical body.

Both Margaret Mahler and Erich Neumann describe this relationship as a dual unity in which the Mother not only acts as the child's Self but also actually *is* that Self for the child. It is an archetypal experience, an uninterrupted continuum of being within the matrix of the Mother that is necessary for the infant to experience a "rightness or wholeness" of self from which to begin his or her separation or development process. The continuity and quality of this primal relationship is crucial, because it begins to form the tone, the archetypal alignments, for all subsequent relationships.

To recap, because the child only has a body reality at this point, the Mother functions as the ego. As the child grows and realizes that his or her body is a separate entity, he or she begins to develop a separate ego. At the same time, the archetypal Self is experienced as slowly withdrawing from the Mother, and a relationship is beginning to form between the ego and the Self. Within the schemas and layers of experiences with the primary caregiver(s), the relationship to others and to the child's own self is forming. As described in the last chapter, herein lie the moods and atmospheres that make up the positive or negative alignments to the Mother archetype existing within the implicit memory, later appearing in the adult as ambient emotional states, sometimes as a disposition or temperament. Let's use this archetypal framework as a backdrop to review attachment theory and subsequent life processes.

Overview of Attachment and Bonding

An infant is born ready and fully wired for a secure attachment; every baby has an innate expectation of a stable, loving, and responsive environment, one that provides basic trust, safety, security, and love. That secure attachment will support the child in creating and exploring.

All too often, however, babies must adapt to the limitations of their caregivers. When a child's innate drive for bonding is consistently met with an inconsistent response, an absence of response, and/or a dangerous response, then an insecure attachment is created through a repetition of this pattern and results in a nongenerative alignment with the Mother archetype. This alignment is pre-cognitive. Encoded in the implicit memory, it is generally not available to the conscious mind. The alignment is also encoded in the child's nervous system and impacts the internal imagery of the child.

When a child has a nongenerative alignment with his or her mother, the internal image of the Mother or caregiver is mixed—with worry or confusion, or with scary, dangerous images—so that when a child needs soothing and calming, his or her internalized image of the caregiver does not carry out that function. This leaves the child with a psychologically and socially dysfunctional "inner refuge." As Daniel Siegel states in *The Developing Mind*, "The pattern of communication between parent and child shapes the way the child's attachment system adapts to the experiences with the attachment figure. In this way, the genetically pre-programmed, inborn attachment system has been shaped by experience. This adaptation produces characteristic organizational changes in the way the child's mind develops."[29]

Depending on the kind of experiences that have shaped the alignment to the Mother archetype, the attachment solutions for coping with a dysfunctional inner refuge will fall into categories of attraction or aversion—"moving toward" or "moving away." That is, an insecure attachment, on a continuum, will reveal "moving toward" with anxiety, "moving away" with avoidance, or "freezing" and not knowing what to do. In the middle there can be a "moving against," which is a feeling of both attraction and aversion at the same time, sort of like having your foot simultaneously on the gas pedal and the brake.

> **Attachment styles** were first thoroughly researched by psychologist Mary Ainsworth in 1978. Since then, the research has been replicated numerous times with the same results. These classifications can be found in Daniel Siegel's book *The Developing Mind*, pp. 72-75.

The common classifications of infant attachment styles are:

- Secure or Autonomous
- Avoidant
- Resistant or Ambivalent
- Disorganized or Disoriented[30]

Following are descriptions of these attachments and their correlating adult responses:

Secure or Autonomous Attachment

Infants who experience their parents as being available, present, loving, close, and responsive to their emotional cues typically form a secure attachment with them. The children sense, "I can explore my environment, even when my parents are not present. I would prefer them but will interact easily with others and be happy to see my parents upon return."

What we generally see in adults who experienced secure attachment in infancy is an inner integrated sense of confidence and security with few or any unresolved issues from the past. These individuals consequently are more able to live in the present. They are able to form coherent and organized narratives about their lives that provide them meaning, and they can easily share these with others and their children.

Avoidant Attachment

Infants who experience their parents as being rejecting, emotionally unavailable, unresponsive, and/or lacking attunement to the infant's needs generally attach in an avoidant manner. These children determine, "It's too disappointing to not 'be met.' I just won't want to 'be met.' I'll deny all the needs that lead to that wanting. I won't respond to her when she comes back. I don't need contact. I don't have any needs.

Relationships aren't important. I'm on my own (i.e., feel like an outcast or alien). I'll just meet my own needs. I'll be self-sufficient and won't need others (and won't need anything). I won't see anyone else's needs either. I'll just focus on the future, then I'll get what I need."

What we generally see in adults who have developed avoidant attachment are people who are self-reliant, don't need others, and think they can take care of life circumstances best on their own. In terms of their life narrative, they tend to be dismissive, vague of childhood details, and may say, "I had good parents and a good family."

Resistant or Ambivalent Attachment
Infants who experience their parents as being *inconsistent* in their availability, presence, attunement, and responsiveness generally attach with themselves and others in an ambivalent or resistant style. These infants become challenging to console and soothe. They believe, "I can't count on anyone to show up. I could die! I just can't feel this fear all the time, but it's there. I keep trying to connect, but, when I do, I feel how mad/anxious/hurt/sad I am. They don't like that, so I'll hide it. I keep trying and trying. I wish I could feel better but don't know how."

Those who develop resistant or ambivalent attachment generally show up in therapy as adults who have a flow of narratives about childhood that has little to no separation between the stories and current life situations because there often is a replication of inconsistent attunement with others, even their children. They have a longing for closeness but simultaneously an intense fear of losing it.

Disorganized or Disoriented Attachment
Infants who experience their parents as being frightened, frightening, insecure, and/or disoriented in how they communicate generally form a disorganized or disoriented attachment. These infants, consequently, respond in a similar fashion (e.g., fall in a fetal position, freeze in a trance, or cling while gazing away from the parent). Actions mimic those of the parents and there is a feeling of: "Come here and go away! It's too dangerous to want connection; I can get hurt or disappointed or hit or scared. I want to feel connected, but then I am hurt by them. I want them and don't want them at the same time. I feel so confused. I don't feel anything at all anymore; I've gone kind of numb. I'll move toward someone and then move away."

As adults, those with disorganized or disoriented attachment generally manifest incoherence in their narrative life story as well as abrupt changes in their states of mind and ways of relating. They also often have challenges in regulating their emotional responses, difficulty coping, impaired abilities in attention and cognition, and tendencies toward freezing or dissociating under stressful or painful circumstances.

Dealing with Insecure Attachment

The steps a child goes through in the continuum of insecure attachment adaptations begin first with a protest. When that is not received and repaired, the child goes into despair (which can be read as anxiety). Then he or she experiences depletion, which can be experienced as confusion or numbness. Then resignation sets in (i.e., "I just won't have any needs"). Finally, there is detachment, freezing, or shutting down (i.e., "I just won't deal with this"), which completes the nongenerative alignment. See our companion chart of **"Insecure Attachment Styles"** for a more detailed look at each adaptation.

Heart-breaking statistics show that approximately forty-five percent of adults in the United States have one of the above forms of insecure attachment.[31] Studies also show that, overall, babies observed to have one of these forms of insecure attachment test the same when they become adults. This means that their inner refuge was not able to mature enough to support them. Consequently, because this nongenerative alignment to the Mother archetype is so strong, people having had insecure attachment to their mother/caregiver tend to see the world through an untrusting lens and project that viewpoint onto relationships, situations, institutions, partners, and children. They often feel like victims or tyrants.

In general, those who have formed insecure attachment styles have integrated a sense of not being good enough or of not having value and importance. Consequently, their early introjected nongenerative impressions—made before conscious memory, verbalization, or cognition—impact their responses to fear. When related to our physical safety and survival, fear is normal and can be a generative response to situations; think knowing that we can get burned if we put our hand on a stove burner. But fear based on our early impressions and attachment experiences (rather than being based on knowing the truth of who we are) creates reactive states that become nongenerative lenses of understanding. These lenses then color all of our life views, perceptions, and experiences.

When we view the world through a lens of fear or a reactive state, our perception and state of mind either feels like "I am a victim of the circumstances of life" or "I am a tyrant." These approaches to life seem to the hurt ego like appropriate ways to defend itself from the seeming danger viewed through the lens. Ultimately, this victim-tyrant polarity maintains an "us-them" way of relating to life and secures the ego in place. This position is typically defended and thought to be the absolute truth of what is taking place. Again, these perceptions are tainted by the life view seen through the nongenerative lens; they do not reflect the truth of the situation.

When caught in living from a victim-tyrant position, we view the world as unsafe and insecure. We believe someone or something is out to get us or has done us wrong.

Insecure Attachment Styles

	Resistant or Ambivalent	**Disorganized or Disoriented**	**Avoidant**
Relational Template	Not focused enough on self Needs other to be regulator	Too much fear to attach Had to go away from relationships "Intimacy is dangerous"	Over focus on self; dismisses others
Time Orientation	Preoccupied with the past Brain stuck on past injuries	Freeze, immobilized, depressed Disoriented in time	Focuses on the future; denies the past
Projection	"No one will be there" The glass is half empty "There is no help or sustaining love"	"The world is a scary place" "There is no truth" Everything really chaotic	"Life is unfair and wrong" "The world is dangerous" "I'll have what I need in the future"
Inner Turmoil	Creates an uncertainty about what is true inside and out; doubt prevails	Creates a confusion and a fractured sense of own coherence	Can create violent and aggressive thoughts and a dislike of harmony and unity
Need	To feel present safety; practice prolonging pleasure Develop inner guidance Inner refuge	Needs trusting, welcoming, steady relationships To develop inner and outer protector Inner refuge	Needs a welcome in the world, kind gazing eyes, corrective experiences Inner and outer refuge

We may respond either by retaliating and being a tyrant toward the other or by becoming submissive and victimized and needing to withdraw to feel safe. This is the major dynamic that causes suffering in the human condition (toward ourselves and others). This dynamic also keeps us from transcending and realizing our true nature as our beautiful essence and being.

Let's examine a common example of this nongenerative dynamic: Someone says something that hurts our feelings, so we go into a rage and then want to hurt that person in return. The rage reaction typically surpasses the actual incident. We are in a reactive state and feel certain that our lens of perception is absolutely true. Our inner dialogue solidifies this and becomes centered on the hurt. We think, for instance, "How dare you do that! If you really cared about me, this would never have been said." Our thoughts then turn to plans of how to retaliate, dismiss, or hold on to the feelings. Do we hurt ourselves or say something to the other person to help understand the hurt? All are forms of either being a victim or a tyrant toward others or ourselves.

A second example is another hurt person, like the above example. This person, however, holds her feelings in. She also blames herself for having the feelings (e.g., "I am too much and need too much") and believes she is the reason the hurt occurred. She then turns the reactive state inward, does not deal with the hurt—and typically becomes physically ill.

Our reactive states are significant in our healing and in bringing consciousness to the early untrue impressions we took in around attachment and connection to another. When we can honor and give voice to these reactive states as hurt places inside, we can use them as guiding forces or pointers to what needs attention. When we remain in our reactive states and cling to our biased positions, however, healing is prolonged and our patterns are continually replicated with little or no established meaning.

To align with our essential being takes transcending the divisive victim-tyrant state. This involves refusing to adhere to an us-them viewpoint—refusing to participate in being either a victim or a tyrant in our relationships and in our worldview. This transcendence is quite challenging. We must ameliorate the results of our early attachment, so we can form secure attachments and realize our true nature. We must change our lens of perception from fear (i.e., "There is something or someone creating difficulty in my life.") and surrender to the belief that "all is as it is." In other words, we need to shift from an egocentric focus to a focus that is neither negative nor positive—to just embracing what is and the beauty of our human experience. When we own our outer projections as our unique perception based on reactive states and early childhood experiences, we ultimately shift into a later developmental stage that brings us into a state of love toward ourselves and others. And then we are empowered to meet life's situations from this place of love!

18

Early Development's Relationship with Our Journey to the Treasure

A generative alignment to the Mother archetype creates an inner refuge that is truly an inner home base of security. There we find love and acceptance. There we find trust, relaxation, and generosity that automatically awakens those same qualities in us.

As explained in the last chapter, our underlying mood atmospheres originate in our early attachments with caregivers and become our archetypal alignment. In order to develop and proceed from our inner into our outer world, for a time we shut the door on the archetypal world and repress both the incredible potential and the deep wounds we received when our needs were not met in early life. Once the ego matures, however, our underlying mood atmospheres reawaken. They, in fact, often push the ego into embarking upon its journey of reintegrating those missing potentials and reactive states[32] connected with early childhood, releasing the repressed atmospheres of early alignments by advancing through the archetypal developmental stages of Rescuing the Captive and Gaining the Treasure. Michael Washburn, in his seminal work *The Ego and the Dynamic Ground*, summarizes this developmental progression when he writes: ". . . [O]nce the ego is strong and fully developed, it no longer needs to be separated from the Dynamic Ground. . . . In time, [the repression of the unconscious] becomes an unnecessary and unwarranted obstacle to the ego's higher developmental destiny. It becomes a way in which the ego is held back from meeting its ultimate spiritual Ground."[33]

Because they reside in the deep, pre-cognitive structures of implicit memory, re-awakening mood atmospheres do not appear as constructed psychological reality and are, therefore, not easily recognizable to the ego. Instead, they manifest as pervasive feeling states, like membranes over natural consciousness. They might emerge at different times as moods such as happiness, sadness, agitation, or inadequacy—depending upon the generativity of a child's early life. We experience them as our pervasive awareness or as a background feeling tone that has no connection to our normal, everyday life. People will say, "I don't know why; I just feel sad today," or "I have an ongoing sense of disappointment, but I'm not sure what I am disappointed about," or "I feel great, although there's no special reason for my happiness."

The Clinical Work with Pre-Cognitive Structures

Clients come to us when their pervasive feeling states are negative. They have underlying feelings of uneasiness anchored in nongenerative archetypal alignments, and yet they sorely want to feel basic trust and safety. As therapists, our job is to help them to develop the ego strength and witnessing power to clear their nongenerative, primitive alignments (which we are calling pre-cognitive structures) so they can fully live their Treasure and full potential. To help these clients, we must revisit their earliest life.

Babies are busy learning what their body is, what the world is, how the two work together, and what being in relationship is like. When a child is not cared for with deep love and sensitivity—and is instead disrupted by unresponsive or inappropriate caregiving—that child cannot attune to his or her own rhythms and often feels as though his or her nervous system is over stimulated. He or she becomes upset, angry, and unsettled in his or her exploration and in being open, loving, and responsive. In addition, learning that the parent is unreliable and unavailable, the child begins to encode that the world is also unreliable and unavailable. This interferes with having a sense of mastery and control over events. The child, instead, believes he or she has little or no power to change things. He or she ultimately develops a sense of helplessness and hopelessness and/or begins to rest in anger and frustration.[34] This alignment is then wired into the child's nervous system—and impacts the child's entire life.

Another way to look at this trajectory is to examine how a client's early experiences developed his or her internal imagery of a caregiver. If as a child the client was met with anxiety, fear, and/or confusion when he or she needed the calming, soothing, and consistency of a consoling Mother, then anxiety, fear, and/or confusion will have become the client's inner refuge, shaping the client's relationships and life in general. Even that most important of relationships with the Self would be shrouded in anxiety, fear, and/or confusion.

Renowned child development expert Ed Tronick, in *The Neurobehavioral and Social-Emotional Development of Infants and Children*, notes: "Mood states function to organize behavior and experience over time. . . . Moods are . . . long-lasting affect states that develop out of the interaction of two individuals, rather than solely being generated intra-psychically."[35] We, thus, attract relationships that reenact the early patterning of attachment and the archetypal alignments that the moods are expressing. (This is why we sometimes have relationships with people who even seem inappropriate to the conscious mind.) When not understood nor addressed, those moods can turn into full-blown reactive approaches toward life in general.

As noted, nongenerative pre-cognitive structures will manifest as moods or reactive states. These emerge as various feelings at different times throughout our lives. In adulthood, we might feel:

- Discontent; life doesn't quite feel right
- Despair; this can be connected to the pervasive state of wanting to die or the fear we will die
- Sadness or a sense of melancholy
- Loneliness, even when we are with loved ones
- Anxiety, even though nothing is coming up we have reason to fear
- Depressed
- Something is missing, but we don't know what it is
- We don't "belong" or wonder if we were adopted
- Like an "alien"
- We don't really exist, that we are not really alive
- We are "fake" and will be found out
- Everything is unfair
- Everything is wrong
- We are unsafe, even when nothing bad is happening
- We want to hide or isolate ourself
- We are unloved

The Archetypal Pattern Analysis approach to therapy takes these underlying feelings seriously. Knowing that the psyche is offering up these feelings as a way to try and bring long-ago experiences into conscious awareness, we strive to translate them into their historical context. Through our trusting relationship with the client and keeping a secure therapeutic container, we work with changing the alignment to a client's inner refuge—because as the inner refuge becomes generative, the patterned behavior, neural webs, and nongenerative moods drop away, like a butterfly leaves the cocoon.

In summary, underlying moods of defensiveness, aloneness, sadness, despair, and the like are nongenerative archetypal alignments to life. They reveal reactive states from long ago that need to be dismantled. Our work as analysts is to help our clients shift their reactions to an alignment with a generative inner refuge that provides:

- A safe environment
- Safe authorities
- A safe world
- Safe people
- In general, a secure place in which to rest
- Opening to and discovering our true nature as safety and unconditional love

Having a generative inner refuge takes the ability to relax completely and to enjoy our deep experience of just being. When there is this real relaxation, judgment and worry begin to dissolve, our defenses begin to fall away, and we become more able to open our hearts to the miracle of our being. Relaxation, however, first requires a basic sense of trust and safety. We need to feel we have a place of protection that is always with us. Grounded in this peace, we can then respond to situations in a trusting and safe way, no matter what life brings.

From an archetypal perspective, a generative alignment to the Mother archetype creates an inner refuge that is truly an inner home base of security. There we find love and acceptance. There we find trust, relaxation, and generosity that automatically awakens those same qualities in us. Trusting in this inner refuge builds an inner and outer environment of trust and safety.

....

Adult Attempts to Attain a Safe and Trusting Refuge

We all have an innate expectation of being held in a stable, loving, responsive environment, one that provides basic trust, safety, and security. When this does not occur, or only partially occurs, our young self attempts to create a stabilization with the limited tools we have when we are young. Each attempt at creating a safe and trusting environment is anchored in a refuge that cannot quite provide the secure base that is needed for real thriving. Each is resting in a pervasive mood that reveals the reactive attitude. In adulthood, people manifest those moods and may attempt to attain that inner refuge in a variety of ways, many that are not generative. Some of those ways follow:

Reactive vs. Generative Refuge

Reactive Refuge	Generative Refuge	Therapist Position
Surviving; trying to be perfect	Really living, thriving	Welcomed and wanted
Believing there is no help; collapsing and despairing	Taking in abundance and support	Supporting and nurturing with good boundaries, morals, and ethics
"I have to rely only on myself."	Trusting there is help	Collaborating with therapist
Focus on power or control	Enjoying others; having real intimacy	Having an equal and intimate relationship with therapist
"I can have myself or others."	Having freedom while also being close with others	Believing you don't have to take care of therapist, that your needs are most important
Emphasis on achieving, proving worth	Accepting intrinsic value and worth	Accepting you are ok just the way you are; deregulating nervous system
"In the future, I will be fine and have what I want."	Believing it's ok to manifest dreams, be grounded in the world, and still feel free	Being a solid presence to bounce off of, keeping solid conditions
Believing life is unfair, wrong, unsafe	Having a just and balanced inner world	Accepting what is in the moment; authority is hearing the unfairness
Not being any trouble is important	Having needs met and being loved	"What are your needs?"
Thinking that thinking and learning will solve everything	"I am more than my thoughts."	Practicing mindfulness and deconstruction

Trying to Get Safety from the Environment
- **Through control:** By trying to control things, events, and/or people, we are acting out an expectation of trust not being met, a fear of something happening that we won't like, or a fear of a reenactment of a past hurt or disappointment. Control also serves to "keep a lid" on all the feelings of chaos and overstimulation of our nervous system. By taking control of everything ourselves, we are attempting to build a safe and trusting environment.
- **Through doing everything "my way":** By fighting for doing things only "my way," we attempt to create a safe and trusting environment. This is very limiting and precludes collaborating or bringing in new ideas.
- **By forcing things to happen:** We imagine we can feel a basic sense of safety and trust once particular things happen. Sometimes we plan excessively for a future event, hoping a sense of safety and trust will occur at that future time. This creates an alignment with the future rather than the present. It is like putting roots in water instead of earth.
- **Through perfection:** We think that, if we can just make everything look or seem perfect, we will have a safe and trustworthy environment. This includes the body being cut into "the right shape," wearing the "right" fashionable clothing, having our hair or home furnishings looking "just right," and having the perfect car, cellphone, house, job, and more.
- **By holding certain beliefs of faith and religious preference:** Although we may believe that religious faith protects us, it can often be an attempt to create a safe environment. It also can easily manifest into fundamentalist thinking. For example, think of the terrorist who believes that suicide by bomb ensures having a safe environment in heaven or in the future.
- **By following rigid rules:** We may believe that, if we follow certain rules of conduct that seem black and white, we will be safe. Unfortunately, true safety is not based upon these rules but on a higher order of being able to deal with whatever life presents.

Trying to Get Safety by Seeing the World as Dangerous or Perverse
- **By distrusting authority figures:** By holding a pervasive protective sense that all authority figures and those in power are dangerous or incompetent, we are attempting to create a safe and trusting environment.
- **By blaming or defending:** By pushing away others through blame or defensiveness, we can pretend we have a safe and trusting environment.
- **By being suspicious:** By believing that everyone can't be trusted, we are attempting to create a safe and trusting environment.

- **Through paranoia:** By assuming that something or someone is "out to get me" (e.g., IRS, government, employer, banks, Monsanto, cable company, etc.), we are attempting to create a safe and trusting environment.
- **Through self-imposed seclusion:** By hiding or being invisible, we are attempting to create a safe and trusting environment.

Trying to Get Safety Through the Mind
- **By wanting to know everything:** Thinking "If I just know what is happening or everything there is to know, I will be safe" is an attempt to create an atmosphere of basic trust and safety through the mind.
- **Through anxiety:** Holding states of tension such as worrying or being anxious about something, as an attempt to ward off bad things, is a way of trying to have a trusting and safe world.
- **By thinking all the time:** By keeping the mind constantly busy thinking and imagining, we attempt to create an atmosphere of basic trust and safety through the mind.
- **By judging others:** By judging or labeling others, we are trying to keep an unsafe world at bay and to rule out what will or won't lead to a safe and trusting environment.
- **Through comparison with others:** By feeling superior in comparison to other people or objects, we are trying to create a safe and trustingly ordered world.
- **Through constant busy-ness:** Being overly busy—constantly doing, doing, doing—keeps the fear of being left or abandoned at bay or helps us to feel that we matter and are important. This attempts to create a safe, trusting environment in the spin of doing.
- **Through activism:** By fighting for justice and balance in the outer world, we are often attempting to make a safe and trustworthy environment inside.

Trying to Get Safety Through People
- **By striving to be the center of attention:** Trying to be clever or the center of attention is often a way of creating the missing gaze of attention and to feel trust and safety.
- **Through constantly pleasing others:** Pleasing and/or caregiving others are often ways of trying to create an atmosphere of trust and safety.
- **By being the peacemaker:** Smoothing things over is another way of trying to create a safe environment.

- **By being a "martyr"**: Enduring an out-of-balance situation or relationship is yet another way to keep a sense of having a safe and trusting environment.

Using the Reactive States in Therapy

The above reactive attitudes toward life flow from the early attachment experiences and the patterns that were created in early alignments with caregivers. They show the way we attempt to create safety from a very young age by trying to solve the problem of having to react and not being able to rest in the trust and safety of our family. These attitudes are developed from a very young perspective. Once they begin to be exposed, they can, with some mentoring, open into a larger perspective.

If a client has any of the above reactive feelings, we begin therapy with the working theory that his or her childhood involved some stress or even danger. If appropriate, we may suggest that the client start gathering information by putting out in daily view old pictures from his or her early childhood or by reviewing information from siblings, relatives, or family friends that may allow memories to surface. We do this because events in the first few years of life are rarely remembered cognitively, yet are encoded and deeply felt. Often, we will find overwhelming stressors in the family's past that help to explain the context of the feelings. Recall that what we have taken in from our parents' implicit memories of their own early experiences is transferred to us unconsciously.[36] Or we might find that a prior generation had horrible circumstances that were passed unconsciously through epigenetics to the client.

Fragments of memories and snippets of information begin to form a jigsaw-puzzle-like picture; the pieces construct a past that has some connection to the unknowable truth. By connecting current unexplainable experiences to a historical context, the client can shift from a self-defeating inner dialogue (e.g., "I must just be unlovable. I'm bad and don't deserve what I want. I don't belong here. I have to put them first in order to feel loved and safe. If I don't hurry up, I'll be left behind.") to self-understanding, self-acceptance, and self-forgiveness. Remember that such devastating early conclusions were made with a very young perspective, and just like computer operating systems, they need to be updated.

In truth, we, as therapists, function as good caregivers. We help our clients to re-align to the generative aspects of self rather than to the experiences that were coded into their pre-cognitive, pre-verbal unconscious nervous system. It is as if the client and therapist are going back in time, with the therapist simplifying and personalizing the child's early experience, so that the client can now make sense of a mood or a reactive state that occurs consistently in his or her present life. For instance, a client might say, "I just feel so sad all the time." Translated, this becomes, "A very young part of me is trying to communicate how sad I felt when I was left for hours alone in my crib while my mother was ill. I just wanted someone to come and pick me up. That's why I have felt so helpless all my life." These moods are like a breadcrumb trail to our wholeness; they exist so that we will find the captive left behind in the early stages of development.

When we could no longer bear being left alone, we begin to disassociate from a deep need. By helping our clients to discover the missing links of early childhood experiences and to see through the dilemmas and impressions of their early childhood, we empower them to translate a pervasive mood and repair their attachment disruptions and early impressions introjected from relationships with the mother/caregiver as well as the father in his role with these early childhood experiences. In this way, we, as therapists, help to set our clients on new paths to realizing their true essence and potential.

19

Unconscious Communication: Translating the Expression of the Psyche

The psyche is relentless in its expression because of its innate need for growth toward wholeness and fullness of being. If not "heard and understood," the psyche will attempt new means for growth, always holding the realization of our true being, the Self, as the destination.

C.G. Jung valued individuation as the developmental process we experience throughout our lives, with the ultimate goal being to align with our soul's purpose and meaning—and to live from this vantage point. This inner journey is one of gaining more and more consciousness by working consciously to bridge the unconscious realms with the conscious domain, gaining later levels of consciousness and developmental stages. The depth of the individuation process comes when we form a conscious relationship with our unconscious domain and are actively engaged in bridging what is conscious with the mystery of the deep unconscious world. Here we commit to going into the underworld to rescue the parts of ourselves left behind and "held captive" in earlier stages. During our heroic quests, we face and resolve many of the shadow aspects, inner demons, and complexes that veil and act as an amnesic barrier covering our true nature.

Setting the Foundation for Growth and Development

It is commonly thought that approximately ten percent of the psyche is the conscious mind, comprised of content that is known, factual, intellectualizations, and associations. The remaining subconscious shadow, deep unconscious, and collective unconscious material is vast and unknown to the conscious mind. In this vastness live our core patterns that were created from beginning life in the womb as well as from our early infant pre-cognitive and pre-verbal experiences as well as the introjections from early experiences with our caregivers, particularly our mother. In general, our early conditioning veils us from our essential nature, like an amnesia barrier, as the ego forms. But the Self and its unconscious messages are a loving force attempting to bring our attention back to the source of our being.

Listening to only the *conscious* mind for information in associations, facts, and what is already known limits the information available from the psyche and keeps our true nature veiled from consciousness. It keeps us trapped in the limitations of the stories and patterns of the inner dialogue of the mind and the superego. Rather, it is the *unconscious* encoded messages conveyed from the Self that, when translated and understood, help us dissolve the veils and awaken to our essential nature as aware consciousness.

The innate wisdom of the unconscious makes itself known through encoded messages, using images given to us repeatedly throughout our daily lives. This wisdom also reveals itself in our intuition and inner guidance and requires conditions, moral standards, and ethics that are generative and support healthy growth and development. Learning how to translate these images and their themes creates a bridge between the conscious and unconscious material in service of our realizing our essential nature.

When these encoded messages are not understood or able to be translated, they cycle back into the unconscious again. Thus, learning to understand and decode these messages is important to our ability to shift our archetypal alignments and patterns to ones that are generative—and to our ability to see the inner dialogue for the untruth that it is. This takes accessing the wisdom of the deep unconscious Self that is giving us what is needed through encoded messages of images and unconscious communication. We are then able to begin living from our potential as the Treasure Within.

Being engaged in this process of being conscious is a major contribution in rescuing the young parts of self in the early symbiotic relationship with the mother and the development of implicit memory. According to Erich Neumann and current epigenetic and neurobiology research, the first seven years of life are body focused, as we are developing our inner emotional life. Early patterns develop based on whether we formed a secure or insecure attachment, and the generative or nongenerative archetypal alignments to the Great Mother. These alignments are based upon whether the mandate of the archetype of Mother is met. This inner life development sets the stage for how the budding ego is shaped as we enter the mental, conceptual outer world of the Father archetype, whether we begin from a limited state or from feeling secure.

The Deep Unconscious Reveals Itself

As will be explored in the chapter on "Images Appearing in Dreams, Visions, and Daydreams in Each Archetypal Stage," the ways the deep unconscious reveals itself to the conscious mind in unconscious communication come in several forms including:

- Narrative stories in the forms of derivative images and themes
- Dreams with derivative images and themes
- Synchronicities
- Wisdom of the body and the psyche
- Illnesses and symptomology in the body

As learned from Michael Conforti, in Archetypal Pattern Analysis we translate images to bring consciousness to what is being expressed and conveyed from the psyche, bridging what is unconscious with the conscious mind. We examine these images and themes as the experience of a person's inner world, perceptions, and projections, and as the patterns and themes being worked in the therapeutic relationship.

Signs of a Captive

In the Body
Illness, disease, chronic structural issues, chronic tension in the nervous system or in specific places in the body. Negative feelings and thoughts about the body such as "I'm sure I smell, I look awful, I'm ugly, I'm fat," etc. Oral addictions and sexual addictions.

In the Emotions
Negative chronic emotional states that show up in thoughts such as "I'm invisible, I feel lost a lot of the time, I'm unlovable, I'm bad, I hate myself, I'm empty inside, I'm always lonely, I'm always hiding, I feel invisible, I feel constricted and want to run, I'm always sad, I'm always angry," etc.

In the Mind
Negative mental states that show up in thoughts such as "I feel like an alien, I must have been adopted, I don't belong anywhere, I'm a fake and will be found out, I chronically distrust, I've been betrayed all my life, I worry all the time about the past and/or future, I have a constant fear of dying, I'll never find love," etc.

In the Spirit
All the above are blocks to opening to our true nature including internal stances toward our highest potential. This shows up in thoughts such as "I'm not worthy of God's love, or I'm really possessed by the devil."

The renowned psychiatrist Dr. Robert Langs (1928-2014), in his groundbreaking book *Fundamentals of Adaptive Psychotherapy and Counseling*, speaks about the "emotion-processing mind" of the psyche as an adaptive system based upon coping strategies that are responding to triggers in our inner and outer world. These emotional triggers prompt the deep unconscious to send encoded messages to help stabilize the system from overwhelm and maintain homeostasis. They also help to metabolize the experiences from our daily life. Langs sees this to be the purpose of dreams, synchronicities, and encoded derivative communication from the deep unconscious.[37]

The messages come in encoded form, because the information is so emotionally charged that it is unbearable to awareness when experienced. Decoding the messages is the primary way the conscious mind can assimilate the deep unconscious intelligence. As a part of that unconscious intelligence, Langs refers to two primary forms of defense: One is the immune system that defends the body against microscopic predators that can cause us harm and illness. The second is the emotional-processing mind that defends against outside predators or fears of being harmed by the world and daily life.

How to decode these triggers is important to understand, because it is what a person is working through that prompts the deep unconscious to respond with a dream, derivative communication, or a message from the immune system. These triggers are emotionally charged happenings from the day or recent events not yet mastered. The triggers in dreams or narrative stories evoke themes to aid in our ability to decode the images.

Derivatives are thematic narrative ways of communicating that need to be decoded like a dream, only in narrative or story form. They are in response and adaptation to these emotional triggers. The source of most of these triggers is locked into the early emotional reactive states in implicit memory where we feel insecure or need to feel respected, adequate, and cared for. These reactive states are highly charged from these unconscious, pre-cognitive memories and are projected onto others or the world, as if they are a true perception. Just as we believe the inner perception of self to be true, we also believe our outer perception holds a similar quality of truth.

....

Translating Images of the Psyche: The Orientational Approach

Jungian analyst Yoram Kaufmann (1940-2009) introduced what he called the "Orientational Approach" in his revolutionary book, *The Way of the Image*.[38] In this approach, Dr. Kaufmann describes how an image arises from an informational field like a wave from the ocean. Each image, by definition, refers to or carries the information from which it arises. By contemplating the image and its essence, we begin to intuit more of the field from which it rises. Its origins begin to present themselves. This field of information the image carries orients us to what world we are entering; it also verifies that we need to have only that specific image to tell the story.

For example, in speaking, the deep unconscious presents us with images in narrative form. Like a good storyteller, its communication can light up the receiver's mind with an image that is a holographic representation of the complete state of the informational field the image represents. Good filmmakers know this and often begin seeding the mind of the movie viewer from the first image; the setting and the music symbolically let us know what the whole movie will be about.

In Archetypal Pattern Analysis, we move from *interpreting* images, themes of dramas and narrative stories, physical symptoms of illnesses, dreams, collective processes, movies, and the like into a direct *translation* of "what is dominant about the image being expressed by the wisdom of the psyche?" "Translating" is staying true to the image, to the objective expression of the image, and to what the deep unconscious is attempting to express. We consider, "What is this image?" In staying with its *objective* meaning, we *translate* it by staying true to what the image is and its essence (its characteristics and properties) rather than *interpret* it by projecting our or the client's personal associations on the image. In fact, the common practice of *interpreting* images most often involves personal associations made by the client and the practitioner; these personal associations are known in our *subjective* experience and are the common content of the conscious mind. *Translating* an image for its *objective* expression, on the other hand, involves a pure listening to the encoded message of the deep unconscious. This message most often disagrees with what is being expressed through the familiar patterns of the conscious mind. In essence, the image in its purest form is attempting to provide innate wisdom way beyond the conditioning of our familiar patterning; this wisdom will help us shift the patterning to be aligned with our wholeness.

As noted numerous times thus far, the psyche is relentless in its expression because of its innate need for growth toward wholeness and fullness of being. If not "heard and understood," the psyche will attempt new means for growth, always holding the realization of our true being, the Self, as the destination. It is our job, as analysts, to help our clients translate their images and patterns in service of knowing their true nature, in service of understanding how they are currently functioning, and in service of learning what is needed for change and wholeness. We do this by asking questions such as: What is this image? What makes this image what it is, versus another image? What is the mandate of the archetype of the image? Why did the psyche pick this image or story out of the millions of possibilities that could have been chosen? Like film directors, we see that the purpose of a client's images is to tell a specific story, unknown and as yet unrevealed to the conscious mind.

We do not view the expression of the psyche as pathological. Rather, we see the psyche's images and patterns as expressions of what is needed for the next step in transformation. When we look at an image and its objective nature, it orients us to its informational field and to what "world" we have entered. For example, in a dream with images of playing an instrument in an orchestra, we have entered the field of being a professional musician. In a dream of being inside a beautiful, large building, we have entered the field of architecture. Both have specific properties and mandates that are different from other fields, and these properties and mandates are important to understand in order to translate the images.

As Dr. Conforti states, every image is archetypal and brings with it a set of mandates and guidelines. So, when we encounter a particular image, we need to determine its objective nature by finding its *dominant* objective nature (i.e., what this image is, its essence, and its characteristics), which also orients us to a set of constraints and mandates involved with the image. Through translating images and the aligning patterning of our clients, we can identify what archetypal fields they are favoring and begin the process of clearing nongenerative patterns. This clearing can interrupt patterns on all levels of being (mental, emotional, physical, and spiritual), allowing new, generative information into the system.

Remember: *Translating* differs from *interpreting*. Interpretation of images and patterns tends to be aligned with what is subjective, in that it includes our own and our clients' personal associations, reflections, and projections already known to the conscious mind. Granted, the subjective does have importance in understanding a person, situation, or collective process, as it points to the dissonance between the conscious mind patterns and what is being revealed by the deep unconscious. However, if we work only with the subjective, we fail to hear the depth of the unconscious process of the psyche and the pattern that is not yet consciously known or revealed. Staying with the subjective can actually facilitate the repetition of a nongenerative pattern. It also can increase the likelihood of entrainment between the practitioner and client or system, holding the patterning in a compulsive, repetitive process.

Entrainment is a process of morphic resonance, when fields influence and vibrate in harmony. That is, like attracts like. As noted in Chapter Four, "Patterns in the Natural World and the Psyche," a common example is when two clocks with varying ticking patterns are hung next to one another and they begin ticking in accordance with the other. So, in our approach to therapy, we are mindful of the commonality of entrainment between people and patterning, and the frequency in which repetition occurs, when we give credence to the subjective realm. For this reason, we attempt to stay true to the objectivity of the image(s). The objective approach also honors the sacredness of what the unconscious is expressing as innate wisdom and as its wish to be heard and understood.

In the Orientational Approach to the psyche, Kaufmann emphasizes the great importance of objective wisdom in translating images. His student, Dr. Conforti, likewise engrained in us the importance of the objective realm, or an image's dominant objective nature, which stays true to a particular image as a direct definition of the archetype: what it is, its defining aspects, where it is found in the natural world, and how it occurs there. Through our work with Dr. Conforti, we learned to stay with objective knowledge while practicing therapy, focusing on how an image would orient us to a specific informational field, innate only to that image. Once oriented, we then encounter an unfolding story, much like the opening paragraphs of a novel or the opening scenes of a play. That story ultimately allows a deeper understanding to unfold and the conscious mind to gain more consciousness.

Applications for reading patterns and translating the objective meaning of the unconscious are numerous. The work may be in therapeutic environments, in consultation with an organization, or in looking at current collective processes in the world. For example, we can pay attention to repeated images and themes in movies or bestselling books; predict the trajectory of a process based on its initial conditions, current situations, and dramas; untangle legal situations and disputes; or even understand nongenerative patterns and processes that are revealed through illnesses and disease processes. To do this, our process involves meticulously researching the dominant objective aspects of the images involved before we translate the objective mandate of the images or patterns into the psychological realm. If this work is done in psychotherapy, we are translating patterns and forming appropriate interventions. If consulting with organizations, we focus on translating the expression of collective processes. If relating to media, books, and movies, or if exploring the likelihood of success for a new product or movie based on its archetypal congruence, we assist in staying true to the archetypal mandate. As an important part of the data we collect, we generally include subjective associations; this allows us to examine any discrepancies between the conscious mind's interpretation and the objective mandate of the images being revealed by the unconscious psyche. Then we can see the patterns and shifts needed to come into full generative alignment with the psyche's wholeness of the Self or with an organization's work in the world. Or we can help clear the patterns innate in the disease process in a body as well as help produce a product or movie that will be highly respected and acclaimed. In short, much can be transformed when we create a bridge between the unconscious information expressed by the psyche and the conscious mind. Once we know and understand the unconscious and its patterning, then we can take action toward change.

The naming of the replicative process of the patterning creates a bifurcation point; the system can choose new growth and meaning, which can then be integrated as a new understanding and change in behaviors. At bifurcations, we are given the opportunity to make a choice—whether to stay with what is familiar and known, keeping the system closed, or to change, allowing new information in and moving into unknown territory that can be unsettling and frightening in the change process. Because new information is made available, there is a movement into greater complexity and an opening in the closed system. This choice for change can create a great deal of anxiety and fear and needs our caring support, listening, and naming the psyche's next step to aid in its success.

As Michael Conforti states, "The nature of closed systems is that they remain refractory to new information and, in so doing, further subsidize the prior replication. The individual has an opportunity to use the repetition either as an opportunity for change and what will disturb the system and move it towards greater complexity and meaning (negentropy) or to remain in the same replicative cycle (entropy)."[39]

We find that when the psyche and its unconscious messages are named and fully heard, when the psyche's purpose is fully understood and honored by the conscious mind of clients, then major shifts toward generativity begin to innately happen. Clients typically feel a sense of relief in finally understanding their repetitive cycle of patterns and feel the support of the psyche's wisdom and guidance. This then helps them feel the confidence needed to make choices on their own behalf at these seminal times of bifurcation.

Derivative Communication Examples in Everyday Life

As a part of daily life, we encounter examples of unconscious communication in narrative stories, both in our communication and with others. Unless we understand how to decode these, we are handicapped in our ability to understand others and what they are attempting to convey. Let's consider this example:

While on a walk one day, I encountered a man sitting alone in his open garage smoking a cigar; a lovely cat was curled up by the man's feet. I had seen the man sitting there alone several times before today. I commented on his beautiful cat, and this was his response: "He is a cat that has been around for about three years. He's a garage cat. He likes to just stay in here and hang out. He isn't much interested in the other animals and people upstairs. He's not afraid of the dog; they pretty much leave each other alone. But he prefers to stay in the garage here. He'll go out a little bit, you know, just a few feet out here, but that's about all. I think he's afraid he will get locked out because that happened once, and we found him in the bushes over there."

As trained analysts, we would be able to see that this man's story about his cat had a deeper message: He was trying to convey that, like his cat, he needed time for himself.

For additional examples of the power of listening to derivative communication, let us turn to the work of Archetypal Pattern Analyst Anna O'Brien. O'Brien has researched derivative communication and examples specifically in conditions of trade or agreements. For purposes of education, she has agreed to share some stories herein that can be helpful to someone in the process of hiring new employees or contractors. By listening carefully to the narrative stories of potential hires, we can learn valuable information (whether the potential hires are moral, ethical, good at their craft, etc.) that will help us determine whether or not to hire them. Remember, each story introduces us to an informational field and a pattern the person is conveying to us.

"Someone hires a contractor to repair a porch. When the job is almost completed, the contractor talks about being 'short changed' at several of his last jobs."

A simple *interpretation* of this communication may be made that the contractor is afraid of being "stiffed" at his current job. This, however, is also the kind of story told by contractors who unconsciously are warning the person that they cannot be trusted to complete the job as per their agreement. Sure enough, the contractor did not do all that was agreed upon and tried to get payment anyway.

"While slicing a cut of meat for a customer, a butcher tells a story about purchasing a shirt online that did not meet his expectations for quality and caused him to be upset."[40]

Such interactions happen to us often on a daily basis, and then we wonder why we are disappointed with what we have received! The comments are not accidental; rather, they are unconscious communication about, in this case, the quality of the meat. The shopper is going to be disappointed if she serves it to her guests.

"The owner of a boutique is very pleased and also surprised with an order of blouses the salesman brought her (which seemed like an unusual opportunity to make extra profit). The salesman tells this story during the transaction: 'This reminds me of a story I once heard about a fortune cookie manufacturer. It seems that this company made two kinds of fortune cookies. One contained standard family-friendly fortunes for the restaurants, and the other offered pornographic fortunes for private parties.

Well, sure enough, they mixed up the orders one day and sent scads of porno fortune cookies off to the family restaurants. Nobody knew until customers began opening cookies at their tables. There must have been some pretty irate people. I don't know if the cookie makers ever recovered.'"

In this communication, the salesman clearly links the blouse order with the mix-up in fortune cookies, and that there was a very undesirable and hurtful outcome. Anna O'Brien explains in her book, *Hawk Wisdom*, how to translate this story. She says, "During any type of transaction, learn to mentally step inside the story you hear. Imagine how you would feel if this story were happening to you. Remember that the thematic 'field' of the story transcends time and place. It can be an unconscious replication of an archetypal pattern pulling toward the truth of a situation."[41] In the case of the boutique owner, when she checked the blouse order, she found that many of the blouses had been gashed, perhaps with a box cutter when they had been re-boxed.

Derivative Communication in Psychotherapy

One of the ways we facilitate translation is through listening to the opening lines and first images that clients use coming into their therapy sessions. We hear their words as derivative communication about how the psyche is currently viewing the therapy process and the therapeutic relationship. Again, out of all the myriad of stories the unconscious could choose from, these are some examples:

"As I was walking here today, I saw this amazing little plant that had broken through a crack in the sidewalk and there was this beautiful little pink flower that had opened."

"What a lovely day! I love the warmth of the sun, and everything is in full bloom."

Both "openers" are validating images that the therapy is viewed to be on track and what the psyche needs for wholeness. Or there can be quite the opposite, when opening lines indicate a misunderstanding, a misaligned intervention, or a break in one of the conditions of the container. For example:

"That plant doesn't look like it is doing very well. Look at all the dead leaves."

"I noticed this morning that there is dry rot on my stairs. Someone could get hurt there."

We pay close attention to what unfolds in these cases. We find that these are not accidental nor coincidental remarks. Rather, they are intentional pointers to direct us to what is being appreciated and needed by the psyche (in validating opening lines), or to what reparations are needed by the psyche (in invalidating opening lines). We then listen closely to the narrative stories that follow, paying special attention to the first two to three stories, their images and themes, and what the deep unconscious of the psyche is expressing. Again, out of the thousands of stories the unconscious could pick from the week, these particular ones are selected to point to a theme and pattern that the person is working in his or her life, and in this particular moment with this specific practitioner. As part of our therapeutic practice, we remember these stories in sequence and then repeat them to the client, pointing out the themes present in each of them. It is interesting how unconscious we are of this process of communication that we engage in so much of the time, until we are taught how to listen to the themes and images.

Here are a few other examples from psychotherapy of a theme in narrative stories that occurs *after* securing the solid therapeutic container:

"I once had a professor who really knew her material and was really intelligent. That was such a good class, and I think I learned the most from her that I ever did in a class."

"I had a friend growing up that I knew really cared about me. I knew I could trust Jake with my secrets, and I was safe with him."

These are examples of unconscious communication *validating* what the therapist had done in setting secure conditions. Themes also can come in the form of invalidating derivatives to let us know we made an error, we have compromised the agreed-upon secure conditions, or we are replicating a pattern. For instance, if a client requests to reschedule and change the routine time set because of circumstances of needing to be gone and we agree to do this, we may get narrative stories in the following session about "a friend who had a miscarriage and her womb was unable to hold the fetus into the second trimester. The couple is so distraught." In such cases, we must own our actions. For example, one might say, "I think in telling me these stories about your friend that you are unconsciously speaking to my inability to hold the container of treatment by changing one of our agreed-upon conditions, the set time we meet. I think you are unconsciously letting me know how distraught you are about my not holding to our conditions by telling me these stories about your friend's miscarriage. In retrospect, what I needed to do with your request was to say that we really need to stay with the same time to maintain a solid holding environment for your growth and development to come to full term rather than 'miscarry' in any way, like what happened with your friend." We see the direct correlation between the derivative communication of the miscarriage to the psyche's unconscious communication of our actions in changing the time and breaking the agreement of the secure conditions of therapy. We then rectify it by discussing the need to keep the time set the same so as to hold full term, as was needed in the case of the friend.

The client may say consciously, "I think it was fine. You don't need to make a big deal of this," but then she might follow up with an unconscious derivative communication saying, "My friend's mother always knows what she needs and has been such a steady and stabilizing person in her life. I have seen her grow so much in having that relationship." In this example, the client's conscious mind thinks that the therapist is making too big of a deal over the situation, but the unconscious communication states clearly that this is just what is needed for the client's growth. This is a common example of the discrepancy between what the conscious mind tolerates, thinks, and communicates (that is based on one's patterns and archetypal alignments) and how the deep unconscious Self holds a standard of morality and ethics that is in service of our highest good.

....

Derivative Communication Through Physical Symptoms

Clients who present with repetitive patterns of self-harm such as cutting themselves are another example of derivative communication. Cutting often is believed to be the result of a wish to release the pain and suffering trapped inside, a way to make known to self and others the extent of this pain. Of course, this is true. We believe, however, this is not the full picture. In researching the origins of the practices of cutting, we have learned that cutting one's body is an age-old tribal ritual among various indigenous cultures, a practice purposely meant for healing; when the skin is cut, large amounts of endorphins are automatically released in the body. Not only do the endorphins potentially heal wounds, but they also can help us emotionally feel uplifted. It seems remarkable that the psyche has access to these archetypal phenomena and age-old practices, with no conscious knowledge of them. So, we can say the psyche used cutting as a means to *heal* the trauma and pain, not only to release it and make it known.

Many clients also present with physical illnesses. As previously noted, the psyche is relentless in pursing what is needed for the realization of our essential being. If it is not responded to or met on a mental, emotional, or spiritual level of expression, the psyche senses no other option but to appear in physical form in the body. To work with clients who have physical illnesses, we research extensively what the illness is, what parts of the body and organs are involved, and what the symptoms are, in order to hear the call of the psyche.

Many of the diseases causing people distress currently in our culture are autoimmune disorders. The responsibility of our immune system, in simplistic terms, is to be our protector. It defends us from microscopic predators that can cause illness. It protects us from becoming ill and maintains a homeostasis in our body through releasing hormonal antibodies to attack viruses, bacterial infections, and other invasive substances. In autoimmune illnesses, what is meant to protect us and maintain this balance is "mistakenly" misguided and actually "overprotects" to the point of harm. For example, in thyroid disease such as Grave's disease, the amount of hormones released into the immune system is in excess, causing hyperthyroidism.

If we look more closely at the Grave's disease example as a part of the assessment process, we would do lengthy research to become familiar with what Grave's disease is and how it functions in the body. We would do this research with the understanding that the psyche is attempting to reveal a psychological pattern through the disease that has not been heard through other means thus far.

Here is what our research as a part of the assessment process would turn up:

According to the Mayo Clinic website, "Grave's disease is an autoimmune disease more common when the person has another autoimmune disease like rheumatoid arthritis, Lupus, or Diabetes Type 1. It involves an overproduction of the thyroid hormone, causing hyperthyroidism. It affects many bodily systems so has a wide range of symptoms and a significant influence on overall well-being. . . . In Grave's, there is a malfunction in the body's disease-fighting immune system, and the cause is still unknown. Symptoms include but are not limited to: anxiety and irritability, tremors, heat sensitivity, weight loss, menstrual and erectile dysfunctions, red, swollen skin, sleep difficulties, heart muscle enlargement, arrhythmia, problems related to the eyes such as vision loss, light sensitivity, and bulging eyes."

Robert Langs referenced one of our primary defense systems as being the immune system of the body. Its purpose is to protect us from harmful outside microorganisms and diseases.[42]

A healthy immune system typically responds by producing antibodies designed to target specific viruses, bacteria, and foreign substances. Normally, thyroid function is regulated by hormones released by the pituitary gland at the base of the brain. The antibody in Grave's disease, thyrotrophic receptor antibody, acts like a pituitary hormone and overrides the normal regulation of thyroid, causing overproduction of thyroid hormone and hyperthyroidism."[43]

As the above three research summaries indicate, in Grave's disease, as is true for most autoimmune diseases we have researched, the process intended to protect us and maintain homeostasis actually goes into "overprotection" and imbalance in the system. This overprotection process, put into action, is actually the cause then of the malfunctioning of the normal body system's functioning and the disease process. What we find is that this frequently matches and mimics a psychological process and a pattern of replication.

In the case of Grave's disease, clients, in our experience, commonly believe there is a need for overprotection of themselves, due to internal fears related to experiences that have been traumatic and frightening in their life. They may believe the world is a very dangerous place that cannot be trusted. In response, they defend themselves accordingly out of fears and beliefs that, in their current life, are actually unwarranted and an exaggerated response.

Healing begins when the psyche is heard and understood by the conscious mind and when the pattern is acknowledged and seen for what it truly is. To begin to release and integrate defensive fears—and for one's healing to take place—we must honor the sacredness of the body's expression and of the associated psychological patterns rather than see the body's expression and its patterns as pathological. Naming the patterns and the psyche's expression through illnesses of the body actually begins a deep understanding so the healing process can unfold.

Translating Dreams

In our work with Michael Conforti, we learned to research images for their objective mandate in narrative stories of waking life as well as in dreams. We ask, "What is the image?" without making associations to the image. We also pay attention to why one image is chosen by the unconscious rather than the millions of other possibilities. For instance, if a train is the mode of transportation in a dream, we look at how the person is transporting him- or herself in life currently. We ask ourselves, "What is a train in terms of transportation? Why a train versus a plane or a cruise ship?" Each orients us to a different informational field. A train goes one way on a track that is set and predictable, has a specific trajectory, has numerous stops in which we can get off and on, is more leisurely, allows us to see the sights, and takes longer than, say, an airplane. An airplane is a fast mode of transportation, high in the air; we are trapped in its body, can't get off until its next destination, and totally surrender to the pilots to get us safely to our destination, although we do get quite an overview of the landscape. A cruise ship is a slow means of being transported to a destination. It orients us to vacationing and entertainment while being out at sea, a symbol of the deep unconscious. Also, cruise ships typically go to specific ports only, and there can be days between port stops.

Each mode of transportation holds a very different informational field and is chosen specifically to tell a story for the conscious mind to understand about its current patterns of living. We then can evaluate whether that pattern is generatively or non-generatively aligned to the archetypal mandate.

Other examples of dream images with which we all are familiar are anxiety dreams: We can't find the proper clothes to wear. People create obstacles so we can't get to work or to an important event on time. No matter how hard we try, we can't get to where we need to be. These dreams usually point to not feeling adequately prepared for an upcoming event or life change.

In looking at dreams, Yoram Kaufmann states that the archetypal forces that create a dream are sending communications from the Self to the ego. The dream is a wisdom that transcends the waking consciousness of the dreamer and a communication from the perspective of being able to see the larger picture. In short, the Self gives a snapshot picture to the ego of where the ego is in alignment with the Self and where it is off track with its own destiny factor.

Kaufmann goes on to say that dream images need to be seen in their entirety—their objective nature (the way science might describe just the facts of the image) as well as the dreamer's subjective experience. In other words, the feelings and thoughts associated with the image provide context and show the alignment of the dreamer to the objective thread of the image. The image also often contains a place in the popular collective culture as well as a thread of the collective unconscious. Within these two is also a thread of the systems that the collective has created that are associated with the image.[44]

In this archetypal approach, we would look at the first dream brought into treatment as the "herald dream," which gives all the information needed in its images to show the major issues and patterns to address in the course of treatment.[45] This dream and each subsequent dream would then be viewed through the lens of three stages: Opening/Exposition, Middle Stage/Dilemma, and Ending/Lysis.

Opening/Exposition

The opening of the dream sets the stage and, most importantly, orients us to a particular field of information, like the first act in a play or the beginning scenes of a movie. We look at each image for the facts of what it is and how it is manifesting the information coming from the Self. We ask questions such as:

- What is the setting?
- Who are the characters?
- In what position is the dreamer in the dream?

- Is he or she viewing it? Involved in it?
- What stage of life is being represented?

Middle Stage/Dilemma

In this stage, our focus is on what drama is being shown. We might ask:

- What is the dilemma being played out?
- What patterns or replicative processes are being represented?
- What stage of life is being shown?
- Is it archetypally congruent with the stage of life of the dreamer?

We are always looking objectively at images and what are the dominant features solely characteristic of a particular image, without projecting any personal associations we may have on the image.

Ending/Lysis

In this stage, we look at the final dilemma and how it is being solved. Our questions include the likes of:

- What is the main dilemma in the dream?
- Is there a generative solution?
- Is it congruent with age and development?
- What is the most generative solution that is archetypally and developmentally congruent?
- Often the dreamer wakes before the dream is solved. To what does this point?
- What is being communicated about the therapy and the relationship to the therapist?
- What is the archetypal message?
- What is the bifurcation point created and archetypal intervention that will help facilitate the dreamer's next step?[46]

As stated earlier, we use the dreamer's associations and the objective image's translation to look at the congruence between the conscious mind and the message coming from the unconscious on behalf of the Self. Understanding a client's associations with his or her dreams is critical to our work as analysts. We know that associations represent part of the self that wants to stay comfortable and with familiar patterns. To prevent a client from choosing a nongenerative pattern just to stay comfortable, we keep the associations in mind as we help the client keep true to the objective nature of the dream, to what landscape we are being oriented, and its context. We pay attention to associations and interpretations from the dreamer to see any incongruence there may be with the objective, unconscious message the images in the dreams are revealing. Let's consider an example:

The dreamer is a forty-three-year-old woman diagnosed with Stage 3 melanoma that began from a mole on her right upper arm. One night she dreamed she had a sore on her right lower arm. She wondered if it were another melanoma and asked people who were there with her (people she did not know). They said, "No, that is not melanoma." She felt relieved.

Associations the dreamer had with this dream felt very positive. In real life, she was relieved there was no more melanoma in her body and could finally relax because of the dream. Let's, however, look again at the same example from an Orientational Approach, keeping in mind the dreamer's associations and conclusions from the dream.[47]

Opening/Exposition
The dreamer orients us to the world of Stage 3 skin melanoma, which, in real life, she had on the same arm as the arm in the dream. This is a very serious form of cancer that can mean life or death, particularly if there is a recurrence, as in the dream.

Middle Stage/Dilemma
The dilemma is seeing another mole on the same arm; she questions whether it is another melanoma.

Ending/Lysis
She solves this dilemma by consulting with people around her she doesn't know, people not medically trained, to find out if this mole is a melanoma. When they say, "No, it is not," she believes them and feels relieved, as though she has no more need to be concerned.

Translation . . . or What is the Message from the Self?
The significant part of the dream is that the dreamer is in what could be a critical place medically, and she consults with strangers who are not medically trained to make an assessment as to whether her mole is a melanoma or not. When they say, "No, it is not a melanoma," she believes them and is relieved. When we asked the client, as a follow up to hearing her dream, "Were those people medically trained and competent to make your diagnosis," she was surprised by the question, answered "No," and was shocked that fact was lost on her. Then we asked: "What is happening in your life that

is very serious, needs your attention, is not attended to in a serious way, and puts you potentially at risk of life or death?" At that point, the client explained what happened before her cancer diagnosis and talked about her long-standing pattern of not addressing serious issues in her life. She had seen the mole on her right arm for at least a year and, at times, thought a doctor should check it out. She kept putting the thought aside, however, forgetting the mole was there until a doctor discovered it during a routine physical. She, in fact, felt guilty she had not attended to it immediately. Perhaps she could have caught it in the early stages and had a good prognosis rather than a Stage 3 diagnosis that is very serious and puts her at risk of an early death.

Exposing this pattern and her guilt opened the client to a wider view of her life. When there are difficult things to face, historically, she has turned away from them with an attitude of, "This is too hard." The dream, flushing out this pattern, set a trajectory for therapeutic work in what needs to happen to shift this way of being and, ultimately, change the pattern. It also exposed the guilt she had not faced that felt too difficult to bear. Seeing that the deep Self had brought this gift to her moved her to tears. Feeling this so deeply allowed her to make a commitment to face this pattern and her guilt and to make it a focus of her psychotherapy.

If we had merely explored the client's *associations* with this dream (she was relieved in real life because of the diagnosis of strangers in a dream), we would not have exposed her nongenerative pattern. In fact, we would have, together, continued to replicate the pattern by not facing the seriousness of the dreamer's actions in the dream. We would have given her the impression that we shy away from things challenging as well and would have become a part of a replicative drama in her life. The incongruences between her associations and the objective translation of images revealed the complex— her nongenerative alignment to caring for herself—and also helped get to the root of the deeper issue that brought her into treatment.

Translating Synchronicities

C.G. Jung referred to *synchronicity* as a "meaningful coincidence" and as "a causal connecting principle"[48] that has a sense of order and connection between mind and body. Synchronicity remains, for some, highly provocative. For many who have experienced its profound, numinous effect, synchronicity is often even comforting.

In David Peat's book, *Synchronicity: The Bridge Between Matter and Mind*, the renowned British physicist quotes Jung's thoughts on synchronicities as "meaningful coincidences, unthinkable as pure chance. The more they multiply and the greater and more exact the correspondence is, they can no longer be regarded as pure chance, but for the lack of causal explanation, have to be thought of as 'meaningful arrangements.' Synchronicities open a window to a creative source of infinite potential. They are the wellspring of the universe itself. They show that mind and matter are not distinct, separate aspects of nature, but arise in a deeper orbit of reality."[49] Jungian analyst Joseph Cambray, in his book *Synchronicity: Nature and Psyche in an Interconnected Universe*, goes on to say: "Jung aimed at expanding the Western world's core conceptions of nature and psyche. By requiring that we include and make room for unique individual experiences of life in our most fundamental philosophical and scientific views of the world, Jung challenged the status quo, urging us to go beyond the readily explainable, beyond the restrictions of a cause-effect reductive description of the world, to seeing the psyche as embedded into the substance of the world. As in so many of his ideas and projects, his genius resided in his capacity to see great depth in the odd, curious, and seemingly erroneous aspects of existence."[50]

In general, synchronicities are the coming together of inner and outer events in ways that cannot be explained by cause and effect. They seem like meaningful coincidences of seemingly highly improbable random events. Because synchronicities are something in the outer world that confirms an inner process and links mind and matter, many people think of these as powerful "accidents" but are left with a feeling that is emotionally charged.

Jungian analyst and mythopoetic author Marian Woodman, in her book *Dancing in the Flames*, describes synchronicities in terms of the activation of an archetype that releases patterning forces that can structure events, both in the psyche and the outside world.[51] They seem to be powerful messages from the Self to really get our attention.

Here are some examples of synchronicities:

A man is sitting having coffee with his best friend, telling about the affair he is having with a woman he met at work. He happens to be sitting on his cell phone, which is in his back pocket, in such a way that he had, inadvertently, speed dialed his wife—who listened to the entire conversation.

A man tells of his parents' favorite painting that always hung in prominence in their family home. On a first date, he went with a special woman to a beautiful, romantic restaurant, and they were seated at a booth. When he looked at the wall behind his date, he saw this same painting hanging above her head.

These two examples show the power of the unconscious that lines up with the message most needed from the Self. Each person is left with a profound feeling of some great force really wanting to get his attention.

Another good example of synchronicity is the all-too-common experience of walking into a room, seeing someone, feeling an aversion to that person, and saying to yourself, "Please, don't pair me up with that person." Invariably, that is exactly what happens. Often in that pairing, we see we need to face some pattern we have not wanted to deal with, but we are now faced with this bifurcation. In fact, Ann Belford Ulanov,[52] noted professor of psychiatry and religion at the Union Theological Seminary in New York, stated in her Assisi Institute lectures on trauma that she believes synchronicities help with healing, that the simultaneous linking of our outer experience with our current inner experience can be extremely powerful. The following are case examples of messages that come in a similar, causal form demonstrating this healing:

Mary is a volunteer with an organization's event. A woman walks into the event and Mary instantly feels an aversion to her. The woman has dyed, bright pink hair, twin toddlers in a stroller, and a baby in her arms. Her jeans are tight and low riding, accentuating a paunch from her recent pregnancy. The woman is loud and walks down the middle aisle doing things to draw attention to herself. Her kids are let out of the stroller and left to wander on their own. The looks and behavior of the woman irritate Mary.

The next day Mary is in a local market. This same woman is there shopping for groceries. The kids are crying in the stroller; the woman continues shopping, ignoring them, while making a commotion of her own which involves several market employees.

The day after that, Mary is in a local shopping mall. She is standing on top of the stairs when this same woman, her kids, and a man come right up to where Mary is standing. They stand in front of her for a while, talking and gesturing and then turn and walk toward another door.

The feeling of aversion, the magnetic pull to look at this woman and her children, the preposterous odds of running into this woman and her children day after day, shows that there is a resonance. To have encountered this person so many times in random public places is highly unlikely. To what is this resonance pointing? The informational field is one of a woman who demands that she be the center of attention. Her children are secondary to that need. Her actions show neglect through a developmental inability to put her children's needs first, and a kind of chaos follows her every move. There is an archetypal alignment to nongenerative mothering and neglect due to developmental limitations on the part of the mother. But what is the message from the Self related to Mary?

When Mary began to explore her aversion to this woman, she was surprised to realize she was looking at a gross form of her own mother. Even the right number and ages of children matched her family of origin, although Mary's mother's need to look good and always put on a public persona was so high that she would have never behaved in this way. In essence, however, all the other nongenerative parenting was present in Mary's mother. Mary was reduced to tears at this insight into her own childhood experience.

Here is another profound example of a healing synchronistic event:

Last winter there were a string of storms. During the third storm of a particular week, a grandmother was traveling at night with her three-month-old grandson on the Wilson River Highway through the coastal mountain range of Oregon. The infant was in a car seat in the back seat. It was very windy, and some trees had fallen across the road. Upon seeing the fallen trees blocking the road, the grandmother stopped the car far from the trees. She got out of the car and went to consult with the several people who were on the road trying to clear the trees. Then a tree fell across her car, while the baby was still in it.

The grandmother ran to rescue her grandson but, in the process, fell. Three people ran to her and learned she was physically fine, but she was hysterical about her grandson being in the car.

The three strangers ran to the car and, fortunately, found the baby unharmed. The tree had come down directly in front of the baby, within inches of where he was sitting. They broke a window to get the baby out, and he had no injuries. If the grandmother had remained in the car, it is likely the tree would have crushed her. There were three storms, three rescuers, and three generations.

As it turns out, the three people who rescued the baby were siblings, and they were coming home from the funeral of their mother, who had recently died suddenly—in a car accident. Although their good deed would not bring their mother back to them, they felt a healing take place because of saving the baby.

We translate synchronicities brought into treatment in a similar fashion as we do dreams. We use the same three stages, look at what informational field to which we are being oriented, and translate the images objectively, looking at their mandate. We also explore the associations the person has to the synchronicity and look for alignments as well as for the objective message of the synchronicity, similar to with dreams. Through this process, we begin to explicate the powerful meaning the Self is bringing to the conscious mind that can allow for behavioral modifications, shifts in archetypal alignments and patterns, and lasting change.

It is through the willingness to engage in a wider lens in life and delve into the archetypal mystery of the unconscious messages from the Self that we gain more and more consciousness, morph the ego into clear states of maturity, and can begin to abide in our true nature as aware presence.

20

Images Appearing in Dreams, Visions, and Daydreams in Each Archetypal Developmental Stage

We have found it useful to recognize archetypal symbols and images and allow them to guide us in the process of supporting our clients in finding what has been lost or cast out into the unconscious. The images help us to locate which developmental stage has captives to be rescued, and those images guide us in supporting the rescue.

Each archetypal developmental stage is encoded in images or symbols. These images are static expressions of both the archetype and the archetypal processes within each stage. When an image comes up in dreams, visions, daydreams and the like, in any form, it stands for an archetypal experience through which a person is currently working. Cinema also uses archetypal images. For example, the image of a particular setting will evoke the archetypal stage a hero enters during rescues of a captive.

Although archetypal images and symbols are coded concepts beyond intellectual understanding, concepts we cannot understand in terms of cause and effect, there is much we do know about them. Note that the undeveloped mind of a child operates only in images, making images our first language, which are almost undifferentiated from the body/self. In modern terms, we call this the "implicit memory," the part of the brain that is not conscious, nor developed, from which perceptions, emotions, sensations, and behavioral patterns of response can be registered or recalled from the past.[53] Interestingly, there are some natural rules to the coding of implicit memory, and it helps to hold these in mind as we explore archetypal images and symbols.

Images from the early archetypal stages of development are a magical confusion of inner and outer experience. The Swiss psychologist Jean Piaget, in his seminal work on cognitive development as outlined in *The Essential Piaget*, noted that, during a human's early stages, the world and the self are one; neither is distinguished from the other. Instead, the undifferentiated wholeness of experience is broken down into parts, which are still not connected in any logical way; they just happen, together or not. Logical relation is shown through the images lying next to one another or appearing in sequence. That means that pre-cognitive images cannot distinguish between one member of a class of things, and each member of a class is confused with the other. Take an archetypal category such as the container: Caves, boxes, wombs, cups, and anything hollow, concave, or "containing" are all part of the class of containers.[54] A child cannot distinguish between the individual items but will use them interchangeably.

Given this early way of being, everything is connected with everything else, and one thing can, and must, stand for the rest.[55] For instance, all "child-eating" father figures stand for the masculine aspect of the uroborus and the masculine, negative side of the introjected parents. Moloch, a Canaanite deity associated in biblical sources with the practice of child sacrifice, is a good example of this negative father image.[56] Even contemporary usage of the term *moloch* in art and literature refers to a person or a thing that requires a horrible sacrifice.

As therapists, we have found it useful, particularly in working with the Rescuing the Captive stage, to recognize archetypal symbols and images and to allow them to guide us in the process of supporting our clients to find what has been lost or cast out into the unconscious. The images help us to locate which developmental stage has captives to be rescued, and those images guide us in supporting the rescue. If an image appears that signals a particular sort of captive, we can help mentor the client by knowing what is occurring in that particular developmental stage, what just came before it, and what comes next in the stage sequence.

In this chapter, we will proceed through the developmental stages, shedding light on the consistent images we have found. We see these images as the psyche's attempt to reveal aspects of the unconscious, which are needed to become conscious and to facilitate the fulfillment of the hero's mandate to come into unity.

We compiled these images over years of study and provide endnotes to make further study accessible.

Uroborus

Experiences of conception and birth are encoded into pre-cognitive structures during the uroboric stage. These encoded experiences, or "experiential repositories of condensed experiences,"[57] show up later in adulthood as pervasive atmospheric moods. For instance, experiences in a toxic womb (through illness of the mother, drug or alcohol addiction, attempts at abortion, to name a few) might be encoded and later experienced as an underlying sense of feeling unsafe in the world, in a range from mild anxiety to paranoia. These feelings also might manifest as image sequences of frightening demonic entities or insidious evil that creates a negative background feeling about the world.

On the other hand, positive intra-uterine experiences can create positive archetypal alignments. These positive alignments might show up as archetypal symbols such as a circle or a mandala, or as kaleidoscopic images of fractal designs. These symbols and representations are often associated with creation stories, as images demonstrating a unity that becomes divided into two, or a unit of two actually being one. Positive experiences of conception and birth also might take the image of the "original paradise" or various celestial realms—safe, beautiful, and nourishing lands—and be longed for.

Intra-Uterine and Birth Images

Through years of research, Dr. Stanislav Grof has found many images that stand for intra-uterine and birth experiences that were encoded during the birthing process. These images include those of being sucked into a gigantic whirlpool, of being swallowed by some mythic creature, or of feeling that the entire world is being engulfed. Images of giant snakes, octopuses, and large aquatic monsters might represent an overwhelming vital threat and come to represent claustrophobia. In addition, during long birth contractions, particularly when labor is gone awry, the baby can encode a sense of utter helplessness, hopelessness, and meaninglessness; this can show up in the adult as pervasive feelings of loneliness, guilt, and existential despair, or that life is absurd.

Dreams also might contain situations that represent the experience as a fetus being caught in the birth canal; these dreams might be of people, animals, or beings caught in painful and hopeless predicaments or of archetypal figures of endless suffering or eternal damnation such as Tantalus and Prometheus.

Once the baby's head is in the birth canal, the encoding of experience can result in images of epic fights or of nature's raging storms, earthquakes, tsunami waves, and volcanoes. Furthermore, the baby might introject the onrush of uterine contractions in various ways that can establish a trajectory toward encoded images of aggression and sadomasochistic sequences, experiences of deviant sexuality, scatological experiences, demonic episodes, and encounters with fire.[58]

Great Mother Oral Stage

In general, the image of mother and child is deeply rooted in our culture and in Christianity. The Great Mother of the oral stage is an image of Mother standing in for the mystery of life. She is seen in her various stages, as the baby's bud of an ego begins to take form. She also is seen as the Mistress of the Animals[59] (as symbolized by free-moving animals) as well as the Great Mistress of the Plants.[60] In this, she symbolizes nurturance and food. Because the child wants to eat the Mother via the breast or food provided later, the child also feels vulnerable to being eaten. The images that flow from this symbol canon are:

- Of being eaten by the world or by an object, animal, monster, or large aquatic beast such as a shark[61]
- The sense that "I will be swallowed or suffocated"
- The cannibal who wants to eat flesh
- The idea that milk is seen as fertilizing[62]
- Of sucking, with the thumb becoming a substitute for the breast

As we recognize our own existence as being separate from Mother, and as we recognize her ability to go away from us, we also see images of food disappearing, images of loss, images of death, as well as images of flying apart and of the terror of being eaten by the unconscious.

Great Mother Anal Stage

As the anal stage dawns, there are images of the child having been fertilized by eating and giving birth by evacuating.[63] Other images convey the fear, "I can be robbed of my body's contents!" We also see images of holding onto our body's contents if caregivers—by making faces while cleaning up a diaper or by saying things such as "Eckkk! Awful! I hate this!"—makes the baby feel repulsive. The baby takes in this repulsion and connects it in a rudimentary way with its own evacuation, its own insides. Evil in some form, thus, enters the symbols,[64] expressing the notion that "I have evil inside me" or "I can be infected by evil and won't be able to eliminate the evil in my own nature." In addition, images of infection, sickness, and death also can stand for the lower anal world. Note, too, that, during his or her birth journey, the baby can be exposed to a variety of biological material such as blood, vaginal secretions, urine, and feces. This can be encoded into images of drinking blood or urine, wallowing in excrement, or participating in repulsive rituals involving urine or excrement;[65] this heightens the sense that "There is something bad inside me."

As the ego gains in strength, it shows its independence by beginning to assume its anthropocentric position at the center of the world, with "me" and "mine" at its core. "Magical thinking" makes this possible. Until this time, the Self was the director of consciousness. Now the conscious ego, rather than the Self, starts to become the executor of the vitality of the personality, and Mother shows up as the image of the Lady of Magic, consort to the magical ego of the child.[66]

As we strive to move from the total domination of the unconscious, power becomes the necessary goal of ego development. This can be depicted as wanting mastery over the Great Mother as the giver of food and as mistress of the plants and animals. One related symbolic image is the rising sun, whose powerful radiance is dominant over the darkness of night (unconscious), which has been defeated. Another coherent group of related symbols portrays the transpersonal hunting-killing principle and includes birds of prey, the eagle, and the self as the animal that kills to eat. Teeth become an important symbol at this stage as well, as they are the implements of eating, of breaking things down in order to easily digest.[67]

Depending on what has been introjected and encoded from life in the womb and birth experiences, images can emerge as huge battles for power—with other people or with the elements—or perhaps battles between Light and Dark. Those who experienced great suffering in the womb or during the birthing process might feel the impossibility of gaining their own authority, and their alignment with this stage may be one of experiencing the archetypal Terrible Mother as a constrictor snake that swallows its prey or as a giant spider that immobilizes, constricts, suffocates, and/or tortures. This can stimulate images of violent scenes of bloody wars, fights, and revolutions during which power is at stake.

Great Mother Genital Stage

As the young ego moves into the third stage of the Great Mother, the genital stage, a mythical correspondence to being the Great Mother's youthful lover ensues. The child is the son or daughter the Mother has borne—as well as the one the Terrible Mother will kill. The child tries to live by the Great Mother's rules but has a hard time doing so. Realizing that caregivers can leave, the child also becomes terrified. In order to sustain a feeling of "all-good" caretaking, the child builds an internal dual system of self-understanding:

1. I am a good child with an all-good Great Mother who is perfect and loving and protective without being smothering; and
2. I am a separate, bad child with an all-bad Terrible Mother who is uncaring, negligent, and hostile when I misbehave.[68]

This splitting solves one problem—the child has a consistent way of feeling safe—but creates another: Now there is a splitting of experiences of bodily pleasures divided into good and bad. The good child has the "good bodily pleasures," and the bad child has the "bad bodily pleasures." The world is now both a garden of delight—and a vast, haunted realm. This duality conjures various images:

- Of having a twin[69]
- Of the Great Mother split in two, being half animal and half human
- Of mutual struggles to dominate
- Of a sense of self-imposed loss

When a caregiver deflates the young ego, or castrates it, the ego does not separate from the Great Mother and tries to hold onto her by being "good." This solidifies the internalization of the split, leaving a captive, the "bad" twin, held fast in this stage. To end the splitting, the "bad" child with the bad mother must find a way to stop its symbiotic dependence on the Mother.[70]

The child also might encode a good mother as an impersonal archetype of nature—such as a tree, garden, forest, home, sky, or the whole world or parts of it—so that a yard or garden in front of the house, or a nearby woods or some particular tree may come to represent a sheltering reality into which the child can withdraw.[71] But, not to be loved is identical with being sick, diseased, or condemned.[72]

Clients with a captive in this stage are vulnerable to seduction and then rejection of some sort. Colloquially, they often have "the rug pulled out from underneath them." They get mixed up with the femme fatale or the male seducer who promises every thing and then delivers a castrating blow. Their bosses, or other authority figures, seem to promise something but never deliver it, to great disappointment. As adults, they are left vulnerable and frustrated as they try over and over to please someone who is demanding and difficult.

Depending on what has been introjected and encoded from existence in the womb and birth experiences, sado-masochistic images, images of sexual torture, abuse, or rape, and images of deviant erotic practices can be translated into experiences with suffocation from the umbilical cord and interactions with blood, mucus, urine, feces, and vaginal secretions of the mother. Stanislav Grof, in his *Psychology of the Future*, says: "It seems that the human organism has an inbuilt physiological mechanism that translates inhuman suffering, and particularly suffocation, into a strange kind of sexual arousal and eventually into ecstatic rapture."[73]

Father Archetype Activated

As the me-and-mine mentality continues to grow—and the Great Mother now is both good and terrible—the young ego is coalescing to form a relationship with the Father archetype. If there is not a father in the home to embody the transpersonal archetype of the Father nor a generative mother who can fulfill this role of movement into the outer world, the child will find a figure, perhaps from sports or comic books, to have a relationship with the Father archetype. Some associated images include:

- The Great Father
- Ascending spiritual currents
- The sun, which has defeated the darkness (feminine unconscious)

The psyches of children match and project matriarchal castration and/or the threat of domination by the Great Mother with a feminine person in their life (often the mother), and children's psyches project patriarchal castration and the threat of domination by the Great Father on a masculine person in their life (often the father). In their dreams and fantasies, this correlation or projection holds; even if the two personal parent figures do not act out the archetypal behavior of crushing the growing ego, the internal images in the child's psyche will still continue to connect the feminine and masculine person to the archetypal castration or to the perceived threat.[74] These images evoke the impressions taken in as the same types of emotions and feelings as if the actual person had acted or behaved in that way. Pertinent images at this stage feature:

- The same sex parent in disguise as a demon or as an animal wanting to kill or annihilate the child[75]
- Fertilizing forces that impregnate
- Rain
- Penetration
- Potency
- A challenged union of some kind
- Triangulation (two people competing for one person or feeling like "the third wheel" in a dyad)
- The number three itself

Separation of the World Parents

As we withdraw from the symbiotic relationship with the Mother, we, unfortunately, simultaneously shield ourselves inwardly against the wonderful, energetic, instinctual, archetypal world we once knew through our primal connection with the unconscious. The psyche experiences this movement away from the archetypal world as a great betrayal. The images that illuminate this stage are:

- Of being made to leave the Garden of Eden
- Of gaining the knowledge of good and evil
- Of losing paradise[76]
- Of killing, sacrifice, and dismemberment
- Of fragmenting the world into separate objects or parts
- Teeth

During this stage, the child also introjects the parents' psyches, in an effort to hold the parents close. These introjects form the superego that will maintain the rules and injunctions of the parents. Such introjection conjures images of eating and assimilating the parents and of taking something inside whole. Teeth are often the instruments used in this stage's images that involve chewing, biting, eating, and assimilating; cutting things into parts and then eating them; or cutting out a heart and eating it.

As noted earlier, the shadow is also born during the Separation of the World Parents stage. The shadow contains all the elements in the child that are part of the "bad" child in the split, elements now condemned as negative values. We all love to hate a good antagonist in a story or film.

The killing, dismemberment, and destruction that occurs in this stage is essential to form an independent ego, but the ego feels its aggression as guilt. Clients dealing with rescuing the captive in this stage often feel a background effect that embodies a sense of guilt. Like the characters in Franz Kafka's book, *The Trial*, they are certain Joseph K. is guilty of something horrible, but no specific charges are ever made and the crime goes unnamed and not understood.

Never fear, however, because the primordial connection that is disavowed as we strive to withdraw from the Great Mother rises up as the ego ideal or the heroic ideal. It is internally embodied in images of a magical figure that can gain mastery of both outside and inside. Indeed, that figure can heal the splitting done in the Great Mother stage. Comic books and movies are full of these heroic figures. In grocery stores and public gatherings, we see children dressed in Superman capes with Spiderman t-shirts or in fairy princess dresses with crowns. These figures can be quite useful in rescuing captives in the early stages of the Great Mother.

Dragon Fights

The archetypal role of the hero is to engage in dragon fights. Dragon fights have three main components: a hero, a dragon, and a treasure. The dragon bears all the markings of the uroborus, including being both masculine and feminine. All great stories of the world include the archetypal image of the dragon. Consider the Hydra, Medusa, the Kraken, and the like. These monsters all simultaneously embody both masculine and feminine aspects.[77]

Symbolically, a dragon fight involves the hero murdering both father/masculine and mother/feminine, not just one of them, in an effort to gain the treasure of the Self. Developmentally, the child in this stage is beginning to find his or her own voice, with the support of peers and institutions, and, in order to attain autonomy, he or she must battle with whatever was taken in from the parents that is not in alignment with the generative Mother and Father. That is, to gain independence, the child must overcome the masculine principle of consciousness as well as the feminine/maternal when it obstructs the ego. He or she also must be strong enough to stand tall against the unlived lives of the parents that push to be included in the child's future. In addition, the hero must fight against the shadow of the "bad child" and against the splitting left from the negative devouring Mother. In general, the fire of the dragon is the devouring and castrating parts of the superego. The images related to this stage include the likes of witches and the terrible mother dragon.

This stage is a long one chronologically, moving from the beginning of school age to completing school and leaving dependency on the parents. The early dragon fights are often engaging with the reptilian monsters, such as the devouring mother dragon, while the older fights often include monsters that have more of a mammal or partial human form.

Birth of the Hero

As the child becomes an adolescent and beyond, the image of a figure standing between two worlds is a perfect depiction of that stage's hero.[78] He or she must conquer the dangers of the unconscious—its rending, destroying, devouring, and castrating character—to move into a better world. These dangers show up as monsters, beasts, and giants that are bisexual, possessing both masculine and feminine symbolic qualities. The monsters always have some human characteristics but are never represented as wholly human. By definition, in fact, a monster cannot be an ideal, perfect, whole human being. If it looks entirely human, it will have some physical abnormality. Think of the Cyclops.

A monster's way of acting is archetypally set: It is either a predator, the guardian of some treasure, or an avenger.[79] Because these archetypes also parallel ways that immature human beings behave, we can learn much by looking at the specific monsters that show up in a client's life and how a client responds to those monsters.

Depending upon how someone responds to his or her developmental challenges, he or she will either conjure a "shining hero" or a "dark hero." The shining hero has realized that the Treasure is in the unconscious. This hero takes various guises: the savior, man of action, seer and sage, founder and artist, inventor and discoverer, or scientist and leader. On the other hand, dark heroes think the Treasure is to be found in the first three stages of the Great Mother—in the body, in power, or in sexual union—and they often have a dual nature: They can be twins, a brother and a sister, one mortal and the other immortal, or, like Superman, the same person who can shift from ordinary to extraordinary.

The emergence of a dark hero indicates that a client is struggling with a captive in one of the three stages of the Great Mother: The dark hero captive in the *oral* stage is the lord of drugs, food, and the physical body. The dark hero captive in the *anal* stage rules through control, violence, and power; has a profusion of great possessions; and is superior to others. And the dark hero captive in the *genital* stage is the playboy who owns cars with throbbing speakers and has women dripping off his arms.

The myth of the hero born of a supernatural father (like Superman, for instance) gives us a hero in service to the collective. This hero feels himself to be responsible for the existence of the world, unlike the hero who is a captive to the Great Mother and only in the service of gaining ego-centric "treasures" such as looking good, having power, or having prolific sex. The dark hero also can get lost in ecstasy of ascending into spirit, attempting to rise above the unconscious aspects that need to be rescued rather than taking on the heroic stance needed to rescue all that is captive. An example is the spiritual teacher who is supposedly enlightened but ends up using his or her position for power, fame, money, or sex. This spiritual teacher, who is usually very charismatic, actually remains in a symbiotic relationship with the Father archetype in order to have a place in the world without really integrating the unconscious captives. Examples include Charles Manson, Jim Jones of Jonestown, and the many other teachers and priests both from Christianity and the East who have large followings and have misused their positions for some kind of personal gain.

As the hero matures, he or she deals with the destruction of an ego system that is hostile to the unconscious. This is symbolized in myths as persecution, dismemberment, and madness—often portrayed as a dark homicidal male force. To depict such myths, images of wild predators such as the boar will be used, but those images will not include animals of noble character, such as the lion. Hitler and the Nazis also are often used as archetypal symbols of this dark, homicidal male force that tries to annihilate the feminine rather than to rescue it.

Because the hero has a mandate to bring in the new, the last dragon fight is the fight against the cultural superego and the old ways, traditions, and taboos. The images often used to reflect this particular dragon fight convey the old giving way to the new: Think of the old king, the boss who won't retire, or something of the older generation that seems to obstruct the new from manifesting. A contemporary example is replacing fossil fuel with renewable resources as our primary source of energy.

To fulfill his or her destiny, the hero must detach from the Great Mother. He or she must move from being enmeshed, as in the case of the "son lover" the Mother will eventually emasculate and keep in her service.[80] Examples of being stuck as a son lover include the marriage in which the man follows meekly in the background and the relationship in which the prospective mate is kept hanging on but never brought close. The only way the hero dethrones or subordinates the Great Mother is by bringing in a "prize consort," which brings us to the anima and animus.

Anima and Animus

Remember that when a caregiver deflates the young ego, or castrates it, the ego does not individuate from the Great Mother. Instead, it tries to hold onto her by being "good." The anima/animus is formed through this split, which began earlier as a fragmentation of the uroboric Mother archetype and the introjection of only the positive aspects of the "good" Great Mother. Then the anima/animus is formed from the early impressions introjected in relationship to the Great Mother, and later the Father archetype, and held unconsciously due to the early development in which this begins. These images can be seen as that of the young prince or princess and sometimes as a young and perfect animal, like a deer. We experience this as a Soul image. Because it comprises only the good aspects of the Great Mother, we are drawn to look for our other half. This other half, or the anima/animus figure, is projected onto a woman or a man and that individual is forced into a human relationship with the carrier of the projection. The anima/animus image then enters the human sphere as a "you with whom I can commune" rather than as the Great Mother, "she who can only be worshipped." This projection also binds us to the collective as well as to our personal unconscious through our partner.

The anima/animus, thus, is a symbolic and archetypal figure made up of magical, alluring, and dangerously fascinating elements, which can bring madness as well as wisdom. That which is actually trying to unite with an archetypal figure can bring madness. Think how hard it is to find and capture a mermaid, the Holy Grail, or any treasure somehow embodied in a form.

For those whose authority is left captive in the Great Mother, the animus will be a powerful, authoritarian man such as the exotic teacher from a far off land or the movie star who has everyone's attention, or the politician who promises he will take care of everything. Examples of the anima are the geisha and the Playboy Bunny, whose only ambition is to serve a man's needs.

By looking at whom your client has chosen as a mate, you can see what is left captive in the Great Mother. You can determine what introjects remain from the Mother and Father archetypes in the client's early years of life. Buried in the unconscious, we don't have a way of working with the introjects themselves, but, by partnering with those who fit those introjects, we can have an outer form with which to work through the internal struggle.

Slaying of the Parents

In this stage, we chew up and analyze our superego, spitting out the parts of our parents that no longer match with our experience and current values and goals. This is a time for young people to develop their heroic knowing of themselves, to begin to recognize their own values that reflect what they think and feel is true, and to establish goals that go with these values. They also need to spit out what was taken in as children from their parents and culture that doesn't fit their new values and goals. This work can include many dragon fights with the actual parents, and it culminates with a strength of identity coming from inside. Outer ideas or demands from family, peers, or culture no longer drive the person; this is the ego at its most separate state from the Self, in a dynamic resonance.

Images of this archetypal stage are of deconstructing—chewing, spitting out, or sometimes vomiting—and often of fighting with an actual parent or a representative of the parents such as a difficult teacher or boss. Because teeth are such an important part of breaking down our food, images of losing teeth, teeth falling out, or missing teeth also often point to a captive in early stages that is interfering with the individuation process. On the positive size of this stage, there are images of completion and digestion. Examples include images of graduating, of getting a good grade on a test, and of running over the finish line in a race.

Rescuing the Captive

Rescuing the Captive is an active process that requires a descent into the foundational stages of the Great Mother and the Separation of the World Parents to collect any of the feminine aspects that were left as our ego was forming and we are making our way into the outer world. As an archetypal example of this, consider the movie *Inception*. In the film, the main character (Leonardo DiCaprio) must repeatedly descend in an elevator to a floor where he must interact with a very distraught woman if he is to complete his mission.

Certain dreams can signal the needed work of rescuing the captive. The mood of these dreams is not a comforting one, although it can feel neutral. These dream images will vary as the memories from our early stages are stored in textures, smells, certain feelings, and often singular images such as a familiar wall color or wallpaper, a particular chair, or a favorite blanket, doll, or truck. Often the childhood home will be the setting of a dream when a captive is trying to escape. Other images of being held captive that show up in dreams include:

- Being lost
- Losing belongings
- Forgetting you are caring for a baby, or a baby is lost and there is a search for the baby
- Losing body parts, or having body parts cut off or fall off
- Being chased (The figures or animals that are the "chasers" can symbolize the memories that need to be metabolized and integrated.)

Because the captive is up against huge forces in the psyche, those forces also can show up in dreams or daydreams as dealing with natural forces such as storms, earthquakes, or big waves. These natural forces symbolize the overwhelming force to which an aspect of the psyche succumbed and signals that a captive is present. There are also many images of the captive being taken over against his or her will, being imprisoned or tortured, trying to escape, and trying to hide. Recall the many images of women being tied to railroad tracks, struggling against their bonds, and waiting for rescue that used to inundate our comics and movies. All are good examples of how, once the feminine component is freed (or rescued, to use the language of the myths), the feminine can then be integrated into the structure of the hero's psyche, and his or her values and actions will become more congruent with his or her own heroic ideal from childhood.

The dream setting also can clue us into times when trauma occurred. Usually trauma leaves a captive in the psyche, an aspect that felt overwhelmed and couldn't be digested. Traumatic memories from under the age of six are undigested sensations, images, smells, background feelings and tastes[81] that are not remembered in a narrative fashion and so often present themselves as images in our dreams or rise in the making of art or reverie. Trauma involving vital threat or physical traumatization to the Mother and fetus leave permanent traces in the baby's system and contribute significantly to the development of psychosomatic manifestations, which can always be traced to unconscious themes on a biographical, perinatal, or transpersonal level.[82] (See "The Wisdom of the Body" chapter for more on this topic.)

Gaining the Treasure

Gaining the Treasure and Rescuing the Captive often alternate with each other. As we make strides in fully facing our inner fears, we will get a hand on the Treasure—and lose it because of some internal captive still waiting to be rescued. Then the hero must return yet again to rescuing what is captive. This process continues as we clear and integrate more and more parts of our shadow.

In the film *Raiders of the Lost Ark*, Dr. Indiana Jones frees the treasure from its guarded place, after defeating all the treasure's dangerous, fierce, demon-like guardians. Once he picks up the treasure and begins to leave with it, a huge boulder, the size of a house, is released. "Not again!" cries Jones. This is a wonderful portrayal of gaining the Treasure. Once the hero in us is strong enough to stand up to all the monsters that our fears symbolize and we are able to get into the "inner chamber" to grab the Treasure, the unconscious will release a huge, overwhelming force to yet again try and bring us under its spell. When we finally overcome the last challenges from the unconscious, we will free the captive feminine, proving that the unconscious is now under the mastery of the hero.

This is why many mythic stories end with a marriage of the hero and the rescued captive. The freed captive is represented by the goddess/princess who is not linked with the Great Mother in any way. And the couple can now have a truly united marriage that is happy ever after. In other words, the feminine image has been extricated from the grip of the Devouring Mother. This is known as the crystallization of the anima from the Mother archetype.[83]

Unification of Opposites: Hermaphrodite

Images of Gaining the Treasure are always of two opposites coming together in integration or unity. The treasure and the hero are no longer seen as two but realized as always being *not* two. There are many symbols of the marriage of opposites: the Yin Yang symbol, the infinity symbol, the pearl in its shell, yantras and mandalas, to name a few. The mythic representation of the unification of opposites is Neumann's mythic image of the Hermaphrodite[84] who:

- Has both genitalia, being beyond gender or the union of the genders;
- Wears the crown of realization, a crown which signals the royal ascendance of the union of mind and heart;
- Has a diamond of many facets glowing in his/her heart, which is resonant with the mind; and
- Stands on the slain dragon (of the uroborus or the unmetabolized unconscious, as he/she is now the ruler of the unconscious).

21

The Wisdom of the Body

"There are two possibilities for thought: either to go outwards in the direction of objects or states, in which case it takes the form of suffering, or to go inwards towards the heart of experience, in which case it dissolves in peace."[85]

- Rupert Spira -

To anchor the later stages of consciousness—which Neumann calls "the archetypal milestones of the Treasure, Hermaphrodite, and beyond"—takes fully embodying our body-mind/ego. It involves releasing subtler and subtler layers of early implicit memory and early patterning from the body and psychological structures. For most people, however, the body, thought constructions, and patterns of mind are their *identity* throughout their lifespan. In this way of being, the kundalini[86] or libidinal[87] energy mostly stays "asleep," other than, perhaps, during sexual arousal.

To attain later levels of consciousness demands that we view our self as a *vast energy system* that includes the body-mind as a temple for our human embodiment. The shift to this higher level of consciousness comes as we move deeply into what Neumann calls introversion, centroversion, and later stages of "awakened" states. This includes not only awakening our essential nature through the evolving relationship between the ego and its return to the Self, but also through the awakening of the body and its kundalini libidinal spiritual energy and aliveness which often entails four stages:

1. Believing we are just the body-mind/ego
2. Seeing we are not just the body-mind and pushing the body-mind away as though it does not matter
3. Realizing the importance of the body-mind, its care as a temple of spirit
4. Embodying the body-mind fully, allowing the mind to move into its purer state

Michael Washburn in his magnum opus, *Embodied Spirituality in a Sacred World*, captures the process of attaining higher consciousness: "This transpersonal body ego becomes restored to full vitality, is undefended, unhidden, radically intimate with others. The ego begins to feel more at home in the body, more comfortable living without defenses, being vulnerable and more comfortable being seen and being touched. Spirit is perceived as transparent in fully manifest form as the ego's higher Self. It becomes evident, in looking back, that the awakening of the body was at the same time Spirit's awakening in the body, and that the ego's return to the body was at the same time Spirit's return. The ego that has been integrated with Spirit is a body ego that has been wedded to embody Spirit. It is an ego that has been married to Spirit in the 'temple of Spirit,' the human body."[88]

Beliefs Held in the Body

To move into this transpersonal body-mind/ego means freeing the unconscious aspects that maintain the veils to the Self and keep the Self from permeating our essence and daily experience. A conscious mindfulness practice and daily meditation are very helpful (perhaps necessary) to assist in this process. Also important is deconstructing the thought structures, priorities, and patterns relating to our bodies that have permeated our life. In addition, we must dismantle our "I, me, and mine" conditioning. We must see the truth of the emptiness and impermanence of that conditioning in order to open to the fullness and numinous of the Self. This, typically, takes a lengthy process of true devotion to our liberation.

One path to this work is by turning to the innate wisdom and guidance stored in the body. Obviously, the body-mind/ego, with its psychological qualities, are quite inseparable. As we discussed earlier, psychological patterns manifest in the body, particularly if they are not listened to and responded to appropriately, through mental or emotional expressions. The psyche, in its continual drive toward wholeness, has no other option but to bring the pattern into the physical in order to get attention and care. This fact leads to our belief that, in order to assist people in attaining and living from their potential, in being fully alive and consciously awake, therapeutic practices need to address somatic expression. For example, as analysts, we begin rescuing aspects of self from the implicit memory of early childhood and subsequent emotional injuries by reading the pattern in its physical form as "disease."

The late Ron Kurtz (founder of the Hakomi Institute) and Jon Eisman (master trainer of the Hakomi and Recreation of Self methods) teach that the mind and our self-consciousness are expressed through the body. This expression reveals both conscious and unconscious aspects of our psychological personality and the central organizing beliefs and patterns we hold. They can be both expressions of us as individuals, or patterns we form into character strategies common to many in our physical embodiment.[89] For example, if someone is angry, he or she typically has tension in the body, enlarged eyes, an expanded body, and a louder voice. He or she also usually exhibits certain movements of the body such as a shaking hand or finger. Similarly, a character pattern of someone who did not feel welcomed into the world or sensed he or she did not belong in the family expresses this in the way he or she carries his or her body: chest protecting the heart; uncomfortable taking up space or being seen; a vacant, hurt look in the eyes; and a general uneasiness being in the body and world.

The bottom line is that what we experience in our *outer* world is registered and expressed through our *inner* world of body, mind, and psychological makeup, both conscious and unconscious. Ron Kurtz, in his book *Body-Centered Psychotherapy*, notes: "There are somatic, emotional, and cognitive experiences that form from our deeply held beliefs, which in turn generate habitual behaviors and perceptual patterns. These are central to organizing our neurologically held beliefs and patterns in the body and may be processed utilizing mindfulness and the careful study of present experience to uncover the underlying formative 'core material.'"[90]

Epigenetics researcher Bruce Lipton, author of *The Biology of Belief*, also writes about our beliefs and experiences and how they affect our body, brain chemistry, and perceptions. For example, he discusses the mother's influence on fetal development. While she is providing nutrition to the fetus developing in her womb, her environment and her environmental experience and perceptions are controlling and changing her biologically. Stress hormones, chemical changes in her brain, and all other biological information (including information from at least four generations of her lineage[91]) cross the placenta with the food and nourishment. So one can see how, if the mother is stressed or in fear, this is transferred to the fetus and the fetus feels the stress, even though that stress does not belong to the fetus.

In short, we are programmed neurologically and chemically, and this affects our beliefs and their synchronized relationship with the body. In other words, from conception through birth, we are "wired," with psychological development and biological development happening simultaneously. Lipton summarizes the process: "Our perceptions of the environment are stored in cellular memory. When early environmental influences are chronically stressful, the developing nervous system and other organs of the PNI (psychoneuroimmunology) super-system repeatedly receive the electrical, hormonal, and chemical message that the world is unsafe or hostile. Those perceptions are programmed into the cells on the molecular level. Early experiences condition the body's stance toward the world and determine the person's unconscious beliefs about oneself in relationship to the world."[92]

Our cells, in essence, impact our overall body-mind functioning. The cell membrane is like the brain of the cell. It has millions of tiny antenna receptors on its surface, receptors that interpret the external messages; the membrane makes decisions about the exchange of messages and substances that are "allowed in." Everyone's antenna receptors look different, demonstrating our uniqueness and core patterning.

Lipton goes on to say, in Gabor Maté's *When the Body Says No*, that our perceptions form our thought structures, which then release different chemical reactions in the brain. These chemicals and hormones are released into the blood, feed our cells, and can change our genes. It is our interaction with the environment, then, that controls our cellular makeup; we are not "genetically programmed." Our beliefs are embedded into our cellular structure and control behaviors no matter what we are thinking consciously. They allow for an openness and healthy growth and development—or defend and shut us down by eliciting an inner voice that badgers:

- I am not good enough or important.
- I have to be strong.
- It's not right for me to be angry.
- If I'm angry, I will be unlovable.
- I'm responsible for the whole world.
- I can handle anything.
- I'm not wanted; I'm not lovable.
- I don't exist unless I do something; I must justify my existence.
- I have to be ill to deserve to be cared about.

Lipton also states that major contributing factors to many of our current disease patterns are directly related to our unconscious beliefs, the stress they cause, and the aligning stress hormones and chemicals released in response. He sees an antidote in our capacity to heal. When we are willing to work with the underlying painful issues, we can reverse our "biology of beliefs" and, thus, change familiar patterns in how we think and have been living our lives.[93]

Psychoneuroimmunology (PNI) Super-System and Its Contribution

Psychoneuroimmunology (PNI) is a fairly new field of study that examines the interconnectedness of the body-mind with the emotional-nervous-immune-hormonal super-system. That is, rather than viewing each system as a separate process in the body, PNI research recognizes that these systems are interconnected as one super-system. Disruptions to one affect all the others. This interconnectedness of the physical and the psychological demonstrates the necessity of treating illness or any dis-ease from the perspective of the super-system itself. Gabor Maté calls this perspective "the healing force within." His work highlights how our experiences, perceptions, thought constructions, emotions, and feeling states are registered physiologically in the cellular and chemical-hormonal systems of our bodies. Unfortunately, this interconnectedness of our emotional and physiological systems is often dismissed by the medical profession and denied by us as individuals. We tend to feel more comfortable believing illnesses are something happening to us from some outside source.

In decades as a family practice and palliative care physician, Maté was struck by the consistent correlations he found between chronic illness and a patient being emotionally shut down rather than expressing "negative" emotional states, particularly anger. He used the example of what Woody Allen said in his movie *Manhattan*—"I never get angry; I grow a tumor instead"—as not being far from what research and the connection between mind and body are revealing to be true.

In his medical practice, Dr. Maté has seen a strong correlation in chronic disease patterns of those who have a tendency to repress their feelings and emotional states. He has found this to be particularly true in a wide array of diseases from "cancer, rheumatoid arthritis, and multiple sclerosis to inflammatory bowel disorder, chronic fatigue, and amyotrophic lateral sclerosis (ALS). Sufferers from asthma, psoriasis, migraines, fibromyalgia, endometriosis, and a host of other conditions also exhibited similar inhibitions."[94] Maté also notes that people who are incapable of considering their own emotional needs feel a strong compulsive sense to take care of the needs of others; in addition, they often have difficulty saying "no." This information has been corroborated by several studies throughout different countries based on interviews of psychologists and thousands of patients that found an overwhelming predictability between whether patients would or would not develop cancer based simply on whether they suppressed their feelings and expression of anger. In unison with these studies are those long-term studies of medical students at Johns Hopkins and Harvard that demonstrated the correlation between teens' emotional states and later illnesses that had no relation to lifestyle choices such as smoking, drinking, or exercise.[95]

The difficult factor for us is the fear we have as humans of being "blamed" for our difficulties, whether physical or psychological. This also may contribute to that desire of professional medical and mental health systems to want to remain separate rather than interlocking systems with the same goal. Maté beautifully expresses a possible solution: "The issue is responsibility without blame. All of us dread blame, but we all would wish to be more responsible—to have the ability to respond with awareness to our circumstances, rather than just reacting. We want to be the authoritative person in our own lives: in charge, able to make the authentic decisions that affect us. There is no true responsibility without awareness. None of us are to blame if we succumb to illness and death. Any of us may succumb at any time, but the more we can learn about ourselves, the less prone we are to become passive victims."[96]

When the Immune System is Confused

As stated previously, Maté and Lipton highlight in their work that disease manifests when there is a disturbance in the PNI, the body-mind mechanism that is our emotional-nervous-immune-hormonal super-system. Much of what is seen in relation to this disruption is related to emotional deprivation, anger (and/or fear of angry feelings), disturbed attachment and its emotional confusion and feelings of inadequacy, and the stress caused with role reversal between parent and child. In these situations, people learn at a young age that their role is to take care of others' needs at the expense of their own. Saying "no" feels like a loss of worth and importance. All these feelings seem to be a threat to self and self-existence. Boundaries between self and non-self become fluid, undifferentiated, and confused.

Maté states that the primary task of the immune system is to differentiate between what is self and what is non-self. It is like a "sensory organ" that, along with the memory of the nervous system, needs to recognize non-self, or it leaves us open to danger. It is important to note that the immune system is our protector. It is in our blood, tissues, and all spaces in the body and acts like a brain, with receptors to detect anything that registers as non-self. Together with the nervous system, the memory of the immune system has been programmed from prior outer world experiences to be either nourishing, neutral, toxic, or dangerous.

In *When the Body Says No*, Maté explains the importance of viewing health in relation to PNI. He states that autoimmune diseases are representative of an immunological confusion in which the body's defenses turn against the self. This immunologic confusion perfectly mirrors the unconscious psychological confusion we have between what is one's self and what is the non-self. Consequently, the immune system attacks the body as if there were a foreign substance present. This parallels how the psychic self is attacked by inward-directed anger and judgment. This confusion reflects the disruptions between the body-mind mechanisms and what Maté calls the emotional-nervous-immune-hormonal super-system, or the PNI system.[97]

When there is a blurring of boundaries and confusion emotionally between self and non-self, there is a question of whose needs matter, and what is safe and what is threatening. This confusion is also detected physiologically in the immune system, with hormones released, in tissues and organs, and in the nervous system. Maté goes on to explain that the immune system becomes too confused to differentiate self from other and then is too disabled to defend against any incoming danger. What is most important to understand is the shared functions of immunity and emotions: First, the awareness that there is a self and a non-self; second, that we have nourishing inputs and the recognition of threat; finally, that we have life-enhancing influence as well as a capacity to limit or eliminate danger.[98]

So much of what underlies pain is the accompanying stress that is in response to threat and the stress hormone, cortisol. Normally the secretion of cortisol from the adrenals regulates the immune system and inflammations. In autoimmune diseases, there often is a reduced amount of cortisol response to stress, and the consequence is confused immune activity and excess inflammation.

In *When the Body Says No*, Maté also emphasizes the role of repressed anger and how to adequately distinguish between what is really a threat and what is not a threat. To know if there really is something potentially dangerous or invasive takes an ability to differentiate the boundaries between what is one's self (and familiar) and what is the non-self (feeling foreign and potentially harmful). Anger is the expression of what feels foreign and dangerous and in need of our response.[99]

Putting PNI into Practice

The groundbreaking research by Gabor Maté and Bruce Lipton shows that our inner experience (perceptions, thoughts, feelings, stories, and emotional states) changes our brain chemistry, cellular structure, and its incoming messages, ultimately affecting our immune-hormonal system, our nervous system, and the functioning of our bodily organs. Lipton also contends this process begins with conception, lasts throughout fetal development, and conditions our first seven years of life (forming most of our implicit memory). From this, we may wonder about the influence of trauma in early childhood on a person's PNI super-system. What would a person have been like without those early traumatic experiences, the generational transmissions of patterns and character strategies, and both emotional and bodily/disease patterns?

The work for those who have traumatic histories (or similar) is to focus inward on unconscious processes. They must mindfully study and inquire into their thought structures, emotional states, belief patterns, and the constructions that form the perceptions they then project onto others as if true. Shifting these thoughts and perceptions, and working with reactive states, will change their archetypal alignments and open them to their fullness, aliveness, and potential. In many cases, even physical disorders will clear with the changing of emotional patterns; an entire system can be restored to health and well-being. In fact, the more deconstruction of shadow in the form of beliefs, thoughts structures, perceptions, and core patterning that they complete, the more experiences of the Self that will become available. When these veils of separation thin, the conscious expression of the inner guiding force gets stronger. Then the Self, the innate archetypal wisdom, can shine through and provide each person with life guidance that is congruent with each individual's higher good.

Given PNI research, it seems critical for mental health professionals to be trained in the integration of somatic patterns and illnesses in their client assessment and treatment. Medical personnel also ought to be trained in including emotional and psychological work in their assessment and treatment. In our opinion, it is not enough to just refer clients or patients back and forth and have medical and mental health professionals consult with one another. This keeps the systems as separate disciplines rather than one. Granted, the current mental health diagnostic manual, the *DSM 5 (Diagnostic and Statistical Manual of Mental Disorders)*, is a small but new attempt by the mental health field to not just study people through a psychological lens but to also view the affect and interplay between the emotional and physiological. But this certainly is not comprehensive enough for what is needed.

To bridge the unconscious to the conscious mind entails the willingness to face all aspects of self—mental-emotional, physiological, and spiritual—not as separate parts but as the unity of the Self. In this archetypal approach, we do just that. If clients present with diseases, we look at the disease's objective meaning. We research what the disease is, what parts of the body are involved, and how those organs function. We also question why those organs are the ones chosen by the psyche, what is attempting to be expressed through the disease, and how it relates to a client's psychological patterns. From this, we begin to have a larger view of the person, what archetypal alignments are in place, and what interventions are needed to realign in a generative expression for full potential and health. If a referral is needed to a physician or naturopath, this, of course, we do. However, many of those who come to us with diseases have exhausted their resources in the medical realm and are feeling disheartened. We are often their last hope.

We find ourselves daily in awe of the beauty of being human, of the loving, relentlessness of the psyche to express what is needed for our higher good. When we have the courage to invite in what the psyche wants to share and listen carefully and deeply to the story being told (whether in narrative form or through somatic expression of disease), we bridge the unconscious communication to consciousness, new alignments and patterns unfold, and people have the opportunity to move closer to realization of the Self and full liberation.

22

Life Fields and Death Fields

Inspired by Dr. Michael Conforti

*Without the proper support of a generative life field,
our potential for having healthy esteem and a course toward
full expression of being is highly unlikely.*

As defined in Chapter Five, fields are nonmaterial regions of influence that have the capacity to shape and form the matter within them. They are a priori and hold all the information and energy in potential while being archetypally driven and influenced. In this shaping, they have the ability to keep out what is not a property of the field and to attract what is similar to the field. When archetypes that are innately nonlocal are constellated into the dimension of time and space, they contain generative and nongenerative alignments to their mandate.

An archetypal field that promotes, encourages, and supports well-being and generative development on a course toward the fullness of life, its potential, and the expression of its true purpose is called a "life field." A life field is in generative alignment with the mandate of the archetype constellated. On the other hand, Michael Conforti coined the term "death field" to delineate a pattern that constellates and replicates under circumstances *adverse* to that which supports the fullness of life and its potential in systems. If conditions are obstructing, limiting, neglectful, abusive, or dismissive, they set up a repetitive pattern of similar nongenerative conditions that play out in a system's development.

Importance of the Strong Container for Healthy Growth and Development

As we described in Chapter Three, an archetypal mandate for healthy growth and development is a strong container to hold and assist in whatever is developing within it. Virtually all living systems need this secure container in order to thrive and be fully prepared for leaving it and for life in the outside environment. If something compromises the secure container, growth and development also is compromised, and the system is not able to reach full potential.

Depending on the extent of compromise to the container, what is growing in it may struggle to survive and even die. If you watch a bird pecking its way out of an egg or a butterfly emerging from a cocoon, you see the requirement of the container to hold securely; without the container, survival can be threatened and questionable. Or consider the likely outcome of an acorn with a hole in it. Will it ever become an oak tree? If it does, will it grow strong and healthy? Similarly, during spring planting, the seeds may all be in good shape; if they are planted, however, in their next container of soil and that soil doesn't have good nutrients, proper drainage, or proper sunlight, those seeds may not germinate. If some seeds do manage to germinate and grow into plants, it is unlikely those plants will thrive.

The same process is obvious in the development of fetuses in a womb, whether animal or human. The container must be secure and provide healthy nutrients throughout the gestation period in order for generative growth and development, healthy birth, and a start in life on a course of thriving. If those ingredients are compromised, the trajectory of the fetus' development is equally compromised. Without proper corrective intervention, the fetus may not survive.

Even after birth, a human newborn is held in other protective environments: the arms of the mother, the presence of the father, the secure home, and the support of extended family, community, and culture. When a mother mirrors to her child the preciousness of his or her being, and the parents and the surrounding community see and encourage the child's full potential to unfold at each developmental stage, the child is set on a course toward wholeness and toward living his or her authentic self. On the other hand, if such generative conditions are not consistently available to the child—the container is unable to hold securely—a different trajectory is formed for the child and his or her inherent potential is obstructed. The child will continue with this nongenerative trajectory unless exposed to other conditions that can shift the course toward an alignment with health and fullness. Without the proper support of a generative life field, the potential of the child for having healthy esteem and a course toward full expression of being is highly unlikely.

How This Applies to Psychotherapy

As Conforti notes, the initial conditions are pivotal to the trajectory and potential course of development for each and every system. If life affirming and generative, the initial conditions set the foundation for flourishing and fulfillment of potential, unless other factors are introduced to change the trajectory. If nongenerative, the initial conditions will negatively impact the foundation and set the developing system on a trajectory for being unhealthy or at risk for survival.

In our psychotherapy practices, we see patterns of relative predictability depending upon initial and ongoing conditions and their alignments to the archetypal mandate of a life field or a death field—one that promotes, encourages, and supports well-being and generative development on a course toward fullness of life and expression of its purpose, and the other that obstructs, undermines, and restricts generative development. If the trajectory is not supportive of providing what is necessary for health and potential, and the archetypal mandate is not met in a generative form, we have learned that a death field is typically underlying it. There are archetypal forces due to archetypal alignments, like a magnetic force field, that pull the trajectory of a client's growth to "killing off" the possibilities for that person's success and thriving.

This takes us back to early childhood experiences. Many children come into the world in situations that fail to promote healthy growth and development. In these cases, unless there is some perturbation in the system of pattern replication, there tends to be a trajectory that continues the pattern of nongenerativity. In our practices, these children show up as adults who display the replication of their early nongenerative patterns; their behaviors and thoughts obstruct their flourishing and reinforce patterns that are neglectful, abusive, abandoning, or rejecting. It seems as though the person's potential is thwarted and "killed off" at each crossroad.

Take, for example, a family in which incest takes place and early trauma is experienced. A familiar contemporary dynamic consists of a father or stepfather who is the perpetrator and a mother who does not protect her children or who is blind to the horror happening around her. In these traumatic situations, children experience a lack of self-importance and value, while the parents' narcissistic needs take precedence over the protection, support, and encouragement of their child's healthy development. Such early beginnings constitute a death field that limits healthy growth: the child's overall purpose and course in life are thwarted. Those unhealthy beginnings also, most often (unless intervention is provided), set up a pattern that repeats boundary violations: What should remain private is violated. Later in life, those who were violated early in life may abuse children, marry dangerous, violent partners, or have a series of miscarriages or abortions—all manifestations of the psyche's attempt to reveal the underlying pattern of a nongenerative alignment to a healthy life and the presence of a death field. Remember: The psyche is continually expressing what is needed for the person's wholeness and ability to move into a field that promotes fullness of life, potential, and purpose.

Life Field Examples
- A herd of elephants will support the pregnant mother during gestation and post birth; all will participate in the development and teaching of skills to the young elephant.
- Many Native American tribes are now teaching their children the native traditions, rituals, and language of their culture. For example, the Plains tribes of the Midwestern United States have schools on their reservations and are providing college scholarships to set a generative course for their future generations.
- Children born into a family that has a good, supportive, healthy holding environment in alignment with supporting and encouraging their healthy growth and development tend to thrive and flourish in their lives and appear in alignment with their life's purpose at each juncture. They seem immune to situations that may take them off course and are able to shake off negative situations. They are firmly established in a generative life field.

Death Field Examples
- Any situation in which children are abused or neglected
- Violent families
- Families in which a parent is alcoholic or drug addicted
- Traumatic situations such as the death of a parent or sibling that is not fully metabolized and resolved with the help of the parents
- The Nazi war camps, where children and adults were held in horrific conditions and taken into gas chambers, put to death, and buried in mass graves
- Chronic illness

Example of a Death Field Shifting to a Life Field
When a person displays symptoms of active post-traumatic stress disorder (PTSD)

or when someone is chronically ill throughout life, there tends to be an underlying death field in place. The repetitive patterns are the psyche's way of pointing to what is needed for healing and for one's wholeness, and they ultimately expose a bifurcation choice point. At this juncture, a new pathway toward generativity is illumined, and the opportunity to turn toward health and fulfillment of one's life purpose becomes available. If this opportunity is taken, a new course in life can be established in a life field. If denied, the pattern of stress or illness will continue in hopes of being heard and understood.

On July 18, 1969, U.S. Senator Edward (Ted) Kennedy, who was then known for excessive drinking and chasing vulnerable women, was driving drunk with Mary Jo Kopechne as a passenger and drove off the Chappaquiddick Bridge. He survived, but Ms. Kopechne drowned in the river. This horrific experience tarnished Kennedy's reputation and the likelihood of his ever running for president, which seemed to be his destiny. In essence, a death field "killed off" Kennedy's fullness of life and potential; he no longer was able to live his full potential as a U.S. president, which had been his trajectory.

A bifurcation or choice point thankfully opened for Ted Kennedy when the children of his two assassinated brothers needed him as a solid father figure. He accepted the responsibility and eventually became a generative expression of the patriarchal head of the Kennedy family. He went on to be a noted and renowned senator who championed major causes, was instrumental in passing major legislation, and was duly honored and mourned at his death.

Situations such as the above are not accidental. They are replications of unresolved prior patterns and archetypal alignments with death fields in one's life that are psyche's attempts to be heard and understood. The example of Ted Kennedy's life, however, demonstrates what is needed to shift a death field to a life field: When a bifurcation is created or naturally arises and is accepted, this shifts the course and a new trajectory is available and possible.

Working with Clients Living in Death Fields

We tend to see primarily five categories of death fields in our work with clients:

- **Early Life Conditions:** The conditions under and into which babies are born set the trajectory for the course of their lives, similar to planting seeds in spring in good or poor soil or in favorable or adverse weather. For example, we red-flag babies who are born to mothers who are addicts; babies born into violent families, chaotic conditions, or situations of incest or sexual abuse; babies who survive childbirth in which the mother dies; and babies who are adopted by a mother who is very unlike the mother with whom the baby spent nine months or more.

- **Extreme Losses:** When people lose loved ones, sometimes the grief process is thwarted in some way and depression, numbing, or dissociating sets in. This can create a death field even if someone has been doing well in life prior to the loss. Some people, however, are able to grieve and metabolize their loss, no matter how traumatic, in a way that is generative and in alignment with a life field in which they continue to thrive. For instance, the death of a child catalyzed a mother to start Mothers Against Drunk Drivers, and the suicide of a son who was a talented musician triggered a father to publish and promote his son's recordings, which are a popular success.

- **Survivor's Guilt:** People who have lost siblings to death, adoption, or abduction; families in which a child has been murdered; people whose family members were on the Titanic cruise ship and lived; a sibling raised in an abusive family who is able to be successful while other siblings struggle to survive—these are all examples of people who might have survivor's guilt. Many clients in these types of situations feel so guilty that they get caught in a death field and are unable to let themselves thrive in a life field.

- **Unconscious Guilt That Is Unknown:** When there have been family tragedies that were not discussed, or deep family secrets, the information tends to be held in the unconscious. Examples include people who had family members in a past generation die in a genocide, babies who were born after a miscarriage or abortion, and babies whose mothers were grieving a significant loss as they were in the womb. These unconscious memories can set people on life courses aligned with death fields. Whether or not they know the origin of their guilt, those people unconsciously "kill off" attempts at success and sabotage having a good life. Michael Conforti brilliantly explains that we suffer far greater from the hurts we cause to others, particularly our loved ones, than our own hurts. These hurts can set up a pattern of unconscious guilt, often preventing people from having a generative life in which they can thrive.[100]

- **Unconscious Guilt Known But Not Acknowledged:** Numerous clients show up in our offices with known yet unacknowledged guilt. They include people who have sexually abused another, those who have hurt their siblings or not been able to protect them, parents who have hurt their children or put their needs first, people who killed animals, sometimes those who have been in war and killed others as enemies, and those who have had abortions or miscarriages. We see the themes of unconscious guilt that keep these people in death fields. They continue to punish themselves and won't allow themselves a good life until the negative, tragic occurrences are worked through and metabolized.

Most clients coming into psychotherapy who have experienced the above situations, who are caught in patterns that are hurtful and painful, do not realize they are living in a death field. We, thus, use our knowledge of death fields and life fields as an organizing principle in early assessment of patterns and pattern replication. We begin by naming the death field for them. Putting a name to their destructive patterns most often brings a sense of relief and a feeling of being seen and understood. A sense of hopefulness often arises. When a client can make a commitment to take the opportunity provided at the bifurcation, a new pathway opens.

But the death field holds its grips with a powerful archetypal force field, like a magnet! Often the client has been in this patterning for a lengthy period in life that has formed a strong course, like a groove in a record. As noted in Chapter Four, we call this a "creode in a canalized pathway." To overcome the archetypal possession with new behaviors that support and promote the fullness and wholeness of one's essential nature and authenticity requires building a life field pathway stronger than was active while in the death field. This is where we are instrumental.

Once clients acknowledge and understand their own death field, we then explain the components and qualities of a life field. We ask them if they feel ready to move out of their nongenerative patterns into a life that can hold deep meaning and purpose. We want to enlist the conscious mind, because we know the unconscious, deep Self has brought them into therapy for just this purpose.

When our clients feel ready, we start to introduce to them behaviors congruent with their thriving and the potential we see in them that needs to be developed. We introduce behaviors consistent with a life field and what those behaviors would look like in their lives. We also reinforce that we see they have the capacity innate within them to shift into a generative alignment.

This therapeutic work can be slow. Wishing to live a life of meaning and purpose does not mean a person can take in the sweetness of life and all the potential and love available to them. When we have lived in a death field throughout our life, there tends to be a "nourishment barrier"[101] that wants to stop the generative flow. Success in dissolving the barrier takes meeting all the challenges, hurt, sadness, and grief that arise in this process, welcoming them, and honoring their purpose.

When clients finally have solid footing in a life field, we then help them imagine the situations that may seduce them back into the old patterns in which they can lose this footing. Remember that death fields hold a very strong magnetic force that can pull them backward. Clients must be able to recognize the typical patterns and behaviors that cause them to revert—and how to stand up to those forces within themselves to remain in a generative way of living.

Example of Specific Therapeutic Stages to Resolve Unconscious Guilt

Frequently, when people are facing guilt, they have a propensity to get rid of the guilt and feel better. If a client has harmed someone, he or she often prematurely wants to make amends to feel better. If that client moves directly to making amends and asking for forgiveness, however, he or she is replicating the destructive pattern with the other who is hurt, because the client is only thinking of his or her own narcissistic needs. He or she wants to feel better by relieving anxiety and getting it over with and is not focused on the needs of the one harmed.

These are the typical steps, which cannot be hurried, for working with guilt during therapy:

1. Client verbalizes the exact details of the harm done and to whom. This may need to be done many times.
2. Client faces the harm that he or she caused. He or she must feel the extent of the other's pain and grieve the remorse for the harmful actions. This usually takes many sessions.
3. When a client has shifted into the ability to feel the other's pain and suffering, it is useful for the client to write a letter to the person, not send it, but bring it into therapy and read it aloud. This needs to be done with feeling, or there is more work to be done on remorse.
4. When the remorse and self-focused feelings are complete, we discuss the process of amends and what is appropriate for the other person. In some cases, it is appropriate to ask to meet with the other; sometimes that may cause more harm. Other options include actually writing and sending a letter to the person or, if contact is either going to possibly cause more hurt or is impossible (i.e., in the case of abortions, miscarriages, or a death), we have the client read the letter over and over in therapy and revise it as needed.

When this process is completed, it will become obvious that the energy within the client has shifted. A sense of relief will be present, and the client will be able to begin the work of moving into a life field that will perpetuate his or her full potential.

Part Five

Three Parallel Maps of Development

"These levels [of development] are the basic maps that human beings use to make sense of their world. They are the hidden maps that govern how we actually see and interpret and feel the world from each of the major developmental levels. Most people think that what they see 'out there' is really out there, and that the same world is available for everybody—all they have to do is look. But, what developmental studies unmistakably show is that, at each level of our development, we actually see and feel and interpret the world in dramatically different ways. Each stage of our development has its own grammar, its own structure, its own map of the territory it is being exposed to. And these vary enormously, so much so that some developmentalists maintain that each of these different stages actually has or is a different world."[1]

- Ken Wilber -

23

Three Models of Developmental Knowledge

"Let's consider ego development and spiritual transformation as forming one unified process of human evolution. A human being grows and develops by learning from experience. Difficulties can occur at any stage of this process, including getting 'stuck' on the ego level. . . . So it is one process of evolution from the beginning of ego development to the final stages of spiritual enlightenment. It is how Being, impersonal and eternal, becomes a person, a human being on earth. So the process is a matter of Being, which is spirit, learning to live in physical embodiment."[2]

- A.H. Almaas -

To move toward our infinite potential and gain the Treasure, we need to rescue enough of our captives to be able to move to later stages of adult development. In this section, we would like to explore how an understanding of three distinct but parallel "maps" of development affords us the clearest approach to rescuing our captives and moving toward gaining our Treasure. We have already introduced two of these maps: the Ego-Self Journey and the Archetypal Developmental Theory. The third is contemporary developmental research.

To really understand rescuing the captive, a practitioner needs a full picture of human development. This is because captives are often still in implicit memory stored somatically in the body, or in the early stages of development. Being able to recognize the captive's capacities at those early developmental stages, what their worldviews are like, and what their predictable features look like at a particular stage allows us to talk with them at their level—which is paramount in facilitating a captive's re-integration. Assessing a client's next developmental stage is also useful, as knowing this information empowers us to plant seeds for the movement into the next developmental level.

In addition, we use an understanding of developmental patterns to work backward from the present-day reactive states of our clients to make fairly accurate guesses about what occurred in their childhoods and now resides in their implicit memory.

We, thus, will present herein a simplified version of the patterns of development that current developmental psychologists doing research have found over the last fifty years. We will spell out the specific developmental tasks, perspectives, and challenges we go through at each level of development and explore how the ego presents itself at each stage. Our goal is to provide a more precise look at what is involved in actually gaining the Treasure.

As a reminder, gaining the Treasure is truly hard work. Each developmental stage is difficult to leave, because leaving requires a change in identity. So we need all the help possible! When used together, the Archetypal Developmental Theory, the Ego-Self Journey, and contemporary developmental research truly provide a fully rounded, powerful tool to assess where clients are now developmentally, where they are headed, and how they might reach the captives left in the very early stages of their development to reach the Treasure that lies in potential. In our later stages of development, the ego is no longer driven by its own importance or the importance of the group. Instead, we are transformed, characterized by a generative inner refuge, and hold a wider lens of being able to have concern for the betterment of all humanity and all life forms.

Our Passion

With this in mind, our passion is supporting clients in their emerging later stages of development. We strive to help people move into their life purpose in order to share all the gifts they bring in their potential. Neumann calls this mature level of being the archetypal stage of Gaining the Treasure. Because we focus on the later stages of the ego's relationship with the Self and the advanced levels of adult development, we look closely at the subtler levels of releasing the patterning of the body and the mind as being in service of removing the veils that keep people and organizations from truly being of service to humanity.

Interestingly, as we have seen the power of Neumann's Archetypal Developmental Theory working with our clients, we also excitedly have found that the later stages of adult development are being studied by several researchers. We have been determined to study the work of those researchers who have been mapping the specific ways in which human consciousness develops and evolves. Of most importance to us have been those researchers who are creating the maps of the later stages of adult development, those who are describing what the human ego becomes as it continues its development—when it naturally goes into a relationship with the wholeness at the center of our being, which we refer to as the "Self."

In particular, we have been interested in post-conventional development (development beyond Piaget's final stage of cognitive growth that allows us to think about abstractions),[3] which we generally reach around the age of eleven or twelve. With our in-depth study of researched developmental theories of later life stages, we were trying to answer certain questions: What is needed to attain the Treasure? What does the ego look like on its way to fulfilling its potential? What enables us to move to a stage in which we can value all ways of looking at the world and create environments for others to grow and evolve toward the Treasure of their potential? What we have pleasantly learned through our study and effort is that Neumann's Archetypal Developmental Theory nicely dovetails with the developmental work of many researchers. Desiring to bring every potent strategy to our therapeutic work, we also have been motivated to incorporate these researched developmental models into our practice.

Overview of Three Models of Developmental Knowledge

The three main models we use to look at human development include the Ego-Self Journey model, Neumann's Archetypal Developmental Theory, and researched developmental models. First, the Ego-Self Journey model focuses on how the ego develops in relationship to the Self—from its birth until it begins to consciously experience more and more unity with the Self. (See Chapter Six, "Neumann's Archetypal Exploration of Individuation" for more on the Ego-Self Journey.) Second, Neumann's Archetypal Developmental Theory shows human progression from the unconscious to consciousness through various stages, including what lies in potential for all beings. (See the **"Archetypal Developmental Theory"** diagram in Chapter Six and the entirety of Part Two of this book for a review of this model.) Finally, the body of research on development by Jane Loevinger[4] and Robert Kegan,[5] elaborated by Susanne Cook-Greuter[6] and Terri O'Fallon,[7] provides the current framework for understanding how meaning is constructed throughout life. This research on the later stages of adult development confirms our findings regarding what is needed to move into the archetypal stage of Gaining the Treasure and beyond. For our purposes, we have synthesized the work of various developmental researchers—to whom we are much indebted—and refer herein to this combined body of research on human development as the "Researched Developmental Model."

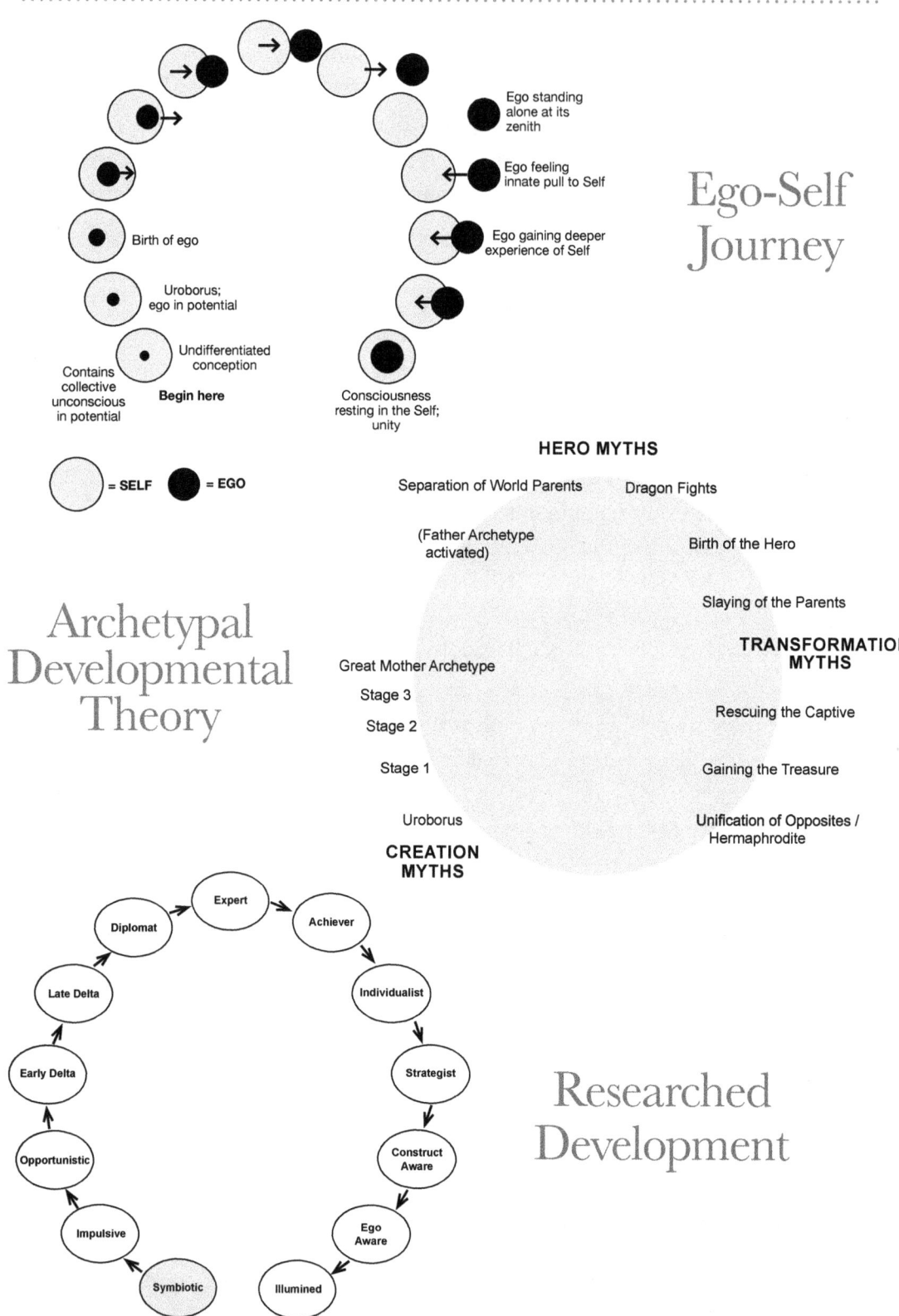

All three of these models show very different views of human development, yet all three portray a process of a sequential emergence of a hierarchy of basic structures[8] of human consciousness that are archetypal in nature and that can be applied throughout humanity. These basic structures lie in potential and contain abilities, capacities, and views of perspectives that are available in the human psyche, yet they must be developed progressively. That is, the lower levels within each of these models are foundational to the succeeding levels; as Ken Wilber teaches, each level is transcended and included in the next. Furthermore, development is not fixed in its timing of unfolding; the stages unfold in a fashion unique to each person, some slower and some faster. Yet the process is uniform in terms of the *properties* of each stage, and each level increases in structural complexity.

Shining through and behind each developmental structure is an archetypal force empowering conscious experience and development: the Self. The Self is not a mental, emotional, nor volitional energy. It may be called a transformational force or an archetype that catalyzes our realization of our innate wholeness, balance, and harmony. It carries the goal of union between consciousness and the unconscious— and a union of all opposites. In Eastern spiritual traditions, the Self is viewed as the "eternal truth," which is simply being in our natural and original state.[9] In Archetypal Developmental Theory, we call this pinnacle of development the "Unification of Opposites" stage.

We all experience the Self as an inner guiding and organizing force that is always seeking union and balance. Like the moon exerts a force upon the Earth by its very existence, the Self exerts a magnetic call for development from stage to stage. In each shift in developmental capacity, the current developmental level is transcended yet still included. Just like our childhood interests were once all encompassing and then we lost that intense interest, we grew into new stages where we can hardly believe . . . that we once had no teeth or that we once craved playing certain kinds of games that now seem immature.

At each step of the ego-Self journey, at each archetypal developmental stage, and at each researched stage of development, progress into the next level carries the deep sense that something in us is dying and no longer needed as we leave behind the old and move into the new stage. That feeling is what keeps us from easily moving from one stage into the next, or what keeps us taking two steps backward for each step forward. The "fulcrum,"[10] or the developmental movement from one stage to the next, functions archetypally as the threshold into the new and unknown, which we seem hesitant to cross. The Polish psychologist, psychiatrist, and physician Kazimierz Dabrowski, who developed the theory of Positive Disintegration,[11] speaks of the lower levels of development disintegrating as growth occurs, which allows for a reordering, a revising, that facilitates the creation of a new, higher level of being.

Maturing has many benefits, but, just as we are reluctant to upgrade our computer's operating system into one that is more complex, we don't want to be in the "unknown," don't really want to give up our familiar way of operating, and don't always want to be in a constant state of learning. Few of us can even remember when we last updated our computer operating system, yet many of us nostalgically remember a developmental stage that now seems as though it were easier to navigate. We just don't know the benefits of the next stage ahead of time, because we haven't experienced them. Yet nature just keeps moving us forward, ready or not! Particularly if we do not have a good foundation in the earliest stages of life, when our worth and value are laid down, shifting into the next developmental stage can seem like running a gauntlet.

With each move from one stage to the next, the psyche is faced with a new fulcrum of development, a leap into a wider, more complex perspective, and the death of what is currently known and familiar. Some of these fulcrums of development are more daunting than others. Keiron Le Grice, professor of depth psychology and chair of the Jungian and Archetypal Studies program at the Pacifica Graduate Institute, captures well the ego-Self drama involved in maturation in his book *The Archetypal Cosmos*. He writes: "The individuation process, mediated by an encounter with the archetypes, effects a radical transformation of the structure of the psyche. The old form of the ego structure is destroyed and a new, more robust, more inclusive psychological structure is formed that better reflects one's psychological wholeness, the entirety of what one is—both the conscious identity and the Self, the other, unknown greater person that stands behind the conscious personality." He goes on to say: "The Self is the center and the totality of the whole psyche, the whole human being, whereas the ego is only the center of consciousness, the part of the psyche that we are familiar with and identify with. To individuate, the ego must face the dark half of the psyche, where the Self resides. It must come face to face with the unconscious."[12] Yet, each stage is an experience of a different world, with a different perspective and a different view of reality.

Research on Ego Development Theory

As defined by developmental psychologist Dr. Jane Loevinger (and added to by Dr. Susanne Cook-Greuter), *ego* is the central functioning of the Self. Theorist and developmental researcher Dr. Terri O'Fallon furthers our understanding of *ego* by noting that it arises from and is permeated with the Self as our essential nature and the

Ego-Self Journey

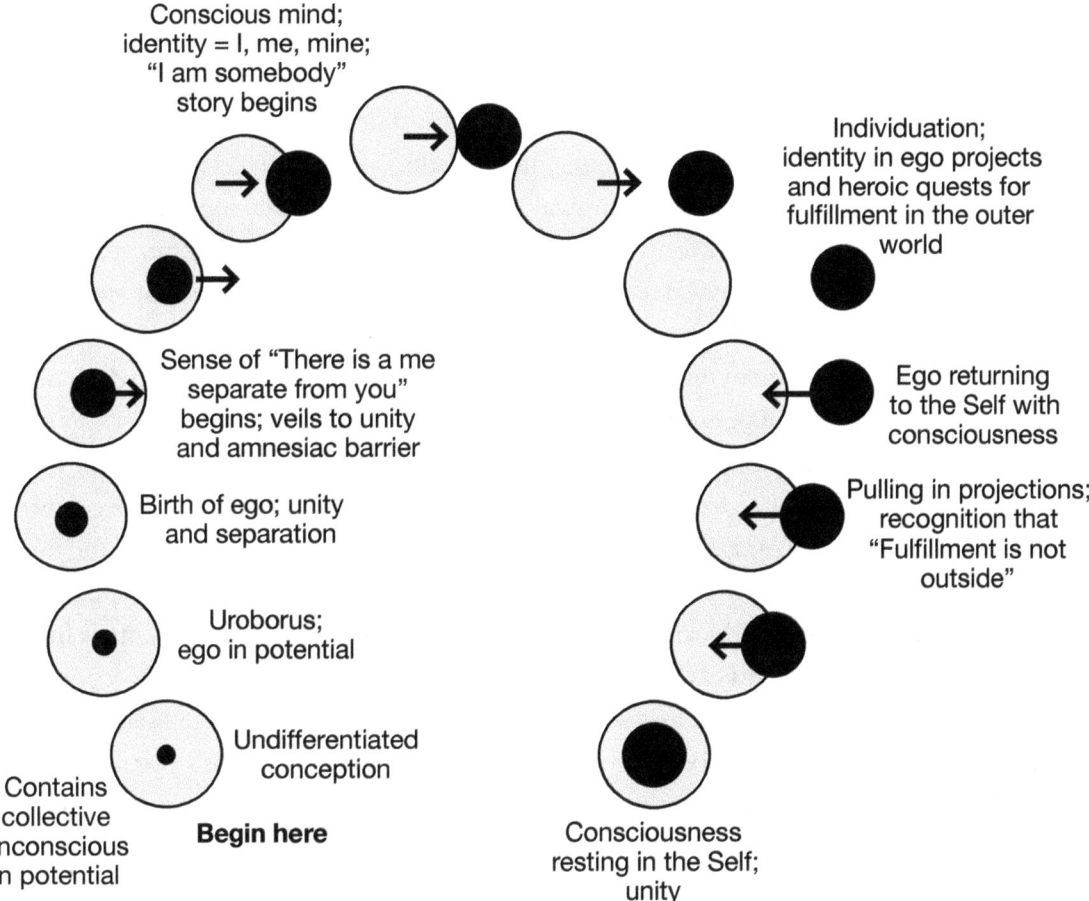

central archetype of human existence. In an article in the *Journal of Integral Theory and Practice*, O'Fallon states: "I use the term *ego* here to denote the underlying principle in personality organization that strives for coherent meaning and orchestrates how we perceive reality. 'Ego development' is the term for the common element in the stage sequence and the corresponding dimension of individual differences. . . . The function of the ego as a process is to organize, synthesize, and integrate experience from both external and internal sources and to mediate among them. The ego is the central processing unit within the rational, personal, symbol-mediated realm of experience. The ego as representation (the 'I' and the 'me' as one's identity) can be understood as the result of this effort at integration. The created identity, thus, changes with the changing levels of integration. Interestingly, at the higher end stages, the ego seems to reflect the possibility of becoming a witness to both the ego's efforts at processing and to the changing results of the process of identity formation."[13]

Developmental psychologist Susanne Cook-Greuter, renowned for her extensive research on ego development theory, delineates the stages that occur prior to the ego reaching maturity as "Survival" stages. She dubs the later stages of development and Self-realization as "Meaning Making." During the later stages, we ask significant questions: "Who am I?" "What is the meaning of life?" and "What is my purpose?"[14]

Moving developmentally from Survival stages to Meaning Making stages is a significant shift, often referred to, when applied in Integral Theory,[15] as moving from "First Tier" to "Second Tier" developmental ability. (Tiers are groupings of similarly patterned stages of development.) The delineation between First Tier and Second Tier stresses the movement into the later stages of adult development that, to date, are attained by only a small percentage of individuals in our culture.

Second Tier stages take a wider view of humanity. We begin to understand our cultural conditioning and how this affects the beliefs of who we are. We move from conflict between developmental stages into acceptance, without judgment, of the necessity of all stages. And we begin taking steps toward deconstructing the apparent duality of there being a subject and separate object of projection. This duality is fundamental to the belief and early life conditioning that "we are a separate self, separate from other beings in our life, and separate from our true nature as the Self." Using Cook-Greuter's model (that began with Jane Loevinger and which has been added to by Terri O'Fallon), we have come to understand that Meaning Making stages of the Second Tier development encompass the mind and the mature ego seeing through and deconstructing thought structures developed and believed to be true prior to this maturity, whereas Third Tier stages, now being researched by Terri O'Fallon, begin moving into an awareness of awareness and eventually to unifiying experiences. (See our "**Researched Developmental Model**" chart later in this chapter.)

Susanne Cook-Greuter also added to the research on developmental stages with an analysis and subsequent theory regarding "perspectives." According to her work, which was added to by Terri O'Fallon, human development can be grouped into various ways of observing things; those perspectives can be grouped and seen as a pattern, with the pattern beginning with a narrow focus and widening with each perspective. These perspectives grow and emerge as we develop.

Descriptions of the Cook-Greuter/O'Fallon perspectives follow and can be viewed in the **"Developmental Progression of Perspectives"** chart:

- **First-person perspective (1P)** = Focus on the self. i.e., "I can only see things from my perspective, and I don't know that any other perspective exists." This perspective is sometimes called being "egocentric."
- **Second-person perspective (2P)** = Focus on self and other. i.e., "I can see that another person has a view, too, and there can be a 'we.'"
- **Third-person perspective (3P)** = Focus on an observer who can focus on another self and other(s). i.e., "I can see there is a third person or thing about which we are speaking. This gives me the capacity to take an objective, scientific, or universal perspective. I can even stand back from myself and form an objective opinion about myself as well as stand outside of historical time."
- **Fourth-person perspective (4P)** = Focus on an observer observing another observer observing another self and other(s). i.e., "I can see there are larger patterns. I also can see that we all have views that are colored by our upbringing and our culture. Because someone has studied something (3P), I can reflect on it, refer to that study, and use it in presenting an even larger picture, like this book, or I can use this same ability to criticize that study." About fifty percent of our current population has this capacity.[16]
- **Fifth-person perspective (5P)** = Seeing the previous pattern of observing observers observing; at this perspective, the perspective and observed can cycle from the 5th to the nth positions.[17] i.e., "I can reflect on how I take perspectives on different perspectives, and I can reflect on how I construct my way of believing."
- **Sixth-person perspective (6P)** = Seeing the nth perspectives and beginning to step outside those nth perspectives. Also taking a perspective using patterns of observation and perspective taking through tiers. i.e., "I can embrace all perspectives at the same time."

Keeping perspectives in mind, let's examine the human developmental stages identified through years of research by Kegan, Loevinger, Cook-Greuter, and O'Fallon.

Developmental Progression of Perspectives

	Narrative	Guiding Principles of Stage	Capacity	Archetypal Developmental Stage
1P and 2P	Momma and Daddy say what's right.	Rules are set by authorities and must be followed	Either/Or It is!	Great Mother
2P	My peer group and society norms now dictate what is right; I begin questioning rules.	Rules are set by my peer groups and society norms	Either/Or I can see there are two sides, but I choose my side.	Separation of the World Parents Stage Two
3P	I can see both sides, but goals take precedence over rules.	Rules give way to goals	I can see there are two sides, but I can still only choose one.	Birth of the Hero
4P	I can't only use goals. They don't always produce the results I'm looking for. I begin to reintegrate lost aspects.	Goals give way to seeing context	Both/And	Slaying of the Parents
4P to 5P		Seeing contexts gives way to awareness of constructs	Witness Neither is nor is not.	Rescuing of the Captive
5P	I experience the Self and self-representation separately. Subtle ego death	Construct awareness gives way to ego awareness	Everything is Constructed	Gaining the Treasure
6P	Causal ego I develop the capacity to experience the Self without a structure based on past experience.	Ego awareness sees through to unity	Everything is in unity	Unification of Opposties or Hermaphrodite

First Tier/Survival Stages

1. Symbiotic Stage

In this early stage, the infant is merged with the mothering one with no separate distinction between self and other. It is an undifferentiated, unconscious state of unity. The ego is in a germ state of potential and not yet formed. In relation to the Archetypal Developmental Theory, this is the non-verbal, first stage of the Great Mother, when the implicit memory is storing information and experiences in relationship to the infant's oral needs. Those needs include being touched, soothed, and seen in the mother's gaze for the preciousness of being. If the infant experiences any level of deprivation during this stage, he or she introjects a compromised message of value, worth, and importance.

2. Impulsive Stage

This is an early stage of ego development that is body oriented around the physical self. The child is preoccupied with basic needs, safety, and what others will provide. Thoughts are very concrete and focus on "me," "mine," "I want," and "no." The child's ego is impulsive, protective, and self-centric. This stage begins the second or anal stage of the Great Mother and focuses on power and one's authority. Because a distinction now exists between what is "me" and "not me," the Impulsive stage begins what Terri O'Fallon describes as a "first-person perspective."[18] With a first-person perspective, one can only see thoughts in a concrete, either/or manner and only see one's own side of any interchange.

3. Opportunist Stage (also known as Self-Centric[19])

This stage, which corresponds to the second (anal) stage of the Great Mother, is only slightly advanced in ego development and is still body oriented around the physical self. The child focuses on how to protect him- or herself and perceives the world as threatening. In this stage, the self is more reactive and automatic than in the first two stages; this is demonstrated by the use of power in service to one's own needs. The child also has an attitude of not needing to be accountable because, in this attitude of "protecting," he or she is only reacting to an outside threat to self. As with the Impulsive stage, children in the Opportunist/Self-Centric stage still respond to life from a first-person perspective.

4. Delta Stage

This immature stage sees the beginning and early focus on self *and* another. Children of this stage also become aware of the quality of concrete operations and are intent on following the rules and not crossing boundaries so as to avoid getting into trouble. They externalize their feelings and project them on others. They have an awareness that the other person can see what they can see, and perhaps what they can't see. This new perspective marks the beginning of the second-person perspective. In the second-person perspective, we have the capacity to see for ourselves (differently than others see). We can talk *with* others, not just *at* them. And there is still a sense of a set of rules by which we must live.

In relation to Archetypal Developmental Theory, the Delta stage correlates with the completion of the third (genital) stage of the Great Mother, including its Oedipal stage. To gain our sense of value, worth, power, and authority as well as embrace our sexuality, we would optimally integrate generative thoughts, feelings, needs, and drives from this early period. If we introject nongenerative messages regarding the nature of our essential being, however, parts of self will be dissociated, split off, and left in the unconscious during the Great Mother period. We would then proceed in development compromised with an underlying sense of betrayal as we turn away from our true nature of the Self. Ken Wilber, who has authored numerous books on transpersonal psychology, explains this dynamic: "If the self fails to adequately integrate any of these elements, it will remain either fused and embedded in these elements (failure to differentiate), thus creating an addiction to these elements (food, sex, power, etc.), or it will disown and dissociate from these elements (failure to integrate), thus creating an allergy to these elements (food, sex, power, etc.). . . . Especially at each developmental juncture, these types of dysfunctions are most likely to occur. In moving from the oral to the genital stage, for example, if the self fails to differentiate adequately from oral drives, it will remain identified with or fused with those drives, thus developing an oral fixation or oral addiction, constantly substituting food for other needs and using food to generate comfort."[20]

5. Diplomat/Conformist Stage (also known as Group-Centric)

This stage correlates with the pre- to early-adolescent state of mind. As such, it is a more mature stage with regard to rules; one follows rules as the norms of the peer group, without questioning or introspection. Also, neatness and/or attention to outer appearance are paramount to conform and be "included" in the peer group. In fact, status, material possessions, reputation, and prestige are in the forefront.

The Diplomat/Conformist/Group-Centric stage is the last of second-person perspective and either/or ways of relating. It reflects a shift from only being able to think about *concrete objects*, to being able to think about the *subtle forms of ego* (e.g., the objects of thought) and thinking about thinking, or visualizing and thinking about feelings.

Although there is not yet a sense of self as a separate adult identity, Cook-Greuter names the Diplomat/Conformist/Group-Centric as the first of the adult stages. Identity, however, is dependent upon one's "groups" and a stance of "us" versus "them." In Archetypal Developmental Theory, this stage correlates with the Separation of the World Parents.

6. Expert Stage (also known as Skill-Centric)

When an individual has reached the Expert/Skill-Centric stage, he or she can look at his or her own self and behavior and see that self as separate from others in an objective way. In general, we can step back during this stage and see we are different from the group and want to be recognized for our own specialness. We become self-conscious and sensitive to the judgment of others. This is the first stage in which we are truly a separate self, distinct from others. It correlates in Archetypal Developmental Theory with the Birth of the Hero.

In the Expert/Skill-Centric stage, we have a third-person perspective and the ability to focus on an observer who is focusing on someone or something else. In other words, we can now concentrate on others and imagine what they are thinking and feeling as well as categorize, prioritize, and bring a hierarchical trajectory to what is visualized. This adds the quality of abstract and formal operational thinking to our awareness; we can visualize symbols of symbols and focus on goals, ideas, and emotions. But we don't yet know that others can do this as well. Building upon what we attained in the Diplomat stage, the Expert stage is the first time in development that we can focus on the larger issues behind physical experience. For example, we can shift from focusing on our difference in skin color to the importance of human rights.

7. Achiever Stage (also known as Self-Determining)

In this stage, rules give way to setting goals; to being success oriented, achievement based, and self-determined; and to a win-lose stance. There also is a new ability to define one's story in one's own terms, an increasing sense of consciousness, and the newfound capacity to see two sides to circumstances.

The Achiever is defined as a mature adult in our culture. We are able to understand ourselves and who we are in contrast to others. We see we are different and can agree to disagree. In this stage, which also correlates with the Birth of the Hero, we have a third-person perspective.

David Yeats, in summarizing Cook-Greuter's work, notes the further categorization of the stages of Cook-Greuter's developmental model. He says, "The Diplomat, Expert, and Achiever are referred to as *conventional* stages of development, as they reflect the adult values of our culture. The next two stages, the Individualist and the Strategist, are referred to as *post-conventional*, in that they are stages that move beyond traditional cultural norms of ego development into other ways of being and experiencing life."[21]

8. Individualist Stage (also known as Self-Questioning)

Individualists are characterized by two distinct personal expressions in terms of ego development: 1) deeply cherishing their own unique orientation in life and in moment-to-moment experience; and 2) shared, egalitarian values of consensus and different justifiable points of view.[22] More specifically, the Individualist focuses on self within the experience of the moment. He or she is able to look inward, take a systems approach, question the norms, and question what family and culture, as being true, define. In addition, the Individualist has an acute drive to develop a coherent self-story. At this stage, we also have an appreciation of varying and differing interpretations. We ask ourselves, "How do I make sense of what I know?" And, we utilize many ways of looking at, understanding, and really knowing something.

During the Individualist/Self-Questioning stage, introspection is a new capacity, and we begin to question, "Who am I?" We tend to turn inward for the truth and turn away from only valuing cognitive information; we place more weight on intuition, dreams, sensory and bodily feedback, our internal wisdom and guidance, and finding patterns and distilling what is most important. In essence, the Individualist moves from goal setting as being of primary importance to being able to see things within a larger context. We start to observe ourselves and understand that truth is a matter of perspective.[23] We also begin to be able to see through and observe assumptions, interpretations, paradox, ambiguities, projections, and contexts. Multiple sides of situations can now be seen and explored, which connotes an early fourth-person perspective, and we move from an either/or to a both/and viewpoint. This mature stage—which corresponds to the Slaying of the Parents in Archetypal Developmental Theory—supersedes the past stages that lack individuation. We can now view ourselves as being unique individuals with our own expression of being.

Second Tier/Meaning-Making Stages

The Individualist/Self-Questioning stage is the last of what are called the First Tier or Survival stages. In the First Tier stages, there is a belief that each stage has the "only" truth and "right" values. Its developmental task is to bring feeling and knowing together. On the other hand, in the Second Tier stages, the developmental task is to undertand the important contributions made by all the previous stages and to cognize that feeling and knowing are a "whole." In this tier, there is an understanding of the extent of our cultural conditioning, steps are taken toward deconstructing the subject/object split (which is so fundamental to our modern scientific paradigm), and the belief of being a separate self is dissolving. In short, the Second Tier moves from "survival" to "meaning making"—and the inevitability and necessity of making qualitative discernments. As noted earlier, the following are considered to be the later stages of development thus far attained by only a small percentage of individuals in our culture.[24]

9. Strategist/Autonomous Stage (also known as Self-Actualizing)
As Strategists, we thrive on complexity and on becoming the most we can be. We look at the larger picture and multi-facetness of life and the universe from the perspective of a separate being. We engage in complex, intertwined parts of life, relationships, processes, and a holistic view. At this stage, we also love shifting contexts, understanding that no story is completely true, and we view all approaches as having equal value. In addition, as autonomous adults now, we take charge of our psychological well-being; we are self-responsible and directive in life. This is the first time we realize that people function from different levels and need to be treated according to their level of awareness. Furthermore, Strategists seek self-fulfillment and define their purpose, taking into account the knowing of constraints and limits of individual control. Deep trust emerges that challenging situations can be handled and solutions found.

Strategists/Self-Actualizers also deeply embody self-authorship, purposeful action, and focus on self-actualization.[25] It is no surprise that the Rescuing the Captive stage of Neumann's Archetypal Developmental Theory corresponds to the Strategist stage, for it is during the Strategist stage that we become strongly anchored in "witness consciousness" as the *context* of a situation gives way to becoming more and more aware of the ego functioning, its storytelling, and thought as *constructs*. However, one vulnerability of Strategists is that, while being able to see others on varying levels of development to which we need to tailor our interactions accordingly, we also are impatient that others don't "get it" and are not on the Second Tier.[26]

In late fourth- to early fifth-perspective, Strategist/Autonomous/Self-Actualizing adults are able to see both sides of a situation and the larger picture and contexts of situations. They can focus on an observer observing another observer observing another self and other(s). An example is our reading other authors who observe others' behaviors. The Strategist/Autonomous/Self-Actualizing adult is now able to experience the emptiness and nothingness of reality—but not yet that reality actually involves both nothingness and the fullness of everything-ness simultaneously without separation. This perspective comes at the next developmental level, the Construct-aware stage. Only approximately five percent of the American population is believed to have reached this level.[27]

10. Construct-Aware/Magician Stage

In this stage, the separate self that has been the center of ego development thus far begins to dissolve and morph. One's identity is no longer centered in an individual self and ego; rather, the person begins to understand that thinking he or she is a separate self is an abstraction, an idea rather than reality. In other words, those of us who are Construct-Aware adults are mindful and aware of ego functioning, storytelling, and thought constructs. We begin to integrate the ego as an idea constructed by humans, our conditioning, and how humans make sense of existence. In other words, we now are aware of the power and limits of language, and we see the idea of self as a constructed story that is seen through the aspects of ego. In addition, although we now see we are nothingness, we also have a deep knowing of our interconnectedness to everything that is the Self. We have come to learn that the need for humans to tell stories and have maps is in service of avoiding feeling our impermanence and mortality, the greatest threat to our egos.[28] Paradox and ambiguity—the radical stance of not knowing versus pretending to know for the sake of the ego feeling safe—and embracing "what is" versus "how things should be but aren't" become the new worldview. And from the limits of not knowing arises a deep appreciation of the mystery of being.

The Construct-Aware stage corresponds to Neumann's Archetypal Developmental Theory stage of Gaining the Treasure, although we continue rescuing the captives from early implicit memory introjects. According to Cook-Greuter, the vulnerabilities at this stage can be loneliness, fear of going insane, feeling rarely understood in our fullness and complexity by others, being aware of our foibles and limitations, and vacillating between feeling the nothingness of being and stepping into the fullness and brilliance of all our being. There also can be a trap in an attachment to transcendent experiences rather than an embracing of the beauty and ordinariness of everyday human experience. Cook-Greuter goes on to say, "Wise compassion is one of the great gifts of positive later stage experience. True maturity in the ego development sense allows one to see all experiences and all others as precious and beautiful in their own right, while the capacity to make distinctions and act with decisiveness and courage is retained. Helping others is more like being a midwife to their own emergence than an act of transforming them for their own good."[29]

The perspective of those in the Construct-Aware stage is early to later fifth-person; the previous pattern of observing observers observing moves into being aware of awareness itself. This process expands as practices of self-inquiry, introspection, and witnessing of the unfindability of the thinker and the "I" to which we refer become more integrated and embodied.

Third Tier/Awareness of Awareness Stages

The Construct-Aware stage is the last stage of the Second Tier, during which one is able to see the important contributions made by all the previous stages and mentally understand that feeling and knowing are a "whole" together. In the Third Tier, now, there is an experience of feeling and knowing uniting through an awareness of awareness itself. In the early stage of the Third Tier, there is a coming to know our own constructed reality, where, in the maturing of this stage, our identity joins with awareness. In other words, there is a direct awareness of the underlying Whole that unites knowing and being. In fact, the awareness of "wholes" marks the Third Tier: of first seeing wholes, but not yet having a relationship with them; next to feeling wholes; then of witnessing wholes; and, finally, of being wholes,[30] experiencing oneself as whole and seeing oneself as intrinsically interwoven with the entire Kosmos and all sentient beings.

11. Ego-Aware Stage

Dr. Cook-Greuter has delineated a transition stage between Construct-Aware and the Illumined/Unitive stage; she calls this transition the "Ego-Aware" stage. Being Ego-Aware, according to Cook-Greuter, takes hypervigilance: One must be aware of the fierceness of the ego's attempts to hold on in subtler and subtler ways in the later stages of development. This advanced stage entails a conscious practice of being aware of thought structures that arise in the forms of inflated or deflated ways of being. Without this conscious practice, the shadow aspects can linger in ways that may not be seen through. Ego-Aware people are able to not only see that everything is a form of constructed reality, but they also no longer feel the need to resist or get rid of what

Researched Developmental Model

Stages of Development Centered in the Body			
Symbiotic	Merged with Mother; no distinction of Self and other	Basic trust, safety, and security	Takes in characteristics of others; introjects
Impulsive	"Me, Mine, No!"	Safety and gratification	Needs are basic; trusts
Opportunist/ Self-Centric	"I win. You lose."	Own needs and wants are foremost	Controls; manipulates; coerces
Development Ruled by Mental Processes			
Delta	Internalized parents	Rules	"If something is wrong, make more rules"
Diplomat/Conformist/ Group-Centric	"I am my group"	Obeys group norms, uses persuasion	Threatened by ambiguity
Expert/ Skill-Centric	Interior of ideas and awareness of emotions comes online	Rules by logic; knowledge-based	Beginning introspection
Achiever/ Self-Determining	Independent Self with own ideas	Coordinated; substitutes goals for rules	Can see past and future selves "I can think about thinking"

Later Stages of Adult Development			
Individualist/ Self-Questioning	Discovers own personal and cultural conditioning	Can see context; adapts rules and creates new ones when needed	Looks inward; questions conventional worldviews
Strategist/ Autonomous/ Self-Actualizing	Becomes responsible for own perceptions and projections	Sees all developmental stages have great vailidity	Sees both sides and makes decisions based on good for all
Construct-Aware/ Magician	Able to see own thought structures; releases shadow	Thinks in terms of systems and paradox	Reframes; reinterprets situations to get all participating
Ego-Aware	Sees the form of constructs and can embrace them all	Engages in constant inquiry while in action	Authentic, truthful, transparent; lets go of ego and OK with "not knowing"
Illumined/ Unitive	Internal experience is of emptiness and outer fullness	Able to experience the Self beyond the influence of past history	Ego no longer in the driver's seat; the Self is the center

Based on the work of Kegan, Loevinger, Cook-Greuter, and O'Fallon, as of 2016 is arising in each moment and are able to simultaneously be in a loving relationship with everything. In Neumann's Archetypal Developmental Theory, this correlates to Gaining the Treasure.

Regarding perspectives, when we are in the Ego-Aware stage, we have a late fifth-person perspective: We can see the causal aspects in others as the interconnectedness of the Self, although we still do not recognize that others see our aspects in return. Instead, the focus continues on our own awareness of awareness of objects and the awareness of constructed reality and its projections. Plus, in this stage, the boundaries between self and other, conditioned and unconditioned, begin to collapse and dissolve, leaving the unconditioned source of all being.

12. Illumined/Unitive Stage

The Illumined being experiences the conditioned and unconditioned as no longer two but as co-arising—not good or bad, but necessary, like two sides of the same coin. We see the Self as part of one reality rather than in a dual view of daily life. Internal experience is of emptiness, and external experience is of fullness of form appearing simultaneously as one.

The Illumined individual experiences a deep cherishing and honoring of all humans, without judgment, and the experience of life is beyond language as has previously been known. In this Unitive state, self-identity is based on inner knowing as the Self. We no longer are shaped by language nor differentiate one aspect of reality from another. We see self and other not separate but of an "ongoing humanity" in a highly evolutionary and creative journey. The universal or cosmic perspective of all is participating in a cosmic dance in eternity. Further, we experience the humanness of people on all levels and the human essence that we all have in common. We welcome and accept others as they are, without judgment, agenda, or need to control. And there is no differentiation between seeing the causal, formless aspects of others as well as they can see our causal aspects. The Illumined person is also oriented to all that exists as being in the eternal moment, resting in the inner knowing of Self and cherishing all human existence. In Neumann's Archetypal Developmental Theory, this is the Unification of Opposites or the Hermaphrodite. This state of unity is continually deepening and integrating throughout the course of life.

The perspective of the Illumined/Unitive individual is sixth-person; the ego is transcendent, and constructions are seen through, as everything is in unity with itself.[31] This mature individual embodies a personhood of love and compassion and embraces all of life. He or she also recognizes there is a never-ending, continual evolution of consciousness throughout our human existence rather than believing that, when we "awaken," that is the end of our journey. The Illumined person also knows that the nondual, unconditioned awareness of the Self is, and always has been, the truth of our being, and that our conditioned humanness is always welcomed and inseparable from the Self. This deep knowing becomes the vantage point from which the Illumined/Unitive individual lives.[32]

Comparison of Archetypal and Researched Development

- Uroborus — 0P Symbiotic
- Great Mother — 1P Impulsive
- Great Mother — 1P Opportunist
- 2P Early Delta
- Father Archetype — 2P Late Delta
- Separation of the World Parents — 2P Diplomat
- Dragon Fights — Late 2P Diplomat
- Birth of the Hero — Early 3P Expert
- Slaying of the Parents — 3P Achiever
- Rescuing the Captive — 4P Individualist, 4P-5P Strategist
- Gaining the Treasure — 4P-5P Construct-Aware, 5P Ego-Aware
- Unification of Opposites — 6P Illumined

Looking at Our Culture Through the Lens of the Three Models

To exemplify, if we look at current culture of the United States through the lens of each of the three models, here is where our culture stands:

- **Ego-Self Journey Model**: Current culture's "center of gravity" is in the farthest position possible from the Self. (Refer to the **"Ego-Self Journey"** chart.)
- **Archetypal Developmental Theory**: Our culture is at the Birth of the Hero stage, the stage in which heroic quests of gaining mastery, power, authority, possessions, winning, and the right mate reign supreme.
- **Researched Developmental Model**: The "center of gravity" of the United States is currently at the Expert level (ruled by logic and rules with a beginning introspection) and the Achiever level (has an independent self with individual ideas; has substituted goals for rules).

Our culture is a long way from the later stages of development, when we begin to see that happiness is not found by outside means and when we can look for and acknowledge our shadow aspects and unintegrated material. *If or when our culture were to mature to its next level*, such maturation within the three models would correlate thus:

- **Ego-Self Journey Model**: Ego beginning to return to the Self
- **Archetypal Developmental Theory**: Rescuing the Captive stage
- **Researched Developmental Model**: Strategist/Self-Actualizing, the stage in which we are able to view all levels of development lower than ourselves as being of value

Each stage of development has a different worldview, different paradigm, and different perspective. Also, each stage is made up of what can be described, articulated, reflected upon, influenced, and changed; what is valued; who we deem worthy of respect; and the time frame we can envision for the stage. Given this construct, we need to understand what kind of therapy and interventions are appropriate for each stage of development.

24

Evaluating Developmental Stages

Leaders in later levels of development notice and actively manage psychological dynamics and support the growth of the "we" space of systems.

As therapists (and consultants), part of our work is to evaluate in which developmental stage a person's (company's, or other system's) "center of gravity" rests. We generally use the Ego-Self Journey model as an *overall picture of the individuation process*, with the Archetypal Developmental Theory *illuminating the unconscious process of gaining conscious awareness*, and the Researched Developmental Model *clarifying the conscious abilities and capacities of meaning making* that are typically available throughout a lifespan. We have found that knowing the guiding principles of the stages, what each stage has the ability to perceive, and the way meaning is constructed in each stage can be quite helpful for assessment and treatment. In fact, having three different systems of appraisal helps us to hone in quickly on the right stage and to determine if clients:

- Are so new to the stage that they are oscillating in and out of it,
- Are "swimming" in the stage but not near integration,[33]
- Have mastered the stage and are in the oscillation of integrating,
- Are stuck in the stage and avoiding the "unknown," or
- Are completing a stage. (At this juncture, clients often want to "push away," feeling, "Oh, that's old stuff" or "I already know that.")

Once we have discerned our client's stage, we are able to help the individual, company, or organization to fully integrate that stage and to seed the foundation for shifting into the next. Then we look for aspects from the shadow that are caught in reactive cycles and attempting to be heard and brought into consciousness. If our client has a history of repeated trauma, recurrent stress, or developmental predicaments, that person (or company) can have facets of consciousness at several different developmental stages split off from access to consciousness. As described earlier in the book, we call these split-off aspects "sub-personalities" or "captives." They are feelings and memories from earlier stages and perspectives that were not able to continue to develop in a normal fashion because of a lack of environmental support or traumatic circumstances.

Although sub-personalities are most apparent in individuals, companies also carry shadow material that functions in similar ways and acts through the employees. Ken Wilber notes that, "Each sub-personality exists as a subconscious or unconscious 'I,' an aspect of the Self that was defensively split off, but with which consciousness remains fused, embedded, or identified as a hidden 'I,' with its own wants, desires, impulses, and so on. The nature of the sub-personality is largely determined by the level (stage) it was dissociated from."[34]

As noted in Part Four of this book, therapists sometimes function as quasi archeologists. We help to dig up aspects from the earliest stages of development that are caught in reactive states needing to be recognized and reintegrated, and then we advocate and interact with those aspects or sub-personalities. Through feeling acknowledged and understood, those sub-personalities begin to integrate into consciousness. As each separate "I" is transcended, it automatically becomes part of the known "me."

In Neumann's Archetypal Developmental Theory, the stage of integrating split-off aspects or sub-personalities is called Rescuing the Captive. During this stage, it is the ego's task, mandated through the archetype of the hero, to find and reunite the split-off aspects. Much of what is rescued resides in the three archetypal stages of the Great Mother and the Separation of the World Parents. In the Ego-Self Journey model, we would find the ego returning to the Self, which automatically begins the process of ego dissolution. This would trigger any aspects of ego development that are not complete to come into the foreground for completion. In the stages of the Researched Developmental Model, we would find that the Strategist/Self-Actualizing level is reaching back to the earlier stages that are centered in the body (the Symbiotic, Impulsive, and Opportunist/Self-Centric stages) and back into the implicit memory of our first seven years.

Using the Researched Developmental Model

When using the Researched Developmental Model in a clinical setting, we code the elements and capacities of the stages that clue us in to how to assess and guide treatment. Following is our shorthand list of each stage's elements, coded by the perspectives to which they have access and by the abilities and capacities those perspectives contain.

Symbiotic Stage
- I am taking in what my caregivers are feeling and how they treat me and feel about me; and I am beginning to encode those feelings and experiences into patterns. I am floating in union with Mother. (0 Perspective)
- I am my body, which is different from the environment. I can only take one perspective: I can only see my side. (1P)
- I am different from my mother! She can leave me! I am my body and am separate. (1P)

Impulsive Stage
- I am an emotional body-self, and my emotions are different from the emotions and feelings of others. (1P)

Opportunist/Self-Centric Stage
- I'm integrating being able to think *and* feel. I'm a conceptual self now and can use my mind to repress feelings and needs that I don't think will help me get what I want and need. (1P)
- Rules are set by my parents and other authorities and must be followed!
- This reflects a very black-and-white system of "This is how it is," "I have no choice," and "I have a very hard time keeping the rules." I still can only take one perspective (1P) and can only see my side.

Delta Stage
- I'm trying to follow the rules so I can belong. There is a lot of me they don't seem to want, so I don't want those parts of me either, and I tend to project those feelings onto others. I am starting to notice that others can see something different than what I see. (2P)

Diplomat/Conformist/Group-Centric Stage
- Rules are set by my friends, peer groups, and my society's norms (e.g., the norms of teenage television networks and social networking sites). I'm beginning to question rules altogether. This reflects a more mature version of a black-and-white system of "I can see there are other ways, but I can't choose them. It's either/or. I can take two perspectives, myself and another (2P), but usually I only take my own perspective."

Achiever/Self-Determining Stage
- Rules give way to goals. I have goals and can see there are two sides to most

situations, but I can't quite yet choose one of those sides. This leaves me seeing two sides but usually choosing my side. I can begin to take a third-person perspective: myself, another, and an observer (3P). Now I can begin to imagine what the other person must be thinking or feeling. This adds the quality of abstract and formal operational thinking to my abilities.

Individualist/Self-Questioning Stage
- I cannot *only* use goals. They don't always produce the results I'm looking for. Goals give way to seeing that everything is in a *context*. This means there cannot be *only* two ways of perceiving; there can be a *both/and*. I can choose both sides at the same time! I can find my own truth from inside me! I can observe there are many sides to any situation. I understand paradox now! I can take a fourth perspective (4P). I begin to shift from doing (as identifying my worth) to the importance of just being.

Strategist/Autonomous/Self-Actualizing Stage
- Seeing contexts gives way to being able to see through thought structures and to knowing that *the mind constructs reality*. I come to know that everything is constructed, so I can't choose a wrong way. There is just a choice. I can be a witness and take a fourth-person perspective, but I'm moving into the fifth-person perspective (5P).

Construct-Aware/Magician Stage
- Seeing constructs gives way to being able to see that my *ego constructs stories and narratives all the time—and those constructed stories and narratives aren't always true*. I experience myself as something beyond my self-representation. I am aware of awareness and see the "I" within the other. My view is that things neither are nor are not. I can take a solid fifth-person perspective (5P) but am beginning to see from a sixth-person perspective (6P).

Ego-Aware Stage
- Seeing that my ego cannot know the truth and that I can deconstruct my ego, I can see that *I am not my ego! Everything is actually in unity*. I have the capacity to experience myself without a structure based on past history or experience. This frees me from all perspectives and constructs, and I can take a full sixth-person perspective (6P) that begins to involve awareness of the unity of opposites.

Illumined/Unitive Stage
- I experience my ego and the Self as not separate. I feel a oneness with all that is in existence. I experience the unity of opposites.

Let's look at an example of assessing a client using the researched stages of development and perspectives in a clinical setting:

A client expresses frustration that he isn't able to meet his goals.

What We Know
- It is very difficult to solve a problem by thinking from the same level.
- Becoming frustrated with goals is actually a desire for a larger way of looking at the world.
- One cannot yet see choices as "both/and" from a third-person perspective.
- The next level of perspective needs to be "gaining context," or the fourth-person perspective.

How We Would Approach the Client Based on This Knowledge
- We would begin the therapy by questioning him about the *context* of his frustrations and the *context* within which he has set the goals.
- We would *refer to the prior developmental level*, where rules are the guiding force, to learn if rules about the way he meets goals might still be in force and be part of his frustration.
- We would endeavor to get the client to *widen his perspective taking* by leading with statements such as: "This frustration can be a sign of maturing. Becoming frustrated with goals can be a sign that you want a larger way of looking at the world."
- We would endeavor to get the client to *shift to a fourth-person perspective* by seeding with questions such as: "Can you see your situation from all possible sides? Could the paradox you find yourself in actually be usable?"

Being able to see the context of things, in general, is a huge step in development. From an Archetypal Developmental Theory perspective, to see the context of things and work with goals, one must have consolidated the archetypal stage of the Birth of the Hero and, at least, be moving into the Slaying of the Parents stage. This can be a difficult passage, because it means learning to function from an inner compass instead of relying on an external, peer-driven, outer compass.

Knowing the movement from rules to goals to contexts to constructs—and the perspectives those embody—can help immensely in assessment and in seeding the foundation for the next developmental stage, whether we are talking about individuals, companies, or organizations. For example, we all have been involved with bureaucracies that function from 2P, where rules are "the rule" and there are no exceptions. Or consider a department store that operates from the belief that "the customer is always right," even though there are rules to that rightness. That store is functioning at 3P. Similarly, stores that take back returns easily at any time demonstrate they understand context and would be coded as 4P. Furthermore, a company that functions with the goal of being in service to the community, hires people who are able to function from a Strategist or above developmental level, and gives its workers permission to do their job without layers of in-house bureaucracy is likely functioning at a 5P level.[35] Finally, here's an example of a company functioning at the 6P level: A nursing company in the Netherlands hires nurses whose sole purpose is to be of service to people's health. These nurses are empowered to function from the wisdom of their years of practicing medicine and manage themselves. Health in their community has dramatically improved, people feel supported, and the company makes enough profit that it has expanded to other communities.

Using Perspectives to Integrate Sub-Personalities/Captives

Another strategy we use to assess a person's developmental stage is to explore the progression of how a person organizes his or her early experience into patterning from infancy through the third-person perspective. This enables us to recognize sub-personalities/captives, locate them in their specific developmental stage, and then interact with them. By exploring context and widening perspective, we are able to question all that was taken in as a child from the family system as well as from the institutions of school and church.

Remember, atmospheric feelings (feelings that seem to always be in the background, such as sadness or separateness) are stored in the implicit memory as pre-verbal structures of meaning at 0P. Then images are eventually connected with those atmospheric feelings, and images of the mother/caregivers become stable as attachment figures, even though the images may contain positive and/or negative connotations. The next progression is that the child is able to symbolize content and have some words for his or her experience. Words then develop into concepts and then into schema or early representations of organized patterns that stand for identity. This all occurs in 0P and 1P (implicit memory). So Rescuing the Captive generally takes going back into a 1P perspective (that is encapsulated in the unconscious) and talking with that captive in its language from that specific developmental level. When the captive feels heard and understood, the sub-personality or aspect integrates within a third-person perspective (3P). See the following "**Rescuing in the Implicit Memory**" chart with perspectives added to reinforce this concept.

In looking at an example of how knowing stages and perspectives can help with integrating a sub-personality, or rescuing a captive, let's continue to use our client who is frustrated with not being able to meet his goals. As his therapy work continues, his frustration gives way to his lamenting, "I can never do anything right. I should just die!" The client feels so bad about himself that death seems to be his best option. Obviously, this very black-and-white solution is from a younger developmental stage. We would assess this stage as beginning in the zero-person perspective and being encapsulated into the unconscious at a first-person perspective, where everything that happens is seen as "my fault."

Even though whatever happened in that younger developmental stage is in this adult client's past, within the session, that past is alive and strong in his unconscious and is active now, in the moment. Taking it very slowly, we begin to interact with his 1P captive. We ask what is going on in this 1P captive's world. He says that his father is shouting all the time, his mother is always in the bedroom with the door shut, and he feels horribly responsible for his younger sister, who cries constantly. Responding to this aspect on his level of development, and in the early historical time frame in which this aspect of him lives, we say, "This must be horrible for you. You don't have anyone to help you or your sister. You can't possibly know what to do, because you are so young. You must think this is your fault. Of course, you would think about dying. You just don't know any other way to deal with how horrible you feel."

He brightens considerably and says that he likes the picture on the wall of the therapy room. We take this as a derivative communication that we are on the right track; he is saying he likes something and seems to come back into current time. As we continue talking about what was happening back then, he seems to be able to bring in more and more perspectives. Taking him into 3P, we ask, "What did that little guy need back then?" He readily responds by saying, "I just needed a grownup to make everything better." Introducing 4P, we ask, "Can you be that grownup for that little guy now, if we go back into that scene together?" He then is able to talk about how difficult it was to see his sister suffer when he was growing up and how he decided he would take on her suffering. Examining this now, he decides it was a wonderful, heart-

Rescuing in the Implicit Memory

Perspectives Taken	Ability of Stage	Capacity	Archetypal Development Stage
0P	Sensorimotor intelligence	Sense of Self in physical brain	Uroborus
0.5P	Sensation, perception	Floating in Mother's womb	Uroborus
1P	Exocept — primitive organization of memory traces and images	Downloads of environment and caregiver's feelings	Uroborus and Stage One of Great Mother
1P Early	Images	Transitional object of caregiver	Great Mother
	Symbols	"I exist as object in the world."	Great Mother
	Endocept — preconscious cognition; an interrelationship of feelings and former experiences	Emotional brain comes "online"; Stage 1 creates magic for events too complex	Great Mother
	Words		Great Mother
	Rudimentary concepts		Great Mother
2P Early	Rudimentary schemas		Great Mother
	Rules, peer group, in/out group		Great Mother
2P Late	Symbols		Separation of the World Parents
3P	Goals	Intellectual brain "online"	Dragon Fights
4P	Contexts		Birth of the Hero

felt goal, but an impossible one. Nonetheless, that goal probably kept him alive and gave him a reason for living—rather than dying in some unconscious, accidental way, which he remembers contemplating as a young child.

Eventually, we reached the root of his problem with goals through exploring the context within which he and his sister were growing up. We helped that sub-personality to recognize its dilemma, which is the first step in reintegration. Over time, therapy proceeded to bring our client into a 4P, while integrating an old, limiting sub-personality and rescuing the captive caught in a 1P world.

Now, let's look at an example of how using the stages and perspectives can help companies and organizations. A larger company bought out Company X in 2008. Six Company X employees retained their jobs, while fifty-five employees were laid off. Management did not allow anyone who remained to see or talk to the laid-off employees, whose jobs were filled within a few days by employees of the new, larger company. By 2015, Company X was struggling with productivity and office atmosphere issues, which seemed worst in the summer months. People were short tempered and irritable with one another, a large number of absences occurred, and meetings were consistently disrupted.

The original Company X operated at 3P. With the handling of employees at the merger, the six remaining employees resorted to their core patterns of terror, hiding, anger, or pleasing and caregiving; they felt they had to compromise themselves to continue to have a job. This left an unconscious dynamic of functioning at 1P; each of those six employees thought only about themselves rather than about the whole team. Until their first-person perspective is acknowledged and talked through, the unhealthy dynamic will continue to cause problems for Company X.

Leaders in later levels of development notice and actively manage psychological dynamics and support the growth of the "we" space of systems. They focus on influencing whole systems rather than on influencing individuals. They look for the larger problem rather than what the presenting symptoms point to, and for the implicit assumptions and principles under which the system is operating that are not being recognized. They look for what is "un-discussable," what is just not talked about, and discover what behavior is rewarded and what behavior is punished.[36]

25

The Difficult Transitions Between Stages

There are fulcrums at each developmental stage; at these fulcrums, we will face a bifurcation. If we choose generatively, we will leave old patterns of being behind, advance developmentally, and adapt to a new way of living.

Recall from our earlier discussion that a *fulcrum* is the movement between the developmental stages—a dance between the stages. Each fulcrum leads us into unknown territory. Consider the dance of the caterpillar that fashions its own cocoon, identifies with it, embeds itself inside it, makes complete use of the cocoon, and then begins to dis-identify and become a butterfly, separate from the cocoon. Eventually, the butterfly de-embeds by breaking apart the cocoon, drying its wings, and flying away, transcending the cocoon altogether.

Note how the caterpillar, at each stage of its development, embraces and integrates the major features of that particular period of its development. So, too, do we need to embrace and integrate all the major features of each of our own developmental stages—all their qualities, thoughts, feelings, needs, and drives—in order to shift to the next stage. This is not easy work. Obviously, if asked, a caterpillar probably would not choose to "melt down" into its elemental parts and then reorganize into an entirely new entity, but it is driven by the same magnetizing force that we are, the innate force that drives us to grow in complexity.

As we explained earlier, maturing has many benefits, but we are usually reluctant to leave the stage we are in, because we don't want to be in the scary unknown and we don't want to give up the comfort of the familiar. Maturing takes work! Experiencing stress, trauma, or abuse makes that work even harder. Instead of being able to shift and move on, we have to put all our energy into defending ourselves.

Each level of self-development has built-in defenses—against pain, disruption, (stress and abuse) and ultimately death. The self will use whatever tools are present at that level to defend itself. For example, at the first fulcrum, the self only has sensations, perceptions, and impulses. It, thus, can only defend itself in the most rudimentary ways such as by fusing with the physical environment or through hallucinatory wishes (of what is really needed) and perceptual distortion. At the second fulcrum the self has the added tools of more intense feelings, emotions, and newly emerging symbols. It, thus, can defend itself in more elaborate ways such as by splitting the world and the self into "all good" and "all bad" representations, projecting its feeling and emotions onto others, fusing itself with the emotional world of others, and creating magical meanings. By the time of the third fulcrum, the self has added concepts and beginning rules. These powerful mental tools can be used to forcefully repress the body and its feelings, displace its desires, and create displacements so that it can confuse itself as to what is occurring and what is really needed.[37] Note there are fulcrums at *each* developmental stage; at these fulcrums, we will face a bifurcation. If we choose generatively, we will leave old patterns of being behind, advance developmentally, and adapt to a new way of living.

In this clinical example, let's explore a case outlined in Nancy Newton Verrier's book, *Primal Wound*.[38] Carrie constantly felt a sense of disorientation and inability to function well in her role as mother and housewife. She could not really feel joy with her children, although she loved them dearly. Carrie's problems manifested as her not wanting to go to her children's school functions, even though she knew her kids really wanted her to go. She did not understand why she didn't want to go, just that it wasn't something she wanted to do. She felt bad and frozen about this. She had no life outside the home. She had decided to try therapy because of how bad she felt about not being able to show her love for her children.

After a few therapy sessions, we learned that Carrie had a cunning voice in her head that doubted everything she did. That voice constantly confused her, caused her to distrust her own reality and perceptions, and accused her regularly of being unkind. When we examined those thoughts and their repeated pattern, Carrie began to remember her mother's responses to whatever she wanted or any emotions she would share: "You don't want that toy. You don't need to cry. You don't think that's funny. You're cold! Put a jacket on! You think you are so smart, but you're not." Eventually, we were able to pair the voice in her head with the misleading parental diatribe (which we call the superego). Carrie was amazed at how different she felt once she was able to interrupt and not believe this confusing voice that had been narrating her life.

The therapy work then led to questioning whether she *was* really bad, because she *had the feeling* that she was a really bad person. She remembered that she repeatedly played a game with her childhood friend that they called, The Princess and the Slave Girl. In the game, Carrie was usually the princess in distress waiting to be rescued.

She recalled the common scene: "I'm being tortured or in prison and someone has to come and rescue me."

So we talked about her feeling that she was waiting to be rescued. This led to the realization that she actually felt this way a lot of the time while she was growing up. She also was able to articulate how much she hoped therapy would rescue her. But she didn't remember being tortured or being locked up, just feeling as if she were.

During one particular session, Carrie was quiet for a long time. Then she began crying and stopped herself. As we worked through that and she began to sob, we discovered that she remembered deciding that there was a "good Carrie" and a "bad Carrie." We sat with that for a while and talked about what that was like. Eventually, we explored the fact that, often, when a child creates a good and a bad self, that child is responding to feeling like he or she has a good mother and a bad mother. This defense strategy is a way of making meaning of not having the kind of love one needs. That understanding seemed to break something open inside Carrie. She sobbed and then remembered that, when she was really little, she used to have a recurring dream of a bad little person coming to get her. She pondered, "I wonder if that bad person was me?"

The next few sessions led us into her memories of spending hours creating fantasy situations and worlds in which she had exactly what she needed. And that she had a special fairy princess who would come and be with her, who she felt really loved her just the way she was. During the next few months, that fairy princess's presence was with Carrie more and more of the time. She was able to play with her kids and even went to their school Christmas pageant.

Once we felt this phase was integrated, we began exploring her feelings of being held in jail and what she thought that might have been. We talked about how those kinds of pervasive feelings were memories stored in a place before there were words to describe a young child's experience. Slowly over the next three months of sessions, Carrie brought in childhood pictures and talked with relatives and close family friends. The pictures were always of Carrie in a playpen, peering through the bars. Family friends said they remembered that Carrie was always in a playpen when they came over and that she was rarely allowed to be outside of it. They remembered that the playpen was in front of the television and that she was given whole bags of cookies to keep her quiet.

Bringing out this very young material from implicit memory involves a slow therapeutic process—and an even longer time to integrate it into the narrative of life. But, it did explain why Carrie felt the way she felt most of her life. The process also seemed to release her soul from the oppression she had always felt. She was relieved to know that she wasn't really bad, but that, of course, is what any child would think under those circumstances. The process also explained why Carrie hadn't been able to play with her own children.

In the weeks and months of therapy that followed, Carrie began excitedly to tell stories about exploring the neighborhood with her children. They would go to the library and read together, and she planned to go on camping trips with her family. Granted, Carrie's inner dialogue of doubt will still pop up when her reactive states are triggered by outer situations, but by also learning mindfulness meditation, she is beginning to build an inner refuge where her fairy princess presence lives all the time and the doubting voice cannot enter.

Difficult Transitions in the Three Different Models

The most difficult transitions occur during the stages in which, like the caterpillar becoming a butterfly, we become a very different creature. Despite the hard work required to complete each stage, remember that, if we haven't completed a stage, nature will push us along and reveal what we have not claimed and integrated through events which may cause great suffering. This built-in check attempts to point us back to working with what we have left behind. In fact, if we really want to embody the later stages of development, we will have even more cleanup work to do.

Following are the stages of our three primary diagnostic models where one might really struggle:

Difficult Transitions in the Ego-Self Journey Model
- Birthing the ego out of the unconscious and then maintaining its development from the great archetypal pull back into unconsciousness.
- Reaching the zenith of the ego's development as the farthest from the Self and then turning toward the Self, now ready to stand strong in going into the unconscious to rescue anything held captive there.
- Returning from the underworld, integrating, and then bringing the gifts received in the unconscious to the community.

Difficult Transitions in Neumann's Archetypal Developmental Theory
- Moving from the three stages of the Great Mother into the outer world. This transition necessitates allowing the ego to take precedence over the archetypal world, a shift that, archetypally, we experience as a betrayal of our self. (See the Separation of the World Parents explanation in Chapter Six.)

> **Particularly Difficult Fulcrums**
>
> * Dis-identifying with the mind that makes concrete distinctions (no longer identifying with the sense as "me")
> * Dis-identifying with the mind that makes *subtle* distinctions (no longer identifying with "me" as a mental "me")
> * Dis-identifying with the mind that makes *any* distinctions (transition into nonduality)

- Moving from Slaying of the Parents to Rescuing the Captive, which correlates with the culmination of the ego's development. The ego, at this point, must turn inward toward the Self.
- Rescuing the Captive. This process necessitates going back into the Great Mother to rescue any parts that were not integrated. Archetypally, it is experienced as going into the cave or underground to fight the demons or dragons that live in the dark. It takes great courage to persevere to attain the prize of the Treasure of one's own being!

Difficult Transitions in the Researched Developmental Model
- I am a body and separate from those who care for me. Yikes! (Separation Anxiety)
- I am an emotional body-self, and my emotions are different from the emotions and feelings of others. I need to have the right to say "no" and "This is mine" and have my words be respected. (The Terrible Twos)
- I am a mind and can use it to integrate or repress the emotions and needs that I have in order to please, get along, or meet my goals in this world.
- I am more than my senses and my body.
- I am more than my emotions and feelings.
- I am more than my thoughts, ideas, and imagination.
- I am my soul. I need to integrate my mind, body, and emotions into my soul.
- I am aware of being awareness.
- I am.

26

Attaining the Later Stages Held in Potential

Gaining the Treasure ultimately results in our realization that our early situation and the ensuing patterning was a gift that forged our uniqueness. We come to celebrate that our creativity flows from this uniqueness and comes into the world in a way that no one else could express. Finally, we are able to embrace our essential nature as the Self and recognize that Self in others as the One Self, with our care and concern going to all beings.

In his book *The Origins and History of Consciousness*, Erich Neumann refers to three different dimensions of personality development that take place over the course of a lifetime, from conception through the adult stages. The first dimension is ego development in terms of *extroversion*; it is the adaptation we make to the outer world of objects, quests for happiness, fulfillment, and ambitions. The second dimension is the turning inward to the objective psyche and archetypal mystery in developing a deep appreciation for and relationship with the unconscious domain. At this point in development, we realize our quest for happiness. Because lasting peace and love are not found in the outer world, we turn inward in search of true peace and happiness in realization of the Self. The third dimension is what Neumann refers to as *centroversion*; this is a continual process of balancing the prior two stages, as there is an innate inner drive helping us become the expansive, self-creative being of our potential and pulling us toward wholeness and Self-realization. This is often referred to as the second half of life.[39] According to Neumann, "Centroversion manifests itself as a directive center, with the ego as the center of consciousness and the Self as the psychic center. The conscious and unconscious work together in a harmonious interplay between persona and anima/animus."[40]

Although the unconscious underlies and dominates most of our life, in the second part of life and through individuation, we have the opportunity to engage consciously in the powerful force of the unconscious, summoning it to be our guide to awakened states of being. In doing so, we shift the focus from ego-driven activities to transpersonal and supra-personal contents toward the Self and the center of the total psyche. The crucial factor is attaining a conscious ego that can remain stable enough to avoid being overwhelmed by the unconscious.

To live from the later stages of development with an ego that has morphed, been purified, and is living in unison with the unconscious and devoted to embodying the Self, we must unify the opposites. We do this by collapsing the inside and outside worlds, the separation between conscious and unconscious, the anima/animus, male and female aspects, daily life and divine life, and individual and collective. The mandala contains all of these as expressions of the faces of God. Neumann beautifully describes this in the later stages of development and the journey we go through to reach these stages: "We began with the ego in the womb of the parental uroborus dragon, curled up like an embryo in the sheltering fusion of the inside and outside, world and unconscious. We end, as in an alchemical picture, with the hermaphrodite standing upon this dragon: By virtue of its own synthetic being, it has overcome the primal situation. Above it hangs the crown of Self, and in its heart glows the diamond."[41]

We have talked in prior sections about the first stage of development Neumann calls *extroversion*, when the focus is on the identity of "I, me, and mine" and on reactive states projected into the world as what is a true perception of self and the world. The second stage of *introversion*, however, moves us from Survival states to Meaning-Making states (from the First Tier to the Second Tier in Cook-Greuter's model)—ultimately to a wider view of human existence. It positions us for the later stages of adult development as the ego matures and layers of patterning, identity, and defenses are released and integrated. A huge shift takes place when we realize that peace, happiness, love, and fulfillment are not attained by outside means other than momentarily. We see that the inner thoughts, feelings, and reactions that have formed our perceptions and been projected on the world and others are just that, projections. Not the truth.

Our intention and motivation turns toward the truth of life and living from our essential nature and its gifts to others—from the Treasure and the jewel of our being. The ego is morphing and changing as we embody more openness and flexibility in emotional states, persona, vulnerability, and expression congruent with our true nature. As more and more layers of unconscious shadow aspects and defense structures are dissolved and integrated, a mature form of ego emerges; projections are retracted and seen through as our perceptions rather than the truth. We live from a stance of emotional maturity.

Neumann speaks to this process when he writes: "In the integration process, the personality goes back along the path it took during the phase of differentiation in reaching a synthesis between the conscious mind and the psyche as a whole, that is, between the ego and the Self, so that a new wholeness may be constellated between the diametrically opposed systems of conscious and unconscious. . . . All the differentiations built up and personality components built up during the first half of life, when consciousness was developing, are now rebuilt. In this transformation process, the ego reaches consciousness of the Self and the Self evolves out of its unconscious activity and arrives at the stage of conscious activity. The mythological stage becomes a psychological reality when the conscious mind experiences unity of the psyche."[42]

To refocus our attention from outside projections and reactivity to owning our inner life states doesn't typically happen without a shift in our center of gravity. We need to stop believing that we are what our thoughts and feelings are telling us from the superego of parental introjects, and that we are only as large as the boundaries of our body. Disengaging from such beliefs, without trying to get rid of them, takes a form of mindful meditation practice, because our thoughts and constructed stories, their related feelings, and the sensations left in the body are so powerful that they influence our perceptions, brain structure, cellular makeup, and even genetic makeup.

The Platform for the Later Stages of Consciousness

Moving into later stages of consciousness toward Self-realization rarely is done without developing and becoming anchored in "witness consciousness." When we rest in that which is aware of all experience, we see we are responsible for our thoughts, storytelling, perceptions, and projections and that they are fictitious rather than real. We are much more interested in finding meaning in who we are, what this life is about, and what we can offer to our community and the world.

As we inquire into these thought patterns and constructs of ego, we see they arise and dissolve without a current thinker. They are based on early impressions of self with parents and our environment that lie unconscious, until activated, in the implicit memory and in splinter personalities. When these early impressions are activated and we become reactive to something triggered in our outer world, the change in the later stages of development manifests as our having learned to own the reactions as our perception based on the early years of implicit memory storage. We can then move from reacting and projecting on others to seeing the pattern and constructed beliefs and stories for what they are. We invite in all that is a part of the reactive pattern of ego, honor the hurts and betrayals felt, and release this layer of the memory. Rescuing these parts and deconstructing and disengaging from these thought structures becomes an ongoing, lifelong task, as the thought structures become subtler and subtler.

In a strong witness state of consciousness, our physical presence becomes more grounded and attentive, and there is a dissolving of boundaries between self and other. The lens through which the beginning witness consciousness views life is one in which there are both a witness and something being witnessed (self and other/subject and object/thoughts and witness of thoughts). Although still a dualist perspective, that view over time dissolves into an increasing awareness in all seeing and knowing, and in awareness itself as not separate but permeated with, and arising from, the Source. As the ego morphs into a purer state and we abide more consistently in awareness of experience, thoughts, storytelling, and constructed reality, the separate self that has been the center of ego functioning begins to dissolve. As the boundaries of a separate self dissolve, we experience being one with a vastness of infinite reality.

Let's examine this evolution from the viewpoint of the Research Developmental Model, as described in Chapter Twenty-Six. For example, completion of the advanced Construct-Aware stage happens when the identity with our life stories is integrated into a coherent self-story, while we also witness that self-story as a story rather than as the reality of our existence. In seeing through our projections as constructions of mind, we begin to withdraw these constructions and see everything as projections of the mind.

Likewise, the stage of becoming Ego-Aware takes hypervigilance in witnessing the subtler layers of ego and thought structures around inflated or deflated ways of being. Subtler forms of young reactive states are felt and not projected onto others. Seeing through them helps thin out structures and quiets the mind, but there may be some reactive states from early childhood implicit memory experiences that still get activated. We then inquire into and work with what needs to be heard, honored, and released. We are devoted to the truth and less engaged with negativity or ego reactivity in others. As thought constructions and reactions of the ego thin and the mind quiets, the beauty of existence takes center stage as the presence in our lives.

Those of us in the Illumined stages experience another major shift into the conditioned body-mind of being fully grounded in our physical presence and embracing our humanness. The experience is of the unconditioned ground and source of all being, not as two separate things, but co-arising—the conditioned being permeated with the unconditioned Source. The internal and external experiences collapse into one experience of simultaneous emptiness and fullness anchored in this eternal moment.

At this developmental zenith, opposites and polarities begin to unify, we integrate shadow aspects of self, the persona is liberated, and we abide more continually in our true nature as that which is aware and awareness itself. We sponsor an integrated approach to life of being present in daily activities of life while abiding in awareness of the Self.

Polarities central to being victim or tyrant, or a subject of projection, become subtle to nonexistent in daily life. When these polarities occur, they are embraced, accepted as our humanness, and seen through as constructions of mind and subtle layers of patterning, honored for their meaning and then released.

Progress into and through these later stages of development means facing our conditioning, ego and persona, and constructions of mind and working with them diligently. We do not push them away or try to make them stop. Instead, we allow, embrace, inquire into, study, and disengage from the conditioning of the mind. Through this process and through a daily practice of mindfulness, meditation, and being aware of being aware, we begin to see thoughts arise and dissolve on their own without a findable thinker. We get more and more anchored in the awareness of all experience that is unfindable and relax into a felt sense of "I am," our eternal nature.

As an example of how a psychotherapist might work with the later levels of development, consider the case of Cathy who came in for therapy. She is a highly developed meditation practitioner, is functioning at the archetypal stage of Gaining the Treasure, and is at a fourth- to fifth-person perspective, the Construct-Aware stage. She has been experiencing what she described as "a weird sense of constantly waiting." She described experiencing a pressure to do something, although she doesn't know what it is, and an ominous sense of being judged. As we sat together, she began to feel that same pressure and judgment. Our conversation went like this:

> *Therapist:* What would I want you to do?
> *Cathy:* You want me to come up with something! Otherwise, you will feel bad about me.
> *Therapist:* Why would I feel bad about you?
> *Cathy:* I know this doesn't make sense. I can just feel it.
> *Therapist:* This is one of those kinds of feelings that comes out of the deep memory of a child. I wonder if someone pressured you about something that made you feel bad about yourself. I wonder what happened.
> *Cathy:* I just noticed how that plant is beginning to bloom. It's so healthy!
> *Cathy, a few minutes later:* I still feel that pressure.
> *Therapist:* Let's just stay with the feeling and see where it goes.

We sat together for another fifteen minutes, quietly sitting in awareness. She was continuing to follow her own awareness in her body. Suddenly, she looked up and said: "Oh, my God! I'm remembering the pictures in my baby book of me sitting on a child's toilet seat at ten months of age."

Therapist: Really? Ten months! I think kids today are twenty to thirty months old before they are potty trained.
Cathy cries for a few minutes and then says: I don't have to produce anything for you. I guess toilet training and performing were linked together.

This is an example of a subtle reactive state being triggered by the movement of development. Having to please by producing or performing can be buried deeply in the implicit memory and can bind a person into "doing" as a way of life. Cathy was lucky to be able to find the origins of this reactive state and can now move on to even higher stages where "doing" is replaced by treasuring existence.

The Archetypal Developmental Stage of Gaining the Treasure

In Archetypal Developmental Theory, Neumann would call the period of moving into the later stages of adult development, Gaining the Treasure. The mandate of this archetypal stage is the creation of a generative alignment to the center of the psyche, the Self, and the morphing of the ego to a mature level of development that supports living from the essence of the Self. Recall from our prior discussion that, in early stages, the archetype of ego is the center of consciousness of the psyche. In the later developmental stages, the alignment of the ego to the Self changes: As the mature ego consciously aligns with the Self, the conditioned self can become a vehicle for the unconditioned awareness flowing from the Self and can then consciously recognize the Self as the central archetype of the psyche.

This work demands the creation of an environment for the spontaneous re-centering of the archetype of the Self and takes more than the magnetic force pulling us toward the Self. It takes conscious intention. The rich, integrated experience of the mature ego also:

- Requires a grounded physical body, which means inhabiting our body from the inside with an ability to fully accept and nurture ourself on a physical level.
- Requires a willingness to clear any repressed emotions.
- Requires the ability to embody those emotions and express them when necessary, but not in a reactive mode.
- Knows that emotional reactive states are shadow parts with roots in implicit memory and the kind of adaptation required for survival and belonging.

- Sees that its strength lies in its vulnerability; it is able to be transparent both to its own reflective process and with others in relationship.
- Has had its persona cleared of the ways it "must/should look," while also retaining the ability to present itself in ways that are acceptable to social norms.
- Has had its personal superego and cultural superego digested so they no longer hold sway from the unconscious.

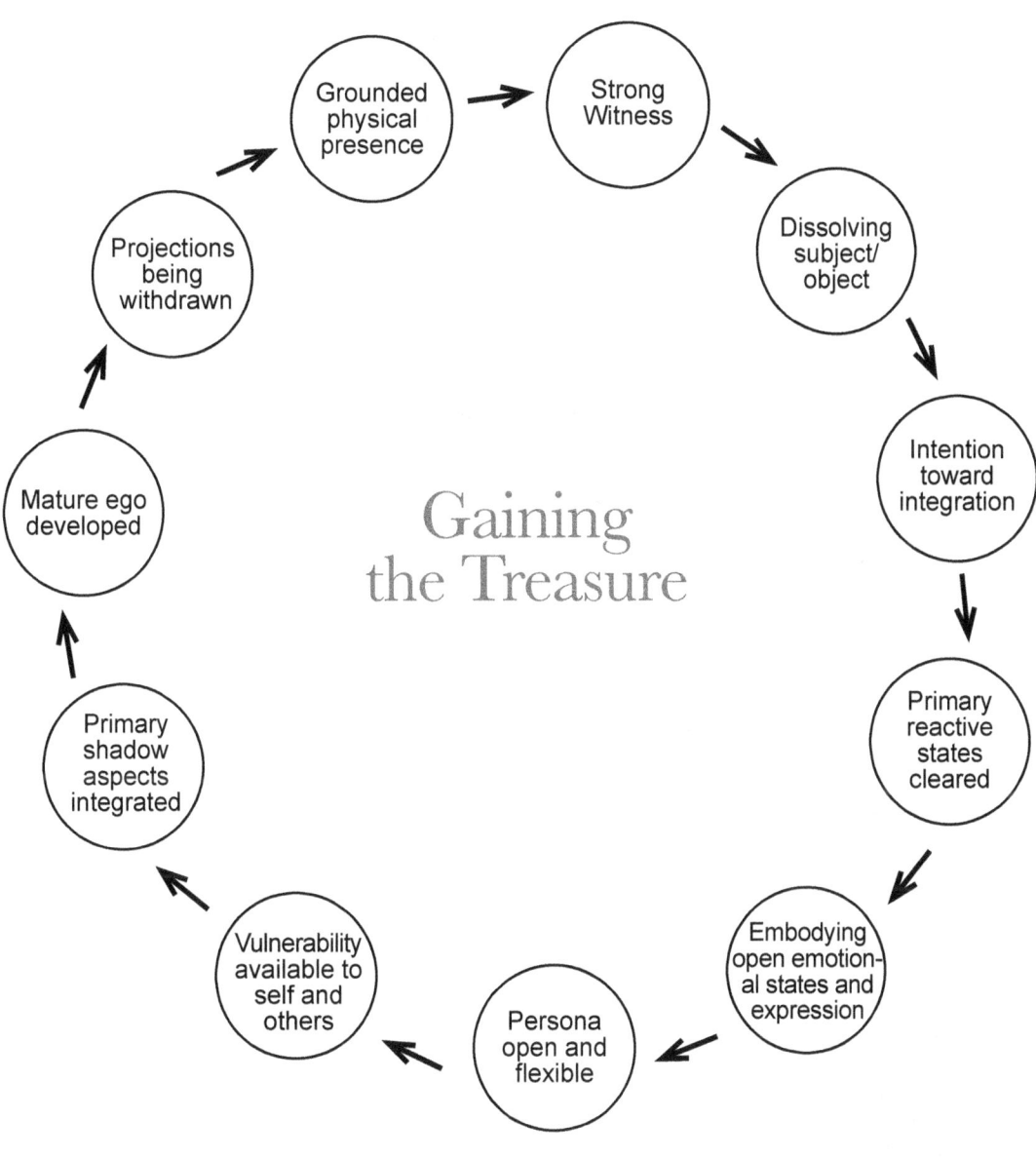

See the **"Gaining of the Treasure"** diagram for a visual synopsis of this later developmental level dynamic.

The process of gaining maturity can be grueling. The witness aspect of the ego must be strengthened to be able to bear the weight of the shadow elements and the process of assimilation. Unconscious psychic content is brought repeatedly into the view of the conscious ego and must be recognized as belonging to its own personality, so that the contents of the shadow are known and accepted by the ego and the persona.

Furthermore, in the later stages, fulfillment no longer comes from outside approval; the "steering wheel" is inside and driven by meaning, altruism, and awareness. There is an integrated feeling of value and worth, which creates an inner stance of authority. We also can welcome all parts of ourself. Because of this, we can accept attacks on our heroic quests or ego ideals and experience them as feedback, when useful. At this level of maturation, the ego spontaneously has access to creativity and allows it to flow into the world in whatever form it wants: gardening, writing, painting, designing or organizing, dancing, playing music, and so on. Addictions to any material objects, particularly the focus of the early stages (e.g., food, substances, power, sex, etc.), fade.

Gaining the Treasure also means having a strong witnessing consciousness that can witness sensations and experience, emotional states and the thought patterns that create them, the stories created with those thought patterns, the ego itself and its structures, along with any sense of separation, and, ultimately, form itself. We eventually see our job as strengthening the experience of self to be flexible and strong enough to continue its own maturational journey—that includes its own dismantling!

We see the Treasure as having realized the larger identity of an alignment to the Self, which includes the experience of: "I am an expression of the Self. I am fully embodied and have access to the full range of my human emotions and can express them. My mind has thought structures, but I am larger than my mind. My behavior is patterned, but those patterns do not define me. I have a persona in the world, but I am not attached to it. I have constructed my identity, but I do not have attachments or aversions to separate states. I am larger than my attachment or aversion to form itself. And I am aware of awareness."

Gaining the Treasure ultimately results in our realization that our early situation and the ensuing patterning was a gift that forged our uniqueness. We come to celebrate that our creativity flows from this uniqueness and comes into the world in a way that no one else could express. Finally, we are able to embrace our essential nature as the Self and recognize that Self in others as the One Self, with our care and concern going to all beings.

27

Challenges of the Later Stages

"The more individuated we become, the wider is our consciousness of the realm of the unconscious which spreads out before us in, as, and through the world.... The process of becoming conscious doesn't banish the unconscious but, rather, aids us in developing the trust to give ourselves over to it time and again, thereby learning how to receive its gifts of wisdom."

- Paul Levy -

When people are moving into the later stages of development, they often are leaving behind the perspectives of their friends and family as well as the cultural worldview. This can lead to feeling quite alone. Companies moving into the later stages are no longer using standard ways of operating and can face criticism. Because the prevailing culture is usually on the center of the bell curve, going beyond the norm takes courage. For example, going beyond our parents is always something we wish for, but the actuality is daunting. Likewise, going beyond what other companies are doing takes innovation and the ability to tolerate great ambiguity and risk.

Feelings of emptiness and insignificance are part of the journey of going beyond seeing contexts to realizing that reality is constructed. Experiences of the innate natural Self begin to emerge, but many sub-personalities can show up during this dissolution. As mentioned earlier, according to Susanne Cook-Greuter, the vulnerabilities at this stage can be loneliness, fears of going insane, feeling rarely understood by others for our fullness and complexity, having a heightened awareness of our own foibles and limitations, and vacillating between feeling the nothingness of being and stepping into the fullness and brilliance of all our being.[43] Rather than embracing the beauty and ordinariness of everyday human experience, we also might become trapped in an attachment to transcendent experiences.

Nonetheless, once people have progressed to a fourth-person perspective, they seem to have an easier time integrating sub-personalities. Perhaps this is because they have moved into Rescuing the Captive and already stand beyond the "system" in which they were raised, are discovering their own personal and cultural conditioning, and have already begun to deconstruct the story of their life. Perhaps this is because they have an easier time now with their own persona being challenged, know they have material in their shadow, and are, nevertheless, confident everything is okay.

Having a spiritual practice seems to increase the ease of integrating sub-personalities and shadow material. Perhaps having experiences of something greater than ourselves creates a feeling of there being help in digesting some of the younger material. For more examples, following is a shorthand version of the shifts we are making as we move toward and through these later stages of development. *The italicized phrases are examples Terri O'Fallon has begun to find in her research into these later stages.*[44]

Transitions in the Later Stages

- **Higher than contexts:** I have a finished narrative of my life and can witness my life now. I can begin to see my projections on the world. I begin to own my reactions as my reactive states and judgments.
- **Higher than constructs:** This narrative of my life is simply a constructed story. It's not necessarily the only way of looking at my life. *I can see there are limitations to my beliefs.* I can feel my deep interconnectedness. Paradox and ambiguity are my new worldview. My personal history is no longer as important.
- **Higher than Meta rules:** I see the foundational rules of the world (or mind or universe). I can see nature's archetypal rules of form. *I recognize my boundaries are expanding.*
- **Higher than Meta goals:** My goals are not tied to specific content but to a general nature of a particular goal. "I want to make money" changes to "I want my company to support change in the world."
- **Thinking in wholes and linking wholes together:** As an example, we have taken many theories that describe whole processes and combined them in this book. Synthesizing is a gift at this stage. *My boundaries are made up!*
- **Seeing total wholes as well as the individual parts within a single whole:** I can see that everything is a constructed reality and be in loving relationship with all of it! The ability to tolerate the fragmentation of my personal image and to live without a sense of identity is an example of being able to see that we are whole, even though we don't feel whole at the moment.

- **Immediately perceiving a whole, through a subtle state of apprehension:** This is the ability to sense into a situation, know it in its totality, and use that intuitive knowing to guide action. *Knowledge is formulating itself on the basis of self-existent awareness. Ideas are not established on logic but on this pre-existent awareness.*
- **Witnessing wholes:** This is an ability stemming from being anchored in witnessing. People at this stage automatically see in "wholes" from a witnessing position. They are aware of an "I" and a "whole" being witnessed. They do not think analytically and break something down into its parts; instead, their experience is of "wholes." *They can see individual examples but do not categorize or put things into a trajectory. They see "wholes" but don't yet have a relationship with them. They are beginning to have new understandings of timelessness.*
- **Being wholes as an ultimate state**: This is the stage in which being and "wholes" are not separate. There is no longer a witnessing "I" and a "whole" being witnessed. The relationship is experienced; there is just being whole. *This is the mind with no categories. Inside and outside are permeated by the whole expansive universe.* This is an experience of united knowing, feeling, and being.

For an example of this seeing, feeling, witnessing, and being whole, let's look at a study done in the late 1980s of advanced Theravadin Buddhist students. The researchers used the Rorschach test to measure the psychological changes at each major stage of meditation practice. This is pertinent here, because psychological changes related to meditation practice correlate to the cognitive and perceptual capacities of adult developmental stages.[45] The findings were surprising. The researchers reported: "Usually Rorschach subjects unquestioningly accept the physical 'reality' of an inkblot and then project their imaginings onto it. These advanced students had very different responses. A most striking feature of all these Rorschach [findings] is the extent to which [the students] view their own internal imagery in response to the shapes on the inkblots as merely manifestations or emanations of energy or space. Here is a typical but especially clear example: 'I feel the energy coming from that, the whole energy of the picture. . . . There's an intensity, a certain power of it, and everything else is just a dancing manifestation of that energy coming out.'"[46]

To summarize the study findings:

- Students had full awareness that they were projecting images upon the inkblots.
- They saw pure perceptual features of color and form and saw the color and form move and change.

- They experienced seeing the shading as particular qualities of states of mind.
- They perceived how forms and images rise and organize into existence and how forms and images dissolve or become absorbed back into space.
- Sometimes they saw the inkblots as pure space from which energy is unfolding.
- They also saw them as depicting the activity of the molecules of the universe or the primal elements within the body, or saw them as interactions of internal organs with energy.
- They saw the inkblot as a projection of the mind itself.
- Seeing all the inkblots as a united whole, one student linked them together in one story. In reaction to that student's linkages, the researchers noted: "Integrating all ten cards into a single associative theme is an extremely rare finding. The student achieved this without any significant departure from reality testing and without ignoring the realistic features of the inkblot.

In sum, "the most distinctive feature of these Rorschach subjects is their unique perspective in which they actually witness energy/space in the moment-by-moment process of arising and organizing into forms and images; and conversely, witness the forms and images become absorbed back into energy/space."[47] From this study and other examples of living from later developmental stages, we have an inside view of some of the challenges we have in daily life in the earlier stages of later development, as well as how these challenges begin to dissolve as we feel the non-separateness and exquisiteness of our lives.

Author Paul Levy beautifully captures the transformation to wholeness when he writes: "The more individuated we become, the wider is our consciousness of the realm of the unconscious which spreads out before us in, as, and through the world. . . . The process of becoming conscious doesn't banish the unconscious but, rather, aids us in developing the trust to give ourselves over to it time and again, thereby learning how to receive its gifts of wisdom. . . . When we shed light on the darkness of the unconscious, it's not that all of its contents become illumined; rather, there becomes a more permeable boundary for the unconscious contents to emerge into consciousness, as well as for consciousness to step into the world of the unconscious. . . . Over time, these two seemingly opposite realms begin to become indistinguishable from and turn into each other, while at the same time, paradoxically, becoming more distinct from each other. . . . It is as if we are connecting with a healed, whole, and awake part of us that, temporally speaking—outside of linear time—has always existed. We begin to cooperate with and surrender to a deeper impulse within us, as if we are allowing ourselves to be drawn into the strange attractor that is ourselves, a process which can only take place in the present moment. By becoming aware of and stepping into this higher dimensional part of ourselves, we are attracting this particular part of ourselves, with its corresponding universe, into materialization; this is the sacred power of dreaming."[48]

28

Unfolding Our Infinite Potential with a Generative Inner Refuge

Pure presence is not a thing or something that can be described. Perhaps the best we can do is attempt to point to "just this," that which is always present in the silent stillness and spaciousness of just being. This is the greatest healing power and the greatest gift we have. Abiding here in "just this" is the ultimate healing power of unconditional love, that which flows through all of us—what Jung and Neumann call, the Self. Having reached this stage, we have attained the Treasure!

To live from our true essence, the Treasure within, we are like the giraffe that sees and observes everything from a higher perspective. This allows us to be graceful and intentional in our approach to life. We can witness our thoughts, explore them, respond with calm in a crisis, treat others compassionately as we would want to be treated, and share our gifts with the world. As we noted previously, attaining this level of being is not easy, and only a small portion of humans actually unfold the potential of their essence.

As described throughout this book, a major deterrent to gaining the Treasure is that we have much work to do with the deep reactive states in ourselves. Our years of study and experience have taught us that, in order to tackle reactive states, facilitate the maturing and clearing of ego's conditioned states, and ultimately move toward living in the pure presence of the Self, we must develop a generative inner refuge. This generative inner refuge, which is characterized by an emotional maturity and advanced development, establishes the foundation to move into the true inner refuge, the thinning of veils to the Self.

Hallmarks of a true generative inner refuge include:

- Embodying confidence, self-worth, and self-love
- Living in our authority
- Living with intention and focus
- Shifting from a compelling drive for *doing* to relaxing into just *being* and to *doing* from *being*
- Accepting *what is* without needing to *know*
- Attuning to our innate inner wisdom and witnessing our thoughts, feelings, and behaviors without judgment or opinion
- Observing thoughts and stories of the mind, detaching from their power and influence, and merely seeing them for what they are: the inner dialogue based upon early childhood impressions
- Facing and befriending what causes us fear; having emotional balance
- Relating to the world and relationships in a solid, intimate, and meaningful way
- Living our potential
- Having inner trust and security
- Embracing the abundance and support available
- Living from an open, vulnerable, loving heart
- Discovering deep meaning and purpose in our daily lives
- Sharing our unique gifts with the world in service to humanity

Embodying these qualities and moving from reactive inner states requires a healthy, secure attachment and the ability to shift from focusing on the outer world and our projections to focusing on our inner experiences. This significant shift leads to a maturing and clearing of our ego (the "I, me and mine" pattern) and to the thinning of the mind stream and its thoughts.

Once again, we must repeat that this process is not an easy one! People are commonly triggered by events, circumstances, relationships, and what other people do or say in the outer world. Reacting to these, projecting our distress, and listening to our inner dialogue as though it is true is second nature for the vast majority in our culture. But we can do better. We can change how we live and relate by becoming more loving, considerate, kind, and compassionate. We can commit to examining and working with our reactive states and the perceptions that comprise our reactive inner refuge. We can shift our focus to our inner life: emotions, feelings, and thought constructions. When we finally own our "outer" life as a mere reflection of our "inner" life and pull back our projections on others, we mature to embody a generative inner refuge, which feels like having a balanced center of gravity. (See Chapter Eighteen, "Early Development's Relationship with Our Journey to the Treasure," for more on reactive versus generative inner refuge.)

How We Work With Integrating Reactive States

For the majority of people, facing the underlying dynamics holding reactive states in place will require a skilled psychotherapist who knows the inner workings of implicit memory and early attachment disruptions, who knows how to welcome and face fears, and who knows how to engage the brain's hippocampus to integrate memories. When the explicit memory is activated, narratives that create meaning from our history can then be integrated and understood; viewing reactive states as an attempt of the psyche to bring information from unconscious core beliefs and patterns into consciousness is key to integration.

An important part of this integration and the therapy process is reading patterns. For example, we explore what is being brought forward by the inner wisdom and what wants to be heard and acknowledged. In the process of reading patterns and working through them, we are building a bridge between unconscious expressions (narrative stories and themes, dreams, and synchronicities) and the conscious mind. At the same time, that bridge is connecting the client to the next stage of development.

As we have expressed numerous times throughout the book, we do not view reactive states as pathological in any way. Rather, we see them as perfect expressions of what the psyche is attempting to reveal and what one needs in order to attain wholeness. In other words, our inner wisdom brings up a particular memory so the nongenerative aspects of our inner refuge (i.e., any hurt, pain, humiliation, anger, depression, anxiety, etc.) can be fully acknowledged for what they are. Once the nongenerative aspects are acknowledged and worked through, they no longer have the power nor need to be one's driving force. Without aspects that are trying desperately to be heard, we can empower our true Self to shine forth, and we anchor more deeply in our generative inner refuge.

One of the reasons therapy works in integrating reactive states and healing the inner refuge is because we set solid conditions around the therapy, beginning with the first session. (See Appendix B for an in-depth look at this practice.) Every living system requires an archetypal solid container for healthy growth and development. This container actually helps repair and heal injuries caused by narcissistic, neglectful, or abusive parenting or caregiving. It also provides a healing vessel that will not replicate the patterning of a client's early conditioning. Instead, new patterns are seeded and tended to, until maturity and integration can be achieved.

In service of maintaining a solid container for therapy, here are some of the conditions to which we hold ourselves accountable:

- Provide an environment in which we see the preciousness of our client's being
- Mirror back to our client his or her preciousness of being
- Hold the value and worth of the person as a given, without question
- See the layers of conditioning and defenses covering the Self and sub-personalities, without judgment

During each therapy session, we invite clients to rest in mindful awareness and in the study of their inner core beliefs, perceptions, and expressions of them. Most of these beliefs, perceptions, and expressions were formed in early childhood and stored in implicit memory, before brain development allowed experience to be encoded in explicit memory and narrative form. The reflection, discussion, and self-inquiry that occurs during therapy helps our clients to move their memories from being unconscious into being conscious.

As we invite all aspects of self to be present and embrace those aspects, good and bad, we mirror their value and worth and underline any ways those aspects are showing up in our client's current daily life. Whenever possible, we provide a context about a client's early childhood that is known from his or her history. This includes implicit memories and reactive states, early experiences and education, as they are also normalized. Remember that an integral aspect of therapy is building a narrative story of one's life that aids in making sense and meaning. From this vantage point, the client can begin practices of self-care and nurturing in all aspects of his or her life.

We also hold in high regard, and a curiosity about, what is trying to be revealed by a particular reactive state, what the pattern and core belief is, and what is underneath that pattern and core belief. Most people have either been told by others or by their own inner dialogue, "Don't think like that," "Just let it go," or "That was in the past." Pushing things out of conscious memory only gives them more weight, and they reoccur repeatedly. Behind these reactions is a story wanting to be invited in, heard, and fully honored.

When we bring a witnessing presence and loving kindness to the memory, we are able to make meaning from the implicit memory, and that layer encapsulated in the unconscious can be released. With each layer released, the more conditioning of the ego is cleared and the more aspects of the Self are rescued and integrated. For example, if someone needs to be the center of attention in social situations, we see this as demonstrating the inner hurt and missing experience of not getting enough positive attention as a child. This aspect of the person desperately wants to be heard, to be deeply listened and attended to, and to be fully acknowledged and honored. We may say, "Of course, you want to be seen and have us pay attention. Your mother was locked in her bedroom for much of your childhood. There was no one taking care of you or giving you the attention children desperately need for their development."

We use the information given from a client's early history to educate him or her about how children take in the information from their parents' limitations, how this conditions and forms one's core beliefs, and how believing these messages caused a turning away from the natural self. Through this educational process, we weave together the past memory that is alive in the moment with the truth of our client's being, while also seeing his or her true essence.

As part of therapy, we also elicit a commitment from clients to see all reactions in the outer world experiences as pointing to their core beliefs and young feeling states. We then explore together what the underlying meanings are. We do not participate in whether they are true or false, but see them as memories. This begins the integration of a mature ego, as our clients are then able to pull back their projections on the outer world and its circumstances. They eventually gain clarity and see their projections as merely perceptions based on their early conditioning.

Reactive Refuge Examples and Underlying Meanings

As noted earlier, in working with clients, we see the Self, their beautiful being, holding that throughout the treatment until they also are able to see this in themselves. In addition to holding this position of unconditional, aware presence, we also hold certain positions regarding a client's particular core beliefs. Following are examples of some typical core beliefs and the positions we hold in the interest of healing and helping our clients shift to a generative inner refuge and their next stage of development:

"Surviving" and trying to be perfect

The lives of these clients are organized around their version of "being perfect" and around an inner dialogue that pushes them to do what is humanly impossible. They don't feel of value or worth or feel they have anything to live for. And, no matter how hard they strive or how successful they are, nothing is ever good enough and they end up merely surviving rather than thriving.

What often underlies this reactive state is not feeling welcomed into the world nor wanted. In this pattern, typically, the mother was unavailable, so the child was not able to fully attach to the mother nor just rest in her arms and presence. Also, the mother did not mirror her child's true essence as being perfection itself. Sometimes under neglectful situations or when parents are not around, children parent themselves by striving for perfection and judge themselves when they are unable to attain that perfection.

Position therapist holds: Clients feel welcomed, wanted, and fully enjoyed for their presence, whatever that may be. There is no need to be anyone different than who they are, and no need to be perfect or not perfect.

Feeling there is no help, feeling despair, and wanting to collapse, sometimes even wanting to die

Typically underlying this despair are early experiences with caregivers not being there when they are needed for support, nurturing, or secure attachment. The experience of the child was that there literally was no help. Collapsing in despair or taking care of the parents' needs seemed like the only options available.

Position therapist holds: We provide unconditional support with good boundaries, ethics, and morals. The environment is nurturing and encouraging, focusing on the client's needs. We demonstrate that help is available now in the therapeutic relationship, and we encourage exploring this in other aspects of life.

Feeling "I can only rely on myself"

This pattern reveals there was either no one to count on in early childhood (except oneself) or the client had intrusive parents from whom he or she wants to pull away. In either case, the only option seems to be to rely on oneself.

Position therapist holds: We offer trusting support and help when needed. We also demonstrate how to maintain a collaborative relationship. Pointing out the attributes of people who can be trusted for help, taking the risk of asking for help, and then noticing the result is therapeutic. We might ask, "Did you get the help you wanted? Are you able to accept it fully? How does being helped make you feel?"

Always needing to be in control

Underneath this power and control is a client who feels powerless. Needing to be in power or control typically demonstrates that a client's early childhood took place in an environment that was either very controlling and undermining or out of control, in chaos, and madness. Becoming controlling is a way to keep a lid on the inner feelings of chaos that feel unbearable. It also keeps relationships at a safe enough distance so as to avoid intimacy that might be hurtful.

Position therapist holds: Keeping the secure container around therapy is particularly important for a client who struggles with this core position, because a secure container is truly a safe environment that is neither controlling nor chaotic. It is a place where one can examine the purpose control serves in one's life, without judgment. Also, modeling the collaborative therapist-client relationship can be the first step toward building an emotionally intimate relationship with another.

Believing "I lose myself if I am in a relationship. I can either have the relationship or my individuality. I don't know how to have both."

A client with this core belief typically had close relationships with his or her parents, but those parents did not allow the child the freedom to be him- or herself. This is a common dilemma with those who have well-developed patterns of taking care of others, beginning with caregivers.

Position therapist holds: We provide an environment that focuses on the client's needs. When attempts to take care of us are made, we may say, "There is no need to take care of me. I know that has been your experience, but, in here, I can take care of myself. Let's look at what you need."

Distinguishing between *taking care* of someone and *caring about* them also can be helpful with clients who hold this belief. We might coach with, "Taking care of people gives them the message that you don't think they are capable of taking care of themselves. I know that is not your intent. Letting people take care of themselves, and helping if asked, can express a way you really care about them."

Proving worth through doing and achieving

This reactive pattern reveals a history of not feeling accepted and important for just being alive. Clients with this core patterning need to prove their intrinsic value and worth through striving and doing rather than just being. Although they think an "end product" will prove their worth, it never quite satisfies their desire to feel important in any lasting manner.

Position therapist holds: We provide an environment that is accepting of being of value and worth just for being alive. Our message continually is that all people have the same value and that value is not based on having to do something; it's based simply on being.

Believing "I will be fine in the future and have what I want in the future."

This pattern reveals someone who had to wait for what was wanted or was continually promised things that were never fulfilled. People struggling with this core belief organize their lives around hoping something will happen in the future.

Position therapist holds: With these clients, we focus on being a solid presence with secure conditions, while helping them to manifest their dreams in the present. We might say, "What if you could have that feeling right now and didn't have to wait?" Or even, "How do you know you have more time that you can afford to wait? You may miss the opportunity here right now."

Believing that life is unfair, wrong, or unsafe

This core belief reveals an early childhood that was unfair and/or unsafe, and this nongenerative pattern wants desperately to be acknowledged.

Position therapist holds: We hold a safe environment for this unfairness to be expressed, and we acknowledge to these clients that their early life circumstances were unfair. We also help them accept "what is" in the moment. Accepting what is does not mean it is okay, fair, or unfair. It just is. Sometimes action needs to happen, but, in the moment, it just is.

Believing "I don't want to be any trouble to anyone."

This core belief reveals early childhood experiences of feeling like being alive was too much trouble for one's caregivers. To survive, these children felt they needed to stay out of the way or they needed to ignore their own needs. Being "trouble" felt dangerous, either emotionally and/or physically.

Position therapist holds: We hold an environment in which our client's needs are important and outright ask, "What do you need?" We also allow much expression around feeling like, "I am afraid I am too much, and you will tire of me and want to leave." We also acknowledge this client's experience of being too much for his or her parents, noting that it was the parents who had limitations and caused much hurt by their inability to be present and mirror attention and affection. We tell this client that he or she has never been "too much," that he or she is and always has been a beautiful being, worthy of being loved, and of loving him- or herself.

Believing that thinking and learning will solve everything

This pattern reveals developing the mind as a defensive structure. This client is often very successful in education and career, based on his or her knowledge. He or she feels a sense of value and worth—for knowing. Staying in the mind and creating fantasy, which began in childhood, is easier than developing a thriving inner world. In fact, underneath this nongenerative pattern is an emotional body that is shut down and painful, making it challenging for the person to form deep, intimate relationships.

Position therapist holds: We create a safe and caring environment where the client can begin to open up to his or her feelings and emotions—and an intimacy not yet experienced. Introducing a mindfulness and self-inquiry practice that helps deconstruct and disengage from thoughts and fantasies of mind is also helpful. This opens a door to seeing, "I see I am more than my thoughts. What I feel is also important, and it feels good to share this with another person."

Attaining the True Inner Refuge

With steadfast commitment and devotion to live our true potential, our true purpose, and gifts of Self in the world, we must work diligently to rescue the aspects of our true self left in the Great Mother during the first six to seven years of life. Witnessing thought structures, feelings, inner stories, and perceptions, and being willing to own our projections allows the ego to mature. As we involve ourselves more deeply in this process, we move from the reactive inner refuge to embodying the generative inner refuge traits—and, ultimately, to a life of increased harmony, balance, and loving presence.

To anchor ourselves in the generative inner refuge, we must develop a good experience of a witness/observer self that merely notices, without judgment or opinion. (A daily meditation and mindful awareness practice can be instrumental in developing this witness/observer self. See Appendix A for an exploration of mindfulness and mindful awareness.) Only then can the separation between the witness and what is being witnessed dissolve. That is, by attaining a generative inner refuge, we can move toward the dissolution of the separate self (There is a "me" and an object of projection.) and experience more openings to the unifying experiences of the Self. In this new state, we can begin to feel the ground or source of being as occupying more conscious, loving presence in our lives. We can experience the unification of all that is arising from this ground in each moment, as it also dissolves back into it in each moment.

Moving into the true inner refuge causes a shift from a sense of duality to an experience of non-separation and a felt sense of unity. We begin to experience life as a numinous co-arising: All is arising and dissolving in each moment from this dynamic source of being but is never separate from it. In fact, all is permeated with this pure, unconditioned presence. This is the beginning of the dissolution of duality into non-duality, but only a beginning. There is an ongoing unfolding and evolving of experiencing non-separation. And thoughts and concepts are viewed as constructions of mind, not to be gotten rid of, but to be seen through, so that thoughts are thinned and eventually quieted.

In the true inner refuge, witness consciousness (awareness of our thoughts and reactive feelings as ego constructions, rather than reality) gives way to an increased focus on being ego aware. There is a hypervigilance needed to be aware of the fierceness of the ego to hold on, and the various ways this happens. Our practice shifts to self-study, self-inquiry into the truth of reality, and deconstruction of the egoic dynamics. In this process, we become increasingly aware of the unfindability of the "me," the thinker, and the origin of thoughts. We begin to experience the "I" we refer to as the eternal "I am," and we rest in being aware of being aware—awareness itself.

As we experience the later stages of development, we see this pure presence is not a thing or something that can be described. Perhaps the best we can do is attempt to point to "just this," that which is always present in the silent stillness and spaciousness of just being. This is the greatest healing power and the greatest gift we have. Abiding here in "just this" is the ultimate healing power of unconditional love, that which flows through all of us—what Jung and Neumann call, the Self. Having reached this stage, we have attained the Treasure!

In closing, we leave you with the inspirational words of Dorothy Hunt, a psychotherapist and spiritual teacher in California's Bay Area: "Nothing in this world is static. Everything moves as Mind. When the mind stops moving, the world returns to Nothing, yet here it is again! We dream creation into being, and then tack on names to make each thing look separate. But nothing is separate. There is Only This! dancing as an infinite display, revealing its mystery of creation. Even the names we imagine are real are part of the endless unfolding of Only This! But as long as the mind insists that its names for things are Reality, we see memory rather than tasting Reality."[49]

Epilogue

"Individuation seems to be the innate urge of life to realize itself consciously. The transpersonal life energy, in the process of self-unfolding, uses human consciousness, a product of itself, as an instrument for its own self-realization."[50]

- Edward Edinger -

This legacy of love and devotion to our mentors, clients, and students, *The Treasure Within*, opened with a review of the foundational theories of those giants on whose shoulders we stand in our humble effort to advance the effectiveness of psychotherapy through an archetypal paradigm for individuation. Of particular focus for us has been the meta-theory work of Dr. Michael Conforti in developing Archetypal Pattern Analysis and Erich Neumann's groundbreaking work elucidating the stage-by-stage journey of the ego during its life-long relationship with the Self. (See the **"Ego-Self Journey"** diagram on page 83 or 307.)

In Parts Two through Four of *The Treasure Within*, we offered a detailed look at the dynamics of each archetypal stage of development, eventually focusing on the transformational stages especially important for adults if they want to unfold their full potential. We reiterated over and over that, in order to attain the Treasure within, adults must return to their deep unconscious and rescue aspects of their Self that dropped out of integration and were left behind during their early years of life. We also spelled out many ways of working with deep unconscious patterning to achieve living from the essence of one's being. (See the **"Archetypal Developmental Theory"** diagram on page 92.)

In the last part of our book, we explored yet a third view of development: the current researched developmental stages from experts in the field of developmental psychology. It is fascinating to see how the abilities and capacities available at each level of maturation—outlined by leading scholars such as Loevinger, Kegan, Cook-Greuter, and O'Fallon—parallel the various stages lying in potential for all beings that are elucidated in Neumann's Archetypal Developmental Theory. (See the **"Comparison of Archetypal and Researched Development"** diagram on page 321.)

364 The Treasure Within

To come full circle and bring these three different models of individuation and development together, consider how the ego identifies with the Self through each of the archetypes in its developmental journey by examining our **"Ego-Self Journey with Archetypes"** diagram.

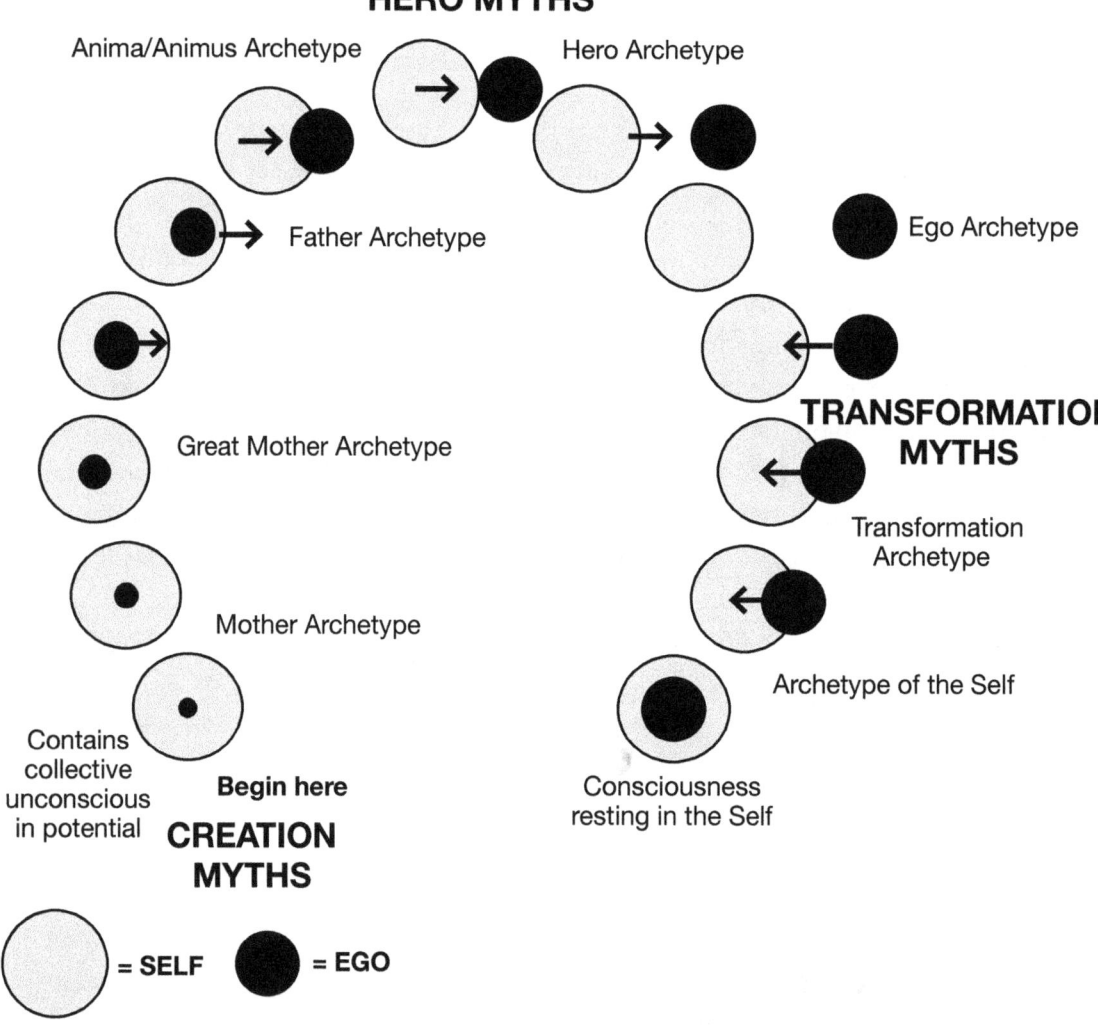

Note how the Self illuminates each successive archetype. Each new illumination fascinates the ego and forces it to release its identification with its current archetype and to reach for the numinous new archetype.[51] Thus, the ego develops new abilities and capacities through letting go, being willing to move to the next developmental stage, and embracing its new identity. To paraphrase the chart:

Development Through the Archetypes

Ego identifies as the Self through the Great Mother archetype

Ego identifies as the Self through the Father archetype

Ego identifies as the Self through the Anima/Animus archetype

Ego identifies as the Self through the Hero archetype

Ego identifies as the Self through the Ego archetype

Ego identifies as the Self through the Transformation archetype

Ego identifies as Self by resting within the Archetype of the Self

To make a long story short: The ego begins its journey in undifferentiation with all that is (through the Mother) and ends its journey in an integration with all that is (through the Self). Along the way, the ego attempts to find refuge in whatever capabilities and capacities it has available in its developmental range. When it is overwhelmed, it regresses—which is why sometimes we end up watching a movie instead of making art. Following are some of the different developmental refuges the ego takes during its journey:

I am	Refuge in un-differentiation
I am me/her	Refuge in fusion
I am body	Refuge in my body
I am sexual	Refuge in my sexual self
I am emotional	Refuge in my feeling, emotional self
I am mind, ideas, imagination, thinking	Refuge in my thinking self
I am mystery	Refuge in my own mysteriousness
The eternal I	Refuge in the Self

Ultimately, our mandate as humans is to find our Treasure within! We do this by strengthening our ego's capacity to accomplish the tasks of the successive developmental stages, by capturing and integrating previous developmental stages, by building a strong witnessing platform and generative inner refuge, and by dissolving into the Self. To support and anchor individuals, other therapists, companies, and the world at large in accomplishing this demanding work, we offer this archetypal approach as a "treasure" map. In addition, with this initial map of the Archetypal Developmental Theory as a key to the "Treasure within," we challenge the next generation of those on the journey to apply this information to build upon the work and share their discoveries, too, for the benefit of all humankind. Such noble use of one's heroic gifts, in due course, will go a long way toward achieving Erich Neumann's dream of creating a future humanity that would cast out the primordial uroboric dragon and reconcile, through integration, a new synthesis for all beings, establishing a structure of consciousness in humankind that can no longer be split apart by opposites, a new synthesis that would eliminate the ability of the uroboric states to manifest in the world and cause the atrocities of war or genocide of any kind.[52]

Take up the mantle. Accept the challenge. Make it so!

Appendix A

Supportive Practices for the Later Stages of Development

Having a mindfulness practice and meditating are simple, meaningful practices to help attain our True Inner Refuge and later stages of adult development.

Mindfulness and Mindful Awareness

"One's mind, once stretched by a new idea, never regains its original dimensions."

- Oliver Wendell Holmes -

Mindfulness and mindful awareness are natural states—when we are in complete acceptance of the present moment, just as it is, whether we agree with it or not, whether we like it or not, or whether we want to resist it or cling to it. In these states, we accept what is and live without resistance. We just notice, without opinion or judgment. We are able to detach from our thoughts and perceptions of our conditioned self, while simultaneously appreciating our humanness as a conditioned being. Living mindfully is our True Inner Refuge. Having a mindfulness practice and meditating are simple, meaningful practices to help attain our True Inner Refuge and later stages of adult development.

If we are asked, "Are you aware?" we respond with a deep knowing of, "Yes, of course." There is a part of us that knows we are aware of our thoughts, feelings, sensations, and that these are fundamental to our being. We are taught, however, to attune to our conditioned self—our inner dialogue of thoughts, stories, and feelings of mind—as the truth of who we are. We also are conditioned to believe we are limited beings. Mindful awareness can help us to re-attune to our awareness of experience and deep knowing without engaging in the conditioned, limited self as truth. In so doing, we become aware of being aware. This is our natural and true nature.

We begin to realize that this awareness is unknowable and unfindable, and not even a thing. At the same time, there is a deep knowing of being conscious and aware. With daily practices of mindfulness and meditation, anchoring ourselves in the witness first and then in pure awareness, we begin dissolving the veils of separation and patterns of being limited. Our thoughts and feelings related to "not good enough or important enough" begin to thin, our reactive states quiet, and we move deeper into Self-realization and living our true nature, the Treasure within. Given the power of mindfulness and mindful awareness practices to support our attaining our True Inner Refuge and the Treasure within, let's look at the current neurobiology research supporting how helpful the practices are in healing the reactive states and dissolving the veils to our natural self.

Neurobiology Research on Mindfulness

To begin, we must review what the mind is and its relationship to the brain, body, and relationships. We can then understand more clearly how a mindfulness meditation practice can be helpful to let go of conditioned thought structures and emotional patterns and stories. This is a necessary part of moving into the later stages of developing a witness and witness consciousness, and of moving into being aware of being aware.

In Eastern spiritual traditions, the mind is thought to create our world. While the mind in its purity and radiance is the mind that arises from and remains permeated with the unconditioned pure presence of awareness, it is also the creator of thought, the thought "'I," all of our inner and outer world perceptions and projections, and the view of there being an inner life and outer world.

Daniel Siegel, a leading researcher and practitioner of mindfulness, tells us: "*Mind* relates to our inner subjective experience and the process of being conscious or aware. In addition, *mind* can also be defined as a process that regulates the flow of energy and information within our bodies and within our relationships, an emergent and self-organizing process that gives rise to our mental activities such as emotion, thinking, and memory. . . . Subjective experience, awareness, and an embodied and relational process that regulates the flow of energy and information are fundamental and interdependent facets of *mind*. Mental activities also include our beliefs, intentions, hopes, dreams, perceptions, reasoning, intuition, and images."[1]

Siegel goes on to differentiate forms of mindful attention and the importance of our focusing mindful attention for our growth and development. *Focused attention* allows us to be aware and to develop a strong witness state to all experience, without being entrained in thought structures as though they are true. It is a gateway to integrating linkages in the brain that facilitate compassion, empathy, and aliveness in our relationships as well as good health and a sense of well-being. Focused attention keeps us conscious and not falling back into the familiar thoughts of the self-limiting hypnotic state of an earlier time.

The more mindful awareness we cultivate, the more explicit memory is activated to allow for creation of a narrative understanding of our experience and life path that can help lead us to lasting change. Explicit memory encodes through linkages of neurons and the activation and maturation of the hippocampus during brain development so that we can remember autobiographical information. Siegel says, "As we practice focused mindful awareness, we begin to be more open and accepting of the current moment, less engaged in thoughts and concepts, and less judging and critical of ourselves and others. It is a key to emotional maturity."[2]

Another researcher, epigeneticist Bruce Lipton says the mind is very important for our very existence. The thoughts that color our lives are primarily from the first seven years of childhood, when we learn to be a part of a family, community, and culture. People tell us who we are, and it is all recorded under a hypnotic-like state. This becomes our programming, habits, and behaviors. These translate into the physiology of the body: Our perceptions, thought patterns and constructions, and chemical reactions in the brain ultimately control our behavioral patterns and genetics.[3]

In essence, Bruce Lipton's current epigenetic research reveals that the mind is an "interpreter." Our perception of our life and our activities in the outer world trigger the release of chemicals in the brain, depending upon our different perceptions. That is, our perceptions create thoughts, which direct the brain to release certain chemicals into the body and blood, which then send messages to our genes that may actually change our genetic makeup accordingly. Like the placebo effect, what we believe then begins to happen. Thoughts of love and gratitude allow us to open our hearts and are different than the thoughts of fear that shut down cells and release stress hormones from the brain. We begin to see that thoughts create the lens we wear as well as shape our world, our perceptions, and our outer projections.

This process highlights how the brain changes with our experiences and is highly influenced by a mindfulness awareness practice. So attention is integral to providing new neural pathways, firings, and the ability to rewire the brain. This rewiring of the brain changes the chemical releases and grooves in the old patterns of neural firings and neuro pathways in the brain and our thought processes. In addition, mindfulness practice has been shown to aid in forming secure attachment within us (as well as with our children), which helps us live our life from confidence and assurance and attain the later stages of adult development.

When the mind is in thought, we are not paying attention or conscious, and we go into the hypnotic programming of the unconscious of an early childhood time of conditioning. Only approximately one to five percent of the time are we truly relating from a conscious state of mind! The rest of the time we are thinking, and consciousness is not present. That means that ninety-five percent of the time we are thinking from the defaulted program of the first seven years of life and the hypnotic conditioning. Those thought structures are often self-limiting and restrictive of wants, hopes, and desires.[4]

According to Siegel's research, attention is integral to building neural pathways and to engaging the brain's hippocampus so as to encode explicit memory narratives. This is what allows us to make sense of our life experiences and to have good health, well-being, and healthy relationships. Further, with mindful awareness and attention, a neuron's firing patterns and connections are strengthened, and there is encoding of events into long-term memory.

Siegal states: "The mind can change the activity of the brain. By harnessing the power of awareness to intentionally focus energy and information in a new way, neural firing can be altered. 'Attention' is the process by which energy and information are focused through the circuits of the brain. When we focus attention in integrative ways, we can cultivate differentiation and then link these differentiated regions to one another. The neuroscientific saying, 'neurons that fire together, wire together,' reveals how the associated activation of neurons changes their linkages to one another. The process using attention to change the activity of the brain is a part of the larger process by which experience changes neural structure, called 'neuroplasticity.'"[5]

Obstacles to Attaining Our True Inner Refuge

Although we are attached to our conditioning—our thoughts, feelings, preferences, beliefs, and resistances—they hinder our ability to be present in our natural state. They, thus, keep us from our True Inner Refuge and from the later stages of adult development. Renowned author and spiritual teacher Peter Fenner delineates the common psychological obstacles to resting in our essential nature:

- Attachment to suffering
- The habitual need to do something
- The need to know what is happening and where we are
- The need to create meaning
- Fearful projections about unconditioned awareness (our natural state)
- Making problems when there are no problems
- The tendency to make unconditioned awareness into something (that it can be a thing—an object of awareness)[6]

These seeming obstacles are merely phenomena that arise in the mind and seem to keep us from the simplicity of resting here now as the Treasure, our true nature and True Inner Refuge. To loosen the grips of our conditioning and rest in our True Inner

Refuge, it is helpful to create space for a regular practice of mindfulness awareness and meditation.

Mindfulness Awareness Practices

As stated earlier, a focused regular practice of meditation is optimal and a gateway to increased experiences of being aware of being aware as pure presence itself. Beyond the psychotherapy experience and rescuing the captive aspect of self, meditation and a daily mindfulness practice are two of the swiftest and most efficient means of realizing our true nature, the Self. If you are not currently a meditator and are interested in exploring its usefulness in your life, here are a few simple practices we suggest:[7]

Meditation Focusing on Breath

Sitting with eyes closed, slow your breath down and begin breathing deeply. Focus your attention on slowly and deeply breathing in. Feel the flow of breath in your lungs and fill your body. Then slowly breathe out, feeling the sensations in the body as you exhale. Continue with this process. There will be times the mind will take your attention. Not to worry. Just bring your attention back to your breath. Over time, the mind will quiet. We ask you to focus on your breath so you cannot focus on your thoughts. Start by setting aside a short time such as five or ten minutes every day and increase that time to what feels natural and nourishing.

Just Sitting

Just sitting is another simple practice we learned from Peter Fenner[8] that often has profound effects. The process follows:

- Find a space absent of stimulation such as computers, television, and people.
- Sit (or lie down) in a quiet, still position.
- Stay awake and attentive to what is happening.
- Then just do what you are doing, which is being.
- Stay in this being space for a set period of time, eventually working up to about twenty minutes per day.

This can be an easy, impactful way to develop a focused awareness of just noticing while doing what you are doing. There is nothing you need to do to do what you are doing![9]

Just Sitting in Awareness
You can also just sit with your eyes closed and focus on being aware of being aware. Notice the still, silent spaciousness that ensues.

....

Other Mindfulness Awareness Practices

We use basic mindfulness practices in psychotherapy by bringing people's attention to their memories, pictures, thoughts, feelings, sensations, and the like. This helps to bring attention to the present moment experiences. As we begin awareness of these and let them be, it helps thin out thoughts and helps us rest more deeply in pure awareness of the Self. Additional mindfulness practices include:

Thinning Our Thoughts: When a thought arises, meet it with impartiality. If we leave the thought alone, it naturally dissolves. This practice is a simple way to meet fears and inner conflicts about the "right-wrong," "victim-tyrant," and "us-them" of our reactive states. At any time we can rest deeply here in this pure presence, fears, conflicts, and concerns will dissolve. We can let life move through us effortlessly without disturbance, without making stories or projecting our opinions and perceptions.

Increasing Our Capacity to Be With What Is: This state finds us without acceptance or rejection, without attractions or grasping onto the things we want, and without rejecting the things we do not like and want to get rid of. In accepting what is and letting things be, "Nothing is wrong or missing, so nothing needs to be done."[10]

Self-Inquiry: This starts with simple questions such as "Who am I?" "Who is the 'I' to whom I am referring?" "Where is this 'I'?" "What is this?" Then we explore deeply these inquiries.

Unfindability: This practice is another simple exercise with far-reaching effects. We can listen to our thoughts and then observe their origins. We ask ourselves: "Can I actually locate the exact place from which they come?" And we explore, "Where did these thoughts go? Can I actually locate exactly where they went?" Then we do the same exploration with the "Thinker." We ask, "Who was it that thought those thoughts? Can I actually find the thinker and its actual location?" Going deeper, we look for "What is it that is aware of all this?" That, of course, brings us to awareness itself. We can even further explore the "I" as we refer to ourselves, by asking: "Can we actually locate this 'I'?" When we look closely, we all point to our hearts when we reference "I." But can we really locate it? This inquiry quiets thoughts and is a gateway to resting in awareness, the Treasure of the Self.

There Is Nothing to Think About: As a practice, this is helpful when we begin to thin our thoughts from their density and "remain present to our experience while gradually reducing the ideas, concepts, and judgments we layer on top of our experience.... [We] reduce the burden of thought by learning how to feel complete in the here and now, and also by increasing the capacity to work, relate, and live our lives effectively without the need to process everything as we do."[11]

Listening to Our Inner Dialogue: We also can hear our inner dialogue and feelings as the psyche pointing to what wants to be heard and honored, as well as what wants to be cleared, released, and rescued in our reactive states and split off parts of Self. In this process, we just listen to the dialogue without believing it or attaching to it in any way. We leave it alone and use it only as information about what wants to be honored and released to further our transformation and development. This is an advanced practice, in that it is beyond the need to project onto others or have a perception about things.

These mindfulness and meditation practices lead us to a self-study that ultimately allows for deep learning and an honoring of ourselves, our hurts, and our journey. They can bring us to self-love of our humanness—and to the Treasure of our true nature resting in our True Inner Refuge.

Appendix B

For Practitioners

"States of consciousness can be transformed if changes in their control variables bring about sufficient alterations in them. This is also true of structures of consciousness. . . . [I]f a large enough portion of the elements which form either a state or structure of consciousness [is] altered, the entire system can be up-ended and sent looking for a new attractor—a new stable pattern. Here in a nutshell is the process that underlies many techniques for personal and spiritual growth. In them, old structures are dismantled and new ones substituted."[1]

- Allan Combs -

The Heroic Journey of Becoming an Analyst

"When a person's physical and mental systems cross critical thresholds of complexity, that person is thrown out of his or her comfortable previous state into a temporary but fertile period of chaos which heralds the appearance of a new stage of development."[2]

- Allan Combs -

Our journey as Archetypal Pattern Analysts started in 1995 when we were introduced to Dr. Michael Confori and his work with Archetypal Pattern Recognition, during what was then called the Portland Seminars. Soon thereafter, we both began meeting privately with him and participating in a weekly peer study group. Both of us were seasoned therapists, had been in private practice for several decades, were expertly trained in subjective therapies, and had undergone years of psychotherapy ourselves. We became excited by the depth of the ideas abounding in this archetypal work—how they resonated with our own studies, discoveries, experience, and deep knowing. Dr. Conforti would make predictions based on the trajectory of an image in a dream or unconscious communication[3] of a client; within months, those predictions would be revealed as true. Amazing! We wondered how he knew, and our passion for learning became even more enthusiastic.

Inspired by Dr. Conforti and the Assisi faculty, we felt called to the work, and then a larger force started to carry us. The work was not what we imagined; something much greater was occurring. Our egos were challenged, and we both lost the ability to do our work in the way we had previously been practicing. As we were exposed to the power of the objective psyche[4] and its predictive ability, we began to see the limitations of practicing from a subjective viewpoint.[5] We found ourselves in awe of the psyche's relentless capacity to stand for what is for the person's highest good, which is so often in contrast to the conscious mind's intentions.

And then the dilemma was presented: "How do I take what I am learning and make it my own?" There was so much to study, so much to integrate, and we were drawn deeper and deeper into an unfolding journey. We both experienced our relationship with Dr. Conforti changing under his supervision, and we started to allow ourselves to be mentored.

Both of us remember that, at first, we tried to keep the system of work we were practicing the same, only adding on the Archetypal Pattern Analysis work. At different times, in different ways, we came to the conclusion that keeping the status quo just was not possible. We found that how the analyst begins the therapy work and structures the session holds the power of the work! What we were resisting at this point was keeping the conditions for treatment secure and avoiding feeling our own fears and death anxiety. Underlying all human fears, ultimately, is fear of death. We typically do whatever we can to avoid this feeling, by distractions or other forms of evacuating our anxiety to avoid feeling this fear.

Both of us remember several ways we attempted to maintain old ways of practicing until our ears could hear the objective psyche's derivative communication[6] and we realized that our own patterns were keeping our clients stuck. The questions arose: "Am I willing to really look at my own patterns? Am I willing to have my mentor see me so clearly, in my worst patterns, and face the fears of what it means to hold the conditions secure for a client? That brings up all *my* fears, blocks, and patterns of being held securely!"

Learning this work, in every session, all day long, called up the inner dialogue of: "I can hear the derivatives, but what are they saying? How do I do this? How do I take this new knowledge and make an intelligent intervention? This cognitive dissonance is so uncomfortable. Okay, I have to restructure my practice. This deeper truth is more important to explore than to stay in my safe little world."

As one can see, in the first stages of learning, you are up against how much *you* have to change, how much *you* must really work the fears you have, both known and unknown. You have to allow your system to open to chaos and be deeply seen and vulnerable to your mentor. In addition, you must face that you are keeping your clients stuck with your own active unconscious patterning and that you must make changes in yourself to really provide quality treatment.

We cannot imagine it is possible to make the necessary changes without allowing someone to mentor you on a consistent basis. Mentoring is needed in order to change an ongoing method of practicing therapy, to learn to hear the unconscious communication, and to make transforming interventions. This is an intense dilemma that most professionals of any field who come to Archetypal Pattern Analysis must face. We did it with weekly help from Dr. Conforti and with consistently turning to each other for peer supervision. Allowing someone into one's deep patterning is a tremendously vulnerable process. This hard work eventually gave us deep compassion for our clients' dilemmas and their need for us to serve as *their* mentor through their archetypal journey.

To go through the initial stage of the journey takes great tenacity: You must be a rank beginner again, study a large body of material, be mentored, make mistakes, and be humbled in the face of the objective psyche's communication. This work is not for the faint of heart! We have seen many candidates turn away from the call of this work, a call that is for deep personal transformation for therapist and client alike.

We will talk later about the many shades of resistance we went through during our journey—the different bifurcation points that each new level presented, the immense personal surrender required, and the need for clearing so many layers of personal patterns. Only through dedication and true grit were we finally able to truly hold secure conditions, a solid container for treatment, and trust in the power of the work.

Each of us had our own personal demons, allies, gifts, and handicaps to be worked in the secure container with our mentor. Each level of releasing defenses took us into a confrontation with our death anxiety and with being able to face our own manic defenses,[7] which attempted to take over and muddy the work. Eventually, each of us felt a final shift in our center of gravity. We sensed our service to the Self, not the ego, and we embraced the challenge of letting our new gift ripple into the community.

We are very grateful for how Archetypal Pattern Analysis and our mentoring from Michael Conforti has changed our lives. We found that the changes we made meant taking the hero's journey. This led us to use the developmental stages of myths to talk about the transformation we both experienced. To become a hero, face your fears,

Stages of the Hero's Journey[8] of the Analyst or Therapist

1. Hearing the Call of Transformation
2. Wrestling with the Call
3. Crossing the First Threshold with a Mentor By Your Side
4. Facing Tests, Obstacles, Inner and Outer Enemies, and Allies
5. Surrendering and Committing to the Call
6. New Level of Wrestling
7. Surrendering and Receiving Gifts
8. Final Ordeal
9. Integration and Sharing the Gift

and go on to rescue the parts of self left in the Great Mother of early childhood changes your life forever!

....

The Hero's Journey of the Analyst or Therapist

Stage 1: Hearing the Call of Transformation
When a therapist first hears about Archetypal Pattern Analysis, he or she might have various experiences that elicit a call of transformation. Those experiences might start with exposure to new ideas in the synthesizing of Jungian archetypal work, Dynamical Systems Theory, The New Sciences, The New Biology, Patterns in Nature, and Unconscious Communication. The "call" might be sensed by feeling excited by the new ideas or by intuiting how deep and rich the theories and material are and how different the material is from what is generally offered in the field of psychotherapy. Eventually, you also might become excited about the correlations between your own inner knowing or what has been developed in your own work and the ideas being heard. If you are open to self-growth, then you will embrace putting yourself in the hands of an expert by finding a mentor established in Archetypal Pattern Analysis.

Stage 2: Wrestling with the Call
At some point, a bifurcation point will make itself known, creating a choice between, "Do I go toward the newness of this archetypal work, or do I maintain my current patterns?" Choosing to move into new territory and leave the old, familiar way means facing fears and anxiety. Tackling the fears and dealing with the anxiety mandates having a good mentor, as well as having sufficient inner and outer resources and the capacity to change.

Thought-provoking questions to ask yourself about your inner and outer resources might include: "Do I have the time and ability to study several fields of information at one time? Do I have the resources, both inner and outer—such as time, money, and energy—to go through intensive mentoring and rewiring? Is my life stable enough right now to take on this kind of journey, or am I already in chaos because of family illness, financial challenges, or something else? Do I have a drive toward the truth of the Self? Do I have a drive to discover and face my own issues as an analyst or therapist?" You need a steady environment and rock-solid commitment to embark upon this journey and stay the course!

Regarding your capacity for change, you might ask yourself: "Is my system open enough to entertain the changes I intuit will have to occur? Do I have the capacity to hold the challenges to my own existing system? Do I have the drive to know the deep truth of myself? Do I have the capacity to integrate the challenges to my patterns in my current way of working? Do I really believe all this objective psyche stuff?"

The bottom line is that you are comfortable with and already know how to work with the manifest subjective content, and it already provides very powerful therapy. So, you need to be sure you want to bother with the new—because the way you currently work and your ego most certainly will be challenged! Can you tolerate this discomfort?

Additional questions can help you discern your capacity to change. Consider also asking yourself: "How will I apply this new information? Can I add it to what I am already doing, or do I let it change my entire practice? Will I go the route toward truth, even if it means facing anxiety, versus shoring up my ego?" These and more are important considerations, because you may feel anxious and off balance. You may not sleep well. You may even dread your supervision sessions. As you take this hero's journey, your center of gravity and your archetypal alignments will change, most assuredly throwing you off kilter until you integrate the new.

Stage 3: Crossing the First Threshold with a Mentor By Your Side
Once you have resolved the bifurcation point and commit to exploring Archetypal Pattern Analysis in depth, much begins to open up. The work seems easier and more exciting, many insights fall into place, and your working relationship with your mentor reaches a new level. Borrowed from Systems Theory, the term *mentor* refers to a patterning force,[9] an influence that tends to move consciousness toward a particular state. In this case, the particular state you are being moved to is a state that embraces death anxiety and claustrophobic moments as an agent of change.

Working with a mentor can be challenging. You need to be able to tolerate having your patterns exposed. Also, feeling seen by the mentor—and allowing *being seen*—demands great vulnerability. Eventually, however, your mentoring relationship will become a stabilizing lifeline in service of your growth and change.

Stage 4: Facing Tests, Obstacles, Inner and Outer Enemies, and Allies
As noted earlier, Archetypal Pattern Analysis, in its application to psychotherapy, is not for the faint of heart. You will face numerous tests, obstacles, and dilemmas during the journey. These range from learning and accepting the truths related to derivative communication to facing your own inner demons and anxiety.

Hearing the truth of derivatives over and over again while being mentored in supervision works something like this: "My mentor is right. Those themes are showing up again and again in my client's stories. My pattern *is* really affecting my client!"

Being able to accept the truth of derivatives takes allowing your viewpoint to open and be affected by the mentoring. You also will need to feel and clear your own reactions to authority and any complexes around authority (i.e., resisting authority in the service of trying to have your own authority). In other words, you must give your trust over to your mentor, which can be difficult.

Clearing your own patterns related to authority brings up another critical challenge in the journey: It means accepting how *all* your own patterns interfere with your therapeutic practice. To do this, your patterns will need to be named in such a way that fits your own deep experience (i.e., abuse, chaos, madness, abandonment, etc.). You also will need to recognize both the positive and negatives aspects of your own therapy and past supervision, acknowledge the psychic introjections you took in for what they were and for how they have affected your work, and proactively decide to release obstructing patterns. This is another bifurcation point. For example, can you feel and name the fear of being alone with another in a deep, intimate relationship? Are you able to step up to being an authority by setting the conditions of what is needed to make a transformative journey and by tolerating the intimacy of the dyad?

Finally, if you accept the call to learning Archetypal Pattern Analysis, one of the greatest tests you will face is to learn about death anxiety and manic defenses. Once you do, you will realize that you must experience your own death anxiety and deal with your own manic defenses while handling the analysis of your clients, because, as an analyst, your own anxiety and manic defenses can interfere with the capacity to read patterns and inferences from the unconscious communication of the clients.[10]

Take heart, though. Along the hero's journey, you will find allies. Your inner resources, your mentor, and the special movie you see or book you read will help you to keep moving forward. Watch for the "magical key" you are given or the "fairy godmother" who appears and helps.

Cultural Obstacles

Our culture's dominant view of therapy sets up additional obstacles with which you must wrestle if you are to embrace this work as part or the total of your practice. For one, our culture currently supports short-term, solution-focused therapies. It is new to Western culture to understand there are higher levels of consciousness and that therapy needs to deal with *all* aspects of one's being, including the deepest levels of the psyche, work that involves the long-term process of transforming core patterns of the ego. And, yet, society does not see introspection as meaningful. Instead, proof or measurable evidence is lauded, and quick, external solutions such as the use of medication (instead of insight) are supported. In reality, trauma, PTSD, attachment disruptions, or dissociative disorders cannot be adequately dealt with in short-term, solution-based therapy.

Another way the prevailing culture deters the learning of transformational psychotherapy and the application of Archetypal Pattern Analysis in psychotherapy involves death anxiety, which is very much a part of the practice. Death in our culture is repressed out of fear and is often not dealt with or processed. Instead, our culture supports evacuating our anxiety and staying away from what causes us fear. It follows that a therapy dealing directly with this anxiety would not be readily supported.

Stage 5: Surrendering and Committing to the Call
When, as a practitioner, you finally surrender and commit to the process of really learning Archetypal Pattern Analysis, you will experience a new version of yourself and shift into new behaviors. Your new experience of self involves a spontaneous knowing of the sacrifice the mentor is making and of the mentor's humanness beyond the masterful grasp of theory and technique. With this spontaneous enlightenment about the mentor comes an understanding that you are "primary" to the mentor and, therefore, primary to yourself and to your clients. This grounds you in your new role as an Archetypal Pattern Analyst, marking your coming into your own maturity and integrating split-off aspects of your self as a person. You are then ready to forge a primary intimate relationship with your clients, strengthening your therapeutic alliance.

Once you experience this shift, your behaviors, in turn, will change. You will tolerate, maybe even embrace, the challenges to your old patterns, the shifting in your psyche's rewiring, and the changing of your own identity. You will begin to integrate the new knowledge by trying hard to implement in your practice what the new ways call for. One such implementation will be the building and maintaining of secure therapeutic conditions. You will see clearly that old ways of setting conditions and holding a container were actually in service of your own needs and in the service of your ego, rather than in service of what is most needed by your clients in order to change core patterns.

Stage 6: New Level of Wrestling
With these new gifts (and a stronger identity in the process), you also will find yourself facing a new level of wrestling with your self and with new challenges. As the consciousness theorist Allan Combs reminds us: "When a person's physical and mental systems cross critical thresholds of complexity, that person is thrown out of his or her comfortable previous state into a temporary but fertile period of chaos which heralds the appearance of a new stage of development."[11]

Some of the new obstacles, dilemmas, and challenges include:

- Facing being a beginner again on a daily basis
- Experiencing the hardships of implementing a secure container
- Dealing with the cognitive dissonance of not doing the old, familiar interventions
- Wanting to change the conditions of treatment in the service of your own needs, both out of anxiety and out of fear of losing income or clients
- Experiencing your own manic defenses
- Knowing you are getting derivative communication and not being able to make sense of it
- Being able to do literal translating from derivatives but still not being able to identify the archetypal pattern
- Seeing the patterns after the session while writing notes but not while your client is in the room with you
- Hearing a good interpretation of derivatives in supervision but struggling with how to put it into your own words
- Facing your own patterns in every session, while simultaneously asking clients to face theirs
- Feeling consistently awkward, embarrassed with a sense of failure and inadequacy, and having to come up with a way of tolerating this process day after day

Stage 7: Surrendering and Receiving Gifts
This level of surrender manifests in stopping the evacuating of your own anxiety—to be quiet, listen, and trust the answers will come. The gifts of this surrender are an increased capacity to trust the unfolding process and to contain your own anxiety. At this point, you begin to really experience the power of the secure conditions and the depth of the changes that can occur from holding this container. For example, when you do not know what to say or do not know an answer during therapy, you trust the answer will become clear through silence, accept you can take the issue to your mentor, or make internal deals to tolerate the cognitive dissonance. Such a deal might sound like this: "I will take my hardest case to supervision, try all the Archetypal Pattern Analysis principles on that specific case, and ease up on pushing myself on the rest of my cases."

Stage 8: Final Ordeal

All the prior wrestling builds to a deep choice point between the new alignment and staying in your familiar and comfortable patterns. This brings up your greatest fears. An active resistance to implementing secure conditions often comes up at this point. It is as though your system cannot stay in chaos anymore, so it reverts to where it feels most comfortable and tries to move away from the new alignments. Your inner voice cries out: "I am out of resources and have to stop for a while!" or "I want to cut back and only have one supervision session per month." You find yourself feeling vulnerable and unable to rest in a loving field. You schedule conflicting activities during supervision time. And you allow claustrophobic reactions and ego defenses to come in and help evacuate your anxiety in ways that are not useful. Then your own denial precludes your ability to read patterns!

Because of the deep fears you will feel at this stage, different problems also will arise in the conscious world. For example, difficult case situations will come that make you want to break the framework in many different ways: You might think you are taking care of your client by staying in conscious mind conversation rather than encouraging your client to allow unconscious communication to be present. You might resist listening to unconscious derivatives, even resist taking process notes after your therapy sessions, and not trust you can hear the derivative communication anyway! Such focus in the conscious world might lead to your evacuating anxiety by actively resisting the implementation of secure container conditions.

Seems overwhelming, doesn't it? We know, because both of us experienced all the ups and downs of the stages we just described. We found it exhausting not to feel consistently successful, but we discovered we could not maintain our old archetypal alignments. Thanks to the fact that our wrestling was also held by our mentor, we finally surrendered more and more to the truth presented to us by the objective psyche. Eventually, fewer and fewer of the troubling scenarios occurred. As *our* archetypal alignments and core patterns transformed, we found we were attracting people into our practices who were ready to engage in their own transformational journey.

Stage 9: Integration and Sharing the Gift

A primary key to reaching the final stage of integration is having a mentor who sticks to the importance of a secure container, assures you of the normal nature of the process you are undergoing, and consistently helps you interpret your experiences in the final ordeal as just that, a final ordeal. With full and secure holding and containing by your mentor, you will be able to import the strength of your mentor's psyche into your own, and the final integration of the new alignment and patterns occurs.

When this happens, you find you have shifted from being in service to subjective conscious mind content, to being in service to your objective psyche. Feeling the capacity to be resonant with people, you also are able to know how the objective psyche of your client sees your unconscious patterns. This knowing empowers you to be able to hear derivative communication, yours and others, both in session and during general communication with others. And your capacity grows for understanding and seeing the effect on therapy of the derivative communication that comes through dreams or thematic stories.

Such a major transformation will take place that, in general, you will be able to track energetically and physically what is happening with yourself as well as what is happening with your clients. You will be able to see clearly your own patterns, while also being able to identify those of your clients. And you will develop the capacity to tolerate anxiety, both within yourself and within your client. In addition to holding a secure container, through the final integration of the new alignment and patterns, you will feel empowered to prepare your clients for their particular brand of dread of secure conditions and support them through their own "wrestling" and "final ordeal" by working with their level of commitment.

Having the strength and fortitude to hold fast to secure therapeutic conditions[12] takes being aware of your own fears of holding a secure container and of your familiar mode of evacuating anxiety. You also need to know your clients' fears related to being held in secure conditions and their favorite modes of evacuating those fears. Once you open to that knowledge, you will ultimately be able to hold secure the overall therapeutic field, while also holding the field of the interplay between client and analyst. This leads into being able to tolerate and actually enjoy the deep intimacy between you and each client.

The gifts that follow at this stage are numerous and significant. Not only do you come into your own authority by being in charge of setting and maintaining the conditions of analysis, but you also realize your generative alignment to your destiny and come into your own authority to take your gifts out into the world.

It is good to remember that your journey to becoming an Archetypal Pattern Analyst parallels all heroic journeys. You face the underworld and all your fears, wrestle inner demons, and slay dragons to capture the Treasure and bring it back to share with the world. Your courage and strength in dealing with harrowing acts will bring you true transformation. Once you become a hero, your life will be forever changed. And, in that change, you can pave a path for others.

Building a Therapeutic Container for Transformation

"The agreements we make with our clients replicate the physical structure of a container for growth and transformation."[13]

- Michael Conforti -

As noted throughout this book, holding and maintaining a secure therapeutic container is critical to this archetypal approach to therapy and for supporting clients through transformation. To refresh your memory about the archetype of the container, please re-read Chapter Three, "The Archetype of the Container and Archetypal Alignments."

The Therapeutic Container

The archetype of a healing environment and "therapeutic" container can be traced to ancient Greece to Aesculapius, the most renowned healing divinity of the Hellenistic world. Aesculapius, the mortal son of Apollo, was cut from the womb of a woman as she was being burned on the funeral pyre for choosing to live with a mortal instead of the god Apollo. Aesculapius was given to Chiron, who taught him healing. Apollo persuaded Zeus to make Aesculapius the god of medicine, but eventually Aesculapius was slain by Zeus for reviving the dead.

Temples to Aesculapius were built as healing temples where people came to seek cures through a technique called "dream incubation." They sought dreams for specific purposes such as healing, guidance, and divination.[14] These temples and their specific conditions constituted the first "archetypal containers" in which healing of the mind and spirit could take place. There was a room held as sacred space, as the need for healing was seen as a loss of alignment with the divine. Rites of cleansing were performed before entering the room, at a specific time. The room held a stone couch where the dreamer rested, awaiting a dream.[15] A specially trained priest entered only after the dream emerged, leaving room for the deep psyche to speak. Then the dreamer would recount the dream as though listening to the voice of God. Knowing he was not a god, the priest understood his role was translating what the person needed to know.[16] Afterward, the dreamer would place a token of what was healed into the sanctuary. From this beginning, we see there are specific properties that need to be present for the archetypal energies of healing to enter. These properties create a framework, like an egg or a cocoon, within which transformation can occur.

Jung spoke about the importance of an alchemical process in psychotherapy—one that turns something common into something precious. Like a cocoon, the alchemical vessel needs to be sealed for the alchemical process to occur. In fact, the term *psychotherapy* comes from the Greek word *therapeuin*, "to heal," although the term originally meant, "service to the gods." Some of the original alchemists were the *therapeuts* who stood for a form of healing superior to that in most cities and whose healing held to the laws of nature and to a sacred context. They were not only interested in healing bodies but in healing souls. So the name *psychotherapy* originally meant, "in service to the psyche," one's soul.[17]

Being in alignment with the initial conditions of psychotherapy then means holding similar conditions as its origins in Aesculapius and the *therapeuts*. When we, as therapists, provide these archetypal therapeutic conditions, we develop an atmosphere in which clients can deepen into the layers of unconscious patterning in order to release them and to feel the safety and strength of the container and the clinician's ability to hold this container. To do this, we must create and protect a container that feels like a sacred refuge—stable, safe, and secure—like an alchemical cauldron that contains the process until the chemicals form into gold. Along with this, we need to act consistently and in a trustworthy way, always holding in mind a picture of the client's wholeness and giving ethical care. We put the client's needs before our own in taking care of the container and always remember that we stand as the representative of a loving presence that perhaps our client never experienced.

How to Build a Strong Container

As explained in Chapter Three, containers in nature—such as eggs, cocoons, and wombs—all require specific times and conditions to produce normal development.[18] If conditions are not met well, abnormalities will develop. For example, consider the archetype of the womb and the archetypal process of birth. The progress of the fetus has been so studied that we can predict very closely when birth will occur. If the timing is interrupted or conditions within the womb are not optimal, the baby will not be fully developed at birth and may be abnormal or not survive.

How does this translate to the therapeutic container? As forms in nature must hold certain conditions for optimal growth and development, so, too, do therapists need to hold certain conditions for the optimal growth and development, the true transformation, of their clients. The archetypal conditions of the Aesculapius temples provide a model for us of how a healing container looks. These secure containers are built through our agreements with our clients and our own abilities to:

- Be consistent, holding the container in a consistent manner;
- Hold space on all levels—physical, emotional, mental, and spiritual;
- Create generative boundaries; and
- Have a generative attitude toward our clients.

Each therapeutic container we create needs to provide coherence, resonance, and balance. It needs to embody generative attractor sites so that alignments and patterning can be shifted. We can do this by creating generative archetypal conditions within the healing environment. The conditions and the holding environment set the stage for the possibility of change and for shifting to new archetypal alignments so that new pathways of patterns can be laid down. Unfortunately, in the therapy marketplace, it is all too common to allow the client to set the conditions of how often they come, how much they pay, and how confidentiality and anonymity are handled. When clients set these conditions, they often replicate the nongenerative patterns they need to change.

So, it is up to the therapist to learn to hold a sacred container with secure conditions. When the container holds securely, archetypal forces support the work and the unfolding of changes. Holding the container securely also allows the therapist to clear his or her own patterning that would interfere with holding these secure conditions for the client. This is a lot to hold for both the client and the practitioner. The archetypal field pushes against both the client's and the clinician's nervous systems, and one can begin to feel like the Sorcerer's Apprentice. Yet, how the container is held directly impacts the quality of growth and development that will follow. Be aware, particularly, of one rule of thumb: The more traumatic the client's stress or trauma, the stronger the container needs to be and the more resistances that may arise.

The Wisdom Mind

Deep in our reptilian brain resides what Robert Langs calls a "wisdom system" or a "wisdom mind" as a part of the psyche that can see the truth of a situation. It keeps track of the conditions and boundaries of an agreement. We hear it as the still, small voice inside or feel it in the gut or in our heart when something is or isn't right.

The wisdom mind gives us "pictures" of what a particular situation should be like if the situation were congruent with the archetypal mandate of a particular agreement. It unconsciously intuits goals, morals, and ethics, picking up and examining deception and lying, or honesty and integrity. It pays close attention to incongruities and encodes any inherent dangers or benefits for our body, psyche, or soul. In general, the wisdom mind closely monitors whether anything will potentially create an overwhelming emotional wave for our psychic structure, if we enter a particular agreement. When agreements hold safety at their core, the wisdom system can relax.[19] Safety to our wisdom system means:

- Conditions are stable and secure
- Rules are clear
- Responsibility for the agreement is going to be honored by both parties
- No change in conditions will occur once the agreement is made
- Small print is disclosed
- The amount of contact and responsibility of both parties is spelled out and honors both parties
- Boundaries are clear and spelled out

....

The Beginning Conditions of Therapy

The reason we are spending so much time on the secure therapeutic container[20] is because of its utmost importance to the outcome of a client's therapeutic work. The container itself serves as a stable attractor site, drawing to it material that resonates with the core of the constellated archetype. In this regard, the events and details emerging within the therapeutic dyad are essentially transpersonal; the psyche works to entrain all members of the therapeutic enterprise into a synchronized alignment to the archetype.[21]

Powerful archetypal forces are at work even in the *initial* conditions of therapy, and those beginning therapeutic conditions will likely show us a predictable trajectory[22] of treatment and a likely outcome or prognosis. Consider the first contact with the therapist. It is actually the "call of transformation" and the first step on the transformational journey. The unfolding of the client's patterning begins with that first phone call,

Holding Environment for Growth and Development

Forms in Nature (e.g., egg, cocoon, cell walls, womb, etc.)	**Aesclepeion Secure Frame**	**Archetypal Pattern Analysis Secure Frame**
All have specific times and set place for development to occur	Specific time Purification before Set place Fee exchange Stone couch Healer enters when dream emerges	Set time Set place Set fee Anonymity Confidentiality

email, or phone text, and a subtle negotiation ensues. Because of the veiling power of repetition, the client's conscious self is asking, "Will you accept the conditions of treatment in which my patterns can continue?" How open or closed the person's system is will determine whether the conditions of the treatment will be accepted. If the clinician agrees to replicate the existing patterning by letting the client set the conditions of treatment, the therapist is then assigned a role in an already existing, ongoing drama being played out in the client's unconscious mind, cast to replicate someone in the client's life who has already played that role. (See the previous section, "The Heroic Journey of Becoming an Analyst.") Because the initial conditions set a trajectory for continued pattern replication, we begin reading the pattern and intervening from this first contact and ask the client to call us to set up an appointment. Once again, this implies that the therapist must take the reins and create secure agreements and contracts featuring the needed archetypal conditions. A good container would include details related to the services:

- How confidentiality and anonymity will be handled
- Specifics of the meeting location
- Specific time involved as well as beginning and ending times of sessions
- Frequency of meeting
- Clarification of roles
- Fee agreement

Confidentiality

Just as the space of a cocoon is solely about the caterpillar, the therapeutic space needs to be solely about the client. Remember that nothing is let into a cocoon that is not needed for transformation. Likewise, protecting the therapeutic container on a physical, emotional, and mental level from any intrusion allows for the transformation of our clients. Also note that all the important work of transformation happens within the space of the cocoon. Likewise, in working with clients, we maintain the security of the therapeutic container by keeping the therapy within the space of the session, considering potential infringements on privacy that may occur because of the likes of interactions with colleagues, emails, or phone conversations. Even waiting rooms may be problematic; whenever possible, we need to give our clients a private place to wait for their session time and then to exit from the therapy room. The gold standard should be to allow clients to have their own private world, letting the therapist-client relationship occur within the sacred space of the therapy room.

Meeting Space

A few principles of the container apply when considering where to meet with clients:

- Meet in the same space each session.
- The space needs to be private, where others cannot overhear the conversations.
- So the space can be kept clear of interruptions, it is helpful for the therapist to be in charge of the space.

Simplicity and symmetry play a key role as well. These attributes convey safety, security, and familiarity. A room overly decorated—and with many personal items—implies the space belongs to the therapist, not to the clients; this also implies a personal rather than a professional space that holds anonymity. On the other hand, a highly symmetrical room allows one to easily and quickly identify anything out of place or potentially threatening. By creating an objectively beautiful space that has harmony and symmetry, we can create an alignment to generativity and an environment that can feel like the clients' psychological home. Remember, in creating the therapeutic conditions, we want to hold as key what the client needs rather than what we personally need.

Time
We want our clients to honor their therapy as a sacred time for listening to their deepest self. We can help them achieve this in a variety of ways:

- By maintaining a consistent meeting time
- By not changing their session time for our own or their scheduling needs
- By giving our clients several weeks' notice if we will be out of the office

Starting and ending sessions in the time agreed is also very important. Going over the time sends an unconscious message that we cannot hold the sacred conditions; our being late sends the same message. The client being late often signals that something unconscious, often about the therapy or the relationship with the therapist, wants to be expressed.

Duration
We want to come to an agreement with our client about how long or short the duration of healing will be (i.e., how long he or she will come to therapy in order to accomplish his or her goals); sometimes the duration is unclear, because of the nature of integrating core patterns and alignments. We can, however, set a future time to review the unfolding of the therapy. Rest assured, the unconscious will clue us in as to the ending time by producing images of completion such as graduating from school, completing a long work project, entering a new stage in life, or the like.

Clarity About Roles and Relationships
Keep in mind the purpose of this special relationship. We clarify our intent with our client to maintain the sacredness of the relationship. We don't create dual relationships with our clients by having coffee with them or by spending time with them outside the session. On a deep level, such meetings are very confusing to that part of our client that wants and needs safety and clear roles.

Fee
We make sure to disclose our fee upfront and to keep our fee consistent. When a client misses a payment, he or she may be unconsciously communicating about the container's trustworthiness as well as the trustworthiness of our relationship.

Beware of the Challenges

Holding a secure frame is not for the faint of heart! This process can bring up our own issues as therapists, issues that need to be worked through. Maintaining an ideal frame helps us find holes in our own upbringing and patterning that have not been healed or resolved. We may unearth a wish for a boundary-less, limitless world, an inability to tolerate frustration, a fear of intimacy, past traumatic memories, or even a wish to be seen in a gratifying way.

In our experience, many of the reasons therapists struggle with holding secure therapeutic conditions relates to the level of anxiety that may surface—anxiety that is challenging to hold. Due to this discomfort, therapists often change the conditions or accept a client's requests to open the container to assuage his or her anxiety or to prevent past memories from surfacing.

The secure conditions of therapy are what are called, the "adaptive context."[23] Maintaining the security or allowing leakage in the therapeutic container directly relates to the issues, patterns, and traumas of the client's earlier life being re-enacted. Agreement violations around the adaptive context are expressed through the client's derivative unconscious communication: When we maintain the agreement of the conditions, validating stories emerge; when we violate this agreement, derivative communication expresses disturbing stories. Many traumas and pattern replications, in fact, are revealed when therapists accept client requests to change agreed-upon conditions. Dr. Conforti says that "frame violations mirror both issues in the therapist's as well as the client's life. These times give both clients and therapists an opportunity to see and work them through."[24] This is one of the beauties as well as the profound power and healing capacity of holding secure the archetypal framework.

In summary, learning to read a client's initial conditions and trajectory, creating a secure holding environment, maintaining this archetypal environment, dealing with the psyche's deep patterns that can then emerge to be cleared, and helping develop a deep relationship with the Self—this is the powerful work of this archetypal approach to gaining the Treasure. In other words, as with the early *therapeuts*, the power of our therapeutic "alchemy" is in allowing the secure cauldron to cook until gold is formed!

Application, Assessment, and Stages of Therapy

With the full completion and integration of the archetypal stages, we feel the hero born in us and the Treasure we have become. Our destiny is now the navigator of our life. As with any archetypal movie or myth, when we truly emerge as heroes, we embody our many gifts of Self and then share them with the world.

Our application of Archetypal Pattern Analysis in psychotherapy investigates:

- What patterns are being expressed,
- What the psyche is attempting to express through the patterns manifesting,
- What archetypal fields these patterns favor, and
- How to archetypally intervene in these patterns.

The outcome of this effort is the creation and mentoring of new pathways that facilitate a client reaching his or her greatest potential, the Treasure within.

Although the same methodology can be adapted and applied to other fields and systems as well, we offer in this particular section an example of how Archetypal Pattern Analysis can be applied in psychotherapy. To begin, consider how this therapeutic work articulates the specifics of the essential patterns of human nature. Whereas most therapies provide understanding, insight, and clarity regarding one's patterning, what inspired us is a method that goes much further and provides deeper and lasting change of core patterns. By working with the underlying archetypal and unconscious material, we can actually integrate patterning by changing prior archetypal alignments, causing a new experience of life.

The reason this method is capable of facilitating such transformation is that, while most other therapies involve developing the *ego's ability* and strengthening capacities to work in the *outer world*, we hold a wider vision of moving people to a *deep level of relationship with the Self*—our inner world. During analysis, we continually examine our client's alignment with the Self and facilitate its greatest generativity. We consistently work to bridge communication between the Self and the conscious mind, to develop a working relationship between the conscious mind and the wisdom of the deep unconscious. Because patterns are holographic and present across each layer of our being (physical, emotional, mental, and spiritual), we work with the patterns on each level as they emerge. We attend to how particular patterns shape the outer world situations, and we are involved in how they manifest between client and therapist within the therapeutic relationship. As the pattern clears, it releases on all levels, both in the inner and outer worlds.

This approach requires us, as therapists, to be willing to continually listen for and address our own shadow material, to look at our patterns and how they are affecting the therapy, and to bear a great depth of intimacy. Holding secure conditions for clients requires that we be attuned to their patterns and ours simultaneously, attempting to prevent entrainment in pattern replication, while holding our anxiety and not assuaging it. From the solid platform, our clients are then able to import this holding into their own psyches, which allows them to begin aligning with their higher potential. The process is, thus, transformational for clients—as well as for therapists.

Assessment

Through mentoring by Michael Conforti and the work of Robert Langs, we came to understand these importlant guidelines for assessment.

Initial Contact

A client's therapy begins with the very first contact. As in all settings and situations, the initial contact demonstrates a particular patterning and marks a predictable trajectory. Aware of the importance of this insight into a potential new client, we begin reading the pattern as it unfolds from our first contact. Some questions we consider include:

- How was this contact made?
- How was the person referred? Is this referral source free of personal or other client contacts?
- How much information is needed to decide on making an appointment?
- Does the person expect personal information about the therapist? If so, what would the therapist be replicating if he or she gave personal information?
- Does he or she need to tell his or her history and reason for seeking therapy in depth on the phone or through email?
- How many contacts are needed to set up the first appointment?

The answers to each of these questions tell a specific patterned story that the psyche is expressing. Through the images, patterns, and archetypal alignments of the stories, the therapist can glean a whole picture. We do not judge any of the information or see it as pathological. We work in an objective manner, listening intently for the communication of the Self—through what images, patterns, and derivative unconscious communications are being revealed by the person's psyche. On the surface, the potential client may seem as though he or she is merely trying to establish a level of safety by getting appropriate information to make a decision. On a deeper, archetypal level, however, this kind of behavior is almost always an attempt to replicate ongoing patterns; replication feels like safety, because it is what is familiar.

Let's examine two different methods of initial contact. The messages are quite different when a person calls or emails and says:

A. "I got your name from my doctor and liked what I heard. I would like to set up an appointment," or "I researched therapists on the Internet and resonated with want I saw and your specialties. If you are accepting new clients, I would like to make an appointment." versus

B. "I want you to know my history of abuse, otherwise you won't know enough about me," or "I need to know personal information about you before I can decide if we can be a good fit. (The "good fit," in this case, typically means that we will replicate familiar patterns.)

The clients of the A examples indicate an ego strength and maturity that predicts a trajectory and likelihood of a good prognosis in the therapeutic setting. Those clients do not require us to replicate the patterns they are coming to therapy to address, unlike the potential clients of the B examples. The A clients, due to their ego strength, are also more likely to make a commitment to their therapy process, be able to see their deep Self's intentions, and agree to the archetypal conditions necessary for a transformation in growth and development without resistance.

On the other hand, the B examples begin to paint a picture of clients wanting us to replicate a pattern of boundary blurring and violation, lack of safety, and maybe even abuse. That replicative pattern also definitely involves distrust if we don't intervene but stay on the phone or email (not a private way to communicate) and participate in therapy before we have even met or without their important history being held in the safety of the therapy room. In general, however, both sets of examples demonstrate the psyche's expression of patterns and what is needed for a client's wholeness and fullness of life. Our attunement from the initial contact further solidifies the initial conditions and trajectory of therapy.

Freud found that repetition was a compulsion and a function of our attempts to remember and to gain control over painful, traumatic experiences. In other words, repetition is meant to keep patterns in place and not move into more complexity. Michael Conforti illuminates this further by saying, "The purposeful dimension of repetition is that it insures the stable and highly regulated unfolding of a performed morphological regime, all in service of maintaining and subsidizing a stable alignment with a specific face of the archetype."[25]

If potential clients are able to metabolize a caring intervention (i.e., the need for their story to be treated with sacredness by it being expressed in a safe container that the phone or email does not provide) and make an appointment, their prognosis is much higher than that of those who become angry that we won't replicate by staying on the phone, giving them the personal information requested, and refusing to make an appointment without this replication. Many times, however, the prospective clients who sought replication do call back in a few days—when the caring intervention begins to metabolize as someone who wants a different outcome, with their higher good at heart. When this happens, therapy commences with a major breakthrough! The first bifurcation or choice point for change has been overcome. It's like stepping over a threshold into a new way of being and then adapting to new footing.

Initial Session

The first session continues the secure, intimate conditions of the therapeutic relationship and is pivotal to the overall success of treatment. With this in mind, new therapists can pay close attention early on to setting the trajectory of establishing new patterns that provide generative alignments to the archetypes involved. Paying close attention to the propensity for entrainment and replication is critical. If at any time in treatment we do get entrained or replicate patterns with clients, we can attempt to repair the replication. We can own what we did to replicate the patterns, who we became and what role we played through this replication in the archetypal drama (often a trauma or situation that shaped the client's life), and what we would have done differently in retrospect. This owning helps clients see their patterns, what happens with replications, and that the therapist has a strong-enough psyche and care for the client to own what was done and begin to do things differently. All such messages hold transformative potential and set new pathways in place by repairing past childhood experiences and providing the missing experiences needed.

In the Waiting Room

Often we already have an extensive amount of data about a client's patterns from the referral, the phone call, and scheduling the first appointment. The information continues to unfold as we meet the client for the first time in the waiting room. We might consider:

- Does the client come really early, is he or she late, or did he or she forget the appointment altogether?
- Did he or she get lost finding the building?
- Is he or she in deep conversation on a cell phone when we come out to welcome him or her for the first session?
- Did he or she bring children? A pet?
- Does he or she want to borrow a magazine from the waiting room?
- Does he or she begin talking intimately with us in the waiting room before the two of us can get into the office?

Again, we ask these questions, not in judgment, but as ongoing information about the new client's patterning and what the psyche is wanting us to see and understand in service to the client's greater good. All actions have a story to tell.

Structure of the Initial Session

General guidelines for the initial session include:

- Start and end on time to demonstrate a respectful framework and boundaries.
- Encourage the client to talk as freely as is comfortable for the first fifteen to twenty-five minutes. This begins the revelation of life experiences, archetypal dramas, patterns, archetypal alignments, and derivative unconscious communication to which we will later respond with adaptive interventions.
- During the time the client is talking, we pay close attention to the narrative stories and look for themes emanating from the deep unconscious of the psyche. Developing the skill to remember each theme and its details, knowing each part is being told for a very specific and unique purpose, takes practice.
- When a natural break in the flow of narrative stories occurs, we restate what we have heard, laying out each story and then its theme. We are sure to tend to each story in its objective form, free from personal interpretations, opinions, or projections. This might sound like: "The first story you told was. . . . The second story you told was. . . . The third story you told was. . . . In all three stories, the common theme seems to be. . . ." The purpose of this process is to offer a bridge from the unconscious (relayed in derivative stories) to the conscious mind for conscious understanding. By being shown this bridge, clients become fascinated with how deeply they are communicating outside

their own conscious awareness as well as how attentively we are listening and attuning to their experience. Listening to or understanding our own unconscious communication without someone's help is difficult. Eventually, through practice, the client develops his or her own "ear" for this listening through the ongoing process of translation. Also, because both the conscious mind and the deep self of the unconscious feel heard and attended to through this process, a trusting relationship between client and therapist is forged.

Commitment to the Self and Its Intentions

One of the primary goals in the first session, and then each subsequent session, is to see the essence of the client's Self, his or her essential nature that was veiled early in development by the conditioning of the ego. We can only serve as the bridge from the client's ego and conscious mind to his or her personal essence by remaining in relationship with the Self, which always holds wholeness and one's fullness as its mandate. To be in relationship with the Self, we must see this natural state in our clients, listen objectively to the narratives in our clients' stories or dreams, pay close attention to the images and themes, and provide this information to the conscious mind for translation, understanding, and integration.

The images from the psyche carry transformative power within themselves. Each image brings with it a set of mandates and guidelines, like an instruction packet. A system of knowledge in its own right (as we learned from Yoram Kaufmann's Orientational Approach), each image serves to orient us to its informational field. It is a hologram that informs us how the person is oriented in life and in his or her patterns and how he or she relates to the world. Images also give instructions as to how one can shift these patterns toward generativity and the client's greatest potential. As discussed throughout Part Four of this book, specific images bring with them an energy and a specific transformational potential selected by the deep unconscious psyche to show what is needed for healing.

Once we know the specific images and themes and have a relationship with both the deep unconscious psyche and the conscious mind, we can bridge these in an effort to move forward. This is done by using the client's images and themes and the conscious intentions for entering therapy along with the intentions heard from the deeper essence of the Self. This might look like: "Your conscious mind said it came to therapy to have better relationships and to find a partner. Your deeper Self and essence said, through the images and stories you shared, that its purpose and deep desire is for you to discover your true purpose in life, be who you truly are, and bring those gifts of Self into the world."

When a client can make a commitment to the Self and its intentions, the second bifurcation or choice point for change is aligned with transformation rather than with remaining in repetitive patterning. The archetypal forces are then able to support the work; growth and transformation unfold with ease and in a beautiful flow. If we only stay with the ego's or conscious mind's intentions, we tend to limit treatment to shoring up the ego and its quests to be better and feel of value, based on performance and accomplishments. By aligning with the Self, however, we enter a larger domain where the landscape reveals the truth of our essence: that we always have been good enough, our value has never been in question, and we have always been a perfect, beautiful being not separate from the Self.

In the process of making a commitment to the Self and its intentions, we also begin to see what we introjected from the early conditioning of our childhood and the untruths around which we formed our life. This knowledge is a relief—and a shattering, when we realize how much we have missed. When a commitment to the Self's intentions through a commitment to therapy is made, or at least considered, we are then ready to discuss the archetypal conditions necessary for growth and development and how these are adapted to the therapeutic container and framework.[26] As stated previously, all living systems are held in a container while growing and developing, and it is common that our client's family's container and boundaries needed for growth and development were compromised. Therefore, for healing to take place, new generative, healthy patterning and alignments will need uncompromised environmental conditions to prevent replication.

Discussing the Secure Therapeutic Container's Conditions at the End of the First Session

At the end of the first session, we set the consistent time and space for continuing the therapy and review policies related to cancellation, fees, confidentiality, and the like. (See the following inset, "The Most Ideal Archetypal Conditions," for recommendations on those policies.) Remember from the introduction of the archetypal healing container that there are specific properties of secure conditions needed for deep transformation of patterns and change in archetypal alignments to occur. We might use our pattern reading to explain the particular conditions needed to successfully make the journey. For example, we might say, "All living systems are held in a secure container while they grow and develop. If that container is compromised in any way, what is growing in the container will also be compromised and may not survive. Think about how a fetus in the womb needs a healthy, secure container or it may not survive. When the infant is born, it needs to be held securely in the arms of its mother, or the growth, development, and healthy attachment will be disrupted and affect the course of the infant's life. In sharing your childhood history just now, you spoke of many traumatic experiences and times your parents were not as available as you needed. In order to shift the patterns that have been prevalent in your life since then, you need different conditions than those you have had so far in your life. I suggest we set different conditions for your therapy that will be secure and consistent and provide what is needed archetypally for healthy growth and development."

Although the inset suggestions pertain to beginning treatment in in Archetypal Pattern Analysis, the same assessment and format is easily adapted for other domains and businesses such as bodywork, health care, law practices, and any contractual agree-

The Most Ideal Archetypal Conditions

To provide a secure therapeutic container, the most ideal archetypal conditions include:

* Conduct the treatment only in the therapy room.
* Have a set time that doesn't change due to life's circumstances (either yours or those of your client) including illness, appointments, vacations, holidays, emergencies, and the like.
* Meet at least weekly for consistent sessions.
* Set a fee at the first session that remains the same throughout the therapy. If at some point a reduced fee is needed, be sure to reevaluate when the client's situation improves and return to the original fee. (We do not raise the fee for existing clients when we increase the fee in our general practice.)
* Maintain confidentiality. What is said in the therapy room must remain there.
* During therapy, always focus on the client's needs, not your own.
* The most ideal cancellation policy for missed sessions is to hold all in place and consistent. To do this, when clients need to be absent, keeping the time and space for them (not seeing anyone else in that time and space) and their paying for this time and space offers the most secure and ideal conditions we can possibly provide. We have found that holding a secure container is integral to healing early compromising experiences and allows clients to import their own internal holding and secure attachment. Other cancellation policies often allow clients to unconsciously keep a foot out the door and replicate patterning that prevents them (and often the therapist) from facing the depth of fears related to intimacy.

ments. When there is an agreement to the secure conditions, treatment often progresses rapidly; major shifts and transformations unfold consistently and deeply. This comprises the third bifurcation or choice point to move toward change from repetitive patterning, with clients choosing to agree (or not) to the therapeutic conditions. Because of childhood family experiences, some of our clients have difficulty with this bifurcation. They might have had parents who put their own needs before those of their children, so conditions holding the clients' needs are of utmost importance. As we have mentioned numerous times, one of the keys to changing core patterns is a secure, uncompromised container that provides an archetypal, congruent environment for generative growth and development.

Using the First Two or Three Sessions for Assessment

From the first contact, to making the appointment, to walking our client from the waiting room and engaging in twenty minutes of derivative communication, we gain an extensive amount of data about the client and the way his or her patterns are trying to shape the analysis. We then use the first two or three sessions to fully assess the course of treatment and initial goals. We base the assessment on the client's:

- Behaviors;
- Images, dreams, unconscious derivative communication, family and personal history, and patterns manifested by the client throughout his or her life;
- Propensity to replicate patterns that concretize his or her archetypal alignments;
- Adaptation to the conditions and container; and
- Navigation of bifurcation points.

During those first few sessions, we also listen intently for any pattern replication. If it occurs, we determine who we may have been "cast to play" in the client's old archetypal alignment. In addition, we listen for images of rectification—communications from the client's objective psyche telling us what is needed to transform to a generative archetypal alignment that aids in gaining his or her fullness of life.

After making this archetypal pattern reading, we listen for the next derivative communication. Does it validate the initial reading, bring another rectification image, or bring negative images that denote a missed reading of the pattern? Sometimes the client's conscious mind gives a reaction to this reading, which shows that the conscious mind is not in alignment with the objective psyche of the Self. We, as therapists, must attune here to the unconscious derivatives to show the accuracy of the reading rather than focus on the conscious mind's reaction.

Stages of Treatment: The Hero's Journey for the Client

Clients who accept the secure conditions and make a commitment to the Self's calling by embarking upon treatment agree on some level to enter their hero's journey. They consciously or unconsciously commit to go into the depths of their psyche and face their fears and inner demons, slay the dragons, and rescue the parts of their authentic Self left in the grips of the Great Mother in early childhood. By completing this process, as in the hero myths, clients capture the treasure of the Self, their authentic nature, full potential, and purpose and meaning in life, so as to live out the gifts they are to offer the world.

Following are the archetypal stages clients take during their therapeutic journey and what they typically experience in each stage. These archetypal stages are that of the hero's journey and what it takes to truly birth the hero in ourselves—to begin to capture the treasure of our true nature as the Self.

Note that, before entering each new stage, clients are faced with a bifurcation: "Do I stay where I am or enter what is unknown?" It is imperative we understand these important choice points in the therapy process in order to bring them into conscious awareness and to help clients navigate through them. Although primarily unconscious, the bifurcation points often manifest as clients feeling, "I am done with therapy" or "I want to take a break." They often just do not consciously know where to go next and fear going further into the unknown. When we point out the bifurcation—that this is part of the typical process of therapy, that their fears are natural, what their next step could look like, and that we will partner with them through it—most agree to stay. They then usually come to value us as mentors they can trust to guide the journey and see the therapist-client partnership as an opportunity for major change in their lives.

Stage 1: Hearing the Call of Transformation

Whatever has prompted a client to call for therapy generally seems to be the ego's or conscious mind's call to change. Underneath, held in the unconscious, is the Self calling to be known. The journey will take looking at whatever is out of alignment with the client's highest purpose and true essence. Reframing this in the first session can help clients feel the importance of being fully committed to this call from the Self, and that there is a much larger goal for their entering therapy: discovering their true nature, the Self.

We found in our training to become Archetypal Pattern Analysts that we, too, embarked on the hero's journey and that journey required us to face our fears and inner demons. Our commitment to make the changes needed to shift into alignment with the Self and the deep unconscious took us through similar stages as are outlined here for clients. We learned firsthand that to fully discover our true nature and open to the Self requires becoming a hero. We all must capture those aspects of ourselves still held captive and rescue them in order to embody our true power and pure essence.

Stage 2: Wrestling with the Call

After hearing about the call for transformation and accepting the conditions of a secure container, the client begins to go through a process of wrestling with whether or not to accept the conditions. The analyst knows what the client is really wrestling with: whether or not to accept the call for deep transformation. This wrestling, which sometimes occurs over several sessions, might involve the client:

- Grappling with the new ideas;
- Beginning to accept the interpretation of the patterns; and/or
- Feeling anxious in the face of being held in a secure container. Whatever ways clients have been hurt or frightened during their life while trusting in another and being held securely—such as riding in a car with a drunk parent and feeling terrified for one's safety—will come to the surface for consciousness and healing in response to this therapeutic container.

Whatever the wrestling, during this process, the client reveals much information about patterning and what he or she needs to begin the journey of becoming a hero.

Stage 3: Crossing the First Threshold with a Mentor By Your Side

Everyone goes through a process if he or she is going to turn away from old patterning, conditioning, and defenses and surrender to discovering his or her true nature. Depending on how much authority has been used to oppress the client in his or her past and depending on how invested he or she is in the ego's goals, the process can be easy or challenging. Once the client decides, however, to move forward with, "Okay! I'll see what happens," the journey can commence and the old alignments and patterns will begin to release.

At this point, the client then comes face to face with the depth and intimacy of his or her relationship with the analyst. As clients allow the analyst to name patterns, they begin to experience the depth of feeling accepted while in deep vulnerability. They feel exposed as they let the analyst see how they have been living and what they have been allowing. The work then deepens into facing the depths of one's shadow.

Stage 4: Facing Tests, Obstacles, Inner and Outer Enemies, and Allies

Clients experience an inner confrontation at this point, as the work now deepens into facing their own inner and outer demons, shadow aspects, unconscious guilt, and nongenerative archetypal alignments. It is like looking in the mirror. They see the negative aspects of themselves that their patterns, complexes, and ego have been defending against truly seeing into the past. Their idea of themselves, their persona, is revealed.

With this new viewing platform, clients gain a new understanding of their pattern reading and translation. They begin to own how their old patterns served to keep them unconscious. They even start seeing the depth of the patterning from both their family of origin and their culture and what it expresses. This leads to their acquiring a deeper understanding of how they have been acting out their patterns and how those patterns have impacted their own life and the lives of their loved ones. What often ensues at this point is deep grief. The process of dealing with this grief begins to align them with their objective psyche, their destiny, and a deep surrender.

Stage 5: Surrendering and Committing to the Call

Out of this deep understanding and surrender often grows a strong need to keep going forward in the transformational process. Although the new way of being is not fully in view, the old way of being is no longer attractive or comfortable. Although the landscape is not known, clients begin to give up the safety of old patterns and move into a new paradigm and new behaviors. This "halfwayness" causes clients to begin to feel hopeful, but their ego may also feel terrified with not knowing or being in control.

Stage 6: New Level of Wrestling

At this next stage, clients face deep, dark fears. The underpinnings of the patterning have emerged, a new bifurcation point appears, and often a "flight into health" occurs. Clients feel they have made the necessary shifts and that they can now handle life in a different way. At this point they also often have an urge to "take a break," leave therapy, and try out their new skills. The analyst knows that urge is really an ego-intuited need to leave before going into the depth of wrestling that has to occur to step *completely* out of the complexes and patterns. In fact, the desire to leave is often an alignment with manic defenses to keep from facing the depth of the next step of the work, the "final ordeal." By listening carefully to derivatives, we can help our clients see what they are really dealing with and help them make the transition to the final stages of the work. For example, we might respond to a client who considers leaving therapy by saying, "You say you are done, but you just told me four stories about leaving things before they are finished and feeling bad about doing that."

For therapists, this stage is very seductive. On the conscious level, we can see the growth the clients are experiencing and we have a tendency to want to support their decisions. Unconsciously, however, we can realize that to align with the decision to leave would be an attempt to evacuate our own unconscious dread and anxiety of standing for our client's greatest good; we also realize the fears of going down into the depth of intimacy that the next stage will require.

Every step of the way, we, as analysts, are faced with our own patterns, fears, anxieties, and need for change—a parallel process through which our clients are going. At each bifurcation point, we, too, must face and clear our own patterning in order to be able to hold the client's journey. A sacred mirroring process is occurring here. We must manage our own anxiety and see it for what it truly is. A failure to do this internal examining and clearing will result in a high probability that our clients will be unable to deepen into the next stage of the journey.

In essence, the bifurcation point of this stage of the transformation journey is really whether to leave with the feeling of some successes and insights or whether to consciously commit to completing the work. The clients are not all the way out of the old system. They can see and name it, but they are still embedded in it. What needs to happen is that the clients deeply trust in the analyst's capacity to hold them in a loving field, to continue to maintain the secure container, and to help interpret the deep fears and defenses about facing their patterns and fears of change. Once the clients feel this deep trust, they then can move into a deep surrender and commitment for their transformation.

Stage 7: Surrendering and Receiving Gifts

With this surrender, there is a whole new level of alliance with the analyst and trust in intimacy. From then on, the work has a whole new feeling and the clients have a new understanding of their own patterns and complexes. The de-embedding process begins to occur, and an ability to witness their own process strengthens. At this stage, clients are often able to interpret their unconscious material in dreams and derivatives and feel much less emotionally attached to that material. The gifts of this stage include relaxing and trusting in the relationship with the analyst and the unfolding relationship with the Self. Clients begin to rest into the transformation and toward stepping out of the old pattern. The call to destiny also makes itself felt strongly, and the alignment with one's true purpose deepens.

Stage 8: Final Ordeal

Feeling the call of destiny brings clients into a final ordeal in which they have the opportunity to completely break the spells of their complexes and transform. During this ordeal, they must face their deepest, darkest fears and hungers, and their old defenses often surface. Just like in myths and movies, there is typically a last battle with horrendous forces—from which a hero emerges. Of course, questions about resources and quitting therapy often reemerge here and need tender translation. Like birth, there is a membrane to break through in order to experience what has always been present—one's true Self.

Stage 9: Integration and Sharing the Gift

Once this "membrane" is broken, the old pattern no longer can assert itself and clients open up to their true potential. They know now that the answers to all their needs and wants are "inside" (rather than projecting onto others), and this shift is felt by everyone in their world. An integration and maturity takes place. Relationships improve. They feel a new orientation in life and a new ability to deal with their deep fears and anxieties. They also encounter a newfound ability to come into their own authority in the world. They feel expanded and are empowered to trust and share in a loving presence in life.

The work now flows out of recounting successes, integration, and a real appreciation for the journey and the analyst. Granted, the old patterning still occasionally shows up, but it is easily recognized and worked through without a struggle. With the full completion and integration of all these archetypal stages, clients feel the hero that was born in them and the Treasure they have become. Their destiny is now the navigator of their life. As with any archetypal movie or myth, when heroes truly emerge, they embody their many gifts of Self and then share them with the world.

Therapist Position in Building a Generative Refuge

Generative Refuge	Therapist Position
Really living, thriving	Welcoming and wanting
Taking in abundance and support	Supporting and nurturing with good boundaries, morals, and ethics
Trusting there is help	Encouraging collaboration between client and therapist
Enjoying others; having real intimacy	Having an equal and intimate relationship between client and therapist
Having freedom while also being close with others	Ensuring client that he/she doesn't have to take care of therapist, that cleint's needs are most important
Accepting intrinsic value and worth	Encouraging client to be OK with the way he/she is; deregulating nervous system
Believing it's OK to manifest dreams, be grounded in the world, and still feel free	Being a solid presence to bounce off of; keeping solid conditions
Having a just and balanced inner world	Accepting what is in the moment; authority is hearing the unfairness
Having needs met and being loved	"What are your needs?"
"I am more than my thoughts"	Facilitating mindfulness and deconstuctions

Glossary

Most of these terms are found in the curriculum of Archetypal Pattern Analysis and are elaborated upon in the text of this book.

Alignments with an Archetype: Like the face of a clock, each archetype has many facets. Inherent in each archetype are certain mandates or ontological features. In each expression of an archetype, it can be noted, by how the mandate of the archetype is being fulfilled or not being fulfilled, whether the alignment is generative or nongenerative. For example, parenting requires the creation and maintenance of consistent conditions. In the archetype of parenting, some parents provide a safe and loving home (generative alignment), whereas others abuse or abandon their children (a nongenerative alignment).

Anima, Animus: These are archetypal figures formed during early development from taking in impressions of our parents as they are in relationship to us. The *anima* represents the psychic feminine, and the *animus* represents the psychic masculine. These are archetypal structures we work to integrate generatively throughout our development. The ideal is a balance of these within our psyches.

A priori: Something already present from which form will later emerge. That which is held latent in potential and predates the existence of form.

Archetypal Coherence: Many see the natural world as a semblance of random events. In looking more closely, however, we can see a consistent ordering process organized around an archetypal theme. For example, while all newly born babies have individual differences, there is a set of morphogenetic constants underlying the design of a fetus and its development over the course of its nine months prior to birth. Coherence is when the archetypal mandate is met.

Archetypal Mandate (see Mandate)

Archetypal Field (see Field)

Archetype: An archetype is a universal constant, a pre-existing pattern in which form can arise. It is a blueprint underlying the innate order and structure of all life form. For example, birds just "know" how to build a nest for their young and for shelter. Likewise, humans search for shelter and a structure in which to make a home to raise children and live life; there are constants in the task of parenting, mandates that are present and preset within the task itself.

Attractor: A term from math and physics that describes any pattern that defines the repetitive motion of a system.

Attractor Site: A configuration or pattern into which a dynamic eventually settles. An alignment to an archetype is an attractor site that begins to configure behavior into a pattern.

Bifurcation Point: A significant point of change in a dynamical system. Like a fork in the road, it is a choice point. For example, your system could reject new information or use it to shift into a more complex order toward change. The choice point is between staying with the familiar pattern or choosing to move toward what is unknown and frightening. There is always an influx of energy at a bifurcation point. The energy reorganizes itself and goes in the new direction when it exhausts. When the system exceeds its original parameters, novelty and complexity then enter. (Conforti, unpublished lectures)

Bio Fields: The intelligent energy of a living system held in energy fields. A living communication network derived from bioelectrical phenomena inherent in our living tissues.

Causal Realm: Where the archetypes and form are held in potential—beyond time, space and form. It can also be referred to as the space we enter during deep sleep.

Complex: Inherent in an archetypal field is a magnetic pull to alignments or attractor sites so that patterned tendencies of behavior are highly organized around a theme or facet of an archetype. The *attractor* is what C.G. Jung called a "complex." As Michael Conforti states in his book *Field, Form, and Fate*, "Jungian analyst Yoram Kaufmann defined the complex as a 'quantum of energy organized around a central theme.'" Examples include: mother complex, father complex, sexual complex, and so on. It is as though the complex acts like an antenna that will tune into or tune out certain frequencies (attractors) like a radio station. We can see that each complex manifests in a different form, having a propensity to follow a generative or nongenerative theme.

For instance, some seek abusive relationships that feel comfortable and familiar while finding that loving relationships feel terrifying and dangerous. Others may only be attracted to loving, generative relationships and be adverse to abusive relationships. In our work, we often refer to complexes as "reactive states."

Creodes (Chreodes) and Canalization: *Chreode* origins are (Greek) *Chre* for "it is necessary" plus *Hodos*, which means "route or path." A creode (or chreode), thus, is a biological pathway or habit "canalized like a groove."

Death Anxiety: Death underlies all human fear. As we develop, images and the reality of death are cauterized off from the conscious mind, particularly in traumatic situations. As we begin to approach these cauterized areas, we feel a dread of and an aversion for anything that might remind us of those areas. The ego then has lost the meaning and the inference of meaning. The whole system "complexes" (a younger reactive state) around it. Anything that comes up that refers to the raw image bounces off this resistant shield into the unconscious and is not available to the conscious mind. (Conforti, unpublished lectures)

Derivative Communication: This term refers to the content in the material communicated between client and therapist. It also is relevant to all communication between people in that there is a recognition that communication can have both hidden and overt or manifest content. In other words, manifest verbal and nonverbal communication carries a hidden meaning. It is the listener's task to hear the nature of this hidden communication by concentrating on the themes and metaphors in a person's stories that carry embedded perceptions and beliefs. This method of listening, called the Communicative Approach in Psychotherapy, was developed by Robert Langs MD.

Derivatives (see Derivative Communication)

Dominant of an Archetype: The dominant of an image relates to the most prevailing and underlying feature(s) of the image: What is the essence of the image, or, simply, what is the image about? How is it defined? What are its significant features? This is also true of the dominant of an archetype: What are the salient features? What is the underlying pattern which sums up, in a phrase, the essence of the archetype?

Dragon Fight: The developmental need to struggle against something or someone in the outer world in order to break out of the current developmental level and move to the next developmental level—to attain our true self rather than be stuck in familial bonds or what we believe others hold important for who we are.

Dread/Secure Frame Dread: Dread is the fear of replicating traumatic experiences of annihilation. The unknown is a free fall into annihilation, death, or nonexistence. As a client readies to face his or her own traumatic experiences, the analyst can succumb to his or her own dread and increasingly sabotage the analysis, keeping it in more manifest content and out of terrifying depth.

Ego: The ego is the underlying principle in our personality organization that endeavors to make coherent meaning and orchestrates how we perceive reality. Its task is to be the intermediary between inner and outer reality.

Ego Ideal: An idealized conception of oneself that combines the mystery and unity of the Self with being a heroic figure.

Entelechy: The innate intelligence of an entity that includes its fullest potential. It holds the blueprint, the goal, and the directing force in the development and functioning of an organism or system. It is what drives our destiny throughout life and journey to wholeness.

Entrainment: Falling into synchronism with something or the attunement process to maintain patterning. For instance, clocks will begin ticking together when put together in the same room. Further, brain entrainment is the practice of entraining one's brainwaves to a desired frequency.

Evacuating Anxiety: The buildup of anxiety that causes a system to lose its homeostasis. Evacuating anxiety means doing something (often breaking the therapeutic framework) to release the built-up charge of energy felt inside in order to feel a stable homeostasis again. It is a process of going away from what one fears to relieve the anxiety that the fear creates.

Field (Archetypal Field): A *field* is the energetic element of an archetype, which exerts its influence over space and time. Fields order the matter within, rather than creating the field and its dynamics. Fields organize all forms, structures, and patterned interactions of systems. They shape all matter, thoughts, behaviors, culture, and societies.

Physical fields in the outside world, such as gravitational and electromagnetic fields, are space-time dependent. Archetypal fields, on the other hand, are not influenced by space and time but are nonlocal, as in the transmission of information in telepathy and synchronicities.

Formative Causation: The inherent memory of a morphogenetic field that becomes the source of information for all future organisms. This makes it possible to continue a species. For example, the information of how to fight off a particular kind of bug becomes part of the memory field for future plants.

Fractal, Fractal Geometry: A structure or object whose shape repeats at ever finer scales. It can look complex but has an underlying simplicity.

Fulcrum: A term coined by Blanck and Blanck, used to describe the shift between the major stages of development. The term is used to speak of the steps that the center of gravity of the Self must move through to develop in increasing complexity. We must navigate through a series of stages by first identifying with a new developmental level and then by de-embedding and transcending the current level, while at the same time including and integrating that current level into the next higher level.

Generative, Nongenerative: *Generative* means moving toward growth and complexity and aligning with a fullness of life. On the other hand, *nongenerative* is the opposite and means moving toward entropy.

Gross: The concrete realm of objects found under the prinicples of time, space, gravity, and the duality of opposites. This state is often related to the waking state and concrete objects.

Implicit Memory: Stored memories from the early unconscious, pre-verbal and pre-cognitive states that create an overall pattern of expectation in life. These memories are prior to that stage of brain development when the hippocampus can translate experiences into narrative stories and memories of experiences that create understanding and perspective of our lives. Implicit memories are held in somatic states that function as background affects (symbolized versions of our early impressions of how we were treated) and they act as mental models of what to expect from others. These memories are not available to the conscious mind. They are experienced as "just how it is" and become our reactive states throughout life.

Individuation, Individuate: Refers to a time in one's life (typically the later part) when we have moved into the Transformational stages of Archetypal Developmental Theory. This is the stage when the ego has gained enough consciousness that the Treasure is revealed and the meaning of life is being lived.

Informational Fields: Inherent in archetypes are the a priori nature of informational fields. These fields contain the energetic potentials stored in information encodings in which form is then manifested. For instance, there is an a priori field of the form in which a human fetus will develop subsequent to the fertilization of an egg by sperm, as well as a predictable trajectory in its development over a nine-month period of time.

Initial Conditions: The conditions present at the beginning of something new that set a trajectory for future outcomes, unless a perturbation intervenes to change the set course toward a new outcome.

Introject (Introjection): A term from Gestalt therapy that describes the psychological process of swallowing whole, without chewing into parts. The introjected, therefore, sits inside the psyche as a whole and is not digested.

Iteration: Feeding back into a dynamic the results in its own dynamics. The act of repeating a process with the aim of approaching a desired end result. Each repetition is called an "iteration."

Mandate (also see Alignment): A requirement or universal law or principle. *Mandate* is often used in terms of archetypal expression or when we look at an image and its objective. For example, the mandate of medicine is healing.

Manic Defenses: From D.W. Winnicott's paper entitled "Manic Defenses," this idea relates to the terror and internal dread felt when one is unable to tolerate the treatment when it fails to follow a replicative format. While defenses are necessary for self-protection, manic defenses are resorted to when one is unable to contain one's anxiety and fears. Instead, the person feels the need to react in a flight from these internal feelings in an attempt to bring the system back to a level of homeostasis and comfortability (familiarity). For instance, consider how we want to rid ourselves of the feelings we have when we hear about terrible abuse. This process is referred to as "evacuating one's anxiety."

Manifest Material: That which is known by the conscious mind. It includes "surface" communication such as facts, associations, and known information.

Mentor: A patterning force that provides new skills. An influence who tends to move consciousness toward a new complexity.

Morphic Resonance: When like things attune to one another—like similar patterns of people who live together or when clocks are put together and eventually tick in unison.

Morphogenesis: The coming into form.

Morphogenic Fields (Morphic Fields): Fields which provide a structure containing all the information needed to organize that particular form into manifestation. For example, consider what keeps an acorn growing into an oak tree instead of some other kind of tree.

Narcissistic Injury: When someone was not the center of one's parents' attention when young, dependent, and growing, that person is injured and his or her young needs are still clamoring to be met. Often, unconsciously, someone with this injury will put themselves in the center of things, demanding that the attention come to them first. They also find it difficult to put their children's needs before their own. Children of narcissistically injured parents are often seen as satellites to that parent, not seen for their own uniqueness and often not forming secure attachment with the parent early in infanthood.

Non-linear Systems: Systems not following linear rules. An example in media is a movie in which the events are not portrayed in chronological order. Other examples include being able to click on a more in-depth point in the middle of an article you are reading, and being able to fast forward through a story on cable TV.

Nonlocal: A concept referring to archetypal fields not being held by the perception of time and space, while electromagnetic fields are time and space dependent. It is a term originating in quantum physics that describes that all quanta (microscopic form) in the universe that share or have ever shared the same quantum state remain intrinsically connected with each other and can share a kind of instant communication, despite any distance between them.

Objective Psyche: This term was used by C.G. Jung to describe the objective nature that is characteristic of the psyche or soul of an individual. It is not culturally constructed through a personal lens. Objective is its true nature rather than associations or personal interpretations.

Oedipal Complex: The term, named for the myth of Oedipus, refers to the developmental quandary of wanting to stay in the emotional-sexual realm (of the feminine mother archtype) while nature is moving one on to the mental realm and the outer world (of the father archetype). That quandry, while not gender related, is typified by a wish to unite sexually and triangulate with the parents while also trying to get rid of one of the parents.

Patterns: Patterns are manifestations of archetypal informational fields expressed in space and time. They are external expressions of an internal process. For example, our outer world is formed by patterns in nature: A particular mushroom will grow only on the side of a tree or in certain conditions in the woods, while an acorn holds all the information it needs to specifically form into an oak tree.

Persona: The aspect of ourselves that we find acceptable and present to the world.

Perturbation: A deviation from the usual, predictable course of an event which causes a disturbed or agitated state of being, so that a new course toward change can occur.

Pleuromatic: An undifferentiated state of unity such as a fetus in the womb or a baby in its first state in the outer world that is extra-uterine.

Pre-cognitive, Pre-verbal: That developmental stage before the brain has developed enough to be able to use language or narrative in storing memory.

Reactive State: Acting in response to a situation from an unconsciously triggered memory—like road rage, when someone cuts in front of you and you experience a rageful feeling—with origins in your childhood, when you often felt treated as though you were unimportant. The situation feels like it is happening currently, but actually there is a larger reaction than is appropriate to the situation. Also, the reaction is often projected on another person or situation rather than being seen as an internal process.

Repetition: The tendency to repeat behavioral patterns is a defense mechanism to avoid fears and anxiety of remembering traumatic events. Repetition or externalizing such events alleviates the anxiety that will surface if the meaning of the event becomes conscious and needs to be integrated.

Replication (or Replicative) System, Closed System: An obsolete and closed system with a lack of plasticity. It is one that stays within narrow paramenters and is not open to new information or to change.

Secure Frame (or Solid Container): The specific properties needed to create a place for transformation to occur.

Self: The ordering and unifying center of the total psyche (conscious and unconscious), just as the ego is the center of the conscious personality. In other words, the ego is the base of our subjective identity, whereas the Self is the base of our objective identity. The Self is also referred to as the "divine presence," which connects all humans into a unified collective unconsciousness.

Self-organizing: A process of patterning or organization arising solely from the interactions between the components of a system, not from outside the system. Its repetition maintains it as being self-organizing.

Shadow: That which is seen by the ego or the persona as undesirable or as something it does not want to face. Shaped by the personal and collective superegos, the shadow holds any aspects of Self that do not fulfill the ego ideal.

Somatic: Of or relating to the body, as distinct from the mind. Usually referring to feelings and memories held in the body (like the implicit memories of infancy and early childhood).

Subjective Material/Viewpoint: That which is related to a person's thinking or emotions and is conditioned by one's personal characteristics and ego. It is information already known or conscious, like facts and associations that are impermanent, as opposed to the objective, which is universally accepted to be reality.

Subtle Realm: In a dream state, we have subtle senses and subtle objects and an environment made of subtle elements. This is also the place of imagination, where we think about our thoughts.

Superego, Cultural: An introjected cultural authority woven from what the culture portrays as "the right way to be," to which we adhere.

Superego, Personal: An internalization of our parents, often experienced as an internal voice that is a set of impressions, suggestions, commands, injunctions, and prohibitions absorbed from early patterned experiences.

System, Open and Closed: Systems that are open receive and integrate new information and change, moving toward their innate potential. Closed systems are canalized to habitual patterns, limit possibilites for change, and can become so rigid that there is no ability to accept new information.

Trajectory: A course or path determined by the forces inherent in initial conditions.

Unconscious Communication: Communication which is an expression from the objective psyche revealed through archetypal images, symbols, patterns, and narrative themes. This communication is encoded in a form not understood by the conscious mind but is intended for our highest good. It offers information pointing toward our wholeness and the Self.

Uroborus: The first stage in the Archetypal Developmental Theory. It is a state of symbiotic union with the Mother associated with the unconscious and a state of being undifferentiated, similar to being held in the arms of the Mother. This is not only an early stage of extra-uterine development but a state to which we often want to return when life's challenges seem difficult and we would rather not face them.

Notes

Part One

1. C.G. Jung, *Memories, Dreams, and Reflections*, reissue ed. (New York: Vintage, 1989), 3.

Chapter 1 (pages 25-30)

2. The quote appeared in a 1919 book titled *A Shadow Passes* by Eden Phillpotts.

Chapter 2 (pages 31-38)

3. Rupert Sheldrake, "Morphic Resonance," a keynote speech at the 2013 International Gathering of Eden Energy Medicine (IGEEM) Conference, a gathering of leading-edge thinkers exploring the powerful effects of energy on our bodies, our consciousness, and our world. Available at https://www.youtube.com/watch?v=MtgLklXZo3U.

4. *Nonlocal* is a term originating in quantum physics to describe that all quanta (microscopic form) in the universe that share or have ever shared the same quantum state remain intrinsically connected with each other and can share a kind of instant communication, despite any distance between them.

5. A term used by C.G. Jung meaning, "the unitary nature of the world with each individual being connected."

6. Michael Conforti. From unpublished seminar lectures held in Portland, OR, 1996-2008.

Chapter 3 (pages 39-43)

7. Michael Conforti, *Field, Form, and Fate: Patterns in Mind, Nature, and Psyche* (New Orleans, LA: Spring Journal Press, 1999), 25.

8. Conforti. From unpublished seminar lectures held in Portland, OR, 1996-2008.

9. Conforti, *Field, Form, and Fate*, 133.

10. The term *attractor site* is derived from Chaos Theory.

11. Rupert Sheldrake, *Morphic Resonance: The Nature of Formative Causation* (South Paris, ME: Park Street Press, 2009).

Chapter 4 (pages 45-57)

12. Conforti, *Field, Form, and Fate*, 61.

13. Scott F. Gilbert, "Induction and the Origins of Developmental Genetics," *A Conceptual History of Modern Embryology* (New York: Plenum Press, 2005), 181-206.

14. Conforti, *Field, Form, and Fate*, 20.

15. Conforti, *Field, Form, and Fate*, 18.

16. Conforti. From unpublished seminar lectures held in Portland, OR, 1996-2008.

17. John Briggs, *Fractals: The Patterns of Chaos* (New York: Simon and Schuster, 1992), 19.
18. Briggs, *Fractals*, 19.
19. Briggs, *Fractals*, 121.
20. Briggs, *Fractals*, 121.
21. Briggs, *Fractals*, 26.
22. Conforti, *Field, Form, and Fate*, 25.
23. Conforti, *Field, Form, and Fate*, 18.
24. Conforti, *Field, Form, and Fate*, 118.
25. Sigmund Freud, "Remembering, Repeating and Working-Through," *The Standard Edition of the Complete Psychological Works of Sigmund Freud*, Volume XII (1914).
26. Conforti. From unpublished seminar lectures held in Portland, OR, 1996-2008.
27. Rupert Sheldrake, *Morphic Resonance: The Nature of Formative Causation* (South Paris, ME: Park Street Press, 2009).
28. *Perturbation* is an alteration of the function of a system, induced by external or internal mechanisms, like a stone thrown into a still pool.
29. *Bifurcation* is a biological term meaning "coming to a choice point."
30. Dorothy Washburn and Donald Crowe, *Symmetry Comes of Age: The Role of Pattern in Culture* (Seattle, WA: University of Washington Press, 2004).

Chapter 5 (pages 59-73)

31. Conforti, *Field, Form, and Fate*, 22-23.
32. Conforti, *Field, Form, and Fate*, 22.
33. Rupert Sheldrake, *The Presence of the Past: The Habits of Nature* (South Paris, ME: Park Street Press, 1995), 99.
34. Michael Conforti. Phone consultation, December 9, 2017.
35. Sheldrake, *The Presence of the Past*, 81-82.
36. Templates on the diagram taken from concepts in ancient Vedanta texts and later written about in Plato's work on eternal form. Reiterated in Ken Wilber's Integral Theory.
37. Ervin Laszlo, *Science and the Akashic Field: An Integral Theory of Everything* (Rochester, VT: Inner Traditions, 2007).
38. Sheldrake, *Morphic Resonance*, 48-49.
39. Conforti, *Field, Form, and Fate*, 41.
40. Babaji Bob Kindler. From individual session, 2007.
41. Sheldrake, *The Presence of the Past*, 371.
42. Sheldrake, *Morphic Resonance*, 62-64.
43. Sheldrake, *Dogs That Know When Their Owners Are Coming Home* (New York: Crown Publisher, 1999).

44. Sheldrake, *Dogs That Know When Their Owners Are Coming Home*.

45. Beverly Rubik, "The Biofield Hypothesis: Its Biophysical Basis and Role in Medicine," *The Journal of Alternative and Complementary Medicine* 8, no. 6 (2002): 703-717, https://doi.org/10.1089/10755530260511711.

46. Rubik.

47. Rubik.

48. Sheldrake, *Dogs That Know When Their Owners Are Coming Home*.

49. Lew Childre, *Science of the Heart: Exploring the Role of the Heart in Human Performance* (Boulder Creek, CA: HeartMath Institute, 2009), 2, http://www.heartmath.org/research/science-of-the-heart.

50. Childre, 2-3.

51. Joseph Chilton Pearce, *The Death of Religion and the Rebirth of Spirit: A Return to the Intelligence of the Heart* (South Paris, ME: Park Street Press, 2007).

52. Michael Conforti. From unpublished seminar lectures on the work of Robert Langs MD, held in Portland, OR, 1996-2008.

53. Bruce Lipton. Lecture on epigenetic research for National Institute for the Clinical Application of Behavioral Medicine (NICABM) Brain Lecture Series, February 12, 2014.

54. Masaru Emoto, *The Hidden Messages in Water* (New York: Atria Books, 2005).

Part Two

1. Erich Neumann, *The Child*, trans. The Jung Foundation (Boulder, CO: Shambhala Books, 1990), 216.

Chapter 6 (pages 77-89)

2. Erich Neumann, *Depth Psychology and a New Ethic*, trans. Eugene Rolfe (New York: , Harper & Row, 1973), 113.

3. Bonnie Bright, "The C.G. Jung–Erich Neumann Connection: An Interview with Dr. Lance Owens." *Pacifica Post* (blog), Pacifica Graduate Institute, June 3, 2016, http://www.pacificapost.com/the-c.g.-jung-erich-neumann-connection-an-interview-with-dr.-lance-owens.

4. Bright.

5. Louis Sewart, foreword to *The Child*, by Erich Neumann.

6. Pacifica Graduate Institute, "A Conversation with Erel Shalit and Joe Cambray," June 16, 2016, YouTube video, 52:20, https://youtu.be/O7jazUTm0Aw.

7. Gerhard Adler, foreword to *Creative Man: Five Essays, Vol. II*, by Erich Neumann, trans. Eugene Rolfe (Princeton: Princeton University Press, 1979), 2.

8. Adler, 112.

9. Adler, 112.

10. *Individuation* is the process in which a unique individual identity develops out of an undifferentiated consciousness. Once the ego has matured by developing its identity, we go on to become fascinated with the purpose of life and the conscious rediscovery of that from which we individuated—the vastness of the Self, the center of our being.

11. Adler, 123.

12. Adler, 134.

13. Erich Neumann, *The Origins and History of Consciousness* (Princeton: Princeton University Press, 1954).

14. Edward Edinger, *Ego and Archetype* (Baltimore, MD: Penguin Books, 1973), 5.

15. Murray Stein, *Jung's Map of the Soul* (Chicago, IL: Open Court, 1998).

16. Charting a series of predictable stages is not a new idea. Shakespeare wrote about it in *As You Like It*, and Erik Erikson posited eight stages of psychosocial development, each transcending and including its predecessor and each with its attendant struggle. In addition, Robert Kegan and Susanne Cook-Greuter have added to the substantial body of theory, research, and interpretation of the developmental path. (Please see Part Five of this book for an in-depth look at this work.) In the next section, we introduce the new kid on the block, Archetypal Developmental Theory, which helps us to understand and negotiate this remarkable journey from a different perspective.

17. Emma Jung, *Animus and Anima: Two Papers* (New York: Spring Publications of The Analytic Psychology Club, 1972), 1-2.

Chapter 7 (pages 91-109)

18. Neumann, *The Child* (Boulder, CO: Shambhala Publications, 1973), ix.

19. Neumann, *The Origins and History of Consciousness* (Princeton, NJ: Princeton University Press, 1954), 8.

20. Neumann, *The Child*, ix.

21. Neumann, *The Child*, ix.

22. Erik Erikson, *Childhood and Society*, reissue ed. (New York: W. W. Norton and Company, 1993), 247-51.

23. A.H. Almaas, *Facets of Unity: Enneagram of Holy Ideas* (Boulder, CO: Shambhala Publications, 2000), 30.

24. Richard Nicoletti, *Fathers' Unfinished Task: Illuminating Contents of Oedipal Blindness with Eros Energy: Men's Power Shadow, Men's Homoerotic Shadow, Intrusive Anima*, Diploma Thesis (C. G. Jung Institute: Boston, 2014).

25. Robert A. Johnson, *Femininity Lost and Regained* (New York: HarperCollins, 1991).

26. Michael Washburn, *The Ego and the Dynamic Ground* (Albany, NY: State University of New York Press, 1995), 37.

27. Neumann, *The Origins and History of Consciousness*, 162-165.

28. Erikson, 255.

29. Neumann, *The Child*, 86.
30. Neumann, *Origins*, 403.
31. Neumann, *Origins*, 403-404.
32. Neumann, *Origins*, 307-317.
33. Neumann, *Origins*, 433.

Chapter 8 (pages 111-120)

34. Ken Wilber, *The Atman Project: A Transpersonal View of Human Development*, 2nd ed. (Wheaton, IL: Quest Books, 1996), 117.

35. Andy Drymalski, "Jungian Psychology Series: The Anima and Animus," private class, October 17, 2013.

36. Erich Neumann, *Art and the Creative Unconscious*, 3rd ed. (Princeton, NJ: Princeton University Press, 1974).

37. Kasiva Mutua, "How I Use the Drum to Tell My Story," filmed August 2017, TEDGlobal video, 12:39, https://www.ted.com/talks/kasiva_mutua_how_i_use_the_drum_to_tell_my_story.

Chapter 9 (pages 121-129)

38. Neumann, *Origins*, 418.
39. Neumann, *Origins*, 418.
40. Charles Poncé, *Working the Soul: Reflections on Jungian Psychology* (Berkeley, CA: North Atlantic Books, 1987).

Part Three

1. Neumann, *Origins*, 206.

Chapter 11 (pages 137-142)

2. Neumann, *Origins*, 213.
3. Neumann, *Origins*, 213.
4. Neumann, *Origins*, 213.
5. Neumann, *Origins*, 199.
6. Neumann, *Origins*, 198.
7. Neumann, *Origins*, 202.
8. Neumann, *Origins*, 204.
9. Neumann, *Origins*, 204.

Chapter 12 (pages 143-174)

10. A.H. Almaas, *The Pearl Beyond Price: Integration of Personality into Being: An Object Relations Approach* (Berkeley, CA: Almaas Publications, 1988), 320.

11. Wilber, *Atman Project*.

12. Wilber, *Atman Project*.

13. Almaas, *Pearl*, 320.

14. Almaas, *Pearl*, 323.

15. Almaas, *Pearl*, 323.

16. Almaas, *Pearl*, 237.

17. Almaas, *Pearl*, 237.

18. Bruce Lipton. Lecture on Epigenetic research for National Institute for the Clinical Application of Behavioral Medicine (NICABM) Brain Lecture Series, February 12, 2014.

19. Lipton.

20. Almaas, *Diamond Heart: Inexhaustible Mystery* (Boulder, CO: Shambhala Press, 2011), 172-173.

21. Almaas, *Diamond Heart*, 172-173.

22. Almaas, *Diamond Heart*, 172-173.

23. Daniel J. Siegel, *Pocket Guide to Interpersonal Neurobiology: An Integrative Handbook of the Mind* (New York: W.W. Norton and Company, 2012), AI-52-57.

24. Neumann, *Origins*, 158.

25. Almaas, *Diamond Heart*, 279.

26. Almaas, *Diamond Heart*, 283.

27. Erikson, *Childhood and Society*, 251-252.

28. Erikson, *Childhood and Society*, 253.

29. Erikson, *Childhood and Society*, 255.

30. Erikson, *Childhood and Society*, 256.

Chapter 13 (pages 175-198)

31. Neumann, *Origins*, 174. Quote includes a quote from Barlach.

32. Neumann, *Origins*, 181.

33. A.H. Almaas, *Being and the Meaning of Life (Diamond Heart Book III)*, 2nd ed. (Boulder, CO: Shambhala Press, 1994), 55.

34. Almaas, *Being and the Meaning of Life*, 55.

35. Wilber, *Atman Project*, 9.

36. Murray Stein, *Jung's Map of the Soul: An Introduction* (Chicago, IL: Open Court Publishing, 1998), 179. Referring to the stages outlined in C.G. Jung's *Collected Works*, Vol. 13, 199-201.

37. For more information on complexes, refer to Jolande Jacobi's book *Complex, Archetype, Symbol in the Psychology of C.G. Jung* (Princeton, NJ: Princeton University Press, 1971), or Lynelle Pieterse's book review by the same title found on the Center for Applied Jungian Studies' website ("Book and Movie Reviews"), February 7, 2017, https://appliedjung.com/complex-archetype-symbol.

38. Neumann, *Origins*, 174. Quote includes a quote from Barlach.

Chapter 14 (pages 199-203)

39. Stein, 141-142.

40. Stein, 141-142.

Part Four

1. C.G. Jung, *Memories, Dreams, and Reflections* (New York: Vintage Books,1965), 302.

Chapter 16 (pages 213-223)

2. Robert N. Emde, "Development Terminable and Interminable: I. Innate and Motivational Factors from Infancy," *International Journal of Psychoanalysis* 69, no.1 (1988): 337.

3. Louis Cozolino, *Why Therapy Works: Using Our Minds to Change Our Brains* (New York: W.W. Norton and Co., 2016), 72.

4. Stanislav Grof, *The Adventure of Self-Discovery: Dimensions of Consciousness and New Perspectives in Psychotherapy and Inner Exploration* (Albany, NY: State University of New York Press, 1988), 6.

5. Ed Tronick, *The Neurobehavioral and Social-Emotional Development of Infants and Children* (New York: W.W. Norton, 2007), 286.

6. Tronick, 289.

7. Daniel J. Siegel, *Parenting from the Inside Out: How a Deeper Self-Understanding Can Help You Raise Children Who Thrive* (New York: Penguin Books, 2004), 103.

8. Louis Cozolino, *The Neuroscience of Human Relationships: Attachment and the Developing Social Brain*, 2nd ed. (New York: W.W. Norton, 2014), 116.

9. Cozolino, *Neuroscience of Human Relationships*, 145.

10. Daniel J. Siegel, *The Developing Mind: How Relationships and the Brain Interact to Shape Who We Are* (New York: Guilford Press, 1999), 4.

11. Siegel, *Developing Mind*,163.

12. Cozolino, *Neuroscience of Human Relationships*, 280.

13. Siegel, *Pocket Guide to Interpersonal Neurobiology*, A1-56.

14. Siegel, *Pocket Guide to Interpersonal Neurobiology*, A1-57.

15. Rachel Yehuda, Julia A. Golier, Sarah L. Halligan, and Philip D. Harvey, "Learning and Memory in Holocaust Survivors With Posttraumatic Stress Disorder," *Biological Psychiatry* 55, no. 3 (2004): 291-295, https://doi.org/10.1016/S0006-3223(03)00641-3.

16. Daniel N. Stern, *The Interpersonal World of the Infant: A View from Psychoanalysis and Developmental Psychology* (New York: Basic Books, 1985), 90.

17. Stern, 71.

18. Silvano Arieti, "Cognition in Psychoanalysis," in *Cognition and Psychotherapy* (New York: Springer Publishing, 2004), 132-133.

19. Cozolino, *Neuroscience of Human Relationships*, 133.

20. Siegel, *Pocket Guide to Interpersonal Biology*, A1-43.

21. Cozolino, *Neuroscience of Human Relationships,* 134.

22. Tronick, 420.

23. Siegel, *Developing Mind,* 50-51.

24. Bruce Lipton. Lecture on Epigenetic research for National Institute for the Clinical Application of Behavioral Medicine (NICABM) Brain Lecture Series, February 12, 2014.

25. Nancy Newton Verrier, *The Primal Wound: Understanding the Adopted Child* (Louisville, KY: Gateway Press, 1993), 10-20.

26. Cozolino, *Neuroscience of Human Relationships,* 284.

27. Siegel, *Pocket Guide to Interpersonal Biology,* 36:28.

Chapter 17 (pages 225-231)

28. Erich Neumann, *The Child*, Unstated ed. (Boston, MA: Shambhala, 1990), 13.

29. Siegel, *Developing Mind,* 76-77.

30. These attachment styles were first thoroughly researched by psychologist Mary Ainsworth in 1978. Since then, the research has been replicated numerous times with the same results. These classifications can be found in Dan Siegel's book *The Developing Mind*, 72-75.

31. Siegel, *Developing Mind,* 76.

Chapter 18 (pages 233-241)

32. The state of fight, flight, or freeze in which an individual is reacting with a sense of threat and is no longer receptive and open to input from others in a flexible way. The concept is borrowed from Dan Siegel, as defined in his *Pocket Guide to Interpersonal Neurobiology*, A1-65.

33. Michael Washburn, *The Ego and the Dynamic Ground*, rev. ed. (Albany, NY: State University of New York Press, 1995), 220.

34. Tronick, 353.

35. Tronick, 357.

36. Cozolino, *Neuroscience of Human Relationships,* 279.

Chapter 19 (pages 243-263)

37. Robert Langs, *Fundamentals of Adaptive Psychotherapy and Counseling* (New York: Palgrave-McMillan, 2004), 9-10.

38. Yoram Kaufmann, *The Way of the Image* (Brattleboro, VT: Assisi Foundation, 2004).

39. Conforti, *Field, Form, and Fate,* 122.

40. Anna E. O'Brien, *Hawk Wisdom: Self Defense in the Market Place* (Great Barrington, MA: The Fair Trade Frame, 2013), 31.

41. O'Brien, 31.

42. Langs, 46, 87.

43. "Graves Disease," last modified July 1, 2014, accessed December 28, 2016, http://www.mayoclinic.org/diseases-conditions/graves-disease/basics/definition/con-20025811.

44. Kaufmann, 8-9.

45. Richard Kradin. From an unpublished Herald Dream Lecture held at the Assisi Institute, Brattleboro, VT, May 7, 2006. Also see Kradin's book, *Herald Dream: An Approach to the Initial Dream in Psychotherapy* (London, UK: Karnac Books, 2006).

46. Conforti. From unpublished seminar lectures held in Portland, OR, 1996-2008.

47. This is not a real-life example taken from our therapy. Instead, we have created the example to demonstrate the technique of translating images via the Orientational Approach.

48. Joseph Cambray, *Synchronicity: Nature and Psyche in an Interconnected Universe* (College Station, TX: Texas A&M University Press, 2009), 2.

49. David Peat, *Synchronicity: The Bridge Between Matter and Mind* (New York: Bantam Books, 1987), 23-24.

50. Cambray, 1 (Introduction).

51. Marian Woodman and Elinor Dickson, *Dancing in the Flames: The Dark Goddess in the Transformation of Consciousness* (Boulder, CO: Shambhala Publications, 1996), 226.

52. Ann Belford Ulanov. Unpublished notes from the Trauma Lecture Series held at the Assisi Institute, Brattleboro, VT, August 3, 2015.

Chapter 20 (pages 265-279)

53. Siegel, *Pocket Guide to Interpersonal Neurobiology*, A-I-38.

54. Ken Wilber, *The Atman Project: A Transpersonal View of Human Development*, 2nd ed. (Wheaton, IL: Quest Books,1996), 19.

55. Silvano Arieti, *The Intrapsychic Self: Feeling, Cognition, and Creativity in Health and Mental Illness* (New York: Basic Books, 1967), 101.

56. Neumann, *Origins*, 178.

57. Stanislav Grof, *The Adventure of Self-Discovery: Dimensions of Consciousness and New Perspectives in Psychotherapy and Inner Exploration* (Albany, NY: State University of New York Press, 1988), 227.

58. Grof, *Modern Consciousness Research and the Understanding of Art* (Santa Cruz, CA: Multidisciplinary Association for Psychedelic Studies, 2015), 74.

59. Neumann, *The Child*, 150.

60. Neumann, *The Child*, 150.

61. Neumann, *Origins*, 154.

62. Neumann, *Origins*, 32.

63. Neumann, *Origins*, 33.

64. Neumann, *The Child*, 124.

65. Grof, *Modern Consciousness*, 83.

66. Neumann, *The Child*, 151.

67. Neumann, *Origins*, 124.

68. Michael Washburn, *Embodied Spirituality in a Sacred World* (Albany, NY: State University of New York Press, 2003), 43.

69. Neumann, *Origins*, 95-97.

70. Neumann, *Origins*, 94.

71. Neumann, *The Child*, 80.

72. Neumann, *The Child*, 86.

73. Grof, *Psychology of the Future: Lessons from Modern Consciousness Research* (Albany, NY: SUNY Press, 2000), 46.

74. Neumann, *The Child*, 133.

75. Neumann, *Origins*, 95.

76. Neumann, *Origins*, 118, 124.

77. Neumann, *Origins*, 178.

78. Neumann, *Origins*, 380.

79. Christopher Booker, *The Seven Basic Plots: Why We Tell Stories* (New York: Continuum Books, 2004), 32.

80. Neumann, *Origins*, 190.

81. Peter A. Levine, *Trauma and Memory* (Berkeley, CA: North Atlantic Books, 2015), 7.

82. Grof, *Adventure of Self-Discovery*, 6.

83. Neumann, *Origins*, 198.

84. Neumann, *Origins*, 418.

Chapter 21 (pages 281-289)

85. Online daily quote sent from Rupert Spira, August 8, 2016 (through subscription on his website at www.rupertspira.com).

86. *Kundalini* is a Sanskrit term commonly used in Eastern Spiritual teachings of Hindu Advaita Vedanta and Buddhist traditions. It refers to the coiled, snake-like energy held at the base of our spine. For most people, this energy is unknown and lies latent. For some meditators and spiritual seekers, this kundalini energy becomes aroused and awakened and moves up through the chakra energy centers in our subtle body to the top of the head. This awakening is taught to be the beginning of spiritual consciousness. Leslie Temple-Thurston, in her book *Returning to Oneness*, states: "We have many bodies other than the physical. Our complete, all-encompassing body is really a body of energy and consciousness. It encompasses a mental body, an emotional body, and a vast light body as well. Our life force is always naturally flowing through, and animating all of our bodies. When we chose to awaken to truth, a particularly powerful and vital force of energy or light is activated in the body. In the East it is known as *kundalini*." From Temple-Thurston's *Returning to Oneness* (Sante Fe, NM: CoreLight Publishing, 2002), 11.

87. *Libido* is the psychic energy of our survival instincts, believed to be the driving force behind all human behavior.

88. Washburn, *Embodied Spirituality in a Sacred World*, 166-167.

89. Ron Kurtz and Jon Eisman. From a Hakomi Mindfulness-Centered Somatic Psychotherapy skills training manual, given to students and teachers at the Hakomi Institute's Character Strategies Training in Portland, OR, in 1989. Contact the Hakomi

Institute in Boulder, CO, at www.hakomiinstitute.org for archived materials. This was unpublished teaching material that was neither dated nor paginated.

90. Jon Eisman quoted in *Hakomi Mindfulness-Centered Somatic Psychotherapy*, eds. Haiko Weiss, Greg Johanson, and Lorena Monda (New York: W.W. Norton, 2015), 76. Eisman was paraphrasing Ron Kurtz's words in *Body-Centered Psychotherapy: The Hakomi Method* (Mendocino, CA: LifeRhythm, 1990), 115.

91. Interview of Bruce Lipton by Steve Farrell of Humanity's Team during a Living in Oneness Summit on June 16, 2015.

92. Bruce Lipton quoted in Gabor Maté's *When the Body Says No* (Hoboken, NJ: John Wiley and Sons, 2011), 230.

93. Gabor Maté, *When the Body Says No: Understanding the Stress-Disease Connection* (Hoboken, NJ: John Wiley and Sons, 2011), 239.

94. Maté, "The Healing Force Within," article posted July 27, 2013, http://drgabormate.com/article/the-healing-force-within/.

95. Maté, "The Healing Force Within."

96. Maté, "The Healing Force Within."

97. Maté, *When the Body Says No*, 173.

98. Maté, *When the Body Says No*, 176.

99. Maté, *When the Body Says No*, 174.

Chapter 22 (pages 291-298)

100. The theories of unconscious guilt, its consequences in one's life, and the steps to its resolution were taught in lectures by Michael Conforti in Portland Assisi Seminars and in private case consultations with the authors.

101. *Nourishment barrier* is a term developed by Ron Kurtz, founder of the Hakomi Institute, in the 1980s.

Part Five

1. Ken Wilber, *Integral Meditation: Mindfulness As a Path to Grow Up, Wake Up, and Show Up in Your Life* (Boulder, CO: Shambhala, 2016), 16.

Chapter 23 (pages 301-322)

2. Almaas, *Pearl*, 161.

3. See a good summary of Piaget's theory of cognitive development at https://en.wikipedia.org/wiki/Piaget%27s_theory_of_cognitive_development#Formal_operational_stage.

4. See Jane Loevinger's work: *Paradigms of Personality* (New York: W.H. Freeman, 1987), and with Augusta Blasi, *Ego Development: Conceptions and Theories* (San Francisco: Jossey-Bass, 1976).

5. See Robert Kegan's work: *The Evolving Self* (Cambridge, MA: Harvard College, 1998), and *In Over Our Heads* (Cambridge, MA: Harvard College, 1983).

6. See Susanne R. Cook-Greuter's work: "Making the Case for a Developmental Perspective," *Industrial and Commercial Training* 36, no. 7 (2004): 275-281, https://doi.org/10.1108/00197850410563902; "Post-Autonomous Ego Development," EdD diss., Harvard University, 1999; *Ego Development: Nine Levels of Increasing Embrace* (Cook-Greuter and Associates, 2005), http://www.cook-greuter.com/9 levels of increasing embrace update 1 07.pdf; and ed. with Melvin E. Miller, *Transcendence and Mature Thought in Adulthood: The Further Reaches of Human Development* (Lanham, MD: Rowman and Littlefield, 1994).

7. See Terri O'Fallon's work: Review of *The Postconventional Personality: Assessing, Researching, and Theorizing Higher Development*, by Angela H. Pfaffenberger, Paul W. Marko, and Allan Combs, eds., *Journal of Integral Theory and Practice* 7, no. 1 (March 2012): 150; "The Collapse of the Wilber-Combs Matrix: The Interpenetration of the State and Structure Stages," Developmental Research Institute, May 1, 2010, http://www.pacificintegral.com/articles; "Development and Consciousness: Growing Up is Waking Up," *Spanda Journal* 3, no. 1 (2012): 97-103; and "The Senses: Demystifying Awakening," Integral Theory Conference, July 2013, https://www.pacificintegral.com/articles.

8. Ken Wilber, *Integral Psychology: Consciousness, Spirit, Psychology, Therapy* (Boulder, CO: Shambhala Publications, 2000), 221.

9. Matthew Greenblatt, *The Essential Teachings of Ramana Maharshi: A Visual Journey* (Carlsbad, CA: Inner Directions Publishing, 2001), 48.

10. Wilber, *Integral Psychology*, 92.

11. Dabrowski's theory of Positive Disintegration describes how a person's development grows as a result of accumulated experiences that precipitate a disintegration into a new level of development. See wikipedia.org on "positive disintegration" for a good summary of Dabrowski's theory.

12. Keiron Le Grice, *The Archetypal Cosmos: Rediscovering the Gods in Myth, Science, and Astrology* (Edinburgh: Floris Books, 2010), 51.

13. Terri O'Fallon, Review of *The Postconventional Personality: Assessing, Researching, and Theorizing Higher Development*, by Angela H. Pfaffenberger, Paul W. Marko, and Allan Combs, eds., *Journal of Integral Theory and Practice* 7, no. 1 (March 2012): 149-155.

14. Susanne R. Cook-Greuter, "Nine Levels of Increasing Embrace in Ego Development: A Full-Spectrum Theory of Vertical Growth and Meaning Making," (Cook-Greuter & Associates, 2013), accessed on December 28, 2016, http://www.cook-greuter.com/9 levels of increasing embrace update 1 07.pdf.

15. Integral Theory refers to a meta theory synthesized by Ken Wilber in which researched models of the later stages of adult development are applied in a variety of psychological and cultural ways. See https://en.wikipedia.org/wiki/integraltheory for a more thorough explanation.

16. Wilber, *Integral Meditation*, 63.

17. Cook-Greuter, "Nine Levels."

18. Terri O'Fallon, "The Collapse of the Wilber-Combs Matrix: The Interpenetration of the State and Structure Stages," Developmental Research Institute, May 1, 2010, accessed December 28, 2016, https://www.pacificintegral.com/articles.

19. Susanne Cook-Greuter has opened The Center for Leadership Maturity with Beema Sharma; they have renamed many of the stages to reflect the major developmental activity of the stage. These names will be presented in parentheses.

20. Wilber, *Integral Meditation*, 22.

21. David Yeats, "Susanne Cook-Greuter's Developmental Model: Part 1, The Pre-Egoic and Conventional Stages," StillPoint Psychotherapy (2011): 3. Accessed December 28, 2016, http://www.davidayeats.com/Cook-Greuter-Development-Model-Part-1.html.

22. Susanne R. Cook-Greuter, "Second Tier Gains and Challenges in Ego Development," in *Integral Theory in Action: Applied, Theoretical, and Constructive Perspectives on the AQAL Model* (Albany, NY: SUNY Press, 2010), 308.
Susanne R. Cook-Greuter, "Second Tier Gains and Challenges in Ego Development," in *Integral Theory in Action: Applied, Theoretical, and Constructive Perspectives on the AQAL Model*, ed. Sean Esbjörn-Hargens (Albany, NY: SUNY Press, 2010), 308.

23. Yeats, "Susanne Cook-Greuter's Developmental Model: Part 1," 3-4.

24. Cook-Greuter, "Second Tier Gains and Challenges," 308.

25. Cook-Greuter, "Second Tier Gains and Challenges," 309.

26. Cook-Greuter, "Second Tier Gains and Challenges," 310.

27. Wilber, *Integral Meditation*, 63.

28. David Yeats, "Susanne Cook-Greuter's Developmental Model: Part 2, The Later Stages of Human Development," StillPoint Psychotherapy, Accessed December 28, 2016, http://www.davidayeats.com/Susanne-Cook-Greuter-s-Developmental-Model-Pt-2.html, 5-7.

29. Cook-Greuter, "Second Tier Gains and Challenges," 315-16.

30. Ken Wilber, *The Religion of Tomorrow: A Vision for the Future of the Great Religions* (Boulder, CO: Shambhala Publications, 2017), 221.

31. Yeats, "Cook-Greuter's Developmental Model, Part 2," 7-8.

32. Notes from a keynote presentation by Ron Stewart on the developmental stages as seen in daily life at a private retreat in Portland, Oregon, 2013.

Chapter 24 (pages 323-331)

33. Terri O'Fallon, private training, Portland, Oregon, November 5, 2011.

34. Wilber, *Integral Psychology*, 100.

35. Frederic Laloux, *Reinventing Organizations: A Guide to Creating Organizations Inspired by the Next Stage of Human Consciousness* (Millis, MA: Nelson Parker, 2014), 58.

36. Terri O'Fallon, "Assessing Organizational Systems." White paper, accessed December 28, 2016. Found under "Awakened and Transformative Leadership" at www.pacificintegral.com/resources/research (webpage discontinued).

Chapter 25 (pages 333-337)

37. Ken Wilber quoted in Terri O'Fallon's "State and Stage Summary." White paper, accessed December 28, 2016. Found at www.pacificintegral.com/resources/research/StAGES (webpage discontinued).

38. Nancy Newton Verrier, *Primal Wound: Understanding the Adopted Child* (Baltimore, MD: Gateway Press Inc., 1993), 73.

Chapter 26 (pages 339-346)

39. Neumann, *Origins*, 88.
40. Neumann, *Origins*, 287.
41. Neumann, *Origins*, 418.
42. Neumann, *Origins*, 411-412.

Chapter 27 (pages 347-351)

43. Cook-Greuter, "Nine Levels."

44. Terri O'Fallon. From her online course "Frontiers of Consciousness: Unfolding 4 MetAware Stages," offered by STAGES International, June 2018. All italicized phrases are quoted from this course.

45. Although the Rorschach test was originally used as a *personality* measure, the psychologists conducting this study found that the Rorschach test also was useful in measuring *cognitive and perceptual change*.

46. Ken Wilber, Jack Engler, and Daniel P. Brown, *Transformations of Consciousness: Conventional and Contemplative Perspectives on Development* (Boston: Shambhala Publications, 1986), 205-212.

47. Wilber, Engler, and Brown.

48. Paul Levy, *Awakened By Darkness: When Evil Becomes Your Father* (Self-published: awakeninthedream.com, 2015), 193-195.

Chapter 28 (pages 353-362)

49. Dorothy Hunt, Open Circle Center Newsletter, September 4, 2015. https://opencirclecenter.org.

Epilogue (pages 363-366)

50. Edward Edinger, *Ego and Archetype*, reissue ed. (Boston: Shambhala, 1992), 104.
51. Neumann, *The Child*, 182-83.
52. Neumann, *Origins*, 418.

Appendix A

1. Siegel, *Pocket Guide to Interpersonal Neurobiology*, 1-1 and 1-2.
2. Siegel, *Pocket Guide to Interpersonal Neurobiology*, 6-3.

3. Bruce Lipton. Internet interview via the website of the National Institute for the Clinical Application of Behavioral Medicine (NICABM), February 12, 2014.

4. Lipton interview.

5. Siegel, *Pocket Guide to Interpersonal Neurobiology*, 3-5.

6. Peter Fenner, *Radiant Mind: Awakening Unconditional Awareness* (Louisville, CO: Sounds True, 2007), 41.

7. We will not go into great detail about forms of meditation practice here, because there are numerous books and teachers of meditation.

8. Fenner.

9. Fenner, 68-69.

10. Fenner, 80.

11. Fenner, 178.

Appendix B

1. Allan Combs, *Radiance of Being: Complexity, Chaos, and the Evolution of Consciousness* (St. Paul, MN: Paragon House, 1996), 61.

The Heroic Journey of Becoming an Analyst (pages 379-388)

2. Combs, *Radiance of Being*, 62.

3. "Unconscious communication" is communication expressed by the objective psyche and revealed through themes of archetypal images, symbols, and patterns. These are told in narrative story form contrary to the conditioned mind's subjective data. This comes from the work of Robert Langs MD.

4. "Objective psyche" is the term used by C.G. Jung to describe the objective behavior characteristic of the psyche or soul of an individual and its unconscious material. It is *not* culturally constructed or viewed through a personal lens.

5. "Subjective" in this sense refers to what is conscious and already known as facts, associations, thoughts, emotions, feelings, and the like. It is data conditioned by the person's personal perceptions, personality, and ego.

6. "Derivative communication" or "unconscious content" in the material communicated between client and therapist has a thematic nature, conveyed through stories, and carries embedded perceptions and beliefs through metaphors. The process of encoding these messages was studied and developed by Robert Langs MD.

7. In his paper, "Manic Defenses," D.W. Winnicott notes that "manic defenses" arise when one is unable to contain one's anxiety and fears. He says that the person feels the need to react in flight from these uncomfortable internal feelings in an attempt to bring back a sense of homeostasis, comfortability, and familiarity.

8. Taken from the work of Joseph Campbell. See https://en.wikipedia.org/wiki/Hero%27s_journey.

9. Conforti. From unpublished seminar lectures held in Portland, OR, 2004.

10. Conforti.

11. Combs, 62.

12. Learned in supervision with Michael Conforti, who learned in supervision from Robert Langs MD.

Building a Therapeutic Container for Transformation (pages 389-396)

13. Michael Conforti. From unpublished notes of the "Threshold Experiences" seminar held during the Portland Seminars, 2005.

14. Ed Tick, *The Practice of Dream Healing: Bringing Ancient Greek Mysteries Into Modern Medicine* (Wheaton, IL: Quest Books, 2001), 11.

15. Diane Steinbrecher and Shannon Pernetti, "The Heroic Journey of Becoming an Analyst," thesis for graduating from Assisi Institute as Archetypal Pattern Analysts, 2006, page 2.

16. Sylvia Behrend. From "Eternal Stories in Dreamscapes" seminar featured during Depth Psychology Alliance online talk, 2014.

17. Edward Edinger, *Anatomy of the Psyche: Alchemical Symbolism in Psychotherapy*, 3rd ed. (Chicago: Open Court Publishing, 1991), 2.

18. Michael Conforti. From unpublished Portland Seminar lecture notes, 1997.

19. Robert Langs, *Death Anxiety and Clinical Practice* (London, UK: Karnac Books, 1997), 189.

20. We learned the conditions for a secure container during mentoring sessions with Michael Conforti, who learned under the supervision of Robert Langs MD.

21. Conforti, *Field, Form, and Fate*, 69.

22. Conforti. Unpublished notes from the Portland Seminars, 2006.

23. Conforti. Notes from Assisi Institute Clinical Teleseminar, November 16, 2016.

24. Conforti.

Application, Assessment, and Stages of Therapy (pages 397-411)

25. Conforti, *Field, Form, and Fate*, 8.

26. Learned through supervision with Michael Conforti who learned from supervision with Robert Langs MD.

Bibliography

Abraham, Frederick David, Ralph H. Abraham, and Christopher D. Shaw. *A Visual Introduction to Dynamical Systems Theory Psychology.* Santa Cruz, CA: Aerial Press, 1990.

Adler, Gerhard. Foreword to *Creative Man: Five Essays, Vol. II*, by Erich Neumann. Translated by Eugene Rolfe. Princeton: Princeton University Press, 1979.

Ajaya, Swami. *Healing the Whole Person: Applications of Yoga Psychotherapy.* Honesdale, PA: Himalayan International Institute Press, 2008.

———. *Psychotherapy East and West.* Honesdale, PA: Himalayan International Institute Press, 1997.

Alexander, Franz. *Psychosomatic Medicine.* New York: W.W. Norton, 1987.

Almaas, A.H. *Being and the Meaning of Life (Diamond Heart Book III).* 2nd ed. Boulder, CO: Shambhala Press, 1994.

———. *Essence: The Diamond Approach to Inner Realization.* Boulder, CO: Shambhala Press, 1986.

———. *Diamond Book One: Elements of the Real Man.* Boulder, CO: Shambhala Press, 2012.

———. *Diamond Heart: Inexhaustible Mystery.* Boulder, CO: Shambhala Press, 2011.

———. *Diamond Heart Book Two: The Freedom to Be.* Boulder, CO: Shambhala Press, 1989.

———. *Diamond Heart Book Four: Indestructible Innocence.* Boulder, CO: Shambhala Press, 1997.

———. *Facets of Unity: Enneagram of Holy Ideas.* Boulder, CO: Shambhala Press, 2000.

———. *The Inner Journey Home.* Boulder, CO: Shambhala Press, 2012.

———. *The Pearl Beyond Price: Integration of Personality into Being: An Object Relations Approach.* Berkeley, CA: Almaas Publications, 1988.

———. *The Point of Existence: Transformations of Narcissism in Self-Realization.* Boulder, CO: Shambhala Press, 1996.

———. *Runaway Realization.* Boulder, CO: Shambhala Press, 2014.

Arieti, Silvano. "Cognition in Psychoanalysis," in *Cognition and Psychotherapy*, edited by M.J. Mahoney. New York: Springer Publishing, 2004, 132-33.

———. *The Intrapsychic Self: Feeling, Cognition, and Creativity in Health and Mental Illness.* New York: Basic Books, 1967.

Ball, Philip. *Branches.* New York: Oxford University Press, 1999.

———. *Patterns in Nature: Why the Natural World Looks the Way It Does.* Chicago: University of Chicago Press, 2016.

———. *The Self-Made Tapestry: Pattern Formation in Nature.* New York: Oxford University Press, 1999.

———. *Shapes.* New York: Oxford University Press, 2009.

Biggs, John. *Fractals: The Patterns of Chaos.* New York: Simon and Schuster, 1992.

Booker, Christopher. *The Seven Basic Plots: Why We Tell Stories*. New York: Continuum Books, 2004.

Bright, Bonnie. "The C.G. Jung–Erich Neumann Connection: An Interview with Dr. Lance Owens." *Pacifica Post* (blog). Pacifica Graduate Institute, June 3, 2016. http://www.pacificapost.com/the-c.g.-jung-erich-neumann-connection-an-interview-with-dr.-lance-owens.

Buber, Martin. *Between Man and Man*. New York: MacMillan Co., 1968.

Burke Harris, Nadine. *The Deepest Well: Healing the Long-Term Effects of Childhood Adversity*. New York: Harcourt Publishing, 2018.

Cambray, Joseph. *Synchronicity: Nature and Psyche in an Interconnected Universe*. College Station, TX: Texas A&M University Press, 2009.

Campbell, Joseph. *Creative Mythology*. New York: Penguin Compass, 1976.

———. *Hero with a Thousand Faces*. Princeton: Princeton University Press, 1973.

———. *The Mythic Image*. Princeton: Princeton University Press, 1974.

Capra, Fritjof, and Pier Luigi Luisi. *The Systems View of Life: A Unifying Vision*. Cambridge: Cambridge University Press, 2014.

Childre, Lew. *Science of the Heart: Exploring the Role of the Heart in Human Performance*. Boulder Creek, CA: HeartMath Institute, 2009. http://www.heartmath.org/research/science-of-the-heart.

Chilton Pearce, Joseph. *The Biology of Transcendence: A Blueprint of the Human Spirit*. South Paris, ME: Park Street Press, 2002.

———. *The Death of Religion and the Rebirth of Spirit: A Return to the Intelligence of the Heart*. South Paris, ME: Park Street Press, 2007.

———. *Evolution's End: Claiming the Potential of Our Intelligence*. New York: HarperCollins, 1992.

———. *Magical Child: Rediscovering Nature's Plan for Our Children*. New York: Penguin Books, 1992.

Combs, Allan. *Radiance of Being: Complexity, Chaos, and the Evolution of Consciousness*. St. Paul, MN: Paragon House, 1996.

Conforti, Michael. *Field, Form, and Fate: Patterns in Mind, Nature, and Psyche*. New Orleans, LA: Spring Journal Press, 1999.

———. *Threshold Experiences: The Archetype of Beginning*. Brattleboro, VT: Assisi Institute Press, 2007.

Cook-Greuter, Susanne R. *Ego Development: Nine Levels of Increasing Embrace*. Cook-Greuter & Associates, 2005. http://www.cook-greuter.com/9 levels of increasing embrace update 1 07.pdf.

———. "Making the Case for a Developmental Perspective." *Industrial and Commercial Training* 36, no. 7 (2004): 275-281. https://doi.org/10.1108/00197850410563902.

———. "Nine Levels of Increasing Embrace in Ego Development: A Full-Spectrum Theory of Vertical Growth and Meaning Making." Cook-Greuter & Associates, 2013. http://www.cook-greuter.com/Cook-Greuter 9 levels paper new 1.1'14 97p[1].pdf.

———. "Post-Autonomous Ego Development." EdD diss., Harvard University, 1999.

———. "Second Tier Gains and Challenges in Ego Development." In *Integral Theory in Action: Applied, Theoretical, and Constructive Perspectives on the AQAL Model*, edited by Sean Esbjörn-Hargens, 308. Albany, NY: SUNY Press, 2010.

Cook-Greuter, Susanne R. and Melvin E. Miller, eds. *Transcendence and Mature Thought in Adulthood: The Further Reaches of Human Development*. Lanham, MD: Rowman & Littlefield, 1994.

Cozolino, Louis. *The Neuroscience of Human Relationships: Attachment and the Developing Social Brain*. 2nd ed. New York: W.W. Norton, 2014.

———. *Why Therapy Works: Using Our Minds to Change Our Brains*. New York: W.W. Norton, 2016.

Doczi, Gyorgy. *The Power of Limits*. Boston: Shambhala, 1994.

Edinger, Edward. *Anatomy of the Psyche: Alchemical Symbolism in Psychotherapy*. 3rd ed. Chicago: Open Court Publishing, 1991.

———. *Ego and Archetype*. Baltimore, MD: Penguin Books, 1973.

Elgin, Duane. *The Living Universe*. London: Berrett-Koehler, 2009.

Ellenberger, Henri. *Beyond the Unconscious*. Princeton: Princeton University Press, 1993.

Emde, Robert N. "Development Terminable and Interminable: I. Innate and Motivational Factors from Infancy." *International Journal of Psychoanalysis* 69, no.1 (1988): 337.

Emoto, Masaru. *The Hidden Messages in Water*. New York: Atria Books, 2005.

Erikson, Erik. *Childhood and Society*. Reissue edition. New York: W.W. Norton, 1993.

Feldenkrais, Moche. *The Potent Self: The Dynamics of the Body and the Mind*. San Francisco: HarperOne, 1985.

Fenner, Peter. *Natural Awakening: An Advanced Guide for Sharing Nondual Awareness*. Richmond Hill, Ontario: Sumeru Press, 2015.

———. *Radiant Mind: Awakening Unconditional Awareness*. Louisville, CO: Sounds True, 2007.

Freud, Sigmund. "Remembering, Repeating and Working-Through." *The Standard Edition of the Complete Psychological Works of Sigmund Freud, Volume XII*. 1914.

Freyd, Jennifer J. *Betrayal Trauma: The Logic of Forgetting Childhood Abuse*. Cambridge, MA: Harvard University Press, 1996.

Gilbert, Scott F. "Induction and the Origins of Developmental Genetics." In *A Conceptual History of Modern Embryology*, edited by Scott F. Gilbert, 181-206. New York: Plenum Press, 1991.

Goodwin, Brian. *How the Leopard Changed Its Spots: The Evolution of Complexity*. New York: Charles Scribner's Sons, 1994.

Greenblatt, Matthew. *The Essential Teachings of Ramana Maharshi: A Visual Journey*. Carlsbad, CA: Inner Directions Publishing, 2001.

Grof, Christina. *The Thirst for Wholeness: Attachment, Addiction, and the Spiritual Path*. San Francisco: HarperOne, 1993.

Grof, Stanislav. *The Adventure of Self-Discovery: Dimensions of Consciousness and New Perspectives in Psychotherapy and Inner Exploration*. Albany, NY: State University of New York Press, 1988.

———. *The Cosmic Game: Explorations of the Frontiers of Human Consciousness.* Albany, NY: State University of New York Press, 1998.

———. *The Holotropic Mind: The Three Levels of Human Consciousness and How They Shape Our Lives.* San Francisco: HarperOne, 1993.

———. *Modern Consciousness Research and the Understanding of Art.* Santa Cruz, CA: Multidisciplinary Association for Psychedelic Studies, 2015.

———. *Psychology of the Future: Lessons from Modern Consciousness Research.* Albany, NY: State University of New York Press, 2000.

———. *When the Impossible Happens: Adventures in Non-Ordinary Realities.* Boulder, CO: Sounds True, 2006.

Hayward, Jeremy, and Varela Francisco. *Gentle Bridges: Conversations with the Dalai Lama on the Sciences of Mind.* Boston: Shambhala, 2001.

Henderson, Joseph. *Thresholds of Initiation.* Middleton, CT: Wesleyan University Press, 1967.

Hillman, James. *The Soul's Code: On Character and Calling.* New York: Random House, 1997.

Ho, Mae-Wan. *The Rainbow and the Worm: The Physics of Organisms.* Singapore: World Scientific Publishing, 1993.

Hollis, James. *Creating a Life.* Ontario: Inner City Books, 2001.

Hunt, Valerie. *Infinite Mind: Science of Human Vibrations of Consciousness.* Malibu, CA: Malibu Publishing, 1996.

Jacobi, Jolande. *Complex, Archetype, Symbol in the Psychology of C.G. Jung.* Princeton: Princeton University Press, 1971.

Jaworski, Joseph. *Synchronicity: The Inner Path of Leadership.* London: Berrett-Koehler, 1996.

Johnson, Robert A. *Femininity Lost and Regained.* New York: HarperCollins, 1991.

———. *Inner Gold: Understanding Psychological Projection.* Hawaii: Koa Books, 2008.

Jung, C.G. *Collected Works of C.G. Jung.* eds. Gerhard Adler, Michael Fordham, Herbert Read, and William McGuire. Princeton: Princeton University Press, 2000.

———. *The Collected Works of C.G. Jung: Complete Digital Edition.* eds. Gerhard Adler, Michael Fordham, Herbert Read, and William McGuire. Princeton: Princeton University Press, 2014.

———. *Man and His Symbols.* London: Aldus Books, 1964.

———. *Man and His Symbols.* New York: Dell Publishing, 1968.

———. *Memories, Dreams, and Reflections.* New York: Vintage Books, 1965.

———. *Memories, Dreams, and Reflections.* Reissue ed. New York: Vintage Books, 1989.

———. *Psyche and Symbol: A Selection from the Writings of C.G. Jung.* New York: Anchor Books, 1958.

———. *Symbols of Transformation.* Princeton: Princeton University Press, 1976.

———. *Word and Image.* Princeton: Princeton University Press, 1979.

Jung, Emma. *Animus and Anima: Two Papers.* New York: Spring Publications of The Analytic Psychology Club, 1972.

Kaufmann, Yoram. *The Way of the Image.* Brattleboro, VT: Assisi Foundation, 2004.

Kegan, Robert. *The Evolving Self.* Cambridge, MA: Harvard College, 1998.

———. *In Over Our Heads*. Cambridge, MA: Harvard College, 1983.

Kindler, Babaji Bob. *Dissolving the Mindstream*. Portland, OR: SRV Associations, 2014.

———. *Jnana Matra: The Wisdom Particle*. Portland, OR: SRV Associations, 2014.

———. *Manasana: The Superlative Art of Mental Posture*. Portland, OR: SRV Associations, 2015.

Kradin, Richard. *Herald Dream: An Approach to the Initial Dream in Psychotherapy*. London: Karnac Books, 2006.

Kurtz, Ron. *Body-Centered Psychotherapy: The Hakomi Method*. Mendocino, CA: LifeRhythm, 1990.

Laloux, Frederic. *Reinventing Organizations: A Guide to Creating Organizations Inspired by the Next Stage of Human Consciousness*. Millis, MA: Nelson Parker, 2014.

Langs, Robert. *The Daydream Workbook: Learning the Art of Decoding Your Daydreams*. Brooklyn, NY: Alliance Publishing, 1995.

———. *Death Anxiety and Clinical Practice*. London: Karnac Books, 1997.

———. *Decoding Your Dreams: A Revolutionary Technique for Understanding Your Dreams*. New York: Ballantine Books, 1989.

———. *Dreams and Emotional Adaptations: A Clinical Notebook for Psychotherapists*. Phoenix, AZ: Zeig, Tucker, and Theisen, 1999.

———. *Fundamentals of Adaptive Psychotherapy and Counseling*. New York: Palgrave-MacMillan, 2004.

———. *The Listening Process*. 3rd ed. Lanham, MD: Jason Aronson Publishers, 1979.

———. *Love and Death in Psychotherapy*. London: Red Globe Press, 2006.

———. *Psychotherapy: A Basic Text*. New York: Jason Aronson, 1977.

———. *Unconscious Communication in Everyday Life*. Lanham, MD: Jason Aronson Publishers, 1983.

———. *Workbooks for Psychotherapists, Vol. 1: Understanding Unconscious Communication*. Mahwah, NJ: New Concept Press, 1985.

Laszlo, Ervin. *Chaos Point: 2012 and Beyond*. Newburyport, MA: Hampton Roads Publishing, 2006.

———. *The Creative Cosmos: A Unified Science of Matter, Life, and Mind*. Edinburgh: Floris Books, 1993.

———. *Science and the Akashic Field: An Integral Theory of Everything*. Rochester, VT: Inner Traditions, 2007.

———. *Science and the Reenchantment of the Cosmos: The Rise of the Integral Vision of Reality*. Rochester, VT: Inner Traditions, 2006.

———. *The Systems View of the World: A Holistic Vision for Our Time*. 2nd ed. New York: Hampton Press, 1996.

Le Grice, Keiron. *The Archetypal Cosmos: Rediscovering the Gods in Myth, Science, and Astrology*. Edinburgh: Floris Books, 2010.

———. *Archetypal Reflections: Insights and Ideas from Jungian Psychology*. London: Muswell Hill Press, 2016.

———. *The Rebirth of the Hero: Mythology as a Guide to Spiritual Transformation.* London: Muswell Hill Press, 2013.

Leonard, Linda Schierse. *Witness to the Fire: Creativity and the Veil of Addiction.* Boston: Shambhala, 1989.

Levine, Peter A. *In an Unspoken Voice: How the Body Releases Trauma and Restores Goodness.* Berkeley, CA: North Atlantic Books, 2010.

———. *Trauma and Memory.* Berkeley, CA: North Atlantic Books, 2015.

Levy, Paul. *Awakened By Darkness: When Evil Becomes Your Father.* Self-published, awakeninthedream.com, 2015.

Lipton, Bruce. *The Biology of Belief: Unleashing the Power of Consciousness, Matter, and Miracles.* Carlsbad, CA: Hay House Publishing, 2005.

———. "Epigenetics: What Really Controls Our Genes and Why We Don't Have to Be Victims of Our DNA." National Institute for the Clinical Application of Behavioral Medicine, February 12, 2014. Webinar video. http://www.nicabm.com/brain2014/b2-info.

Loevinger, Jane. *Paradigms Of Personality.* New York: W.H. Freeman, 1987.

Loevinger, Jane, and Augusta Blasi. *Ego Development: Conceptions and Theories.* San Francisco: Jossey-Bass, 1976.

Martin, Hugh, and Kaye Martin. *The Human Odyssey.* Sebastopol, CA: AK Publishing, 2014.

Martineau, John. *A Little Book of Coincidence.* London: Walker Books, 2002.

Maslow, Abraham. *Toward a Psychology of Being.* New York: Van Nostrand Co., 1968.

Maté, Gabor. "The Healing Force Within." Posted July 27, 2013. http://drgabormate.com/article/the-healing-force-within/.

———. *In the Realm of the Hungry Ghosts.* Berkeley, CA: North Atlantic Books, 2008.

———. *When the Body Says No: Understanding the Stress-Disease Connection.* Hoboken, NJ: John Wiley and Sons, 2011.

Mutua, Kasiva. "How I Use the Drum to Tell My Story." Filmed August 2017. TEDGlobal video, 12:39. https://www.ted.com/talks/kasiva_mutua_how_i_use_the_drum_to_tell_my_story.

Neumann, Erich. *Amor and Psyche: The Psychic Development of the Feminine.* Translated by Ralph Manheim. 3rd ed. Princeton: Princeton University Press, 1971.

———. *Art and the Creative Unconscious.* 3rd ed. Princeton: Princeton University Press, 1974.

———. *The Child.* Translated by The Jung Foundation. Boulder, CO: Shambhala Books, 1990.

———. *Creative Man: Five Essays.* Princeton: Princeton University Press, 1979.

———. *Depth Psychology and a New Ethic.* Translated by Eugene Rolfe. New York: Harper and Row, 1973.

———. *The Fear of the Feminine and Other Essays on Feminine Psychology.* Princeton: Princeton University Press, 1994.

———. *The Great Mother: An Analysis of the Archetype.* Rev. ed. Princeton: Princeton University Press, 2015.

———. *The Origins and History of Consciousness.* Princeton: Princeton University Press, 1954.

Nikhilananda, Swami. *Self-Knowledge.* English trans. of Adi Sankarahcarya's *Atma bodha.* Chennai, India: Sri Ramakrishna Math, 1947.

O'Brien, Anna E. *Hawk Wisdom: Self Defense in the Market Place.* Great Barrington, MA: The Fair Trade Frame, 2013.

O'Fallon, Terri. "The Collapse of the Wilber-Combs Matrix: The Interpenetration of the State and Structure Stages." Developmental Research Institute, May 1, 2010. http://www.pacificintegral.com/articles.

———. "Development and Consciousness: Growing Up is Waking Up." *Spanda Journal* 3, no. 1 (2012): 97-103.

———. Review of *The Postconventional Personality: Assessing, Researching, and Theorizing Higher Development*, by Angela H. Pfaffenberger, Paul W. Marko, and Allan Combs, eds. *Journal of Integral Theory and Practice* 7, no. 1 (March 2012): 149-155.

———. "The Senses: Demystifying Awakening." Integral Theory Conference, July 2013. http://www.pacificintegral.com/articles.

Pacifica Graduate Institute. "A Conversation with Erel Shalit and Joe Cambray." June 16, 2016. YouTube video, 52:20. https://youtu.be/O7jazUTm0Aw.

Paulsen, Sandra L. *When There Are No Words: Repairing Early Trauma and Neglect from the Attachment Period with EMDR Therapy.* Bainbridge Island, WA: Bainbridge Institute for Integrative Psychology, 2017.

Pearsall, Paul. *The Heart's Code: The New Findings About Cellular Memory.* New York: Broadway Books, 1998.

Pearson, Carol S. *Awakening the Heroes Within.* San Francisco: HarperOne, 1991.

———. *The Hero and the Outlaw.* New York: McGraw Hill, 2001.

———. *The Hero Within: Six Archetypes We Live By.* San Francisco: HarperOne, 1986.

Peat, David. *The Infinite Potential: The Life and Times of David Bohm.* Reading, MA: Helix Books, 1997.

———. *Synchronicity: The Bridge Between Matter and Mind.* New York: Bantam Books, 1987.

Perera, Sylvia Brinton. *The Scapegoat Complex.* Ontario: Inner City Books, 1986.

Pieterse, Lynelle. Review of *Complex, Archetype, Symbol in the Psychology of C.G. Jung*, by Jolande Jacobi. *The Center for Applied Jungian Studies*, February 7, 2017. https://appliedjung.com/complex-archetype-symbol.

Pollack, Gerald. *Cells, Gels, and the Engines of Life.* Seattle, WA: Ebner and Sons, 2001.

Poncé, Charles. *Working the Soul: Reflections on Jungian Psychology.* Berkeley, CA: North Atlantic Books, 1987.

Portmann, Adolf. "Metamorphosis in Animals: The Transformations of the Individual and the Type," http://www.assisiinstitute.com/uploads/1/3/2/3/13231455/apa_portman_article.pdf.

Prendergast, John, and Kenneth Bradford. *Listening from the Heart of Silence.* St. Paul, MN: Paragon House, 2007.

Prendergast, John, Peter Fenner, and Sheila Krystal. *The Sacred Mirror: Nondual Wisdom and Psychotherapy.* St. Paul, MN: Paragon House, 2003.

Rossi, Ernest. *Dreams and the Growth of Personality.* New York: Pergamon Press, 1972.

Rubik, Beverly. "The Biofield Hypothesis: Its Biophysical Basis and Role in Medicine." *The Journal of Alternative and Complementary Medicine* 8, no. 6 (2002): 703-717. https://doi.org/10.1089/10755530260511711.

Sewart, Louis. Foreword to *The Child,* by Erich Neumann. Boulder, CO: Shambhala Books, 1990.

Shalit, Erel, and Murray Stein. *Turbulent Times, Creative Minds: Erich Neumann and C.G. Jung in Relationship (1933-1960).* Asheville, NC: Chiron Publications, 2015.

Sheldrake, Rupert. *Dogs That Know When Their Owners Are Coming Home.* Rev. ed. New York: Broadway Books, 2011.

———. "Rupert Sheldrake ~ Morphic Resonance." Donna Eden Energy Medicine, October 1, 2013. YouTube video, 1:11:16. https://www.youtube.com/watch?v=MtgLklXZo3U.

———. *Morphic Resonance: The Nature of Formative Causation.* South Paris, ME: Park Street Press, 2009.

———. *A New Science of Life.* 2nd ed. London: Icon Books, 2009.

———. *The Presence of the Past: The Habits of Nature.* South Paris, ME: Park Street Press, 1995.

Sheldrake, Rupert, Terence McKenna, and Ralph Abraham. *Chaos, Creativity, and Cosmic Consciousness.* South Paris, ME: Park Street Press, 1992.

Siegel, Daniel J. *Brainstorm: The Power and Purpose of the Teenage Brain.* New York: Penguin Books, 2014.

———. *The Developing Mind: How Relationships and the Brain Interact to Shape Who We Are.* New York: Gilford Press, 1999.

———. *The Mindful Brain: Reflection and Attunement in the Cultivation of Well-Being.* New York: W.W. Norton and Company, 2007.

———. *The Mindful Therapist: A Clinician's Guide to Mindsight and Neural Integration.* New York: W.W. Norton and Company, 2010.

———. *Mindsight: The New Science of Personal Transformation.* New York: Bantam, 2010.

———. *The Neurobiology of "We": How Relationships, the Mind, and the Brain Interact to Shape Who We Are.* Louisville, CO: Sounds True Publishing, 2011. Audio book, 8 hrs. 9 min.

———. *Parenting from the Inside Out: How a Deeper Self-Understanding Can Help You Raise Children Who Thrive.* New York: Penguin Books, 2004.

———. *Pocket Guide to Interpersonal Neurobiology: An Integrative Handbook of the Mind.* New York: W.W. Norton and Company, 2012.

Singer, June. *Androgyny.* Newburyport, MA: Nicolas Hays, 2000.

Sri Aurobindo. *The Life Divine.* Pondicherry, India: Sri Aurobindo Ashram, 1970.

Stein, Murray. *Jung's Map of the Soul: An Introduction.* Chicago: Open Court Publishing, 1998.

———. *In Midlife*. Asheville, NC: Chiron Publications, 2014.

———. *The Principle of Individuation: Toward the Development of Human Consciousness*. Asheville, NC: Chiron Publications, 2013.

———. *Transformation: Emergence of the Self*. Rev. ed. College Station, TX: Texas A&M University Press, 2004.

Steinbrecher, Diane, and Shannon Pernetti. "The Heroic Journey of Becoming an Analyst." Thesis, Assisi Institute: The International Center for the Study of Archetypal Patterns, 2006.

Stern, Daniel N. *Diary of a Baby*. New York: Basic Books, 1992.

———. *The Interpersonal World of the Infant: A View from Psychoanalysis and Developmental Psychology*. New York: Basic Books, 1985.

Stevens, Anthony. *Archetype Revisited: An Updated Natural History of the Self*. Ontario: Inner City Books, 2003.

Temple-Thurston, Leslie. *The Marriage of Spirit: Enlightened Living in Today's World*. Sante Fe, NM: CoreLight Publishing, 2000.

———. *Returning to Oneness*. Sante Fe, NM: CoreLight Publishing, 2002.

Thompson, D'arcy. *On Growth and Form*. Cambridge: Cambridge University Press, 1961.

Tick, Edward. *The Practice of Dream Healing: Bringing Ancient Greek Mysteries Into Modern Medicine*. Wheaton, IL: Quest Books, 2001.

———. *War and the Soul: Healing Our Nation's Veterans from Post-Traumatic Stress Disorder*. Wheaton, IL: Quest Books, 2005.

———. *Warrior's Return: Restoring the Soul After War*. Louisville, CO: Sounds True, 2014.

Tronick, Ed. *The Neurobehavioral and Social-Emotional Development of Infants and Children*. New York: W.W. Norton, 2007.

Van der Kolk, Bessel. *The Body Keeps the Score*. New York: Penguin Books, 2014.

Van Eenwyk, John R. *Archetypes and Strange Attractors*. Ontario: Inner City Books, 1997.

———. *Clinical Chaos: The Strange Attractors of Childhood Trauma*. Ontario: Inner City Books, 2013.

Verrier, Nancy Newton. *The Primal Wound: Understanding the Adopted Child*. Louisville, KY: Gateway Press, 1993.

Vivekananda, Swami. *Jnana Yoga*. Hollywood, CA: Vedanta Press, 1997.

———. *Vedanta: Voice of Freedom*. St. Louis, MO: Vedanta Society of St. Louis, 1996.

Von Franz, Marie-Louise. *Archetypal Dimensions of the Psyche*. Boston: Shambhala, 1994.

———. *Archetypal Patterns in Fairy Tales*. Ontario: Inner City Books, 1997.

———. *The Interpretation of Fairy Tales*. Boston: Shambhala, 1970.

———. *The Problem of the Puer Aeternus*. Ontario: Inner City Books, 2000.

———. *Projection and Re-Collection in Jungian Psychology*. Chicago: Carus Publishing, 1995.

———. *Psyche and Matter*. Boston: Shambhala, 1992.

———. *Redemption Motifs in Fairy Tales*. Ontario: Inner City Books, 1980.

———. *The Shadow and Evil in Fairy Tales*. Boston: Shambhala, 1974.

———. *The Way of the Dream*. Boston: Shambhala, 1994.

Wade, David. *Li: Dynamic Form in Nature.* London: Walker Books, 2002.

———. *Symmetry: The Ordering Principle.* London: Walker Books, 2006.

Wangyal, Tenzin Rinpoche. *Awakening the Luminous Mind.* India: Hay House, 2012.

———. *Wonders of the Natural Mind.* Ithaca, NY: Snow Lion Publications, 2009.

Washburn, Dorothy, and Donald Crowe. *Symmetry Comes of Age: The Role of Pattern in Culture.* Seattle, WA: University of Washington Press, 2004.

Washburn, Michael. *The Ego and the Dynamic Ground.* Rev. ed. Albany, NY: State University of New York Press, 1995.

———. *Embodied Spirituality in a Sacred World.* Albany, NY: State University of New York Press, 2003.

Weiss, Haiko, Greg Johanson, and Lorena Monda, eds. *Hakomi Mindfulness-Centered Somatic Psychotherapy.* New York: W.W. Norton, 2015.

Whitmont, Edward C. *Psyche and Substance.* Berkeley, CA: North Atlantic Books, 1991.

———. *The Symbolic Quest.* Princeton: Princeton University Press, 1969.

Wilber, Ken. *The Atman Project: A Transpersonal View of Human Development.* 2nd ed. Wheaton, IL: Quest Books, 1996.

———. *Eye to Eye: The Quest for the New Paradigm.* Rev. ed. Boston: Shambhala, 2001.

———. *Integral Meditation: Mindfulness As a Path to Grow Up, Wake Up, and Show Up in Your Life.* Boston: Shambhala, 2016.

———. *Integral Psychology: Consciousness, Spirit, Psychology, Therapy.* Boston: Shambhala, 2000.

———. *Integral Spirituality.* Boston: Shambhala, 2006.

———. *No Boundary: Eastern and Western Approaches to Personal Growth.* Boston: Shambhala, 1979.

———. *The Religion of Tomorrow: A Vision for the Future of the Great Traditions.* Boston: Shambhala, 2017.

———. *Up from Eden: A Transpersonal View of Human Evolution.* Boston: Shambhala, 1981.

Wilber, Ken, Jack Engler, and Daniel P. Brown. *Transformations of Consciousness: Conventional and Contemplative Perspectives on Development.* Boston: Shambhala, 1986.

Winnicott, D.W. "The Manic Defense." In *Through Paediatrics to Psycho-Analysis: Collected Papers.* New York: Basic Books, 1974, 129-144.

Woodman, Marian, and Elinor Dickson. *Dancing in the Flames: The Dark Goddess in the Transformation of Consciousness.* Boulder, CO: Shambhala Publications, 1996.

Yeats, David. "Susanne Cook-Greuter's Developmental Model: Part 1, The Pre-Egoic and Conventional Stages." StillPoint Psychotherapy. Accessed December 28, 2016. http://www.davidayeats.com/Cook-Greuter-Development-Model-Part-1.html.

———. "Susanne Cook-Greuter's Developmental Model: Part 2, The Later Stages of Human Development." StillPoint Psychotherapy. Accessed December 28, 2016. http://www.davidayeats.com/Susanne-Cook-Greuter-s-Developmental-Model-Pt-2.html

Yehuda, Rachel, Julia A. Golier, Sarah L. Halligan, and Philip D. Harvey. "Learning and Memory in Holocaust Survivors with Post-Traumatic Stress Disorder." *Biological Psychiatry* 55, no. 3 (2004): 291-295. https://doi.org/10.1016/S0006-3223(03)00641-3.

Index

Note: Page references for diagrams are italicized. Note material is indicated by the page number followed by "n" and note number.

abandonment, sense of, 42–43, 65, 208, 219
abortion, 218
Abraham, Fred, *27*
Abraham, Ralph, *27*
Achiever/Self-Determining Stage, in ego development theory, 313–14, 325–26
acupuncture, 68–69
Adler, Gerhard, 78
adoption. *See* orphans and adoption
advertising and branding, application of Archetypal Pattern Analysis in, 29
Ainsworth, Mary, 227
Akashic field. *See* Causal realm (Field 1)
Almaas, A.H., 99, 145–46, 147, 150, 154, 183
amygdala, 213–14, 217
anal stage, *97*, 99–101, 103, 144, 148, 155–58, *155*, 189, 221
  See also Gaining the Treasure, therapeutic approach to; images, in dreams/visions/daydreams, by Archetypal Developmental Stage; Rescuing the Captive in Creation Myths, therapeutic approach to
analysts. *See* For Practitioners
ancient wisdom traditions, contribution to domains of knowledge in Archetypal Pattern Analysis, 27
androgyne. *See* hermaphrodite/androgyne
anger, defined, 287
anima/animus, 84, 85–86, 116–17, 118, 143, 276
  See also Rescuing the Captive in Hero Myths, therapeutic approach to; Rescuing the Captive in Transformation Myths, therapeutic approach to

appendices
  Supportive Practices for the Later Stages of Development, 367–75
  For Practitioners, 377–411
archetypal alignments
  attractor sites and, 42–43, 48, 216
  impact of container on, 42–43
  to Mother archetype, 215–18
  practical application of change and, 43
archetypal containers, 39–43
  as archetypal fields, 64–65
  creating archetypal alignments and, 42–43
  in dream images, 266
  examples of facets of, 39–40
  for growth and development, 40–41, 292–93
  practical application of archetypal alignments, 43
  unstable containers, 41
  See also Great Mother
The Archetypal Cosmos (Le Grice), 306
Archetypal Developmental Stages of Life, 79–80, 131, *132–33*, 223, 330
  See also assessment of stages of development; images, in dreams/visions/daydreams, by Archetypal Developmental Stage; transitions between stages; *specific stages*
Archetypal Developmental Theory (Neumann), 77–129, 302–3
  authors' Archetypal Developmental Stages of Life and, 79–80, 131, *132–33*, 223, 330
  correlations to Researched Developmental Model, 311–16, 320–21, *321*

Creation Myths, 86, 91–109, *92*
difficult transitions between stages, 336–37
eight great myths, 79–81
Hero Myths, 86, 88, 111–20
Mythological States in the Evolution of Consciousness, 86–89, *87, 92, 129, 304*
overview of individuation, 78–79
overview of theory, 84–86
Transformation Myths, 88–89, 121–29
Unification of Opposites as pinnacle of development, 305
view of current culture of U.S. and, 322
See also Ego-Self Journey Model; *specific mythological states*
Archetypal Developmental Theory, therapeutic application of
archetypal approach to Gaining the Treasure, 205–9
diagram of, *138*
evaluation of stages, 323
importance of Rescuing the Captive, 137–42, 324
Rescuing the Captive in Creation Myths, 143–74, *164*
Rescuing the Captive in Hero Myths, 175–98
Rescuing the Captive in Transformation Myths, 199–203
See also assessment of stages of development
archetypal domain, mystery of, 31–38
alignment with mythical figures, 33
bridge as archetype, 32
container as archetype, 32
facets of archetypes, 36–38
forms of modern folklore, 33–34
generative vs. nongenerative alignment, 36–38
mandates of archetypes, 34–36
Mother Archetype, 36–38, *37*
oral traditions and, 33–34
origins and definitions of archetype, 31–33
power of symbols, 33
archetypal fields
morphogenetic fields within, 66
quantum fields within, 69
within Field Theory, 63–65
archetypal mandates, 34–36, 248
Archetypal Pattern Analysis, in therapy situation
application, assessment and stages of therapy, 397–410
assessment of initial conditions, 51–52
assessment of open/closed systems, 52–53
behavior of people without generative fathering, 109
bifurcations and choice points in, 56–57, 80
derivative communication in sessions, 252–54
Four-Tiered Field Theory in, 71
as integral approach, 26, 28
life fields and death fields, 293–98
physical diseases and, 281–89
For Practitioners (appendix), 377–411
reactive vs. generative refuge, 237
repair of attachment disruptions, 233–41
seeing the Self in the client at all times, 138, 200
translation of images of the psyche, 247–48
use of Archetypal Developmental Stages of Life for congruence, 131, *132–33*
using reactive states in, 240–41
victim-tyrant polarity dynamic, 201, 209, 230–31
work with pre-cognitive structures, 234–36
See also For Practitioners; images, in dreams/visions/daydreams, by Archetypal Developmental Stage; unconscious communication, as expression of the psyche

Archetypal Pattern Analysis, introduction, 25–30
 domains of knowledge in, 27
 as integral theory, 26
 international certification program for, 30
 multidisciplinary application of, 26–29
 underlying archetypal forces, 25
archetypal purity (Neumann), 195, 197
archetype, origins of word, 31
archetypes as nonlocal, 32, 423n4
Arieti, Silvano, 217
Aristotle, 31
arousal: genital satisfaction, impulses, and bodily union, in genital stage, *97*, 101–4, 159–63
Art and the Creative Unconscious (Neumann), 118–19
the arts, application of Archetypal Pattern Analysis in, 29
assessment of stages of development, 323–31
 guidelines for, 398–406
 initial session, 400–404
 Rescuing in the Implicit Memory, 329, *330*
 sub-personalities/Captives, 323–24, 328–31
 using combination of three models, 323
 using developmental progression of perspectives, 328–31
 using Researched Development Model, 324–27
Assisi Institute: The International Center for the Study of Archetypal Patterns, 26, 30
atmospheric feelings. *See* pervasive atmospheric moods
attachment, archetypal nature of, 225–31
 avoidant attachment, 227–28, 229
 dealing with insecure attachment, 230–31
 disorganized or disoriented attachment, 228–29
 insecure attachment styles, *229*
 overview of attachment and bonding, 226–31
 resistant or ambivalent attachment, 228–29
 secure or autonomous attachment, 227
attachment disruptions, in adults, 233–41
 attempts to attain safe/trusting refuge from external environment, 238
 attempts to attain safe/trusting refuge from seeing world as dangerous/perverse, 238–39
 attempts to attain safe/trusting refuge through people, 239–40
 attempts to attain safe/trusting refuge through the mind, 239
 reactive vs. generative refuge, *237*
 See also Archetypal Pattern Analysis, in therapy situation; generative inner refuge, therapeutic approach to
attachment theory, 216
attunement with fetus/baby, 70–71, 214–16
autoimmune disorders, 255–56, 286–87
autonomy, control and empowerment, in anal stage, *97*, 99–101, 156–58, 209
avoidant attachment, 227–28, *229*

Barber, Michael, 29
Bastian, Adolf, 31
being, as self-existing value, 155
bifurcation
 as conscious choice points, 56–57, 80, 85, 89, 250, 295, 334
 patterns and, 55
biofields (Rubik), 68–69
biology
 archetypal fields in, 64
 canalization, 55
 contribution to domains of knowledge in Archetypal Pattern Analysis, 27
 morphogenesis, 65, 67–68
 repetition and patterns, 46–48
 symmetry in, 56
The Biology of Belief (Lipton), 72–73, 283–84
birth defects, 41

Birth of the Hero, 86, 87, 111, 113, 117–18, 119, 274–75
    See also Rescuing the Captive in Hero Myths, therapeutic approach to
birth process and implicit memory, 219
Body-Centered Psychotherapy (Kurtz), 283
body-mind/ego embodiment, 281–89
    autoimmune disorders and, 286–87
    beliefs held in the body, 282–84
    contribution of psychoneuroimmunology and, 283–89
    stages of awakening of libidinal energy, 281–82, 432nn86–87
bodywork, application of Archetypal Pattern Analysis in, 29
Bohm, David, 27
bonding. *See* attachment, archetypal nature of
Bowlby, John, 215–16
breath, in mindful awareness practices, 373
bridge as archetype, 32
business, application of Archetypal Pattern Analysis in, 29

Cambray, Joseph, 261
Campbell, Joseph, 31
canalization
    archetypal alignments and, 54
    in biology, 55
    closed systems and, 52
    creodes and, 46, 297
    defined, 46
    of emotional, mental, behavioral patterns through repetition, 49–50, 54–55
    and strange attractors, 48
    See also archetypal alignments; bifurcation
Captive, signs of, 245
Carrie (case study), 334–36
castrating/crushing aspect, of Father archetype, 113, 141
castration complex, 103–4, 161–62
Causal realm (Field 1), 61–63, 62, 64, 65
centroversion (Neumann), 194–95, 281, 339–41

Chaos Theory, 47
The Child (Neumann), 93, 225
Childhood and Society (Erikson), 98–99, 100, 103
child sexual abuse, 104, 162, 221, 293–94
Cicero, 31
cinema
    application of Archetypal Pattern Analysis in, 28
    archetypal knowledge in, 33, 36
    comic book and superhero characters, 107, 169
    depiction of dragon fights in, 88
    depiction of Rescuing the Captive stage in, 124, 125, 181, 265
    fractal geometry in special effects, 48
    heroes and higher power in, 182
Clash of the Titans (movie), 140
closed-systems, 52–53, 250
collapse into a singularity (Conforti), 46
Combs, Allan, 385
companies, applicability of developmental progression of perspectives to, 324, 328, 331
complexes (C.G. Jung), 193
conception and implicit memory, 218
concrete operational thinking (Piaget), 106
Conforti, Loralee Scott, 29
Conforti, Michael, 131
    on archetypal alignments, 42
    as archetypal cinematic consultant, 28
    authors' work with, 379–81
    on closed systems, 250
    contribution to domains of knowledge in Archetypal Pattern Analysis, 27
    on dragon fights, 102–3
    Field, Form, and Fate, 47
    Field Theory, 59–73
    as founder of theory, 26
    Four-Tiered Field Theory, 71, 72
    on frame violations, 396
    on images as archetypal with mandates and guidelines, 248
    on mandate of archetypes, 34, 248

on objective knowledge in therapy, 249
on patterns, 46, 48, 49
on repetition in person's life, 49–50, 400
study of initial conditions, 51
use of Sheldrake's scientific language, 66
See also Assisi Institute: The International Center for the Study of Archetypal Patterns; life fields and death fields
conscious mind, as percent of psyche, 243
Construct-aware/Magician Stage, in ego development theory, 316–17, 326
containers
and examples of archetypes, 32
origin of term, 39
See also therapeutic containers
Cook-Greuter, Susanne, 303, 306–21, 347
cortisol, 287
Cozolino, Louis, 214–15, 217
Creation Myths (Neumann), 86, 91–109
activation of Father archetype, 84–85, 86, 92, 102–3, 105–9, 160–61
diagrams of, *92, 129*
dragon fights, 113–14, 119, 179
Great Mother archetype, 95–96, 105
Separation of the World Parents, 92, 104–7
three stages of Great Mother, 96–104, *97*
uroborus/mother as primal relationship, 93–95
See also Rescuing the Captive in Creation Myths, therapeutic approach to
creativity, 126
creodes, 46, 297
cultural superego
dragon fights, 118
examination of during Rescuing the Captive stages, 171–74, 176, 178–79, 182–83, 277–78
integration of, 107
culture
archetypal fields and, 65
shadow and gender norms, 106
symmetry in, 56
Western cultural beliefs and transformational psychotherapy, 384–85
cutting, 254

Dabrowski, Kazimierz, 305–6
Dalai Lama, 111
Dancing in the Flames (Woodman), 261
death anxiety and manic defenses, 384, 385
death fields. *See* life fields and death fields
Delta Stage, in ego development theory, 312, 325
Depth Psychology and a New Ethic (Neumann), 78
The Developing Mind (Siegel), 226, 227
developmental knowledge models, overview, 301–6
See also Archetypal Developmental Theory; Ego-Self Journey Model; Researched Developmental Model
Developmental Progression of Perspectives (diagram), *310*
developmental stages of life. *See* Archetypal Developmental Stages of Life
devouring aspect, of Great Mother, 86, 94, 95–96, 97–98, 102–3, 113, 142, 143, 157–58
Diplomat/Conformist/Group-Centric Stage, in ego development theory, 312–13
disorganized or disoriented attachment, 228, *229*
Dogs That Know When Their Owners Are Coming Home (Sheldrake), 70
dragon fights, 86, 88, 102–3, 113–14, 115, 118, 119–20, 125, 128, 179, 273–74
See also Rescuing the Captive in Hero Myths, therapeutic approach to
dreams
ending/lysis of, 258–59
herald dreams, 257
Kaufmann on images in, 257
middle stage/dilemma in, 258, 259
opening/exposition of, 257–58, 259
translation of dreams, 256–60

See also images, in dreams/visions/daydreams, by Archetypal Developmental Stage
DSM 5 (*Diagnostic and Statistical Manual of Mental Disorders*), 288
Duggan, Annie, 29

Eastern spiritual traditions
    Akashic field, 61, 62
    Kali (goddess), 95
    kundalini, 281–82, 432n86
    mind in, 370
eating disorders, 98, 153
Eckhart, Meister, 111
Edinger, Edward, 80, 82
ego
    achieving unity and balance, 88–89
    C.G. Jung on phases of development, 82
    as masculine aspect, 81
    See also cultural superego; personal superego
The Ego and the Dynamic Ground (Washburn), 102, 233
Ego-aware Stage, in ego development theory, 317, 320, 326
ego development theory, 81–82
    See also Researched Developmental Model
ego ideal
    birth of the hero and, 111–13
    examination of during Rescuing the Captive stages, 169–70, 183–85
    heroic quests and, 115–16
    during Separation of the World Parents stage, 107
    the unconscious and, 85
Ego-Self Axis (Edinger), 80
Ego-Self Journey Model
    diagrams of, 120, *304*, *307*
    difficult transitions between stages, 336
    focus of, 303, 323
    individuation, 81–84, *83*
    with Myths/Archetypes, *364*, 365
    sub-personalities, 324
    view of current culture of U.S., 322
Eisman, Jon, 282–83
electromagnetic fields, 68
Embodied Spirituality in a Sacred World (Washburn), 282
emotional-nervous-immune-hormonal super-system. *See* psychoneuroimmunology
emotion-processing mind (Langs), 246
Emoto, Masaru, 73
emptiness, of seeking in outer world for happiness, 139–40, 154
empty center (C.G. Jung), 192
Endocept stage (Arieti), 217
endorphins, 208, 254
energy fields, 60
    See also Field Theory
energy medicine, 68–69
enforcing agent. *See* personal superego
entelechy
    birth of the hero and, 112, 114
    as control of morphogenesis process, 66
    defined, 66
    parental introjections and, 167
entrainment, defined, 51, 248–49
environmental illness/sensitivity, 153
epigenetic research, 149–50
Erikson, Erik
    on Autonomy vs. Shame and Doubt stage, 100, 157
    on Basic Trust vs. Basic Mistrust stage, 98–99
    on Initiative vs. Guilt stage, 103
Eros, as desire for unity, 89
The Essential Piaget (Piaget), 266
eternal memory of archetypes, 64
Expert/Skill-Centric Stage, in ego development theory, 313
explicit memory, 217–18, 222, 355, 370–71
extreme loss, 296

Father archetype, 84–85, 86, 92, 102–3, 105–9, 160–61, 271–72

See also castrating/crushing aspect, of
    Father archetype
Fenner, Peter, 372–73
Field, Form, and Fate (Conforti), 47
Field Theory, 59–73
    archetypal fields, 63–65
    diagrams of, 62–63, *62*
    energy fields in all systems, 60–61
    examples of morphic fields, 69–73
    fields, defined, 60
    morphic resonance, 67–73
    morphogenesis and self-organizing
        systems, 65–67
    quantum fields, 69
films. *See* cinema; *specific films by title*
formative causation, 66
For Practitioners (appendix), 377–411
    application, assessment and stages of
        treatment, 397–410
    building therapeutic container for
        transformation, 389–96
    Hero's Journey for the Client, 406–10
    Holding Environment for Growth and
        Development, *393*
    stages of Hero's Journey of Analyst/
        Therapist, 379–88
    therapist positions in building a
        generative refuge, *411*
foundational theories, 25–73
    archetypal containers and alignments,
        39–43
    Field Theory, 59–73
    introduction to Archetypal Pattern
        Analysis, 25–30
    mystery of archetypal domains, 31–38
    patterns in natural world and psyche,
        45–57
    See also specific theories
Four-Tiered Field Theory (Conforti), 71, 72
fractal-like patterns, 47–48
Franz, Marie-Louise von, 27, 31
Freud, Sigmund, 50, 400
fulcrums of development, 305–6, 333
    See also transitions between stages

*Fundamentals of Adaptive Psychotherapy and
    Counseling* (Langs), 246
Gaining the Treasure, *87*, 88, 89, 115–16,
    125–26, 128, 197, 278–79, 302
Gaining the Treasure, therapeutic approach
    to, 205–9
    anal stage experience, 208–9
    conception, pre-birth experience and
        uroborus, 207
    oral stage experience, 207–8
    process of, *345*
    requirements for, 344–46
Garden of Eden myth, 168
gender alignment, 170–71
generative, defined, 36
generative inner refuge, therapeutic
    approach to, 353–62
    conditions for solid container in
        therapy, 356–57
    integration of reactive states, 355–57
    movement into true inner refuge,
        361–62
    qualities of inner refuge, 354
    reactive refuge examples, meanings
        and therapist positions, 357–61
    therapist position in building a
        generative refuge, *411*
generative vs. nongenerative Mother
    archetype, 36–38, *37*
genital stage, *97*, 101–4, 144, 148, 159–63,
    159, 190, 222
    See also images, in dreams/visions/
        daydreams, by Archetypal
        Developmental Stage
Gestalt therapy, introjections, 105
glossary, 413–22
Grave's disease, 255–56
Great Mother, 84–85, 86, *87*, 88
    See also Creation Myths; devouring
        aspect, of Great Mother; Gaining
        the Treasure, therapeutic approach
        to; Mother archetype; Rescuing the
        Captive in Creation Myths, therapeutic

approach to; Rescuing the Captive in Hero Myths, therapeutic approach to
Grof, Stanislav, 267, 271
Gross forms (Field 4), 62, 63
guilt, 103–4, 106, 296–98

Hansmann, Brigitte, 29
Harry Potter movies, 88
Hawk Wisdom (O'Brien), 252
the healing force within (Maté), 285–86
health care, application of Archetypal Pattern Analysis in, 29
heart energy field, 70–71
HeartMath Institute, 70–71
hermaphrodite/androgyne, 88, 105, 126–27, 194, 279
   See also Unification of Opposites
heroes, archetypal images of, 185
heroic ideal. *See* ego ideal
heroic qualities, as idealizations, 184, 203
heroic quests, 114–17, 140, 186
   See also Rescuing the Captive in Hero Myths, therapeutic approach to
Hero Myths (Neumann), 111–20
   anima/animus, 116–17
   Birth of the Hero, 86, 111, 113, 117–18, 119
   description of, 86, 88
   diagrams of, *87*, 112, 129
   dragon fights, 113–14, 115, 118, 119–20, 179
   heroic quests, 114–17, 140
   nongenerative heroes, 114
   Slaying of the Parents, 117–20
   See also Rescuing the Captive in Hero Myths, therapeutic approach to
Hero's Journey of Analyst/Therapist, stages of, 379–88
   crossing the first threshold with mentor, 383
   cultural obstacles and, 384–85
   facing tests/obstacles/enemies/allies, 383–84
   final ordeal, 387

hearing the call of transformation, 382
integration and sharing gifts, 387–88
new challenges, 385–86
surrendering and committing to the call, 385
surrendering and receiving gifts, 386
wrestling with the call, 382–83
   See also For Practitioners
hippocampus, 222, 355
Ho, Mae-Wan, 27
hoarding, 94, 148, 158
homeodynamics, 68
homeopathy, 68–69
hundredth monkey effect, 34, 67
Hunt, Dorothy, 362
hyper alertness, 214, 216

I, me, and mine pattern, 282, 340, 354
idealizations, heroic qualities as, 184, 203
Illumined/Unitive Stage, in ego development theory, 320–21, 327
images
   of archetypal heroes, 185
   Conforti on as archetypal with mandates and guidelines, 248
   Kaufmann on arising from informational fields, 246–47
   of mother during oral stage, 220–21
   translation vs. interpretation of, 247–48
images, in dreams/visions/daydreams, by Archetypal Developmental Stage, 265–79
   anal stage, 268–69, 274–75
   anima/animus and, 276
   Birth of the Hero, 274–75
   dragon fights, 273–74
   Father archetype activation, 271–72
   Gaining the Treasure, 278–79
   genital stage, 270–71, 275
   inter-uterine and birth, 267–68
   oral stage, 268, 274
   Rescuing the Captive, 277–79
   Separation of the World Parents, 272–73, 277
   Slaying of the Parents, 277

Unification of Opposites, 279
    uroboric stage, 267
immune system, 246, 255, 286–87
implicit memory, 213–23
    during anal stage, 208–9, 221
    coding of the inner world of child, 213–18
    during conception, pregnancy and birth process, 95, 207, 218–19
    during genital stage, 101, 222
    Great Mother archetype and, 220–23
    during oral stage, 207–8, 219–21
    of prior generations, 150, 240
    reawakening of structures in adulthood, 233–34
    Rescuing in the Implicit Memory and stages, 329, *330*
    Rescuing the Captive by stages and, 147, 148, 167, 223
Impulsive Stage, in ego development theory, 311, 325
Inception (movie), 277
Indiana Jones movies, 88, 140, 279
Individualist/Self-Questioning Stage, in ego development theory, 314, 326
individuation
    C.G. Jung on, 243
    defined, 425n10
    in Ego-Self Journey Model, 81–84, *83*
    in Neumann's Archetypal Developmental Theory, 78–79
    See also specific stages of life
informational fields, 60–61, 67
inherent memory, 66–67
initial conditions, 51–52
inner dialogue, listening to, 375
inner refuges, 182, 215–16, 226–27, 236, 237, 365–66
    See also attachment disruptions, in adults; generative inner refuge, therapeutic approach to
insecure attachment, 227–31, 229
Integral Theory, 308
internal approval, 88

The Interpersonal World of the Infant (Stern), 216
introject/introjections
    in C.G. Jung's stages of consciousness, 191–92
    defined, 105, 165
    examination of during Rescuing the Captive stages, 124, 166–68, 174
    heroic quests and, 115
    sexual projections and, 116–17
    See also dragon fights
introversion (Neumann), 123, 198, 281, 339–41
invincibility, sense of, 113
iteration, defined, 46

Journal of Integral Theory and Practice (O'Fallon), 307
Jung, C.G.
    on activity of archetype and psyche, 33
    on alchemical process in psychotherapy, 390
    on anima/animus, 116, 143
    on archetype as bridge of individual to unitary world, 32
    classic theoretical sources of, 31
    on complexes, 193
    contribution to domains of knowledge in Archetypal Pattern Analysis, *27*
    on empty center, 192
    on individuation, 243
    on nothingness as unconditioned essence of our true nature, 154
    on phases of ego development, 82
    on the Self, 61
    Stein's description of five stages of consciousness of, 190–94, 202
    on synchronicity, 260–61
    on transcendent function, 194
    work with Neumann, 77–78
Jung, Emma, 84
Jung's Map of the Soul (Stein), 190–94, 202
just sitting practices, 373–74

Kali (goddess), 95

Kaufmann, Yoram, 27, 246–47, 249, 257
Kegan, Robert, 303, 306–21
Kennedy, Edward (Ted), 295
Klein, Melanie, 94, 97–98
kundalini, 281–82, 432n86
Kurtz, Ron, 282–83

Langs, Robert, 27, 96, 246, 391–92
Laszlo, Ervin, 27, 60
later stages of development, 339–51
    challenges of, 347–51
    Gaining the Treasure, 344–46, 345
    Neumann on extroversion/introversion/centroversion/later stages of awakened states, 339–41
    platform for, 341–44
    Theravadin Buddhist student study (1980s) and, 349–50, 436n45
    transitions between stages, 347–49
    See also generative inner refuge, therapeutic approach to; Supportive Practices for the Later Stages of Development
Le Grice, Keiron, 306
Levy, Paul, 350
libidinal energy, 281–82, 432n87
life as numinous co-arising, 361–62
life fields and death fields, 291–98
    death field, defined, 291
    death fields due to early abuse, 153
    early life conditions and, 295–96
    examples of death fields, 294
    examples of life fields, 294
    extreme loss and, 296
    importance of strong container, 292–93
    psychotherapy practices and, 293–98
    shift of death field to life field, 294–95
    survivor's guilt and, 296
    unconscious guilt, 296–98
Lipton, Bruce, 71, 73, 149, 283–84, 287–88, 371
Loevinger, Jane, 303, 306–21
Lord of the Rings (movie), 88

love
    as experienced archetypally, 155
    as platonic form (Almaas), 145
    romantic love and morphic resonance, 70
    sexual union and, 163
    See also later stages of development

magic-phallic stage, 106
magic-warlike stage, 106
Mahler, Margaret, 225
mandate of archetypes, 34–36, 248
marriage archetype, 35
masturbation, 94, 101, 104, 160, 162, 163
Maté, Gabor, 284, 285–87
meditation, 282, 349–50
mental representations, 216
mentoring
    in Archetypal Pattern Analysis, 26, 29–30, 57, 141, 160, 168, 201, 240, 266, 380–81, 383
    by fathers, 109
    new generative alignments and, 114, 177
mind
    Eastern spiritual traditions on, 370
    Lipton on, 371
    percentage of time spent in conscious state of, 371
    Siegel on, 370–71, 372
Mindfulness and Mindful Awareness (appendix), 369–75
    Fenner on psychological obstacles to attaining our True Inner Refuge, 372–73
    mindfulness awareness practices, 373–75
    neurobiological research on mindfulness, 370–72
mindfulness practices, 181, 201, 282, 370–75
modern folklore, 33–34
morphic fields, 68–73
morphic resonance, 42, 53–55, 67–73, 248–49
Morphic Resonance (Sheldrake), 65

morphogenesis, 64, 65–67
morphogenetic fields, 65–67, 69
Mother archetype, 36–38, *37*, 215–18
   See also Great Mother
mothering one
   attunement with fetus/baby, 70–71, 214–16
   held image of, 220–21
   merging with, 146–47
   Neumann on mother-child relationship, 93
Mother Teresa, 111
movies. *See* cinema; *specific movies by title*
Mutua, Kasiva, 119–20
mythological states. *See* Archetypal Developmental Theory

narcissistic wounding, 94, 157–58
natural world. *See* patterns in natural world and psyche
negative merging, 147
Neumann, Erich
   on anima/animus projection and relations between sexes, 116
   on archetypal purity, 195, 197
   on awakening of hero, 197–98
   on being reborn as total man, 126–27
   contribution to domains of knowledge in Archetypal Pattern Analysis, 27
   on extra-uterine embryonic phase, 225
   on extroversion/introversion/centroversion/later stages of awakened states, 123, 194–95, 198, 281, 339–41
   on guilt, 104, 106
   on importance of Father archetype, 109
   on liberation of captive and assimilation, 140–41
   on mother-child relationship, 93
   on symbology of artist in Slaying of the Parents stage, 118–19
   on uroboric castration, 94
   vision of integration of humanity, 127–28
   work with Jung, 77–78
   See also Archetypal Developmental Theory
Neurobehavioral and Social-Emotional Development of Infants and Children (Tronick), 234–35
neurobiological research on mindfulness, 370–72
neuroplasticity (Siegel), 152, 216
The Neuroscience of Human Relationships (Cozolino), 214–15, 217
A New Science of Life, The Presence of the Past (Sheldrake), 65
Nicoletti, Richard, 101
nongenerative, defined, 36
nourishment, as platonic form (Almaas), 145–46, 147
nourishment barrier, 297

obesity, 148
Obi-Wan Kenobi (character), 111
O'Brien, Anna, 251, 252
obsessive repetitive rituals, 173
Oedipal conflict, 101–2, 160–62
O'Fallon, Terri, 303, 306–21, 348
open-system families, 52–53
Opportunist/Self-Centric Stage, in ego development theory, 311, 325
oral fixations, 98, 146, 152–53
oral stage, 96–99, *97*, 144, 148, 149–55, *149*, 189, 220–21
   See also Gaining the Treasure, therapeutic approach to; images, in dreams/visions/daydreams, by Archetypal Developmental Stage; Rescuing the Captive in Creation Myths, therapeutic approach to
Orientational Approach (Kaufmann), 246–47, 249, 259–60
The Origins and History of Consciousness (Neumann), 77–78, 80, 93, 126–27, 339
orphans and adoption, 42–43, 65, 219, 296

Pan's Labyrinth (movie), 140
parenting archetype, 35
participation mystique, defined, 191

patterns, defined, 47
patterns in natural world and psyche, 45–57
   application of systems in nature to human systems, 49–50
   initial conditions and, 51–52
   morphic resonance and, 53–55
   open and closed systems, 52–53
   repetition and patterns, 46–47
   symmetry and, 55–57
   therapeutical approach to, 50–57
   types of patterns, 47–49
Pearson, Carol, 29
Peat, David, *27*, 260–61
perception and thought fields, 71, 73
persona, as defensive projection, 202
personal superego
   activation of Father archetype and, 84–85
   alienation of true nature and, 105–6
   dragon fights and, 118
   examination of during Rescuing the Captive stages, 171–72, 175, 177–78, 181–82, 185–87, 277–78
   formation of pure form of anima/animus and, 118
   projected onto peer group, 107
pervasive atmospheric moods, 217, 220–21, 233, 266, 267, 328–29
phantom limb experience, 68
physical diseases
   archetypal therapeutic approach to, 281–89
   derivative communication and, 254–56
   signs of a Captive and, 245
   stage identification and, 148
   unconscious beliefs and, 284, 288–89
   See also specific diseases/disorders
physics, 27, 56, 69
Piaget, Jean, 106, 266
Plato, 31, 46
Pliny, 31
pornography addiction, 104, 148, 162, 163
Positive Disintegration theory (Dabrowski), 305–6

post-traumatic stress disorder (PTSD), 294–95
pregnancy
   archetypal fields and, 64
   attunement with fetus/baby, 70–71, 214–16
   implicit memory and, 218–19
   mandate of archetype of, 35
   stress of mother during, 149–50, 214, 216, 218–19, 283
   transmission of multi-generational information during, 150
premature birth, 219
pre-verbal structures of meaning. *See* implicit memory
Pride and Glory (movie), 28
Primal Wound (Verrier), 334–36
primitive somatic states, 193, 214, 217–18, 220
   See also pervasive atmospheric moods
prostitution, 162
Psychology of the Future (Grof), 271
psychoneuroimmunology (PNI), 283–89
psychotherapy. *See* Archetypal Pattern Analysis, in therapy situation; For Practitioners
puberty and contrasexual images, 194–95
Pythagoras, 46
quantum physics/fields, 69
reactive states, 193, 218, 230–31, 234–36, 240–41, 246, 324
   See also generative inner refuge, therapeutic approach to
Reike, 68–69
Rescuing the Captive, 85–86, 87, 88, 89, 99, 106, 123–25, 128, 137–42, *138*
Rescuing the Captive in Creation Myths, therapeutic approach to, 143–74, *164*
   Almaas on platonic forms, 145–46
   archetypal aspects of Great Mother stages, 144
   based on anal stage experience, 148, 155–58, *155*

based on genital stage experience, 148, 159–63, *159*
based on oral stage experience, 148, 149–54, *149*
examples of, 147–48
in Great Mother stages, 143–63, *164*
integration of anal stage through, 158
integration of genital stage through, 163
integration of oral stage through, 154–55
merging with the mothering one, 146–47
See also Separation of the World Parents stage, eight activities and Rescue of
Rescuing the Captive in Hero Myths, therapeutic approach to, 175–98
    anima/animus projections and, 180, 187, 190–98
    as applied to heroic quests, 180–90
    Birth of the Hero stage and, 180–83, 187
    centroversion and, 194–95
    during dragon fight #1: beginning of stage/with Great Mother, 175, 176–77, 180
    during dragon fight #2: middle of stage/with personal superego, 175, 177–78, 181–82
    during dragon fight #3: end of stage/with cultural superego, 176, 178–79, 182–83
    ego ideal and, 183–85
    listing of dragon fights, 179
    quests and stages, 188–90
    Slaying of the Parents, 187, 195–98
    substitute gratifications due to disruptions in early stages, 188–90
    superego and, 185–87, 196–98
Rescuing the Captive in Transformation Myths, therapeutic approach to
    anima/animus projections and, 203

    during stage one, 199–201
    during stage two, 201–3
Researched Developmental Model (Loevinger, Kegan, Cook-Greuter, O'Fallon), 306–22
    Achiever/Self-Determining Stage, 313–14, 325–26
    Construct-aware/Magician Stage, 316–17, 326
    correlations to Archetypal Developmental Theory, 311–16, 320–21, *321*
    Delta Stage, 312, 325
    developmental progression of perspectives, 308–9, *310,* 348
    diagrams of stages, *304, 318–20*
    difficult transitions between stages, 337
    Diplomat/Conformist/Group-Centric Stage, 312–13
    Ego-aware Stage, 317, 320, 326
    Expert/Skill-Centric Stage, 313
    First Tier/Survival Stages, 308–14
    Illumined/Unitive Stage, 320–21, 327
    Impulsive Stage, 311, 325
    Individualist/Self-Questioning Stage, 314, 326
    Opportunist/Self-Centric Stage, 311, 325
    overview of, 303, 323
    Second Tier/Meaning-Making Stages, 308, 315–17
    Strategist/Autonomous/Self Actualizing Stage, 315–16, 324, 326
    Symbiotic Stage, 311, 325
    Third Tier/Awareness of Awareness Stages, 308, 317, 320–21
    view of current culture of U.S., 322
resistant or ambivalent attachment, 228, *229*
romantic love and morphic resonance, 70
Rorschach test study, 349–50, 436n45
Rubik, Beverly, *27*, 68–69

safety, trust, and security, in oral stage, 91, 98–101, 151, 153

See also attachment disruptions, in adults
secure or autonomous attachment, 227
security. *See* safety, trust, and security, in oral stage
self-harm, 254
self-inquiry practices, 374
self-organizing systems, 47–49, 65–67
self-worth and value, in oral stage, 96–99, *97*, 151–52, 153, 154–55, 220–21
separation anxiety, 98, 152, 220
Separation of the World Parents, 84–85, 86, *87*, 92, 104–7, 112, 119, 272–73, 277
Separation of the World Parents stage, eight activities and Rescue of, 165–74
    #1: completion of introjection of parents' psyches, 165, 166
    #2: pushing sense of unity into background of awareness, 168–69
    #3: separation of consciousness into two entities, 169
    #4: projected ego ideal, 169–70
    #5: gender alignment, 170–71
    #6: personal superego, 171–72
    #7: creation of shadow, 172–73
    #8: cultural superego, 173–74
    listing of, 165
sexual addictions, 101, 104
sexual objectification, 104, 148
sexual projections, 116–17
shadow
    examination of during Rescuing the Captive stages, 123, 124, 172–73, 181–82, 187, 202
    gender alignment and formation of, 106
    heroic ego ideal and, 113
    heroic quests and, 115, 140
shared resonance, 70
Sheldrake, Rupert
    on archetypes as dynamic, 32
    Conforti's use of scientific language of, 66
    contribution to domains of knowledge in Archetypal Pattern Analysis, *27*
    on energy fields, 60
    on entelechy, 66
    on morphic resonance, 42, 53–55, 67–68, 71
    on morphogenetic fields, 65–67, 69, 70
shopping addiction, 98, 153, 158
Siegel, Daniel J., 152, 216, 226, 227, 370–71, 372
Slaying of the Parents, 86, *87*, 88, 117–20, 277
    See also Rescuing the Captive in Hero Myths, therapeutic approach to
Socrates, 31
solar-warlike stage, 106
Son Lover in myths, 180, 275
Source of all existence/the Self (Field 0)
    archetypal fields and cusp with causal realms, 64
    in Eastern spiritual traditions, 305
    in Field Theory, 61–63, *62*
    as guiding and organizing force that seeks union/balance, 305
    Illumined/Unitive Stage and, 320–21
    non-separation from, 81
    seeing the Self in the client at all times, 138, 200
    Unification of Opposites as, 305
spiritual practice, as aid to process, 348
spiritual teachers, when seen as dark heroes, 275
spitting out, defined, 118
split-off parts. *See* shadow; sub-personalities
stages of life. *See* Archetypal Developmental Stages of Life
Stein, Murray, 190–94, 202
Stern, Daniel N., 216
strange attractor, defined, 48
Strategist/Autonomous/Self Actualizing Stage, in ego development theory, 315–16, 324, 326
sub-personalities, 323–24, 328–31, 348
substance abuse, 94, 98, 146, 153, 294
substitute gratification behaviors

addictive behaviors and oral stage,
    152–53
  anal stage heroic quests and, 189
  genital heroic quests and, 190
  oral stage heroic quests and, 189
  uroboric heroic quests and, 188–89
  See also specific behaviors and addictions
Subtle realm (Field 2), *62*, 63, 67
superhero characters, 107, 169
Supportive Practices for the Later Stages of
    Development (appendix), 367–75
survivor's guilt, 296
Symbiotic Stage, in ego development theory,
    311, 325
symbols, power of, 33
symmetry, 55–56
synchronicities, 125–26, 260–63
*Synchronicity: Nature and Psyche in an
    Interconnected Universe* (Cambray), 261
*Synchronicity: The Bridge Between Matter and
    Mind* (Peat), 260–61

therapeutic containers, 356–57, 389–96,
    393, 404
Theravadin Buddhist student study (1980s),
    349–50, 436n45
thinning our thoughts/veils to the Self, 288,
    342, 353–54, 374
thought fields, 71, 73
thyroid disease, 255–56
Time & Space (Field 3), 62, 63
toilet training, 209, 343–44
transcendent function (C.G. Jung), 194
Transformation Myths (Neumann), 88–89,
    121–29
  diagrams of, *122*, *129*
  dragon fights, 125, 128, 179
  Gaining the Treasure, 125–26, 128
  Rescuing the Captive, 123–25, 128
  return with the Treasure, 127
  Unification of Opposites, 126–27, 128
  See also Rescuing the Captive in
      Transformation Myths, therapeutic
      approach to

transitions between stages, 333–37
  difficult transitions in Ego-Self Journey
      Model, 336
  difficult transitions in Neumann's
      Archetypal Developmental Theory,
      336–37
  difficult transitions in Researched
      Developmental Model, 337
  fulcrums of development, 305–6, 333,
      337
Treasure of the Self, 78, 88–89, 140–41, 273
  See also later stages of development
Tronick, Ed, 234–35
trust. *See* safety, trust, and security, in oral
    stage

Ulanov, Ann Belford, 262
unconscious
  achieving unity and balance, 88
  ego ideal and, 85
  as feminine aspect, 81
  as percent of psyche, 243
unconscious communication, as expression
    of the psyche, 243–63
  derivative communication examples in
      daily life, 250–52
  derivative communication through
      physical symptoms, 254–56
  and foundation for growth/
      development, 243–44
  orientational approach to translation
      of images of the psyche, 246–50
  revelation of deep unconscious,
      245–46
  signs of a Captive, 245
  translation of dreams, 256–60
  translation of synchronicities, 260–63
unconscious guilt, 296–98
unfindability practices, 374–75
Unification of Opposites, *87*, 88, 126–27,
    128, 140–41, 194, 279, 305
uroboric castration, 94, 101, 102, 159
  See also devouring aspect, of Great
      Mother

Uroborus. *See* Great Mother
us-them viewpoint, 230–31

value, as platonic form (Almaas), 145
Verrier, Nancy Newton, 334–36
victim-tyrant polarity dynamic, 201, 209, 230–31
void, toleration of periods of, 181

Waddington, C.H., 46, 55
Washburn, Michael, 102, 154, 233, 271, 282
The Way of the Image (Kaufmann), 246–47
When the Body Says No (Maté), 284, 286–87
Wilber, Ken, 188, 305, 312, 324
Winnicott, Donald, 94
wisdom of the body. *See* body-mind/ego embodiment
wisdom system/mind (Langs), 391–92
witness/observer self
  generative inner refuge and, 361–62
  in later stages, 348–49
  thoughts and, 181, 182, 187, 200, 201
  See also Supportive Practices for the Later Stages of Development
The Wizard of Oz (movie), 139–40
Wonder Woman movies, 88
Woodman, Marian, 261

Yeats, David, 314

About the Authors

Diane Steinbrecher LCSW is an Archetypal Pattern Analyst, Hakomi Somatic Psychotherapist, and Addictions and Integral Psychotherapist working with individuals, couples, and families for over forty-five years. She also provides consultations and supervision to clinicians and those attaining licensure.

Diane has studied with Michael Conforti PhD since 1995. She has integrated Archetypal Pattern Analysis into her clinical practice and serves as a faculty member of the Assisi Institute: The International Center for the Study of Archetypal Patterns. She specializes in helping clients resolve the effects of childhood traumas as they begin to realize their natural state, the Self. Central to her therapy and teaching is reading patterns in behavior, thoughts, the body, and diseases that are viewed as a perfect expression of what is needed to shift these into generativity and one's wholeness.

Diane also is the co-founder of Archetypal Associates through which she co-teaches "Fundamentals and Application of Archetypal Pattern Analysis" in ongoing groups and trainings. In addition, she is a Radiant Mind coach and group facilitator in Dr. Peter Fenner's Radiant Mind program and provides nondual psychotherapy and spiritual mentoring.

In addition to her clinical work and teaching, Diane is on the Advisory Board for Peace in Schools, the first for-credit Mindful Studies program in high school curriculums in the United States. Plus, she is a therapist for the A Home Within program, offering free therapy for those clients who are or have been in the foster care system.

Diane lives in Portland, Oregon, and can be reached at d.steinbrecher@comcast.net.

Shannon Pernetti is an Archetypal Pattern Analyst and Integral Therapist who has been in private practice in Portland, Oregon, since 1975. Working with Dr. Michael Conforti since 1995, she co-teaches "Fundamentals and Application of Archetypal Pattern Analysis" in workshops and monthly training and application groups and is on the Assisi Institute: The International Center for the Study of Archetypal Patterns faculty.

Shannon also is a Nondual Therapist and a Radiant Mind Coach.

A skilled group facilitator, Shannon is a co-founder of Opening to Life, a Healing Arts Center in Portland, Oregon, and a Founding Board Member of Returning Veterans Project. She offers therapy, consultation, training, and supervision. Her work focuses on shifting core patterns and archetypal alignments to facilitate a fundamental unity with the Self.

Shannon can be reached at spernetti@gmail.com.

www.ingramcontent.com/pod-product-compliance
Lightning Source LLC
Chambersburg PA
CBHW080353030426
42334CB00024B/2856